Dynamics of Difference in Australia

Dynamics of Difference in Australia

Indigenous Past and Present in a Settler Country

Francesca Merlan

PENN

UNIVERSITY OF PENNSYLVANIA PRESS

PHILADELPHIA

Published by
University of Pennsylvania Press
Philadelphia, Pennsylvania 19104-4112
www.upenn.edu/pennpress

Printed in the United States of America
on acid-free paper

10 9 8 7 6 5 4 3 2 1

Library of Congress Cataloging-in-Publication Data
Names: Merlan, Francesca, author.
Title: Dynamics of difference in Australia : indigenous past and present in a settler
    country / Francesca Merlan.
Description: 1st edition. | Philadelphia : University of Pennsylvania Press, [2018] |
    Includes bibliographical references and index.
Identifiers: LCCN 2017036450 | ISBN 9780812250008 (hardcover : alk. paper)
Subjects: LCSH: Aboriginal Australians—History. | Aboriginal Australians, Treatment
    of—History. | Australia—Race relations. | Australia—History. | Ethnology—
    Australia.
Classification: LCC DU123.4 .M46 2018 | DDC 994/.0049915—dc23
LC record available at https://lccn.loc.gov/2017036450

CONTENTS

Region, Position, and Ethics of Representation

This book is about relationships between indigenous and nonindigenous people in Australia at different points in time and especially about "differences" as detectable and active in those relationships. I take differences to be identifiable forms of being in common, together with some sense of commonly shared values, that contrast with other forms similarly held in common by "others." The aim in each following chapter is to explore kinds of difference and the extent to which difference has served as a mode or pathway of engagement or a delimiting boundary, in the first place between indigenous and nonindigenous actors but subsequently in ways that make those categories more complex and more directly contested. The book's aim is not to examine "culture/s" as if entirely separate but to examine what we understand as cultural by considering difference in indigenous-nonindigenous engagement and its implications. I have found it plausible and indeed illuminating to consider differences over long time spans, so the material in this book moves between moments of early indigenous-nonindigenous encounter and the present.

Many nonindigenous people in southern Australia say that they infrequently meet and do not know any indigenous people. That this is possible is some indication of the relatively peripheral position and small proportion of indigenous people and communities in urban and especially southeastern Australia. Like many who set out to do research with indigenous communities, my intention on coming to Australia was to go north, where indigenous people constitute a much larger proportion of the population and it is unlikely that one would not "see" them. Seeing is different from getting to know, and in this Preface I set out the conditions in which I came to know Australia's north and became involved in the indigenous-nonindigenous relations this book explores.

The book is concerned with historicity but is also ethnographic, based partly on my own ethnographic research, as well as on my search to win ethnographic insights from historical material. The link between ethnography and analysis in the book raises two issues that need to be addressed here. The first is what is nowadays often called in the human sciences "positionality"— the call for us as researchers and authors to reflect on our own position in relation to the people we write about, focusing on issues of relative privilege and our ethical responsibility to avoid exploitative research. The other is the matter of "relationship." The book is about indigenous-nonindigenous relationships, and this account focuses on relationships I came to have with indigenous people and communities over time.

I came from the United States in 1976 to take up a three-year research fellowship in the Top End of the Northern Territory of Australia. I had never been in Australia before. What made me think I could arrive and do this kind of research? I had some personal preparation and inclination. As a child I had spent periods of time in North American Indian communities in which Indians were the majority, and as a PhD student I had done research in communities where relations between Indians and outsiders were marked by a high degree of physical and social separation, but influences from dominant North American society were also pervasive. Both of these things are true of northern Australia too. There had been in my family history some relationships with indigenous people in northern New Mexico where I was born, and I felt a continuing interest in those Native American settings that seemed as interesting as others I knew, including that of the first-generation Italian immigrants in Brooklyn on my father's side of the family with whom I also spent much of my childhood. I cannot, however, recall any personal feeling of nostalgia for traditional lifeworlds other than the ones I found around me (cf. Rosaldo 1989). But I did have a sense from early on of different social milieus, their uprooting and reconfiguration. At the time I set out for northern Australia, I had few specific preconceptions about what life would be like there or the character of relationships between indigenous and nonindigenous people. An entire framework of supported academic research made it all possible.

I had applied for and been granted a research fellowship from the Australian Institute of Aboriginal Studies in Canberra, the national capital, to investigate the changing locations and languages of indigenous people in an area of considerable social diversity, three hundred kilometers southeast of Darwin, the Northern Territory's capital.[1] The town of Katherine was the supply center and focus of the region for both indigenous and nonindigenous people,

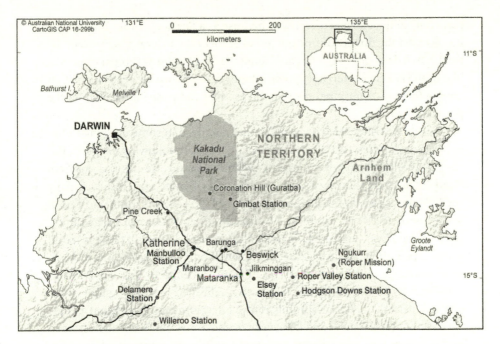

Figure 1. Katherine region and locations in Australia. CartoGIS, Australian National University.

inhabited by about five thousand people when I arrived. A number of Aborigines in the town had long lived there, but they had become a minority among the Aboriginal population as new arrivals came in and stayed, mostly on the town's fringes. Several hundred Aboriginal people were camping on the fringes, many of them recently displaced by changes in the conditions of rural work. Some of these communities were expelled by pastoralists and/or fragmented as Aboriginal people came to be more fully included in an economy of government welfare benefits.

Unknown to me, changes were being set in train in the relations between Aboriginal people and other Australians that were to shape much of my activity for years to come. The biggest was the Australian Parliament passing the Aboriginal Land Rights (Northern Territory) Act in 1976, enabling Aboriginal people to claim traditional ownership of territory they regarded as theirs. This law was the product of years of activism by and on behalf of indigenous people, mainly taking place in Australia's urban centers but imaginatively stimulated by remote Australia. Land rights were politically possible on a large scale only in the Northern Territory because as a territory rather than a state it was under the direct control and jurisdiction of the federal government. By the 1970s federal government endorsement of land rights was bipartisan (unlike in the Northern Territory itself, where there was widespread opposition among the non-Aboriginal people who by then composed a majority of the population there).

From Katherine, I also became familiar and lived in some outlying indigenous communities, two of which especially figure in following chapters: Barunga, seventy kilometers southeast of Katherine on the Central Arnhem Road (then largely unpaved, now paved); and Jilgmirn.gan (locally usually spelled Jilkminggan) on Elsey Station about 114 kilometers south and east of Katherine on the Roper Highway. A range of other towns, town fringe camps, stations (ranches), and other locations interconnected with these were all places I spent time, partly because interlinked kindreds whom I came to know lived in a range of different places (see Figure 1). Communities like Barunga (and Beswick to the northeast) had been established or reconfigured in the postwar period, with the administrative intention that Aboriginal people could be contained there and kept away from town. Others like Jilgmirn.gan on Elsey were long-term station communities, places of settlement reconfigured on pastoral properties where Aboriginal people were living on small excision areas of the homelands of at least some members of the community. Many of these station communities had been much larger until around the time of implementation of the minimum wage, phased in from 1966 to 1968, when they were turned off many of those properties or discouraged from living there. The new conditions meant that pastoralists were unwilling to accept the continuing residence of numbers of indigenous people. Indigenous camps on some stations were now greatly reduced or only seasonally occupied. Others like Jilgmirn.gan on Elsey—not too far from the small town of Mataranka (about thirty kilometers), in the homeland of most camp residents and familiar to others married in or present for other reasons—continued to hold their populations.

I received mixed but generally welcoming treatment from indigenous people in the various living situations I got to know, through links of kinship and shared experience among members of the various camps and settlements. My becoming "adopted" shortly after my arrival as a "granddaughter" to two principal women in two different camps in Katherine provided a framework and transferrable elements of recognizability for my receptions elsewhere; this, I came to understand, was the genius of indigenous regionalism, its

network-like character and tensile strength (Chapter 5). These elements structured the kin identity I could be assigned in new locations and, on a personal
level, my reception by particular people. My hosts and their families welcomed my interest in where they had come from, their languages, their connections to home territories. Many spent considerable time involving
themselves in our shared travels, recordings of language, biographical, and
story material of all kinds. In part, this was because some people (of those
who had been displaced) harbored desires to return to where they had come
from, but not all did. Nor did all see the recording of this material as something relevant to the future of their own families and people: "It will be good
for white people, not for my family," one man memorably said. Alongside
these research concerns I became very involved with how indigenous people
were managing in their present, and in this we made considerable common
cause.

I spent at least two years (1976–78) in the north before the Northern Land
Council asked me to be involved in a land claim over a spectacular national
park, the site of Katherine Gorge and River, considered by local (nonindigenous) townspeople to be the premier attraction of the Katherine region, and
a centerpiece of the regional economy. I therefore had a clear idea how contentious this case would be. Nonindigenous townspeople were worried that
indigenous ownership of the park would exclude them. They were worried
about the effect on tourism. No favorable public view had yet formed concerning the possible tourist values of indigenous presence and ownership; that
was to come only later.

The people I was getting to know had been enormously changed by colonization, from around the 1880s, when gold mining began around Pine Creek
(and with lesser intensity, near the growing town of Katherine) and pastoral
properties (ranches) were taken up and stocked where environmental conditions seemed favorable (and even where they did not, leading to repeated
failures).[2] Indigenous people had moved to these places of settler colonial
occupation—mines, towns, pastoral stations. As well, they had been subject
to large-scale exterminatory violence arising from settler occupation during
what many older indigenous people recalled as "killing times," or sometimes
"wild times."[3] Indigenous people who "came in" to pastoral properties from
the colonially appropriated bush remade their lives there but were affected by
continuing violence, disease, and eventually, by concentration in army camps
during the Second World War.

These experiences gave rise to differences among indigenous people in their relations among themselves and in their relations to white people. Those who had lived as the labor force on (especially larger, continuous) pastoral properties tended to have a greater sense of cohesion among themselves (a context of parts of Chapters 5 and 6) and had found white bosses to whose predictable expectations they had learned to accommodate; while those who had lived in the mining fields tended to have experienced continuing exposure to volatile and changing work regimes, substance abuse (opium, methylated spirits, alcohol), and sexual exploitation (Chapter 6). Somewhat different kinds of personalities were to be found within these sets of people.

After World War II, some resided in the government settlements or communities established to contain them, others returned to outlying pastoral properties whence they had come, and still others, often illicitly, lived on the fringes of regional towns. There was movement among all these locations in Aboriginal walkabouts, which became ever less common. Aboriginal presence around towns was prohibited to all but officially employed Aborigines until 1948. Alcohol was prohibited to them until 1964, and paternalistic employment situations of low or no wages, with some keep, were common until 1968. Their influx into regional towns began as nationwide union activism resulted in the implementation of a minimum wage. Pastoralists had warned that wage parity would result in Aboriginal people being turned off cattle stations. Exploitation of indigenous labor, according to Patrick Wolfe (1999:27), was a "contradiction, rather than an inherent component" of replacive and tendentially eliminatory settler colonialism (although see McGrath 1987 for an important qualification to this view). Indeed, pastoralists rapidly replaced indigenous labor with technologies; as well, they began to employ indigenous workers casually.[4]

The nonindigenous people of Katherine had made little or no provision for the fringe-dwelling Aborigines, and, with few exceptions, they repudiated the fringe dwellers for being who they were and for the squalor of their conditions. Many indigenous people in the postwar settlements built to contain them had nevertheless begun to orient more regularly toward towns as sources of supply and because of the increasing Aboriginal social intensity there. Administrative moves began to gain tenure for camps and to give the residents basic services. Their increasing access to cash (wages and the monetization of welfare) and the removal of controls on their access to alcohol in 1964 had contributed to their becoming a troubling presence in town. Legal purchase of alcohol had been symbolically coded by some Aborigines as achieved "citizenship" (see Sansom 1980), but alcohol undoubtedly became an enormous medical and social burden on Aboriginal people and communities, and it has remained so.[5] The nonindigenous town's negative image of Aborigines as fringe dwellers contrasted with more romantic and traditional imagery prevalent in urban Australia. Northern white Australians, on the other hand, felt their understanding of northern conditions to be far superior to that of nescient southerners.[6] The prospect of "traditional ownership" of the beautiful Katherine Gorge national park, as far as most townspeople were concerned, was incompatible with the region's developed tourism. Aboriginal ownership would only impede tourism, and their presence would spoil town amenity.

As I spent most of my time with Aboriginal people living around the town, camping in fringe locations, I noticed many things that have stayed with me ever since. Most obvious was the woefulness of their fringe-camp living conditions. Indigenous people were vulnerable to exploitation. Shortly after I arrived, a woman limped into a fringe camp where I had become a regular visitor and part-time resident some kilometers out of town. She needed to recuperate from having been abducted (evidently lured with alcohol), driven away, and raped by several white workers who were haunting Aboriginal camps for just such purposes. The woman was concerned with recovering and with the rage and retaliation (against herself) that she feared from her husband. I notified a recently appointed community affairs officer in Canberra to try to bring about an investigation of this event and others like it. The victim declared that she did not want police involvement, but I soon received a letter stating that investigation would require certain kinds of evidence and witnesses and asking if we could provide them. Alcohol consumption in almost all cases like this contributed to a general moral alarm in such towns and supplied a reason for blaming the victims.

Further, an Aboriginal family living in town[7] with whom I spent a great deal of time ducked their heads, or otherwise took evasive measures, at the sight of police, no matter whether we were sitting in the open outside their house as they frequently preferred to do or just walking or driving around in my car, doing nothing at all that would normally be considered suspicious. "Yinyigben, yinyigben" (police, police), the older people would hiss to others in Wardaman, the language of this kindred, and everyone knew that meant: Duck! A long, remembered history of interaction was reflected in their behavior. There was little sense among them that the police might be helpful, although that feeling has changed to some extent since then.

As my involvement developed in conveying information about land claims to indigenous people, or attending while it was being conveyed, I saw that there was an enormous gulf of incomprehension between information givers and supposed receivers (see Thiele 1982; Merlan 1995; Cowlishaw 1999). None of the institutions or motives involved in the process was initially at all familiar to most Aboriginal people. It was not (simply) a matter of language but a mutual lack of institutional familiarity and a dearth of meanings that could be exchanged between people who had limited fluency with each other's everyday and imaginative worlds. The situation was paradoxical: while older Aboriginal people were among those most likely to know something about land areas that might be claimed in terms contained in the Land Rights Act, they were the least likely to understand why representatives of the Land Council and others were now coming to talk to them about these things. Many had never spoken to outsiders about the kind of mythological and sociological information that was required to pursue claims; they even regarded some of it as not to be widely disseminated (Michaels 1985), and they were understandably nonplussed by, and sometimes mistrustful of, outsiders' intentions. They also had, at first, little sense of what kind of information would help them in their claims. How could they intuit what had been consolidated as expert understanding and was now required as proof of relationships to land they might claim? They often said things that would be decidedly unhelpful, and some were concerned that with proof of their ownership they would be made to go back to where they came from. In addition, many had only limited knowledge of the places under claim. Such information was not evenly distributed among them (Chapter 7).

Some of the Aboriginal people, especially around town, wished to claim areas where they were now living, so that they could carry on with their lives as they were. Yet the Northern Land Council was encouraging them to make much wider claims.[8] The wishes that such people expressed were negatively evaluated, dismissed, or subordinated by the Northern Land Council's grander sense of the opportunities.

It has taken some time for me to comprehend that scene. I first felt satisfaction that this transition, from complete dispossession to the possibility of repossession, had occurred. But then I noticed that the Northern Land Council had little feel for the actual effects, on people's current outlooks, of the violent and dislocating histories that many had experienced either directly or as survivor generations of earlier colonization. The Land Council expected these dispossessed people to be involved in making the claims that the legislation and the Land Council were now enabling, but the process to which the dispossessed were being brought was unfamiliar, and the wider national negotiations over indigenous-nonindigenous relationships were unknown to most of the former.

I subsequently reflected on these mismatches between the authorities pursuing land rights and the people that they were established to help. The topics of these papers ranged from increasing indigenous awareness and use of money in the context of generalized kin relatedness (Merlan 1991b) to the question of their participation in land claims (Merlan 1995). My 1998 book *Caging the Rainbow* suggested that the entire land claims process might be best interpreted as attempted governmental mimicry of what had become understood, through legal precedents and anthropological involvement, as "traditional" forms of indigenous relationship to land. Aborigines were then expected to reproduce evidence of these forms of relationship in order, belatedly, to reclaim country from which their forebears had been dispossessed. Claimants could win cases if they could demonstrate their traditionality, thus both benefiting from policy and reinforcing their distinct status; while those who could not meet criteria of traditionality could neither win cases nor change the disadvantaged and prejudicial condition in which they lived.

In particular, I have been vexed that the indigenous people with the longest-term attachment to the area of Katherine town were considered by relevant authorities, legal representatives, and others to be a liability to the land claim because they no longer lived their relationship to the town in the expected traditional modalities of myth and dreaming[9] and associated embodied relationship to places. History was not supposed to have occurred in order for claims under the Northern Territory Land Rights Act to be successful. Guided by the statutory requirements, my land claim research showed that *these* were people who had formerly been of the Katherine area in terms of long-term connection and validating mythic identity. Their attachment, though changing in character over time, was why they were still there. However, the impact of settler appropriation was that they were largely unaware of many of the elements of their past that would have allowed them to be identified as its long-standing occupants. Written records and stories serendipitously recorded from their elder relatives by a locally residing agronomist and by a passing anthropologist (Arndt 1962; Reay n.d.) attested their longstanding occupation of the Katherine town area. However, circumstances had changed their collective memory and store of information, and they had become townspeople of a (marginalized, disadvantaged, racialized) sort. They did not match expectations of the new land claims dispensation, despite their own strong sense of relationship and homely belonging to the town. An impatient senior barrister, acting for the Katherine land claim, had dismissed them as a "cancer" on the case. Such selective recognition of indigenous claims has become known as "repressive authenticity."[10]

This situation brought home to me that we cannot expect successful land claims to heal all the injuries of dispossession. The terms on which claims were to be made were unavailable to many. To satisfy the enormous machinery of administration and governance required to restore land ownership many of the Aboriginal people I knew in the 1970s had had to reorient their lives away from the bush, toward town and community where they lived an increasingly cash- and store-dependent life. While their aspirations to claim land grew as they came to understand what was possible, claiming land was only one concern in their lives. The intensity of emphasis on claiming land seemed to be a symptom of a much larger mismatch in indigenous-nonindigenous relationships (Merlan 2007). Land rights, like the current "Recognise" initiative, which figures in my Introduction and Chapter 8, has been a settler preoccupation, and this requires interpretation.

I nevertheless went on to be involved in as many claims as I could manage in the region I knew well, on the basis that here, at least, was some provision for indigenous futures. Was this a good choice? The processes have indeed resulted in the return to Aboriginal landholders of large areas of otherwise vacant Crown land. The resulting changes have not necessarily included clear improvements in life conditions broadly understood. The claims era has left in its wake many landholding groups, many institutions (governmental and otherwise) that have responsibilities for looking after and managing the affairs of such groups, and related business groups and arms. Government policy has encouraged indigenous people to form corporations through which they could interact with the formal and informal institutions of Australian society.[11] The Aboriginal people who provided the information and experience that helped to win land claims were made signal members of corporations, but their inclusion was often titular rather than empowering, in my experience. These corporations are now staffed and led by younger people with different, and usually less intensive and extensive, experience of country.

Observing this transition over almost forty years, I have been led to write this book and to explore what we may understand as cultural that persists in circumstances of radical change and how differences change and emerge.

Persistent Difference

This book is about relationships between indigenous and nonindigenous people in Australia engaging with one another across major disparities of knowledge, cultural orientation, and power since the first arrival of Europeans. It is about how they engage with each other in ways that define and redefine the understood meanings and implications of these differences.

Writing about Australian indigenous social orders has emphasized continuity of difference (with variable emphasis on colonizing assaults on it); race and racialization as defining of indigenous-nonindigenous relations; and the power of the state, the state culture of bureaucracy, and its self-preserving circularity.[1] In Australia any portrayal of indigenous lives is written in knowledge of the intensity of public debate about indigenous issues. I think this is, in fact, particularly so in Australia: as historian Patrick Wolfe (2016) recently repeated, indigenous issues reverberate in the public sphere well beyond indigenous proportion in the population. Indigenous issues in Australia are topics of almost daily front-page news and debate, differing in this way in degree from Fourth World (Native American) matters in the public sphere of the United States.

Recent ethnographic, anthropological, and historical works concerned with Australian indigenous people have had at their conceptual core incommensurability of indigenous and nonindigenous social orders (Povinelli 2001, 2002; Clendinnen 2005), the experiential specificities of the collisions between these orders (Austin-Broos 2009), as well as the relation between anthropology and history (Wolfe 1999, 2016) and the importance of mutually supportive partnership between these two disciplines. The colonization of Australia and its aftermath shaped broadly similar, continent-wide structural patterns of domination, expropriation, and subsequent state interventions (Wolfe 1999, 2016). Ethnographers have persistently observed patterns of colonialism viewed as "structures,"[2] remarking on the histories, in different parts of the continent, that have given rise to specific forms of experience (Macdonald 2000; Austin-Broos 2009). Through all these generalizations and specificities, indigenous-nonindigenous difference is clearly seen as neither eliminated nor fully transformed despite the intensity and enormity of colonial and postcolonial events.

As I stated in the Preface, I take "difference" to denote identifiable forms of being in common, together with some sense of commonly shared values, that contrast with other forms similarly held in common by "others." What reflexive senses of these differences those involved may have is a matter for discovery and interpretation. Anthropologist Elizabeth Povinelli (2001, 2002), her work ethnographically grounded in a neighboring region of the Northern Territory to the one I write about, has for some time proposed a view of differences as evidence of incommensurability between indigenous and nonindigenous ontologies: ways of being that are irreconcilably different, which nonindigenous institutions and agents seek to police and make commensurate with their own terms.[3] Her concerns first focused on what she represented as European heterosexualization of indigenous experience, against evidence of indigenous diversity of modalities of attachment to land and persons (Povinelli 1993). She also traced scientific and other colonial sanitizing efforts that purged indigenous lives of their "repugnant" aspects, sexual and other. This book aims to identify some of the dynamics of difference in indigenous-nonindigenous relations. In it I draw on both historical and ethnographic materials from my research to illustrate and interpret dimensions of difference that emerge in different times and situations of encounter. All of the chapters explore what I take to be persistent dimensions of difference that continue to play a significant role in indigenous lives and in indigenous-nonindigenous encounter.

Chapter 1 treats the earliest recorded arrival of Captain James Cook in Botany Bay; it relates how Aborigines apparently refused to "see" the arriving outsiders despite their physical proximity. It presents evidence of two modes in which indigenous people attempted to shape early colonial encounter: one, surprisingly, by refusing to react; and the second, by recognizing arriving colonials, not only as spirits of the dead[4] but as specific relatives. This encounter could be called an instance of indigenous "nonrecognition," argued to have cultural specificity but also ubiquitous in human interaction. The book goes on to examine somewhat different questions of seeing, knowing, recognizing, at different points in time. Chapter 2 addresses an often-raised issue of the imitative behavior of indigenous peoples in encounter, aiming to reinterpret its social significance in this circumstance. Chapter 3 examines great disparities between indigenous and nonindigenous attitudes to "things." Chapters 4 and 5 contrast nonindigenous and indigenous ways of stereotyping the actions of the "other": colonial generalization of indigenous character as "treacherous," the indigenous retrospective evaluation of nonindigenous action as "cruel." This contrast opens out into consideration of indigenous modes of recognition with their avenues for incorporation of even unbiddable outsiders, prompting reflection on how this has sometimes made them vulnerable to different, powerful others. Chapter 6 brings in questions of state and nation in shaping exclusion, inclusion, and changing emphases on difference as a matter of race; the chapter discusses recent governmental liberalization of definitions of "Aboriginal." The book ends by turning to the current Recognise initiative in 2016. The material in this book gives us insight into social and bodily affective and recognitional modes shaped over a long term. I do not suggest unqualified continuity but point to the historical and social embeddedness of the modalities involved, no doubt affected but perhaps in some ways intensified in encounter with outsiders.

The Present Moment: "Recognise"?

As I write this Introduction, Australia continues to contemplate, hesitantly, a referendum that would write into the constitution the recognition of indigenous Australians.[5] The Australian constitution does not mention indigenous Australians, and the Australian government has not yet proposed the terms in which the constitution could refer to and thus recognize them. "Recognise" (as the initiative is called) is being debated and urged by supporters as an appropriate and necessary step in repairing and renewing relations between indigenous and nonindigenous people at the national level. Opinions on it differ. Some argue it should happen; others oppose it as marking out a special place for indigenous people in a way that is divisive. Still others argue that this move is a distraction—"useless"—and that other measures to adjust this relationship would be of far greater value. Increasingly, the latter are indigenous spokespeople, who seek something they can see as realizing their demand for a meaningful and rightful indigenous place in Australia today.

The Recognise initiative reveals Australia as attempting, and wanting to be seen to attempt, to engage with its indigenous population in a new way and accord it some kind of official commendation at a new institutional level. Collective acknowledgment is now sometimes said by people of varying political and social persuasions to be necessary to Australia's national "completion." This is phrased on the Recognise website in various registers. An indigenous man from Cape York, Harold Ludwick, is quoted as saying: "If the Constitution was the birth certificate of Australia, we're missing half the family." This places the "birth" of "Australia" at the time of federation, 1901, occluding the temporal dimension of what is often acknowledged as thousands of years of indigenous presence on the continent. Another part of the website urges: once we write in "this missing first chapter of our national story, it will formally become part of the shared story of every Australian." In other words, the indigenous story will no longer be a thing apart but will be included on the terms of the nation-state as a whole.[6]

At the same time, Recognise marks out the fact that the "indigenous" is felt by many nonindigenous Australians to represent "difference" that remains problematically unassimilated. Indigenous people and presence, though valued in some ways, remain to be reconciled with national being or more fully included. With one exception—a finding of native title in a High Court case discussed below—indigenous Australians are, however, not attributed legal forms of recognition deriving from their having been the original people of the continent. Would the present initiative amount to this kind of recognition or not? That is the underlying tension, the elephant in the room, of Recognise, a seemingly celebratory proposal. If it were to be originary status that is recognized, what would be the consequences? And if not, what then?

Not far below the surface of the Recognise initiative is a question about the terms of Australian sovereignty that was raised but not resolved to everyone's satisfaction in the famous *Mabo* case (1992). In judgment of a claim to possessory title of the island of Mer in the Torres Strait by virtue of longstanding possession, advanced by Eddie Mabo and other islanders, the High Court found that native title exists, and it may survive colonization. On the other hand, the High Court made clear that native title may not survive if it is deemed to have been lawfully extinguished by governmental action. That is, despite its foundational-sounding name, native title is residual and relative, a bundle of rights that remains and is recognizable at common law only insofar as these rights do not conflict with other forms of legal title to the land in question. Thus the court confirmed received doctrine on sovereignty, putting that matter beyond the reach of review in domestic Australian courts.[7] The *Mabo* judgment thus upholds a conventional view of sovereignty as completed and unassailable, resulting from originary colonization. But there are many lurking legal and other potential issues. For example, if native title may in principle persist at common law and does persist in particular cases, does sovereignty (in some meaning of the term) persist with it (Patton 1996; Reynolds 1996)? Is the finding of persistence of native title consistent with a notion of Australia as a colony of settlement, as is usually assumed, or of invasion? And what, in broader terms presupposed by these questions, if sovereignty were regarded not as a juridico-political absolute but as what many take it to have been, a practice of colonial domination and governance (Muldoon 2008:63; Biolsi 2005)?

These issues suggest the likely limitations of the Recognise initiative. Maintenance of a discourse of finished sovereignty limits and frames those uncertainties; but refusal to address the issue may appear to many to be, as Ari Kelman (2013:5) puts it regarding a North American indigenous context of commemoration, a "hollow offer of painless healing."

In two senses, Australia has never decolonized. It grew out of British colonies that federated as a constitutional monarchy in 1901. Still today the queen remains the head of state and is technically designated queen of Australia (though in practice, an appointed governor general carries out all the functions usually performed by a head of state, without reference to the queen).[8] Second, no treaties or other negotiations were ever held with indigenous people/s that might be considered a moment of formal recognition. Despite a lengthy history of governmental management of indigenous affairs, there has never been a formal moment of decolonization: colonization was not marked by formality, so how can a moment of decolonization be marked? Yet that is what is clearly being sought in Recognise: an act of recognition that will make a decisive difference. There has been, in theory at least, such a moment in many other former colonies. In the extractive colony of South Africa, where colonists were always a minority and went about seeking resources and subordinating local people as labor, decolonization took place and Nelson Mandela became president.

Terra Australis: The Great, Late, Southern Liberal Settler Continent

Australia was a late settler colony in comparative global terms. While Columbus's first voyages led to lasting European contact with the Americas from 1492, the Dutch navigator Willem Janszoon only made the first recorded European landfall on the Australian continent, on the western shore of Cape York in present north Queensland, in February 1606. Though there were a few brief contacts in between, the next portentous European arrival came a full 164 years after Janszoon in 1770, when English navigator Captain James Cook sailed into what is now Botany Bay at Sydney, naming eastern Australia "New South Wales" on 22 August 1770 at what has been henceforth most widely known as Possession Island, a small island in the Torres Strait Islands group off the coast of far north Queensland (which includes Mer, the subject of the *Mabo* case referred to above).[9] Cook's favorable reports on the prospects led to British settlement from 1788, beginning with the arrival of the "First Fleet" of eleven ships. Commodore Arthur Phillip, transporting on this first trip of settlement 759 convicts, their marine guards and families, and a few civil officers, came with instructions authorizing him to make regulations and land grants in the colony.

British colonization proceeded apace; competition with the French, who had also launched expeditions of exploration, ebbed in the early nineteenth century. British colonists came to settle, explore, expand their reach, and develop the continent economically as they might find possible. Officially they were instructed to conciliate the natives to the extent necessary to form penal settlements, replacing the American colonies as a convict destination. However, New South Wales soon also became a colony of free settlement: the first immigrant free settlers arrived in 1793. Notables of the colony began to argue for abolition of convict transportation and for the establishment of representative government. The colony began to grow rapidly as free settlers arrived and pressed on, well ahead of government regulation, into new lands to farm and, soon after, establish sheep and cattle pastoralism. Despite the long and arduous sea voyage, settlers were attracted by the prospect of making a new life on virtually free Crown land.[10] This was accomplished by widespread indigenous dispossession and little conciliation.

Mobility was an expression and an instance of emergent power.[11] Colonists had crossed the ocean and meant to establish a social order, the character of which changed but the intended longevity of which was not in doubt. The nature and implications of settler colonialism have been more fully shaped in a relatively recent literature (Wolfe 1999, 2016; Veracini 2007a, b, 2010), as has the ongoing historical entwinement of settler colonialism and forms of liberalism (Humpage 2005; Povinelli 2002, 2005; Strakosch 2015; Watson 2004).

Australian writer and historian Patrick Wolfe (1999, 2016) characterized colonial settlement as a structure, not an event. By this he meant that certain lasting structures subtend and channel settler colonialism. The intent to stay, expand, and take over the land has meant replacement, not conciliation, of encountered peoples. It is one thing to colonize and intend to rely on newly subject peoples as a source of labor. It is another to arrive and rapidly begin to render the indigenous people physically, civically, and morally superfluous. Replacement involves the latter: what Wolfe calls a logic of elimination. The term "logic" is perhaps too rigid, or at least does not of itself make allowance for situational variability. But the drive to dispossession and elimination was certainly evident. Wolfe sees the logic enduring into present times in changing terms. The way and extent to which underlying structures have changed is a question we may ask concerning settler colonies like Australia. Kinds of change that have occurred are especially addressed in Chapters 5–8; the historical trajectory of settler colonialism becomes manifest and is in fact evoked in initiatives like Recognise. They are a moment of reckoning that calls forth competing perspectives on past, present, and future.

Anthropology and Difference

Anthropology in general was subject to searing postcolonial critiques in the 1980s. One critique said that anthropologists created their "object," the "Other," through an "allochronic discourse" of "other men in another Time," as Africanist anthropologist Johannes Fabian (1983:143) put it. Thus, I feel obliged first to reflect on changes of focus in anthropology and on related questions about the ethics of anthropological research.

Anthropology's othering was paradoxical, Fabian argued, in that ethnographic research is inherently communicative and intersubjective: people in the same time and place, talking to each other, produces much of the empirical material of fieldwork. Anthropologist and subjects typically occupied very different social positions, however. The conditions of the growth of anthropology were colonialist-imperialist expansion and the spread of forms of capitalism, taking over space—the homelands of anthropology's initial subjects.

This brought with it what Fabian called one-way "chronopolitics," contemporary research that excluded the subjects from colonial time and located them in their own time.

Much Australianist writing has been in terms of evolutionary and structural-functional paradigms, treating indigenous subject matter in isolation from its contemporary real-world colonial context. The theorization of early work typically involved intellectual partnerships of field-workers and scholars, as in the cases of missionary Lorimer Fison and explorer-administrator Alfred William Howitt, biologist W. Baldwin Spencer and postmaster F. J. Gillen in Central Australia. However, we still can learn from the storehouse of early field ethnography, as much of it does not "distance" indigenous people and social orders. William Lloyd Warner's *A Black Civilization* (1937), concerning the Yolngu of northeast Arnhem Land, was deliberately titled to signal a significant departure from earlier stadial and primitivizing views of human societies: "civilization" was a call to evaluation of Aboriginal societies in terms of their social/moral worth. Much of what Warner (1937:10) discusses, for example, as the "primary articulation of Murngin [northeastern Arnhem Land] society with its natural environment" that is discernible in the relation between the Murngin ceremonial cycle and the environmental contrast between wet and dry seasons, resonates with many contemporary positive views of indigenous particularity and ethical environmental concern (Rose 2004, 2011). Mervyn Meggitt's *Desert People: A Study of the Walbiri Aborigines of Central Australia* (1962, from fieldwork of 1953–55) featured a fulsome structural account of kinship, social and ceremonial organization, the first lifelike depictions of indigenous people's contemporary lives in a remote settlement, in the process showing some of their continuing self-assertive style. Meggitt said little about settler impacts on their lives, nor much about their location in a settlement. Anthropologist, administrator, and public intellectual W. E. H. Stanner's positive, recuperative take on aboriginal religion (1966) and subsequent Boyer Lectures (1968)[12] helped to create a climate of opinion more favorable to Aboriginal interests, particularly to land rights, from the 1960s.

Throughout much of the twentieth century, and true to anthropology's beginnings, anthropologists have undoubtedly tended to conduct research with bearers of the most distinctively indigenous ways of life: "othering" has taken the form of seeking out the "most other" indigenous difference. Much Australianist field research and writing from the 1960s onward originally pivoted on themes concerning ecology and human adaptation to the harsh environmental conditions here, a particular materially based form of interest in difference. But the concern of these researchers expanded in many different directions once they had established themselves with indigenous people and communities. One may without prejudice include here Fred Myers, best known for *Pintupi Country, Pintupi Self* (1986), who, from initial interests in the social organization of human mobility and aggregation in the desert environment, came to frame the most lasting account of emotions, autonomy, and relatedness among desert people and later came to study the rendering of landscape in aboriginal art. He also wrote on the relation of Pintupi to the welfare state and the awkward relationship between their political culture of "nurturance" and the government policy of self-determination. Elizabeth Povinelli's original research interests related squarely to hunting and gathering. However, her questions about the characterization of "labor" and her involvement with indigenous people caught up in the land claims process led her to a critique of "late liberalism" and to the question of survival of alternative ways of being, the "otherwise" (Povinelli 2002).

Anthropological research work was largely done by men in remote Australia, with a few notable exceptions (e.g., Englishwoman Phyllis Kaberry and Catherine Berndt in partnership with her husband Ronald), until quite recently. This was evidently quite deliberate. According to Jeremy Beckett (pers. comm.), Sydney University doyen of anthropology Professor A. P. Elkin (1933–56) urged young women students to work in "settled" Australia. Thus Aborigines in urban contexts attracted the attention of (mostly female) sociologists and geographers (e.g., Fay Gale, Ellen Biddle, Judy Inglis). The urban literature featured global analytical concepts of "adaptation," "assimilation," "acculturation," "integration," some of which were (also) policy terms (see Langton's 1981 critique); while the anthropological work in remote communities, studying "kinship" and "traditional" social organization, was short on ways of treating the indigenous-nonindigenous encounter. This work had a foundational thematic: the Other. But it was becoming clear that this thematic was seriously flawed, or at least that it made far-reaching exclusions that were morally intolerable.

From the mid-1960s, in a decolonizing climate that regularly cited "self-determination" as desirable internationally (McGregor 2011:58–59), another postwar change filtered into Australianist work. Efforts began, largely on the part of historians, to break what anthropologist W. E. H. Stanner, in his Boyer lecture of 1968 called the "Great Australian Silence." Stanner diagnosed a "cult of forgetfulness practised on a national scale" that had resulted in scant attention to indigenous history or presence in Australia and denied adequate representation of indigenous conditions. Stanner's awareness had been shaped in part by a large research project initiated in 1964 by an Australian scholar, teacher, Pacific administrator, and Aboriginal rights advocate: Charles Dunford Rowley. Accepting a three-year appointment to the Social Science Research Council of Australia, Rowley studied (and commissioned others to study) the situation of Aborigines in Australian society. He wrote the first three volumes of a series, *The Destruction of Aboriginal Society* (1970), *Outcasts in White Australia* (1971a), and *The Remote Aborigines* (1971b). The books conveyed a hitherto little-known history of the encounters between Aborigines and non-Aborigines and a masterly survey of present relations that helped to determine the agenda of the Whitlam Labor government (1972–75). In a final work (*Recovery: The Politics of Aboriginal Reform,* published posthumously in 1986) Rowley remained hopeful, suggesting possibilities for forms of Aboriginal autonomy in a continent whose white people, unlike those of Papua New Guinea where he had worked, would not go away and whose indigenous people still had "some business together which is not the business of other citizens" (Inglis 2012).

This was followed by work of a growing number of Australian historians, some of whom began to attempt representation, as Henry Reynolds (1981) put it, from "the other side of the frontier."[13] "Resistance" became one of the signature themes not only in history but also in anthropology (Scott 1985; Ortner 1995) as authors sought to cast historical materials in more relational, sociological, and ethically inflected terms that attributed agency to indigenous people. There began to emerge in Australia a new picture of the colonial past, with previously little or unknown Aboriginal heroes and stories of resistance (Willmott 1987; Pedersen and Woorunmurra 1995), which could be celebratory only up to a point because of their tragic subject matter. Such research has placed the character of Australian nationhood in question with unprecedented intensity, provoking "history wars" between conservative defenders of a benign view of Australia as a colony of settlement and vigorous and confrontational reinterpretations of the colonial past as violent and dispossessory (see, e.g., Windschuttle 2002; Macintyre and Clark 2004; Manne 2003, 2009; Attwood 2005).[14]

While many research projects arose from indigenous difference, those researchers also registered profound impact and influence on indigenous lives that was not always easy to specify or analyze, partly because of the fraught political field into which any such representation enters. In recent decades, there have been some analyses using the terms and tools of colonial studies (Tonkinson 1978; Trigger 1992, applied to mission contexts), the effects of bureaucracy and administration on everyday indigenous life (Collman 1979a, b, 1988), Foucauldian theorization of the disciplining state and of resistance (Morris 1989), and research conducted in a variety of locations (outback towns, remote-area camps, cities) under the principal rubric of race and racism (Cowlishaw 1988, 1999, 2004). Among newer emphases have been ethically inflected approaches to history, social relations, and ecology (Rose 1992, 2012, 2015), and the concept of "ontological shift" through which Diane Austin-Broos (2009) reads two signal moments of change in Central Australia: Arrernte dislocation from their land, and their subsequent incorporation into an expanding welfare state.

Exposure of indigenous people to the state in northern Australia in the land claims processes (Merlan 1998; Povinelli 2002), as Austin-Broos has argued (2011), deflected Australianist anthropology into reexamining traditional indigenous relationships to land. Presenting collectivities as possible "traditional owners," as required by claims processes, was remote in many ways from the way Aboriginal people now live. Increasingly over the last decade (but see earlier Thiele 1982; Cowlishaw 1999), anthropology and other social sciences have turned to examine and critique liberal and neoliberal bureaucratic and policy processes focused on indigenous people (see also Strakosch 2015).

As some following chapters will show, some of the people I have worked with in the north came from families that were survivors of the violence of settlement. They have narrated some of this past as they experienced it, leaving me with little doubt about where I stand in the history wars. I have more doubts about how to assess the nature of continuity in colonizing and dispossessory practice, especially in the ways that representations of difference play in relations of indigenous people with bureaucracy and in policy processes. Some historians and anthropologists have considered it more ethical to withdraw from any representation of indigenous people and to focus on the settler colonial state and society. Anthropologists have examined the evidently nonbenign, circular, and remedialist character of the social democratic and neoliberal state, trained on shaping and domesticating indigenous difference (Lea 2008a, b; see also Strakosch 2015). As well, anthropologists have studied Australian state and bureaucracy, its whiteness (and especially its antiracist dimension, the fear of being oppressive), which shapes bureaucratic approaches to indigenous people and communities in the guise of help (Kowal 2015). In anthropological, historical, and other related settler colony literatures (especially those of North America) there are critiques of (usually) state-framed concepts of "recognition" (Coulthard 2007; A. Simpson 2014), and there are many statements of preference for "refusal" by indigenous scholars: claims to the right to unknowability of indigenous people and communities. There are many policy- and practice-related critiques of recognition as well (e.g., for Australia, see Pearson 2014): that "recognition" does not really accept the possibility of an autonomous indigenous position, but is always seeking to subordinate and subsume it. As I earlier indicated and will return to discuss in Chapter 8, that is exactly the elephant in the Recognise room.

Arguing for an "anthropology of anthropology," historian Patrick Wolfe (1999:3, 214) has sought to write, not "the agency of the colonized, but the total context of inscription." He takes the further step of saying that one can ethically examine anthropological constructions and discourses but not indigenous ones. For indigenous people, Wolfe says, survival is the issue; survival is a matter of not being assimilated. Any claims to authority over indigenous discourse made from within the settler-colonial academy necessarily participate in the continuing usurpation of indigenous space; there are "no innocent discourses" regarding Aborigines (Wolfe 1999:4). To refer to indigenous discourse is inherently invasive, he avers; invasion continues in new forms. I do not agree that the study of indigenous discourse necessarily claims "authority over indigenous discourse." Indeed, I dispute that we can neatly separate indigenous from nonindigenous discourse. This book tells a story of indigenous action, but in ways that could not be told simply with reference to settler or indigenous arrangements as if these were separate. I believe that we need ethnographically grounded accounts of the indigenous experience of change in their relationships with others.

Material in this book draws on my experience with indigenous people and communities. It is grounded in features of problematic relationships that are not over yet, as well as in largely positive relationships that I developed with people that allowed me to participate in their lives. I present indigenous positions that I came to know, and which would otherwise not be heard, as important.

Recent works critical of liberal and neoliberal governance acknowledge the significance of understanding indigenous action, orientation, and practice. In her examination of recent (2000–2006) indigenous policy in Australia, political analyst Elizabeth Strakosch (2015:180) argues that there is intimate entwinement between formations of settler colonialism and neoliberalism, which "thrives in the gap between liberalism's promise of full inclusion and its practice of sifting actual claims to inclusion based on the 'capacity' of the claimant." Older frameworks of capacity assessment, framed by sovereignty, she concludes, need to be transcended as the exhaustive site of political order. This "opens up the possibility of redress between different orders rather than within the liberal state framework" (186). The state is only one kind of political institution, she points out, urging us, "as settlers, to understand and encounter the other forms of political life that already exist" (ibid.). Yet, notably, Strakosch says little about what those other forms may be.

Similarly, Tess Lea's (2008a) ethnographic study of health bureaucracy and its remedialist practitioners convincingly shows how projections of indigenous "neediness" are produced and along with it an institutional, bureaucratic, magical "real" replete with incantations such as "involve young people," "provide funding," and so on. The work describes a hegemonic logic that "cannot imagine betterment without some form of government intervention" (Lea 2008a:233), and which reproduces rationales for such intervention. Lea asks how someone like herself, both bureaucrat and anthropologist, can comprehend bureaucratic cultural habits and *not* reproduce them: "I say simply: forget the agony of trying to be pure; concentrate instead on being as technically proficient as you possibly can. Dare to draw upon evidence to inform your interventions. . . . The field does not need more good-willed generalists mouthing safe platitudes; it needs people who are competent at their profession and dignified in their analysis" (ibid., 235).

As I understand Strakosch and Lea, each points to looming aporias if one tries to understand history, action, and difference as if from the settler side only. There are too few ethnographically grounded accounts of the indigenous experience of change and its relational aspects.

The story of indigenous action cannot be told simply with reference to settler or indigenous arrangements as if these were separate. I have gotten to know people on both sides of that divide. My field experience in northern Australia has imbued me with a sense of indigenous views about what their forebears had lived through and of how they relate that to their own experience. The views of indigenous people tend to be less known, less accessible. At least, some of the most impressive indigenous people I knew were unlikely to articulate their views in ways that reach nonindigenous publics, partly for lack of opportunity, but not only for that reason. Some older people were shaped by particular local circumstances, at particular times, and some of those circumstances have changed or will change, making them less likely to address nonindigenous publics than their descendants who are the products of different times.

Relationship, Mediation, and Power

The first chapters in this book concern encounters of explorers, colonists, and indigenous people, and depict meetings that certainly had a stark, even shocking, face-to-face dimension: some of them involved people coming into each other's presence with little or no prior warning, producing visceral reactions, shouts, embrace, tremblings, evasions, and so on, none of which could have been premeditated or enacted in conventional ways. But there was an entire repertoire wielded by explorers, as we will see, a range of ways of thinking about and dealing with "Indians," "natives," "savages" that sprang from forms of organization and the systematization of understandings about what kinds of reactions might be encountered and how to steer them in particular directions. Likewise, indigenous people had a store of ideas about the strange, uncanny, and unknown that they brought to bear on these meetings to some extent and clearly also proceeded on occasion to further engage outsiders more fully.

Later chapters reflect on encounters that retain a dimension of the face-to-face, but in which indigenous-nonindigenous relations are mediated by "things," material objects that explorers and settlers pressed upon indigenous people and today are often a main basis for evaluations of indigenous difference. Here too there is obvious contrast and a great deal of incomprehension in how materiality figures in encounter, early and later. Further chapters reflect on the changing nature of indigenous-nonindigenous relations when a much more clearly demarcated, geographical set of frontier spaces bounded by hostility had been established and there was an ever larger number of settlers who consider themselves to be on one side of it, wherever they may be geographically. In this circumstance settlers produced and circulated widely among themselves understandings of indigenous persons, behavior, and character, while an ever smaller proportion of the former had any significant face-to-face interaction with indigenous people. Several later chapters deal with what I have experienced as indigenous responses to these frontier events and to intensifying conversion of social spaces and persons into ones infiltrated by and linked to settler institutions. This includes the emergence of persons of mixed race, what indigenous and nonindigenous people made of it, and state efforts to control it.

The final chapters consider the nature of relationships in recent years when Australian governments had changed their modes of dealing with indigenous people to the point of consulting them with respect to resource development projects. Power becomes stretched across a more complex set of linking relations between indigenous and nonindigenous people and institutions; and indigenous people deal on a personal level with those who come close to them but also increasingly apprehend the difference among levels and people as representing them rather than as authoritative or powerful in their own personal right. Through an analysis of a particular prominent "sacred sites" dispute, Chapter 7 shows, mutatis mutandis, how persons as highly placed as the prime minister of Australia have interpreted aspects of disputatious situations in terms that they took to be reflective and respectful of indigenous action and belief very foreign in character, in that case with decisive political consequences. There as in other cases there was a chain of mediated links across a complex set of relations.

In all forms of action it is often the case that the interacting parties are unequally resourced, endowed with forms of technological and other material, as well as ideological and social backing, sources of inequality between them. We regularly talk of differences in power. What do we mean by this? Power, though a notoriously contested notion, is often referred to by Max Weber's (1947:152) formulation: "the probability that one actor within a social relation will be in a position to carry out his own will despite resistance." Despite undefined notions of "will" and "resistance," this statement usefully points to the issue of unequal capacity. In the encounters studied in this book, such unequal capacity shaped thinking and acting, but it did so in different ways at different times.

As noted above, mobility—global and local—on the part of outsiders was a first key indicator of power differential. Explorers and settlers were able to arrive on the continent with a "pre-accumulation" (Wolfe 2016) of ideas, preconceptions about who the natives might be and how to deal with them, technical expertise, and plans. None of this would have been evident to indigenous people for some considerable time. Settlers were able to make use of it in order to press on with exploration and expansion even under the direst of circumstances, which indigenous people obviously sometimes misjudged as likely to extinguish their efforts. Never was that the general outcome, although individual explorations were occasionally disastrous. Also locally mobile wherever they went, explorers were able to co-opt people to assist them, but in specific and sometimes ambiguous, evasive, and duplicitous terms,as Chapter 4 illustrates. Settlers were able to move, resettle, and introduce large numbers of animals whose presence put indigenous-nonindigenous relationships on a collision course (Roberts 1969; Reid 1990: chap. 4; Barta 2008:524–26).

There are instances of direct, physical effects of power upon indigenous people, obviously in the form of physical violence but also, more subtly, in the ideas and ingenuity by which outsiders attempted to engage them and win their compliance. There were accumulations of power in the relationships that growing settler numbers and institutions were able to actualize among themselves and from which indigenous people were excluded. In episodes of the recent past and present, structural conditions enabled government officialdom to determine the separation of children from families based on categorizations of human types and associated ideas of education and improvement; indigenous people were and are variously allocated and reallocated outside and inside bureaucratic and administrative schemes of management. Late in the piece, in the final decades of the twentieth century, indigenous people come to be "recognized" as meriting a role in processes that channel the exploration of natural resources, ostensibly in the name of community consultation.

Sometimes, outsiders' forms of power become structuring conditions of indigenous people's lives, without their necessarily focusing on how that has come about and without these conditions being directly taken account of in their forms of action. However, when indigenous families seek to avoid the police or regularly occupy town spaces so as to minimize interaction with whites and with other indigenous people, we see people dealing knowingly with structures of power. It is more difficult, but important, to render account of how forms of power and influence operate when social landscapes, soundscapes, money transactions, and many other kinds of events and actions penetrate people's lives in new ways.

We need a general term for a form of life that persists in difference, having and recognizing qualities of its own, while it is lived in the shadow of potentially dominant power and hegemonic cultural influences, whether the latter come in the form of foods, labor, music, visual culture and technology, welfare, or churches. Neither "autonomy" nor "subordination" describes this form of life. I have sometimes referred to this general condition as "intercultural" (Merlan 1998, 2005) with reference to relations between indigenous people and communities and wider Australian society, but that deliberately leaves such a space open to be specified more closely. To do so is difficult. It is important to recognize forms of indigenous difference, both continuous and innovative, in people's lives, but without resorting to holistic concepts of continuous cultural logics that fail to account for change and conditions.

Difference is partly an effect of power. While the history of indigenous-nonindigenous relations includes some encounters with the potential for equality at the personal, often corporeal level, these moments were fragile before the larger forces in play. In longer-term colonization, zones and boundaries of difference are demarcated in a power-laden regulatory way that indigenous people were to observe as persons and collectivities. We see indigenous people responding in a variety of ways that bespeak some fragmentation as they become entangled, if not encapsulated, within the fields of value that these practices subserve.

Today we continue to witness an ongoing struggle over the nature of indigenous difference. There is competition between ideas of the timeless difference of traditional "Aboriginal culture," which can be highly valued, both by indigenous and nonindigenous people; and the unruly differences of many everyday indigenous settings—including conditions of people, houses, the use of things and money, the nature of relationships to people and institutions—which administrators and many others typically read wholly as consequence of "disadvantage" requiring remedy and reformation (Strakosch 2015:139–43, 157–58). This has policy implications, creating spaces for further state involvement (Lea 2008a, b; Strakosch 2015). I take to heart Povinelli's concerns about suppressive power. This book, like her work, is concerned in many places with realities that persist beyond the pressures to commensurate and that are discernible and expressed in indigenous people's own reactions to and musings on nonindigenous difference. As will be demonstrated in this book, incommensurability often appears not as classically "cultural" but at a mundane level, carried in the structures and practices of socioeconomic and racialized inequalities that are so much the medium of indigenous-nonindigenous relationship today.

CHAPTER 1

Nobodies and Relatives

Nonrecognition and Identification in Social Process

This chapter examines two modalities of indigenous-nonindigenous engagement in early encounter. One was their complete refusal to engage. The second was identification by indigenous people of Europeans as spirits of the dead. The Europeans were at an advantage. They had some general reports concerning Australia's natives and some reported knowledge and experience of other Pacific peoples. Aborigines probably had variable experiences and ideas about degrees of otherness on the part of people outside their immediate region and within the range of their own form of life,[1] but they had no inkling of the existence, cultural repertoire, and mind-set of these strangers. Thus the outsiders had enormously greater power to control the terms of engagement between themselves and the Aborigines. I will argue that nonengagement is a major modality of social orientation, fundamental to building and maintaining social boundaries. Nonengagement is arguably part of a family of practices, a spectrum of involvement. In the historical context examined here, the nonengagement, or deliberate indigenous refusal of engagement, was a first-response tactic, before some other kind of response became imperative. The identification of people with spirits, I will argue, was often relationally specific: Europeans were identified as specific personalities or attributed particular social characters. Though deeply embedded in indigenous practices concerning people's identification with others, the identification of Europeans with spirits could be rapidly questioned in this new context, as we will see.

They "Scarce Lifted Their Eyes"

Joseph Banks, the botanist accompanying Captain James Cook's first great voyage (1768–71), observed parties of indigenous people in what came to be called Botany Bay, an area only a few kilometers south of what is now Sydney's central business district. From the ship *Endeavour*, Banks saw the natives fishing from small boats within easy sight of the English. Despite that proximity the Aborigines paid no attention to them. Banks (1962: vol. 2, p. 54) observed that they "scarce lifted their eyes" as the *Endeavour* passed "within a quarter mile of them" (Banks 1962: vol. 2, p. 54).[2]

There were other sightings of indigenous groups by the English. Yet twice in his journal entry for 28 April 1770, Banks mentions the ship being within close proximity of "Indians" who appeared "totaly unmovd at us." A few days later, Banks describes how twenty or so natives, seen walking along a beach, "pursued their way in all appearance intirely unmovd by the neighbourhood of so remarkable an object as a ship must necessarily be to people who have never seen one" (ibid., 63).

Perhaps the strangeness of a ship, a watercraft of an entirely unfamiliar kind, allowed this "remarkable object" to be unseen. While a ship would have been unfamiliar, we cannot leap to the conclusion that the natives did not physically see it. The diary does tell us that the "Indians" made different responses to the English over the period of several days, including these nonresponses. The entry of the same day, 28 April 1770, makes it clear that the ship had indeed been noticed by some "Indians" gathered about a fire. That they had seen it was inferred by Banks from the fact that they retired to an eminence from which they could watch it. Earlier in the day, the sailors were also waved at, invited to land, and menaced by men brandishing "pikes and swords." It was only later, when the ship entered an inlet, that it was completely ignored by people within easy eyesight. That vision was good at the mentioned distance of a quarter mile is shown by an entry of 8 June in which things went quite differently at a location on the ship's northward travel along the coast: "Still sailing between the Main and Islands; the former rocky and high lookd rather less barren than usual and by the number of fires seemd to be better peopled. In the morn we passd within ¼ of a mile of a small Islet or rock on which we saw with our glasses about 30 men women and children standing all together and looking attentively at us, the first people we have seen shew any signs of curiosity at the sight of the ship" (ibid., 76). Thus, "not seeing" was only one kind of early event among others.

There are other recorded instances of indigenous people's refusal on early encounter to make sensory contact, even on occasions when outsiders, men of ordinary stature, were physically copresent or in close proximity with them.

In 1844, India-born Charles Napier Sturt (1795–1869), soldier, pastoralist, then explorer, set out from Adelaide northward on his third and final Australian expedition. Notwithstanding the seven decades' difference between his incursion and Cook's, he was moving into uncharted parts of the continent.[3] His party frequently encountered Aborigines who had not seen Europeans before; and it seems likely that many had not yet received reports of them. On one such occasion the explorers ascertained that "some natives were encamped at a little distance above us; but although we went to them, and endeavoured by signs and other means to obtain information, we could not succeed; they either did not or would not understand us; neither, although our manner must have allayed any fear of personal injury to themselves, did they evince the slightest curiosity, or move, or even look up when we left" (Sturt 1849: vol. 1, p. 414).

Sturt's party tried to engage the Aborigines face-to-face, but evoked little reaction. This lack of reaction, we are entitled to assume, must have been deliberate. Perhaps even more surprising, when the party abandoned those efforts and were leaving, the Aborigines seemed to take no notice of them at all. They appear to have been looking down, not up or at them.

This null reaction is recorded often enough, in different parts of the continent. We immediately suspect studied avoidance, but what is to be made of that as a form of relation?

Maurice Merleau-Ponty (1962:361) wrote that "the refusal to communicate is still a form of communication" and that recognition is a sociocultural practice, effected through habituated bodily practices, and embedded in social convention and experience. By refusing to look, Aborigines were denying the others a subject status and refusing to engage with what they might be doing. The reciprocity inherent in exchanging visual recognition was being blocked from the outset. To meet the gaze of another, as Merleau-Ponty (1968:142) puts it, is to see oneself from without, that is, to acknowledge an external perspective on oneself.[4] Thus not to see is also to defer being seen and the redefinition that occurs when one places oneself in the gaze of another. Though in near face-to-face contact, Aborigines were constituting the other as outside the sphere of what social theorist Alfred Schutz (1967:164–72) calls a "We-relationship." Avoidance here apparently involves attending but presenting to the avoided other as if not doing so.

A relation constituted by nonrecognition is usually asymmetrical and power-laden, involving incipient or established dimensions of power, perhaps also awe and fear. In this case there is a politics of withholding on one side (the Aboriginal one), and (typically) what was an eager attentiveness to the possibility of direct interaction, if not invasiveness, on the other. Nonrecognition is a denial of the other as encounterable, of commonality or (in a broad sense) common objects that could be the subject of negotiation between them.

How long can nonrecognition go on, under what circumstances, and what may it morph into?

Nonrecognition at early encounter was a tentative, transitory experiment. Would the ignored strangers disappear or at least remain distant? The indigenous people may have dealt with other unfamiliar or unexpected creatures in this way. They may have felt themselves to be in the presence of something weird or threatening. They were not eager to further the engagement (while the outsiders typically were), but they no longer had the capacity to shape their actions autonomously of those outsiders. Their nonresponse was under external influence.

First Contact

The phrase "first contact" often refers to first contact between entire peoples previously unknown to each other, usually "moderns" and "preindustrials." In commenting on various terms applied to the quincentennial celebrations of Columbus's Bahamian landing, Caribbeanist anthropologist Michel-Rolph Trouillot (1995:114–15) noted that the term "conquest" was challenging the conventional term "discovery." He considered the rising popularity of the term "encounter" as evidence of "the capacity of liberal discourse to compromise between its premises and its practice." "Encounter" sweetens the horror, he argued, as it evokes give-and-take. A reminder of indigenous agency, "encounter" is part of recent rehabilitation of the category of the indigene who had all too long been portrayed as simply vanquished. Trouillot objected that emphasis on give-and-take fails to acknowledge the hugely unequal resources and outcomes that "conquest" places more clearly in focus. There is much about the historical outcomes, as Trouillot observed, that refuses sweetening.

For Tzvetan Todorov, author of *The Conquest of America* (1999), what took place after 1492 was not only the invasion and progressive subjugation of one group of peoples by another; it was principally, and perhaps predictably, the fatal meeting of two different sign systems, two ways of interpreting the world. The predominantly preliterate Aztecs lived in a world that, according to Todorov, was tradition- and past-oriented and with an inherent or internal relation to what we call "nature" rather than one of externality. In what probably counts as the dénouement of the book, the Aztecs, confronting a critical situation in which "the art of improvisation matters more than that of ritual" (p. 87), were unable to counter the arrival of Cortés because they were paralyzed in the conviction that he was a god. Europeans were able to assert themselves through their different (let us follow some of Todorov's wordings and say "superior") ability to use and manipulate signs; *logos* over *mythos*.[5] Indigenous people and conquistadors lived in different worlds of meaning.

Todorov's story of European capacity to understand others better than those others' capacity to understand Europeans is pervaded by moral critique, and he refers to the resulting destruction of pre-Columbian society. But is this the only way to narrate processes of culture change? Studying the Yucatecan Maya, following the Spanish conquest and throughout the colonial period, William F. Hanks (2010) provides evidence of the adoption of aspects of an originally alien culture. He thus offers an alternative to Todorov's story of cultural collapse. To raise this point does not downplay the drastic nature of colonial impact—in Mexico or in Australia. However, positing of complete collapse implies that little or nothing of interest remains in its wake, and it fails to deal with the specific courses of colonial histories.[6]

Perhaps the best-known first contact account to North American and European academia is Marshall Sahlins's (1985) treatment of the Hawaiian adventure, then misadventure, of Captain Cook. In his last voyage to the South Pacific (1777, after his first visit to Australia in 1770), Cook was (mis)recognized as Lono, the deity of seasons whose arrival Hawaiians awaited and celebrated annually. Sahlins's "first contact" theorem is that people greet the unexpected or novel in categories and forms of action already familiar to them. There is evidence that after first associating with the annually returning god, Hawaiians rapidly found this identification contentious and became disabused of it. The seeming felicity of Hawaiian and English coincident identities imploded (partly because of competition between priestly and chiefly factions that came to involve Cook), and Hawaiians killed him and some of his crew at Kealakekua Bay on the island of Hawaii in 1779.

Sahlins suggested that the events of encounter proceeded, initially at least, in terms of a Hawaiian cultural logic (Sahlins 1985). The assertion was, for him and some others, important for its preservation of the relevance of "culture" and as a riposte to other analysts seen as reducing or fitting non-European histories to the history of global capitalism (cf. Wolf 1982). Just as important, however, seems to be the fact that the original identification was short-lived. According to Nicholas B. Dirks (1996), Sahlins deals only with a dramatic first moment of culture contact; he argues that the notion of distinct "cultural orders" survives Sahlins's analysis relatively intact. His emphasis is on the question how cultural *categories* change, rather than on the openings produced in the historicity of social life.

Though their accounts differ in some ways, both Todorov and Sahlins emphasize indigenous people's dealing with otherness by deploying conventional, preexisting forms of categorization: in both Mexico and Hawaii, this involved misrecognizing arriving Europeans as gods. Even accepting the likelihood that this may have occurred as part of the spectrum of first contact responses, what part does this play in our understanding of the relationships that went forward from those moments? We need to recognize greater openness in what is meant by "culture" and to be wary of holistic notions of culture/s. Of course people will bring aspects of their existing ways of thinking and doing to engagement with the strange and unknown. But perhaps the situations have prompted indigenous people to think and respond in alternative ways, and produced something new?

Richard White has coined the term "middle ground" to draw attention to the new culture generated beyond the "first contact." In *The Middle Ground: Indians, Empires, and Republics in the Great Lakes Region, 1650–1815*, the "middle ground" is "some common conception of suitable ways of acting" (White 1991:50). It is not entirely anybody's, but a product of European-Indian interaction. The "middle ground" was a historical phase, entailing that each "side" (complex assortments of Indian and European actors and groups) strove to attain cultural legitimacy in terms that the other could recognize, under conditions in which neither side could achieve its ends solely through force. This produced outcomes in which Frenchmen and Algonquians act more as they think the other will recognize, in ways thus influenced by them, than they otherwise would. This asserts the importance of dimensions of mutuality in circumstances of ongoing contact across boundaries of difference—continual awareness of being (visible) in an interactive zone.

Australian historian Henry Reynolds (2006:7) has denied the existence of any such "middle ground" in Australia in which those in encounter sought to achieve mutual recognition and intelligibility. Effectively, the power relation was at no stage as nearly equal as in the Great Lakes case. Reynolds is correct insofar as the scale and density of settler-indigenous relations in Australia gave less opportunity for whites' enculturation into indigenous ways. With the possible exception of subsistence graziers and dingo scalp hunters on the most marginal pastoral country (Finlayson 1952:116), there was no Australian frontier equivalent to the continual involvement of French fur traders with Indians on the Great Lakes. Nevertheless, White's historicization of frontier culture invites us to consider the roles of violence and material exchange in the quest for mutual intelligibility in all encounter material.

The Openness of Copresence, and Interaction Rituals

We need to consider the timescales at which nonrecognition occurs and its social extension: how does something that initially happened between small encountering groups such as these become characteristic of a broader relationship? And what role does it play there, as in indigenous-nonindigenous relations in contemporary Australia? Encounter between indigenous people and outsiders proceeded and intensified over the following decades from such moments as the nonresponsive ones discussed at the start of this chapter. Expansion of interaction resulted in changes in the ways that these people "on the ground" dealt with each other and fed back into and accompanied other changes occurring elsewhere in the larger frameworks in terms of which they did so, over time producing *changes in kinds of persons*, understandings and surmises concerning each other resulting from such interactions.

While contemplating nonrecognition and its possible persistence, we also find evidence of the extent to which participants in early encounters did engage and did manage to comprehend each other's meanings and intentions, despite great gulfs of difference, typically, the absence of any common language and, frequently, of any verbal mediation. Within minutes of encounter participants were gesticulating to each other: sometimes to warn each other off, to discourage approach; but also sometimes to convey messages concerning details and immediacies of direction of travel, nature of the landscape, availability of water, and presence of people in other locations. All of these communications would have involved basic elements of "interaction ritual"

(Goffman [1967] 2005) between the different parties to the extent of trying to make themselves comprehensible to each other through gesture, tone of voice, gaze, positionings, and (no doubt with considerable room for misunderstandings) indications based on assumptions about what the other party was asking or wanted. No doubt many verbal statements were uttered, a large number of which would have remained unintelligible or sometimes intelligible to an extent via intermediaries whom explorers and settlers engaged to accompany them. It would go against everything we know to assume that capacity to interact is completely blocked off, even in cases of minimum commonality in background; a great deal can be conveyed, particularly in face-to-face mode, including aspects of orientation, emotion, intention, and propositional meaning. Yet we must also assume that there were great gulfs of intended meaning, evaluation, and substance that were *not* conveyed.

Indigenous nonrecognition as a first way of dealing with outsiders suggests a number of questions. How deliberate was it? How concerted? How "cultural," that is, how can it be contextualized in relation to other practices? We need theory that allows us to understand how these interactions could be both determined by the cultural formations in which agents were embedded and yet not determined by them, so that agents changed as they interacted. We get some help here from "practice theory" and some of its predecessors engaged with the effort to come to grips with social process understood as relatively open and dynamic rather than as enclosed and channeled. Another helpful source is phenomenologically based conceptualizations of differential "sedimentation," or more versus less entrenched and incorporated quality of practices and their openness to change. Let us briefly consider these two theoretical topics.

Culture and Sedimentation

Thinking about the concept of "culture" as it evolved in the nineteenth and twentieth centuries has had to grapple with the issue of conscious awareness and the depth of actors' awareness of practices as meaningful. For some major culture theorists, culture has never been simply a matter of products, material or otherwise. Anthropologist Franz Boas, in reinterpreting the "culture" notion away from evolutionist as well as broad, traditional humanist usage (such as that of E. B. Tylor) and identifying it instead with the burden of custom and tradition, attributed to "culture" a strenuous hold over people's behavior

(Stocking 1966), a kind of "second nature." In his hands, culture was transformed into a comprehensively behavior-determining medium that was no longer to be a basis for demeaning (such as primitivizing) comparisons, but understood as a word for a common human condition, considered extremely difficult for people everywhere to get outside of. It was also in these Boasian transformations that "culture" became definitively, anthropologically pluralized (into "cultures").[7]

Boas's transformative usage, in representing people as subject to their culture/s, also involved a new apprehension of the role of unconscious social process. It became no longer necessary (or even plausible) to attempt to explain customs in terms of "conscious reasoning" or a directly utilitarian origin; rather, in Boas's (1904) terms, culture was rooted in general conditions of life.[8] In fact, Boas (1904:246, 253–54) argued that the more a piece of behavior was repeated and unconsciously imitated, the more difficult it was for people to break with it. Secondary rationalizations or explanations of custom—why do we do X?—though not "true," came to the fore especially at generational or other breaks at which, for example, children might ask questions or in other circumstances that denaturalize custom. Thus, for Boas, reflexive appreciation and articulability involve a state of exception that breaks through ordinary practice, or culture, which is largely associated with unconscious, routinized, or taken-for-granted behavior.

Boasian notions of culture as largely second nature have some parallels with Pierre Bourdieu's (1972) much later concept of habitus. Bourdieu drew on phenomenology, and it served for him to incorporate the social into the body (a dimension that did not play an explicit part in Boas's views of culture). By "habitus," Bourdieu refers to the inculcated and accumulated dispositional structures that social actors come to incorporate or embody: why do we feel at home in certain kinds of environments rather than others, or act in certain ways rather than others we feel to be unfamiliar? The concept of habitus was aimed at circumventing what Bourdieu saw as both objectivist and subjectivist fallacies in social theory: attributing to ethnographic subjects the analyst's objectifications on the one hand; and the limitations of a personal perspective on the other.

There has been considerable debate over how dynamic (or otherwise) the concept of habitus may be, whether it manages to overcome the enclosures of notions of "structure" and the implications of conceiving habitus as deepseated bodily disposition without representational content and only limited availability to reflection. Bourdieu (1994:122) certainly intended habitus as a theorization of generativity rather than determination, of an active and creative relation (*ars inveniendi*) between the subject and the world. He does, however, suggest the priority of experiences, for example, early childhood ones, which he thinks prevail in the systems of disposition that constitute habitus and lead to relative closure to others (1994:134). With notions of habitus and field and the concept of symbolic violence, Bourdieu provided an alternative perspective to (especially early) determinist Foucauldian "domination" of subjects by regimes of knowledge and power. In these and other terms, social theorists have tried to explain our orientations to the world as encultured beings.[9]

It is useful to loosen up a rather undifferentiated notion of "habitus" by considering a gradation, spectrum, layering, or differential sedimentation of practices: their relative significance to the way people act and the kinds of awareness people have of them. One might think of "habitus" or embodied dispositions, some of which are more firmly incorporated and entrenched, but others of which are more unstable and temporary; some that people are aware of and others less so. Let us imagine some dispositions may perfuse a range of distinguishable practices, without the underlying common thread necessarily being itself salient or recognizable to actors. The notion of a spectrum of more and less entrenched habitual orientations, permeating assumed knowledges and forms of practice, could usefully be associated with a modulated concept of dimensions of subjectivity more or less open to fashioning and refashioning (whether by self-conscious "reflexive transformation," willed change, or otherwise). To entertain such dimensions would also help to cast personhood in more sociohistorical terms and culture in more distributive ones, that is, as distributed in forms of action and conceptualization. This would also allow a more diversified picture of the varying, overlapping, and sometimes conflicting ways in which people apprehend contexts and are shaped and transformed, profoundly or in more transitory ways.

Time and Resonance

The indigenous people with which this chapter began reacted to sightings of outsiders in a number of ways: by brandishing spears, by flight, by direct gazing, and, on occasion, no (evident) response at all. Nonrecognition was the most difficult for explorers to define as an event. They had awareness of themselves—they had made themselves visible, sometimes waved, called out—but the indigenous people failed to react in circumstances in which re-action seems fully expectable. Was this a kind of (non)response that indige-nous people would have named or described? We cannot know. At some point the indigenous people must have seen enough of Cook's ship and men to concert, whether explicitly among themselves or "instinctively," a nonre-sponse that lasted over an unknown but extended period of time—minutes if not longer. The same is true of the encounter with Sturt. On that occasion, the explorers tried even harder to elicit response, so indigenous nonresponse must be seen as deliberate ignoring of repeated efforts on the part of the out-siders to attract attention.

Processes relevant to meaningful human action, notes Stanton Wortham (2006:8), take place across characteristic time intervals, from milliseconds (for neuromuscular activity), to seconds, days, years, and centuries (cf. Lemke 2000). Over what times may nonrecognition, the refusal of exchange of gaze and awareness in the context of immediate copresence, characteristically take place? In the episodes that I have recounted, I suspect, the characteristic in-terval of nonrecognition in face-to-face situations occurs only over a very limited time span. Where people come together for longer periods of time and do not interact or react, it is usually in terms of a clearly framed and recognized kind of activity: a long and deliberate coming together in which initial talk is uncharacteristic and even held to be rude or proscribed for some reason; or where introspection rather than outward engagement is normative, as in a Quaker meeting. It is hardly likely that nonrecognition endured very long in early colonial encounter without turning into another form of action (as we shall see). It was probably relatively fleeting and sometimes culminated in indigenous people leaving the scene, moving away if they could, or some-thing else.

Such early encounters probably resonated well beyond their brief occur-rence. Indigenous people would no doubt have talked about them among themselves. Each event of this kind is likely to have been reported in particu-lar ways by those who were present. We are unable to know exactly what their reports were like or how varied they were. But we may assume they would gradually have become part of regular accounts to others who had not yet seen explorers or other colonials, perhaps involving interpretation of the clothes, animals, and other aspects of the outsiders' behavior. Where violence occurred—and it often did, as further discussed below—this would have also been reported in some form.

For a considerable time, in different parts of Australia, there would continue to be people who had never seen outsiders such as these Europeans. But that was to change, as was the range of responses. "First" moments were platforms for subsequent ones. Phillip Parker King of the British Royal Navy in 1821 was greeted by Aborigines in a harbor at King George's Sound on the south coast of the present Western Australia by "Indians ... hallooing and waiving to us" (Shellam 2009:4). This bold greeting, so different from nonrecognition, has to be understood in the knowledge that these people had been visited the year before by another ship, from which they had learned the word "water" from the Port Jackson (Sydney) language (ibid., 5) on the other side of the continent. The area had also been briefly visited by explorers George Vancouver in 1791, Matthew Flinders in 1801 and 1802, who went inland and met Aboriginal groups, and French navigator Nicolas Baudin in 1803, who found a sealer brig in a bay. The question that we might be able to answer is not: when was first contact here? But: what variable responses emerge and go forward from early encounter?

Earlier in this chapter, I discussed some approaches to first contact in which indigenous "culture" resulted in at least temporary alignment of Europeans with indigenous gods. To consider culture as a spectrum of action and disposition of which actors are more and less aware enables us to imagine forms of first response as at various points on the spectrum; it also suggests that responses would, correspondingly, be more and less likely to change if and when interaction continues and depending on the course it takes. Such encounters are nothing if not "historical," and so the notion of what is "cultural" in them needs to be flexible. Let us experiment with some of these ideas by considering what seems to have been a much more widely remarked commonplace of colonial contact in Australia—the idea that whites were ancestors or returned ghosts.

Were We Dead?

In many cases of colonial contact, outsiders seem to have been identified with out-of-the-ordinary beings. In the case of Hernán Cortés, Todorov's typecase in Mexico, the conquistador is said to have been taken to be a returning god, and this to have rendered the Mexicans incapable of response. We also saw an identification of Cook with Lono in Hawaii. In North America, something different is commonly recorded: first European arrivals are cast by narrators as already foretold in story or legend (Ramsey 1983; Miller 1985). Perhaps casting encounter in this way mitigated the shock of impact or had the effect of attributing power or distinction to the foretellers.[10]

Indigenous people, not universally but very commonly across the Australian continent, first applied to Europeans words that otherwise referred to "ghost," "spirit" of the dead (also, sometimes, terms the principal meaning of which was "white"). This suggests that, to some degree, they cast the new arrivals in terms of the persons and spirits of their imaginative and cosmological peripheries, mainly the dead. A mapping of terms for (Pama-Nyungan) Australian languages reveals their continent-wide distribution. The pattern is also common in other[11] languages of the continent, including in the region of my own field experience. We have a few explicit accounts of this sort of identification.

George Grey—soldier, explorer, colonial governor in Australia, New Zealand, and South Africa—led two (fairly disastrous) expeditions into uncharted country in northwest Australia (presently Western Australia) in 1837 and 1839. He was observant, but also much assisted by an accompanying Nyungar Aborigine (from the southwest area of present Western Australia), Kaiber, who undoubtedly helped him understand a good deal in their interactions with indigenous people as they moved across country. Grey (1841: vol. 2, p. 129; see also p. 363) mentions a man, apparently one just encountering whites for the first time, asking him repeatedly in the "Swan River language" (i.e., Nyungar, near present Perth, Western Australia), "Were we dead?" The asker apparently took it to be quite possible that the dead may have human form and be able to engage with others and answer such questions. There are many clear instances of indigenous people having made an identification of this kind in early contact, on the basis of an understanding that ghosts and ancestral beings (with whom arriving colonials were often first identified) could exist in the same space-time with living people.[12] But notice that, though evidently presupposing such an identification, in the situation of encounter, which he clearly takes to be extraordinary, the man is moved to ask, "Were we dead?"—questioning the identification directly of a being who, he supposes, may be of this kind. The query "Were we dead?" is also a kind of meta-question as to whether these creatures belonged to a category of "spirit" usually referred to by that term, already imaginatively prefigured? Possibly, but it is hard to know how consistent ideas about spirits of the dead may have been. It is important, in any case, to see this as the man's questioning matters previously assumed as commonplace but probably rarely put to such a salient, startling practical test.

Figure 2. Map of Australia showing distribution of "ghost" and "ancestor" terms in Pama-Nyungan languages. CartoGIS, Australian National University. Courtesy of Claire Bowern at Yale University Pama-Nyungan Laboratory.

It seems that identifications often did not remain at the level of a broad category of ancestral spirits, but were person specific. In another place, Grey (1841: vol. 1, pp. 300–302) recounts how an old man (north of Perth, and belonging to an apparently newly contacted group) gazed at him with great curiosity, then went off to fetch his wife, who, "throwing her arms round me, cried bitterly, her head resting on my breast. . . . At last the old lady, emboldened by my submission, deliberately kissed me on each cheek, just in the manner a French woman would have done; she then cried a little more, and at length relieving me, assured me that I was the ghost of her son." Again, Grey was no doubt assisted by local interpreters in understanding this fairly intricate message.

These stories evoke the interacting parties' differing perspectives. The old man (and woman) look at Grey, see him as their son because of his appearance and on the basis of acceptance of the possibility of the dead appearing among them, and they communicate this to him. Notice that difference in "color" was not prohibitive to their identification of Grey; in fact, they may have expected "ghosts" to be somewhat pallid. They seem to have seen other similarities, perhaps in features. Identification of a newly arrived European as ancestor might appear preposterous to readers who imagine racial difference would prevent the identification of personalities across such a solid-seeming barrier—to say nothing of the underlying notion involved, that a personality may resurface later in time as another individual.[13] Grey wrote that he was loath to disabuse them of their notion; he left the conviction with them, or at least did not firmly answer the question put to him in the negative.

In any case, the parties appear to be interacting over who or what Grey is, with the old lady firmly persuaded that he is her returning son. Grey realizes this and allows himself to be embraced and kissed. His conscience-ridden response neither completely confirmed this identification nor dispelled it, but this seems unlikely to have altered the old woman's certainty.

Indigenous identification of outsiders with the dead sometimes persisted well beyond early contact, even after the white outsiders were more numerous and their presence had become more widely known. Mary Bennett (1928:109), daughter of Robert Christison, who from 1863 established a station he called Lammermoor in far north Queensland, recounts that one old man wanted to claim him as a "defunct brother" who had "jumped up whitefellow." This reflects more explicitly an idea involved in the episode above: that their own people who had died could return as (what were by then called in Pidgin English and understood to be) "whitefellows" (not simply, that whitefellows generically were spirits of the dead). Presumably, however, identification of whitefellows with the dead and with specific personalities at some point became less common or thoroughgoing, even with respect to outsiders who were in close contact with indigenous people. This kind of assertion of identity is now rare or takes a somewhat different form in my experience.[14]

The identification illustrated by these episodes seems to have been highly asymmetrical. I know of no instance of Aborigines' regarding someone of their number as the ghost of a white person; always the converse, Aborigines regarding a white person as someone known to them. Nor are there reports of any white person claiming an Aborigine as a predecessor. These forms of interaction, early and late, seem to have been strictly unidirectional and sometimes phrased as claims by Aborigines of relationship or identification with whites.

The reasons for the asymmetry of this identification were, first, that Englishmen and Europeans would not have entertained notions of the dead as regularly capable of reappearing in everyday life, nor would they have identified people of different generations as embodying the "same" social personality; and, second, that they would have seen Aborigines as different in kind from themselves and found implausible specific identification of Aboriginal persons with themselves in life or death. Aborigines would surely have differed on the first count; and these episodes indicate that they did on the second as well. They did not draw a boundary around human "kinds" in the same way as did their "whitefella" contemporaries.

This difference in conceptualization and practice concerning human kinds as self and other is related to questions of power and influence. Clearly whites saw themselves as separate and distinct from Aborigines; while the latter, in circumstances that permitted, entertained the question whether they might not be the same or identifiable with each other. Solidification of a category difference as "racial" in Australia was by no means immediate or unbridgeable on the part of Aborigines (see Chapters 5 and 6). Race was not a fixed, given dimension of otherness for indigenous people but emerged as a historically and interactionally produced category. Racial difference was possible, from the indigenous side, because they noticed certain differences of the outsiders (alongside certain similarities); for the outsiders, "race" built on a "preaccumulation" of ideas about the kind of category to which natives belonged.

For Aborigines, things were different. Accustomed as Aboriginal people were to living in small-scale regional systems and patterns of movement, with modalities of extension outward beyond familiar populations, their relational repertoires were fine-grained as well as channeled in social categories (Chapter 5). This combination facilitated attention to differences, as well as building upon widely available relationship or social category types as means of social reckoning with people with whom they came in regular contact. This kind of practice of relationships did not tend toward absolutism, categorical solidity, or complete boundedness; rather it encouraged modalities of identification according to minor differences and similarities. Clearly many Aborigines rapidly resorted to categorizing outsiders as "ghosts" or "spirits" and also experienced fright and dread of them, probably partly because of this sense. Nevertheless the association of outsiders with the dead was also subject to question (as by the Nyungar man) in what were undoubtedly experienced as unusual events of contact and possibly to change and dislodgement. Casting whites in terms of an available cosmologically peripheral category occurred widely and immediately, given that complete and unexpected unknowns coming in unfamiliar guise was simply not an available idea on this continent (nor apparently one that could be projected onto a particular transcendent figure, as happened with the Cook-Lono identification in Hawaii). The category itself may have been without neat empirical correlates: what do ghosts look like? And how do they act? Thus the labeling of outsiders may have been spontaneous and definite, but their identification with whatever was taken to be the general sense of the category seems to have been open to modification in the course of events.

To consider the British as ghosts neither shielded the Aborigines from their troubling otherness nor enabled practical dealings with them. There is much evidence that early categorization of the outsiders occurred in the context of a good deal of uncertainty, as well as disequilibration (Chapter 3). The question by an indigenous person whether someone is dead, or a particular returned ancestor, is not only a practical effort to achieve understanding but a particular platform with respect to what comes next. What role does identification of outsiders with ghosts play in an ongoing process? How does its ideational and emotional content change?

The category (white man as "ghost") is historical in the sense that its meaning changes as indigenous circumstances change. In my own research I have known older Aboriginal people who have memories of the first white, or whites, they ever personally saw. But by their time—the early twentieth century—it was widely known that whitefellas were about, ran stations, mines, or other businesses, were often dangerous or problematic to deal with, but had important resources. Older people I have known have told of first meetings with whites, reporting that they were afraid. The substance of meetings as they remember them had to do with whites showing them how to use matches, giving them flour and sugar and tea to try, and so on, often paired with humorous accounts of how thoroughly they misunderstood these things—using flour for body decoration as if it were white ochre, mistakenly putting sugar in water and dissolving it all, and so on,[15] almost a narrativization of their own inexperience and simpleness. One gets the impression from such older people that they saw these whites as "other," perhaps even as somewhat uncanny. But in many cases they began to live (usually on unequal terms) alongside them and with them—some of the women having their children in more or less routinized domestic arrangements. The example of whitefellas as "ghosts" also helps us to consider what happens when preexisting cultural categories are put to work. Processes of encounter with whites may have unsettled understandings about the dead in general; they may also have led (more immediately) to questioning of the identification of outsiders with the category of the dead. In many places in Australia whitefellas are still referred to by Aborigines as they were in the past, but they are not assumed to be dead. Many northern indigenous people I know continue to sense the presence of spirits of "old people" in their vicinity and in the landscape (but this too is changing). What seems to have shifted definitively is this way of proposing commonality with whites, coinciding with a longer term of common awareness and new ways in which self-other boundaries are shaped. I have commonly encountered the conviction on the part of indigenous people that they think and experience differently than do whites and are much more likely to encounter and believe in spirits.

An appropriately historicizing view of encounter must recognize that, over time, Aboriginal people have been incorporated into a larger, colonizing world. The relations over time have typically been asymmetrical (unequal) with the consequence that, in one form or other, indigenous people and their sociality have been changed more than that of the now nonindigenous majority. By illuminating the temporally and spatially specific sources of inequalities, this book will develop some general conception of power and influence in a context of fundamental and foundational inequality.

Practices as Cultural: A Return

If we notice the plasticity of "culture," its openness to history, why should we continue to frame the underlying logic of responses to the unexpected as "cultural"? Let us review this chapter's examples: early "nonrecognition" of outsider presence, the recognition of whites as ghosts, and the identification of accessible whites as particular indigenous personalities. Can we find in the ethnographic record of "classical" Aboriginal culture the precedents of these responses?

Refusal of sensory contact is not recorded frequently in documentary accounts, but it appears often enough to suggest the systematic nature of this response. That is, it seems to have been patterned (not simply contingent) and recurrent. Therefore, in some sense it belongs to an interactional and socially transmitted repertoire within specific populations. There is much evidence for continental Australia suggesting that refusal of sensory uptake is a significant dimension of a spectrum of practices, some of which lie in the background of actors' perception and capacity for explicit articulation. What follows suggests a long-term historical context for indigenous Australia that seems to have fostered this as a constitutive dimension of practice.

Precolonially, indigenous copresent groupings were typically of relatively small scale (varying with seasonal availability of resources, livelihood rounds, and events of meeting, celebration, and the like). Most were mobile over seasonal cycles within regions and meaningful landscapes well known to them. People moved in and out of local groups according to specific personal connections and circumstances.[16] Ubiquitous modes of kinship and social classification provided the social means for continuing bonds and ways of orienting people's relations with each other in this situation of generally small scale, mobility, and regular dispersal across a known, meaningful landscape.

The setting of small group life in which some people, intimately related, saw each other and cooperated every day, was/is nevertheless not aptly characterized by what is sometimes romantically imagined to be immediacy or unmediated availability of persons to others. First, there were always significant others who were not immediately present. Second, there was variation and specificity in how persons were understood, and there were relationships along dimensions of kinship and other kinds of social classification and relation, age, and gender. Some relationships were stereotypically characterized by closeness and intimacy, others were lived out at least partly in terms of highly formulated prescriptions of behavior. Consider, for example, the "joking relation," with its "organized obscenity" enjoined in some regions between grandparents and grandchildren (Thomson 1932), and the explicit "avoidance" relations enjoined between categories of affines, notably son- and mother-in-law, on a very wide continental basis.[17]

Everyday life was lived with minimal built structures and other material means of separation within camp spaces. In these circumstances, direction of attention and orientation to others, on the one hand, and nonorientation, on the other, seem to have been major modalities for formulating, reproducing, and practicing relationships in differentiated ways. In terms of maximal contrast, with some people one could be physically close and involved. In relations with certain others, especially in-laws (with whom one might nevertheless be encamped) one had to maintain explicit physical and sensory nonengagement, conforming to notions of the proper behaviors among people related in this way. Such avoidance behavior cannot be understood as people just "staying away" from each other; it signals deliberate nonorientation that is socially significant and marked (Merlan 1997b). "Avoidance" is at one end of the sedimentation spectrum, where what one does is considered imaginatively and ideologically salient and highly communicable as a marker of what is important in social relations.

The famously complex social category systems of Australia—valued by indigenous people as foundational—can be understood as the context for their practiced modulation of directness versus indirectness, or for avoidance. Their continuing practice inculcated a more or less articulable sense of sensory circumspection. Their aversion of gaze and their other bodily orientations were relevant to culturally particular forms of agency and social relationship. These modalities developed as cultural under specific conditions of life. While their variable persistence today is conditional on life circumstances, circumspection and aversion still play a significant role in many indigenous settings.

For example, among all Aboriginal people of the Northern Territory I have known, direct gaze is considered intrusive and impolite; in the thought repertoire of older people, not explicitly reproduced as far as I know among younger people, direct gaze may even be lethal in some circumstances. Women I have known shared the idea that senior men could kill a child in utero by looking intently at the body of a pregnant woman. Women had to act appropriately to prevent this. Paperbark coverings were worn for the purpose; but more important, this was one dimension of gendered sensibilization, with women internalizing a sense of caution about behaving in ways that would invite aggression. Language encodes invasive direct gaze in a term of opprobrium that indigenous people translate as "lookin'-at bugger," that is, one who causes a feeling of disquiet and makes one ill at ease by looking too directly. Anybody who has spent time in communities of (remote?) Australia will recognize the demand for appropriate behavior in the "growl":[18] "No more lookin' at!" (i.e., don't look, stare).[19]

In many places in the continent, particular relationships are constituted through norms of circumspection and avoidance. Some of these are also highly normative and ideologically salient. In southern Arnhem Land, women are to avoid their brothers, not speak directly to them, nor give them anything except through intermediaries (W. L. Warner 1937; Hiatt 1966; Burbank 1985; Merlan 2016a). Women who fail to live up to norms are threatened with violence. Stages of life—initiation into adulthood, as well as bereavement—were also marked by circumspection, avoidance, retreat into silence, and deliberate blockage of the visual and other senses.

Older sources on greeting behavior among local groups or persons coming into contact after a period of time report typical forms of spatial and bodily circumspection that suggest the constitutive and channeling quality of this dimension on forms of practice. An ethnographic report on the Edward River in Cape York in the early twentieth century renders the muted tenor of encounter:

> Three men, each carrying a bundle of spears, spear-thrower and fire stick, appeared out of the scrub to the north of the camp. Although their approach was at once observed, causing an under-current of excitement in camp, no apparent notice whatever was taken of the men, who approached slowly to within about 40 feet of the northern fringe of the camp, where each squatted on the ground a few feet apart, placing his weapons in front of him. Not a word was spoken, and apparently no notice whatever was taken of their presence for about 10 or 15 minutes. Then a "big" man left the camp unarmed and strolled casually towards the man on the left, scraped a shallow depression in the ground close to him with his foot, as a native does before sitting down, and then squatted on the ground about a yard away from the visitor. Still not a word was spoken. They did not even look at one another, but kept their eyes downcast. After a few minutes had elapsed the old man of the camp spoke a few words in a low tone—inaudible to me where I stood a few yards away—and the other replied in the same casual way. Still neither looked up—lest he might betray to the watching camp the slightest interest or emotion. At length the old man called the single word *Bat* (fire) and a boy brought out a small piece of smouldering wood which he handed to the old man from the camp. This fire the old man then placed on the ground between himself and the visitor to whom he had spoken. In former times this no doubt concluded the ceremony, but on this occasion a tobacco pipe was lighted and handed to the visitor. A second man now left the camp, strolled casually over and spoke to the man at the other end of the line,

making a present, which was reciprocated. A little later all entered the camp, to be followed in the evening by a larger party of which they were the forerunners. (Thomson 1932:163–64)

From Central Australia, based on observations of the late nineteenth century, we learn that visits to people with whom interaction was sporadic or irregular were characterized by the visitors first making smoke so that their intention to approach was made clear; then by placing themselves within sight of the camp. The visitor

> does not at first go close up to it, but sits down in silence. Apparently no one takes the slightest notice of him, and etiquette forbids him from moving without being invited to do so. After perhaps an hour or two one of the older men will walk over to him and quietly sit down on the ground beside the stranger. If the latter be the bearer of any message, or of any credentials, he will hand these over, and then perhaps the old man will embrace him and invite him to come into the camp. . . . Very likely he may be provided with a temporary wife during his visit, who will, of course, belong to the special group with which it is lawful for him to have marital relations. (Spencer and Gillen 1927: vol. 2, p. 505)[20]

These examples from different regions indicate that bodily and orientational circumspection, including silence, downcast gaze, and the damping down of sensory availability in close proximity of others, was a highly developed dimension of the conduct of relationships and of special events in which the question of ongoing or resumed relationship was sensitive (Stanner 1937). This may be called "cultural." In contemporary settings that have undergone much change, such behavior is evident. In camps and settlements that I have visited indigenous people consider it intrusive to directly enter an indigenous camp or housing area where one is not a regular resident or otherwise well known. This is especially so for a white person, but this etiquette is observed and demarcates boundaries of greater and lesser familiarity among indigenous people themselves. Preferred protocol involves sitting or standing some distance away to await recognition; or a circumspect and very visible, slow approach while remaining at some distance. One's gaze is best indirect or averted (Burbank 1994:84). Yasmine Musharbash (2016) describes a contemporary Central Australian community, Yuendumu, in which improved opportunities for Aboriginal people to access housing now sometimes result in their living next door to white service personnel. But in her experience of twenty years' observation in the community, Warlpiri do not attend to nonindigenous neighbors visually or in any other way, nor do they talk about them, she reports, in their own daily conversations.

One of the most widely remarked emotions associated with indigenous social life is that of "shame" (Myers 1986; Harkins 1990; Burbank 1994), and this seems relevant. Shame is often manifest as a bodily enacted shyness (involving aversion of gaze, withdrawn demeanor) and sometimes explained by indigenous people as what comes from uncertainty, public exposure, a feeling of inadequacy or wrongdoing. To be guided by shame, to be withdrawn in these ways, removes from others the opportunity and reason, as indigenous people might say, for "lookin' at."

Nowadays, physical and sensory circumspection is an aspect of indigenous behavior that is often judged to require modification by schoolteachers (Harkins 1990) and others seeking to make indigenous children conform to valued models of attentive and productive behavior. This has helped to make it a subject of conscious awareness and a dimension of what indigenous people see as proper behavior, informing their explicit understanding of themselves. They often contrast circumspection with the outgoing behavior of nonindigenous others who "got no shame." As indigenous people, over a long period, have been made to feel inadequate and subordinate, circumspection may have been amplified or taken on special salience in relations with nonindigenous people.

Circumspection in all forms is very much part of what is abandoned by indigenous people under the influence of excessive alcohol: drunken behavior often seems to flaut the usual norms of deportment by deliberate intrusiveness and provocation (and is also often marked by complaints of social abandonment by others; Merlan 1998:198).

Indigenous forms of life have been radically altered in all parts of the continent, varying somewhat with the extent of colonial-era and later disruption and relocation of indigenous people, their conversion into semisedentary workforces, their institutionalization in missions, schools, and so on. However, it seems plausible to claim that sensibilities concerning bodily practices based upon the modulation of gaze, proximity, and other forms of bodily orientation continue to be significant through (and to some extent as a result of) some of these quite dramatic changes. They have acquired contrastive significance and value for indigenous people as specifically "blackfella" behavior.

Summing Up

Meeting aliens, indigenous people had to shortly adapt and adopt practices, change what they did, and perhaps explicitly change their minds. In the first instance, they sometimes refused perceptual contact and may have thought that these apparitions would go away. But of course they did not. We have posed questions about nonrecognition: Was it deliberate? Was it concerted? In what sense was it cultural? In relation to identification of whites as spirits of the dead, we have more specific guidance from the accounts. It often seems to have been very explicit and specific; and it was certainly based on quite explicit prior conceptions and categories. We noted also, however, that it seemed to be immediately available for questioning in unusual circumstances, either in terms of the general category, or whites' identification with it, or both.

Vignettes of refusal of sensory uptake and the identification of outsiders as spirits of the dead have provided material for exploration of culture and what is cultural. Preexisting cultural practice is important to all encounter, but accounts that examine it in such terms have been problematic in the extent to which they narrow the discussion to categories and changes in them. This works to thin out the notion of what is cultural and limits a historicizing approach. While attention to preexisting cultural influences reproduced in ongoing social process is important, scholarship has been principally oriented toward the question "What remains the same?" Attention to the preexisting practice does not provide the material for understanding the evident disequilibration, both positive and negative, that often accompanied encounter across boundaries of difference (Chapter 3).

Our concept of culture must enable a relational account of interaction across considerable boundaries of difference. Our perspectives on social process need to recognize culture's potential for openness, historicity, multiscale temporality, and its power-laden character. Culture refers to practices that are differentially entrenched, layered, or sedimented and differentially available to reflection and change. Change may occur through taken-for-granted assumptions being suddenly cast into question by events—such as the startling emergence of explorers whose initial identification as "ghosts" certainly did not settle ongoing questions of what to make of them and how to deal with them. Modalities such as nonrecognition and aversion continue to perfuse and constitute forms of everyday practice across perceived boundaries of difference whether these are internal or with respect to people seen as outsiders.

In the final part of this chapter I returned to its first theme—the somewhat unexpected form of encounter manifested in nonrecognition and refusal of sensory uptake. I suggested that this response is distinctly "cultural," in that sensory circumspection (e.g., "greeting behavior," "in-law avoidance")[21] is regarded by indigenous people as highly marked and as value bearing and worthy of mention as part of who they are, as part of their "culture," or "blackfella rule" now contrasting with "whitefella."

The chapter suggested that, in its wide and diverse distribution, sensory circumspection marks out a dimension of conduct that is deeply culturally entrenched, different from some more common acceptations of "culture" in being a modality of behavior rather than identifiable as thinglike. Some forms of this circumspection were and are more extreme than others and may merit being called "avoidance."[22] I sketched the general conditions under which such cultural forms became fundamental. These involved a small-scale and often highly dispersed, only periodically intensified, kind of sociality. This kind of life was supported in specific cultural forms (such as inclusive, extensible kinship and social categorization) that enabled long-term interdependence, continuity of connection, mitigated small scale and dispersal, and enabled seasonal and social flexibility (see Stanner 1958).

Such circumspection, deeply sedimented and distributed in indigenous practice, is more enduring under particular and even changing conditions of life than is any specific practice (such as avoidance of certain categories of kin or specific ways of showing respect). Forms of action in encounter—sensory circumspection, particular kinds of categorization—have some element of prior cultural content and shape, but the range of matters to which people may orient as new or salient is too varied for us to insist that responses are contained in distinct or necessarily accessible cultural terms. Change in these forms points to changes in indigenous-nonindigenous relationship, as an increasingly shared (but unequal) social world and mutually recognized forms of action were taking shape.

There is another question that can be asked, which continues to acknowledge the importance of the past but is less insistent concerning continuity: What gets repositioned and revalued and how? The ethnographer may also ask, what is happening now, what happens next, how do people see it? Thus inherently these questions make us pay attention to temporalities at different scales and recognize a plurality of patterning.

The next chapter focuses on first encounter that proceeds quite differently from sensory circumspection: the often-discussed issue of imitation between "primitives" and "civilized" parties in encounter. The chapter attempts to re-pose the question: not "What does imitation say about the indigenous other?" but "Is imitative behavior a practice especially oriented to identification and relationship?"

CHAPTER 2

Imitation as Relationality in Early Australian Encounters

Mere (?) Imitation

Europeans came to new lands such as Australia prepared to see and emphasize radical cultural, indeed civilizational difference. Sometimes, they succeeded in doing otherwise and recognized the quickness, the observational
acuity, the mirth, and other characteristics of the people they were meeting.
In many early journals of exploration, Europeans in direct, face-to-face contact with indigenous people remarked on those people copying what they
themselves had done: imitation at close quarters. They recognized the model,
the source material, as their own actions, copied by their indigenous
interlocutors.

For example, Nicolas Baudin, the leader of the French expedition to map
the coast of Australia, 1800–1803, reported that Bruny Island natives came to
them in the vicinity of what he called Port Cygnet, in the southern part of
present Tasmania, in the hopes of obtaining presents (or so he thought), and
they received "what we gave them with great outbursts of joy." He goes on,
"They imitated easily and with gestures, and repeated clearly several French
words" (1974:345).

The natives' repetition of words of foreign languages and of the texts of
songs accurately amazed Europeans. The outsiders considered it something
they themselves could not easily do. The French explorer and naturalist with
the Baudin expedition, François Péron, candidly compared himself with
Bruny Islanders (Tasmanians) in this regard: "Generally, they appeared to me

to have much intelligence; they grasped my gestures with ease; from the very first instant they seemed to perfectly understand their object; they willingly repeated words which I had not been able to seize at first, and often laughed when, wishing to repeat them, I made mistakes, or pronounced them badly" (in Roth 1899:36). "Imitation" implies not only a model and copy of it but also *mutual* awareness of this copying in some degree. Imitation, like nonrecognition, is best seen as a family of relational practices. Imitation requires focused attention upon what another is doing, and in this sense it differs from nonrecognition examined in the previous chapter. However, refusal of uptake also involves attentiveness, but presentation of oneself as *not* attending. The two modalities are therefore not completely opposite.

Early accounts of imitation sometimes noted it as a talent characteristic of primitive people. Contrary to this view, this chapter argues that imitative behavior may be a practice especially oriented to identification and relationship. As well, the occurrence of imitation in early encounter suggests that it was highly honed and developed in indigenous Australia.

Common to Men in a Savage State?

Early observers of indigenous Australians saw their imitative (mimetic) behavior as evidence of their primitive character, *mere* imitation, rather than creativity. During the long voyage of the *Beagle* (1831–36) Charles Darwin visited the locales of many groups then considered primitive, including Patagonia, Chile, New Zealand, and Van Diemen's Land (Tasmania). He had both an evolutionist and comparativist perspective. In his *Journal of Researches* he says of the Tierra del Fuegians:

> They are excellent mimics: as often as we coughed or yawned or made any odd motion, they immediately imitated us. Some of our party the officers began to squint and look awry; but one of the young Fuegians (whose face was painted black excepting a white band over his eyes) succeeded in making far more hideous grimaces. They could repeat with perfect correctness each word in any sentence we addressed them, and they remembered such words for some time.... All savages appear to possess, to an uncommon degree, the power of mimicry. I was told, almost in the same words, of the same ludicrous habit among the Caffres: the Australians, likewise, have long been notorious

for being able to imitate and describe the gait of any man, so that he may be recognized. . . . How can this [mimetic] faculty be explained? Is it a consequence of the more practiced habits of perception and keener senses, common to all men in a savage state, as compared with those long civilized? (1896:206)

At the end of his stay in Australia, Darwin witnessed a White Cockatoo "corrobery" ("great dancing-party"),[1] which he characterized as "rude" and "barbarous." He noted the dancers' close imitation of the emu in one dance, of the kangaroo in another, and though he was otherwise unable to find in the performance "any sort of meaning," he observed that "the [indigenous] women and children watched the whole proceeding with the greatest pleasure" (Darwin 1896:451).

To see imitation as a particular talent, or capacity, of such "primitive" people as Australian Aborigines is a recurring theme in colonists' observations. The report of the New South Wales Board for the Protection of Aborigines for 1910 (Legislative Assembly 1911) noted that children in the school at Ngoorumba (near Bundarra, New South Wales) display great interest in gardening, though it "is new to them," and make fair progress "in such subjects as give scope to their imitative faculties." The primitives' imitative faculty is one item in a wider apprehension of their weakness. Nineteenth- and early twentieth-century ideas about Australian Aborigines were often cast narratively, in terms of civilizational difference between "them" as primitives being overwhelmed by "us" as civilized people. In Darwin's time, the assumption was generally made that primitives were to disappear and would be unable to survive the changes overcoming them. Tasmania astonished Darwin, in this respect: "I do not know a more striking instance of the comparative rate of increase of a civilization over a savage people" (1989:329). To most readers of our time, this seems an intolerable amalgam of direct naming of wrongs perpetrated upon and by indigenous people, followed by a scientific-sounding objectification of events in terms of inexorable forces: "rate of increase" and the like.

In later views of the vulnerability of Aboriginal society, its collapse was due to the high degree of integration among societal institutions: if one thing gives, so do all the rest (see Chapter 1, n. 6). The idea that change entails collapse has been countered (in a usually fraught and politicized atmosphere) in recent decades by an equally mistaken position that continuity entails no deep change (or at least none that can be readily admitted to discussion). And, rather than regard them as "primitive," Australian Aboriginal society has been promoted as one in which the person-land relation is primary and continuous, and indigenous social practice is fundamentally to be seen in terms of kinship and relationality (cf. Glaskin 2012). In re-presenting Aborigines as kinds of persons, this revised account also suggests that their capabilities persist through major alterations in context.

The alternative to these collapse and survival tropes is to acknowledge that the person is a social category continually reconstituted—though partially rather than entirely—as social circumstances change. On this view, imitative behavior is historically and socially specific and exists in relation to other practices at particular times. But practices and dispositions are certainly not entirely mutable. Imitativeness is also clearly part of a general human repertoire. Persistence of such cultural phenomena may be in terms that are not explicit but more tacit, as discussed in the previous chapter.

We should recognize the relevance of a general human capacity for mimesis, while also attending to its sociohistorical specificity. This opens the way to theorize different forms of the phenomenon and to suggest, if not fully illustrate, a spectrum of imitative behavior. In such a spectrum questions of the structure and dimensions of variation become interesting and significant. Clearly, not all instances of imitation are equally intentional (one may sometimes imitate something about a model without meaning to), nor are they equally accessible to reflective consciousness of the parties involved or equally exact replicas of given models.

Imitation as Human Capacity

Imitation is a focus of research in many disciplines: in experimentally oriented fields including comparative, cognitive, developmental, evolutionary and social psychology; cognitive neuroscience; ethology; primatology; and robotics. In the more traditional human sciences, from Aristotle to Erich Auerbach, imitation, or mimesis, has been treated as a topic in ontology, philosophy, and aesthetics. Imitation has been recognized as fundamental in interaction as a modality for the linking of phenomenal experience and shared meaning in a way that creates a platform for more conventional, systematic, and symbolic expression-content linkages and kinds of interaction (Zlatev 2005).

Whatever the phylogenetic distribution of the innate bases of imitation, higher primate observational and experimental data suggest that these are "open programs" requiring substantial environmental input before there develops a significant imitative capacity. Imitative behavior is seen not as definitive of the difference between humans and other animals but as a modality that, strictly defined, is not easily or fully attributed to even higher animals, despite the fact that some of our common imagery of imitative behavior is based on ideas of it as animal-like, simian in particular. With such experimental and primatological evidence there is no contradiction between seeing imitative capacity as phylogenetically (though not uniquely) human and seeing it as strongly susceptible to long-term contextual (cultural) influence.

Relatedly, imitation is seen by many of these experts as a possible key to understanding empathy. While there is still much debate around the extent to which babies and higher primates imitate, or merely emulate, outputs,[2] there is good evidence for the ubiquity of unconscious imitation or mimicry in human interaction. This phenomenon, dubbed the chameleon effect, refers to the unconscious or subliminal tendency to mimic the postures, mannerisms, and facial expressions of one's interaction partners. This level of imitation often seems to be "under the radar," or relatively unavailable to reflection.

Measures of electromyographic (EMG) activity show that people rapidly and unconsciously imitate the facial expressions of others, even when the presentation of these faces is not consciously perceived (Chartrand and Bargh 1999). Social psychological studies show that the mere perception of another's behavior seems to increase the likelihood of engaging in that behavior, facilitating interactions and increasing liking between interaction partners. High scorers on empathy tests are more likely to exhibit the chameleon effect. Unconscious mimicry could lead to an empathic response by biasing the facial motor system, which has been shown to influence mood. Contributing to the picture of the role of unconscious imitation are well-attested imitation deficits associated with autism, hypothetically related to early inattention to social stimuli (including adults imitating the autistic infant) and deficits in joint attention reducing the frequency of synchronous movement (Williams et al. 2001). Together, these results suggest that perception, socially relevant imitation (even if unconscious or only liminally perceived), emotional experience, and empathy are highly integrated. Integration of imitation and affect is relevant to evidence of mutual attention to emotional states from the early colonial encounter material.

However, much of what is recorded as imitative behavior in early Australian encounter, as we shall see, is at a different level than any chameleon effect, more "on the radar": in most events recorded (usually indigenous) people are described as engaging in imitation in which one person's action—typically complex in a sensorimotor sense and sometimes experimental, that is, seemingly intended to elicit reaction—is directly imitated, and this imitation is apprehended by the imitated person as such. Imitation is to this extent shared, entailing an exchange of perspectives between those in the imitative action: model action, interlocutor imitation, model apprehension of the imitation and the intent to imitate. The imitation remains pre- or only loosely conventional, experiential, and often evidently emotion-laden but unschematized, perhaps in some instances not completely voluntary, but in many others clearly so; cross-modal (involving sensorimotor coordination), highly iconic of the "original," and seemingly not oriented to making any particular statement or representation, but simply analogical. More examples of early journal recordings of such imitative behavior follow below.

Anthropologists on Imitation

The work of psychologists on imitation (e.g., Piaget and Inhelder 1969; Donald 1991; Zlatev 2005) has tended to focus on issues of bodily and cognitive capacity, on the question of human distinctiveness or otherwise in capacity to imitate, on the implications of imitation for definition of self and other, on spatiotemporal variations (immediacy, deferral) in imitation, on its proto-conventional and nonrepresentational character, on its relation to consciousness, on the capacity to imitate, on the relationality that imitation presupposes, as necessary to other aspects of human communication and interaction. Anthropologists, on the other hand, have tended to focus on imitation as a modality of relating to and defining oneself in relation to others at relatively high levels of social categorization of relationship between self and other. Recent explorations of this kind have therefore, not surprisingly, tended to come from consideration of the highly asymmetrical relations of colonialism.

In *Mimesis and Alterity*, Michael Taussig (1993) not only rejects primitivizing views of imitation that see it as animal-like; his focus on the fundamentally social, relational, and power-bearing enabled his critique of a colonial politics of representation of the other as completely different and separate. He argued that imitation is a useful trope for getting at processes of *producing* alterity, the mutually involved differentiation of self and other. Taussig (1993:19) epitomizes the "ability to mime . . . [as] the capacity to Other." He cites Walter Benjamin's remark that the "mimetic faculty" is the rudiment of a former compulsion of persons to "become and behave like something else" (Benjamin 1982). Taussig retains from Benjamin the insight that mimetic practice appears in every form of life, but also his conviction that it is diminished in modernity.

Taussig's commitment to this idea is rooted in romantic yearning. He aims to "reinstate in and against the myth of Enlightenment, with its universal, context-free reason, not merely the resistance of the concrete particular to abstraction, but what [he deems] crucial to thought that moves and moves us—namely, its sensuousness, its mimeticity' (Taussig 1993:2). Related to this is his concern to challenge capitalist reification, to restore tactility in order to understand how the world may be comprehended through the body. Little islands of imitativeness, sensuousness and tactility make themselves manifest everywhere, even if adults among us discover this by entering into what we imagine to be the child's world (Taussig 1993:77).

While Taussig follows a Benjaminian line grounded in the idea of sensuous correspondence between something and that which repeats it mimetically, Derrideans contest the kind of totalization that would allow for there to be an original to copy. They value continuing deferral and argue that anything that seeks that kind of totalization produces a radical and disruptive concealment and some form of excess. Performative repetition and inherent instability are the conditions of always-partial identity.

Homi Bhabha belongs to this Derridean camp in the way that he has made widely cited use of the notion of not mimesis broadly speaking but mimicry— his focus is on the artifice of imitation and the asymmetry that underlies it. A key textual provocation for him is British politician and essayist Thomas Babington Macaulay's famous "Minute on Indian education" (1835) in which he had written of creating "a class of interpreters between us and the millions whom we govern—a class of persons Indian in blood and colour, but English in tastes, in opinions, in morals and in intellect" (Bhabha 1994:87).

Bhabha's point is that mimicry produces people who are anglicized but emphatically not English, meant to be "almost the same, *but not quite*. This gives rise to what he calls the "*ambivalence* of mimicry . . . which fixes the colonial subject as a 'partial' presence" but ensures that there is a strategic limitation that makes mimicry "at once resemblance and menace" (86). Bhabha considers mimicry not a harmonization but a resemblance that is not presence. This does not seem to directly deny the original as presence in the way that some Derrideans might, but to delimit the possibility of imitation. "Sly civility" arises in the gap between colonizers and their mimicked versions, accompanied by desire on both sides: on that of the colonizer, for the colonized to become more like them; and on that of the colonized, for quite a range of things, sometimes amounting to Anglophilia, and for what we might call the ideal "real," such as British justice, which they want to be realized as promised. Hegemony exists in the structure of colonial dependence that reinforces this gap, that is, power rules through a surrogate synthesis.

For Taussig imitation is dialectical, an exchange. He accentuates the joint and continuing *production* of otherness rather than simply its prior existence as brute fact—the position he intends to counter. Bhabha as theorist of colonialism places strongest emphasis on the impossibility of totalizations, both at the levels of "original" and "copy," as a function of power relations. Both Taussig's opening of the space of production of otherness and Bhabha's concept of power-laden partial resemblance are useful. Also useful are the impulses, briefly mentioned above, from cognitive psychology, which suggest to us the utility of closer attention to identifying the dimensions of imitation as psychosocial action.[3]

Prevalence of Imitative Behavior

We can consider early Australian encounters by attending to the framing that both parties applied and that affected how they understood the "empirical situation." By "framing" I mean the ideas brought to interaction that strongly affect how it is understood. Here I examine two framings of mimesis: instruction and comic. Such ideas were provisional and experimental, and humor was one way for those interacting to try out framings.

There were many circumstances in which diarists record indigenous people imitating some kind of action they had seen the Europeans perform, observing them, as it were, from a less directly engaged perspective; and in noting their intention, the Europeans sometimes assisted them to perform the action more effectively. This was not direct imitation by indigenous people of Europeans in interaction with themselves but based on observation by indigenous people of what Europeans did or sometimes what Europeans explicitly showed them. For instance, La Billardière (in Roth 1899:29) observed several forms of imitation and collaboration:

A native, to whom we had just given a hatchet, displayed great dexterity at striking several times following in the same place, thus attempting to imitate one of our sailors who had cut down a tree. We showed him that he must strike in different places, so as to cut a notch, which he did immediately, and was transported with joy when he saw the tree was felled by his strokes. They were astonished at the quickness with which we sawed the trunk in two; and we made them a present of some hand-saws, which they used with great readiness, as soon as we had shown them the way. These savages were much surprised at seeing us kindle the spongy bark of the *Eucalyptus resinifera* in the focus of a burning-glass. He, who appeared the most intelligent among them, was desirous of trying the effects himself, threw the converging rays of the sun upon his thigh by its means; but the pain he felt took from him all inclination to repeat the experiment.

In short order, means of using a metal hatchet, a handsaw, and a magnifying glass were imitated. This was imitative instruction of a purposeful kind. On another occasion, a person referred to as a "chief" had observed a woman using a comb that had been given to her. He wanted to use it also but could not get it through his tangled hair. He was assisted, with difficulty: "I . . . was soon obliged to hold his hair back with the one hand, and pull the comb with the other. From this he did not shrink, but encouraged me in my work, saying frequently, '*Narra coopa*—very good.' And when the work was accomplished he looked at himself in a glass, with no small degree of pleasure. He was a man of an intelligent mind, who made rapid advances in civilization, and was very helpful in the preservation of good order in the Settlement" (in Roth 1899:44).

In cases that contemporary diaries record, the imitated content seems generally to have been derived from the bodily actions of Europeans and frequently their words. Such mimesis is not mere action learning, it is also results oriented. To note mimesis as imitative instruction is to depart from Darwin's framing of Fuegians' skill as comparable "to the instinct of animals," as "not improved by experience" and as static ("their most ingenious work . . . has remained the same, for the last 250 years" [1989:178]). What would Darwin have said if he had spent time closely engaged with people, trying to modify their tree-chopping technique with a new tool? Would he have conceded a greater comparability of them with himself in respect to the improvement of their technique by experience?

Our consideration of humor can begin with West's ([1852]1966:88) report on imitative ability as a general capacity of the natives of Tasmania: "They were fond of imitation and humour; they had their drolls and mountebanks;

they were able to seize the peculiarities of individuals and exhibit them with considerable force." The link that is made between imitation and humor is important, relatable to the extent to which good humor, drollery, and expressions of exuberance seem to have been a regular feature of some early encounters that remained of a relatively positive kind. (Many encounters did not remain so.) Playfulness did not escape Darwin's notice. We learn from him that indigenous people appreciated capacities of Europeans to imitate: members of the *Beagle*'s crew in Tierra del Fuego were apparently not averse to engaging in antics and imitative behavior, we are told; although imitative of what and whether it was of the indigenes we do not learn. The Fuegians "were highly pleased by the antics of a man belonging to the boat's crew, who danced well and was a good mimic" (in Keynes 1979:96).

Antics appear to have been most notable when visitors played with children, when opportunity arose. Gaiety and forwardness of children are mentioned on a number of occasions by Baudin. After a short time, the children behaved "as if we had known them a long time," as if the visitors were old acquaintances. The children seem to have accommodated to the difference that the outsiders originally represented and were carrying on as usual. At least for the children, French reassurance enabled a restoration of affect as usual. And the French were able to play and engage in antics with them in a way they would not easily have done with adults.

Playfulness, antics—these seem to be exercises in bridge building. Darwin instinctively treated reproduced language in these encounters as something that is not first and foremost propositional but something uttered and taken up, a form of engagement. Similar forms of bridge building, the intent to produce shared feeling, can be seen in Darwin's observation that Fuegians expressed: "satisfaction or good will by rubbing or patting their own, and then our bodies" (in Keynes 1979:96).

Darwin implies that they are, in effect, suggesting an affective meaning content: satisfaction is shown by their rubbing their stomachs. They then do this to the outsiders, in the absence of the latter imitating the original gesture. The intent seems clear: to establish a mutuality of experience and feeling. Rubbing and patting (so Darwin suggests) were iconic of good feeling and satisfaction. (Presumably, all were smiling or seemed amiable in other ways during this exchange.) Darwin also notes the importance of reciprocity when he writes of having accompanied an old Fuegian man, who offered him evidence of friendly intent by "three hard slaps, which were given me on the breast and back at the same time"; and who then "bared his bosom for me to return the compliment, which being done, he seemed highly pleased" (Darwin 1896:205).

Imitation could turn into parody. George Mortimer (in Roth 1899:41) gives the following account of an interview in order to make the point that French discoverers often found it difficult to open communication with the natives: "Our third mate on landing, saw several of them [natives] moving off. He approached them alone and unarmed, making every sign of friendship his fancy could suggest; but though they mimicked his actions exactly, and laughed heartily, he could not prevail upon them to stay." Thus, imitation was not always a means of achieving greater contact with the other (by "becoming and behaving" like him). It could be a way of achieving some interaction but also bounding it off. Many diarists remarked on the great "shyness" of the natives, the difficulties of approaching them. Shyness is not what we see in the following anecdote, however. The French at Bruny Island encountered a group of women, one of whom stepped forward and made signs to the French to sit and lay down their guns, the sight of which frightened them, says Péron (2006:198). (And so it might have: Baudin [1974:323] reports having aimed at people and says he only had to shift his gun to see how much people feared it. We may guess they had experience of its use.) After they sat, the women were all vivacity, talking, laughing, gesticulating, twisting and turning—when "M. Bellefin began to sing, accompanying himself with very lively, very animated movements. The women were immediately quiet, watching M. Bellefin's gestures as closely as they appeared to listen to his songs. At the end of each verse, some applauded with shouts, others burst out laughing, while the young girls (undoubtedly more timid) remained silent, showing nevertheless, by their motions and facial expressions, their surprise and satisfaction" (Péron 2006:199). After M. Bellefin finished, the most confident of the women "began to mimic his gestures and tone of voice in an extremely original and very droll manner, which greatly amused her friends. Then she, herself, started to sing in so rapid a fashion, that it would have been hard to relate such music to the ordinary principles of ours" (Péron 2006:199–200).

Here the woman's action is clearly recognized as imitative of what the Frenchman did; but Péron seems to imply that she does it as much or more for her companions' amusement as to amuse or engender any sort of commonality with the French. We may interpret this as a targeted mimicking for the benefit of the other women.

Here a participant (Bellefin) is the apparent focus of comment rather than (only) of intended communicative engagement. Where the person copied is an interlocutor like Bellefin rather than a nonparticipant in the interaction and copying is addressed to another intended audience, imitation often becomes a form of mockery and ironic comment rather than a bridge between those seemingly in direct interaction. The effect is to make an ostensible participant an outsider and to make those who receive the message the actual nearer ("in the know") interlocutors. This episode seems to suggest a certain confidence on the woman's part in drawing the distinction she did between insiders and the French outsiders.

Indeed, it may be that Bellefin's attempt to engage the attention of the indigenous women had misfired or gone slightly astray. As we will see (Chapter 3), European venturers thought about how to engage the "natives," whether by offering them various kinds of material items or by other forms of interaction. Often, imitations by indigenous people were of bodily actions that Europeans themselves deliberately deployed as part of a certain received and continually evolving set of ideas that these were the things that would captivate native audiences and serve as a way of evaluating their dispositions, a matter to which the visitors, as we shall see, paid considerable attention. This might be termed one kind of "framing" of imitative action, clearly arising from European preconceptions.

At this point, though, the woman does build a bridge more directly and materially with the French:

> taking some pieces of charcoal from a reed bag, she crushed them in her hand and prepared to apply a coat of this dark paint to my face. I lent myself willingly to this well-meant whim. M. Heirisson was equally obliging and was given a similar mask. We then appeared to be a great object of admiration for these women: they seemed to look at us with gentle satisfaction and to congratulate us upon the fresh charms that we had just acquired. Thus, therefore, that European whiteness, of which our race is so proud, is nothing more than an actual deficiency, a kind of deformity that must, in these distant regions, yield to the colour of charcoal and to the dark red of ochre or clay. (Péron 2006:200)

On this occasion, then, having imitated the song in a way that seemed more directed toward her companions—though certainly provoked by and also directed to the French—the woman explicitly created a ground of commonality between herself and the Frenchman by acting on him, almost certainly with the general aim of making his skin more like hers. This identification—perhaps also partly addressed to her Aboriginal audience and almost certainly in a spirit of fun—was seemingly her intention, and Péron clearly took this, in any event, as an effort to cancel his unusual whiteness. It is more typical in these journals to read of the natives imitating the Europeans; but here we read of the natives taking the initiative to make the Europeans more like themselves, without the French having authored the exchange but with their amused acquiescence.

Further to the episode involving charcoal, above, it is notable that difference of skin color was an object of wonder for indigenous people all over the Australian continent, and they often sought to investigate it (along with some other properties of the visitors, such as sex; see Chapter 3). Indigenous people often at first apparently entertained the question whether light skin color of the Europeans was permanent or temporary, deep or superficial (and also, as in Chapter 1, whether it meant that these beings were ancestors or ghosts). We see in the woman's gesture a play upon an issue that we might term one of relationality: what might arise interactionally from changing that color?

What Is Mimesis in These Encounters?

Imitation, in the above examples, typically involves a visible and/or audible, if small-scale and fleeting, behavioral icon of an act that thereby becomes shared. This production seems particularly significant in situations where the parties have little in common, relative to the commonalities they share with much more familiar others. The episodes reported also yield some sense of the complexity and embeddedness of imitation in larger flows of interaction. Imitation works within an emotional and affective economy of uncertainty, lability, volatility, and apparent continuous attention on the part of both outsiders and indigenes to each other's emotional states. The visitors' inferences of indigenous emotions are sensitive to preconceptions that they held—such as that indigenous people were coming to get "presents," that they would react in certain ways, want particular things. The boundary between engaging and not engaging is unstable, and the journalists are unsure about what is menacing and what is peaceable. We form a picture of a moving border zone of mutual awareness between parties in which one form of action was often rapidly transformed into another and in many of which violence was either clearly feared or actually ensued.

This volatility can continue to appear, or reappear, to the extent that encounter is not stabilized, or becomes destabilized, even after a period of time. It is a zone in which action on the part of the natives may relate but is not subordinated to outsiders' guidelines or framing ideas for the organization of interaction. These guidelines include elements of the outsiders' evaluative and moral framework and notions based on their growing experience of the range of native behavior: what works, what is risky, how to entice and reward, and how to guard against unwelcome developments. Outsiders were constantly bringing to their assessment of indigenous action their ideas of temperament, intelligence, and of moral qualities such as generosity, cruelty, kindness. Though uncertainty can be discerned often enough in early moments of encounter, it can recur after periods in which natives and outsiders have had a certain amount, sometimes even a lot, to do with each other. Uncertainty resulted from a lack of regularization of interaction, of shared affect and understanding of intentions between parties. Initially compliant-seeming or unremarkable behavior on the part of the natives could turn into hostility.

Uncertainty and fear lie behind the journalists' frequent relieved descriptions of indigenous "joy" and "pleasure" at the presence and presents of the visitors. For example:

> As soon as the boat came, we invited some of them to go on board. After taking a long while to decide about it, three of them consented to get into the boat; but they got out again in great haste as we prepared to push off from the shore. We then saw them walk quietly along by the sea, looking towards us from time to time, and uttering cries of joy. The next day we returned in a large party. Some of the natives soon came to meet us, expressing by their cries the pleasure they felt at seeing us again. A lively joy was depicted on all their features when they saw us drawing near. (Péron, quoted in Roth 1899:28)

What emotions were these people experiencing and expressing? A mother in the group had to cover her infant's eyes in order to calm him. Also, some of the natives in this group were concerned to prevent the French from moving in certain directions, so much so that they were entreated not to go in certain directions, with women uttering cries to alert others. Can this have been unalloyed joy? Yet it was so interpreted.

Imitative behaviors in early encounter are best understood as thoroughly relational, built upon mutual awareness. They were evocations rather than determinate messages. They were fleeting and unstable and also evidently frequently asymmetrical. Asymmetry in imitative relationships is a dimension that figures in both Taussig and Bhabha and calls for further comment here.

Of course, our data are themselves asymmetric: they come from one side. They suggest that indigenous people imitated outsiders more than the reverse (although instances are reported of Europeans engaging in imitative behavior, often a response to what they clearly took as imitative on the part of indigenous people). No doubt native imitation drew upon capacities strongly developed culturally among Australian indigenous people—in hunting, dancing, everyday sensibilities and capabilities developed in cultural forms of observation, body movement, and interaction (see, e.g., Ellis 1980, 1984; Marett 2000; von Sturmer 1987; Wild 1977–78). However, the reported imitation must be placed in the context of the instability, volatility, and uncertainty in the relations between the parties. In that world-historic context, there was—as the journals show—great attentiveness on the part of outsiders and indigenes to each other's emotional states. In such circumstances, imitation is one way of recognizing and drawing out and probing the condition of the other, as well as signaling identification with him.

That the economy of mimetic behavior was typically unbalanced, in that the Europeans were more imitated than imitating, is not surprising. It may be partly explained in terms of the wider framing in which imitative behavior occurred. Europeans came equipped with prior ("framing") ideas about what savages were like and, accordingly, were less oriented toward building bridges to them than were indigenous people toward the Europeans; and Europeans were certainly inclined to see their interaction with indigenous people in channeled, experimental, purposeful, and often quite overtly instrumental terms.

To engage in some of the kinds of imitation we see described in various colonial journals—copying of the other, understood by the parties as such—was not to use signs to convey some kind of question or message formulated outside the encounter. Many of these acts of imitation were not conventional nor tokens of regular expression-content relationships but focused upon the immediate encounter itself, making it interactive and at least fleetingly collaborative by doing what the other does and having the effect of creating and prolonging a moment, temporarily deferring questions of what was to come next.

This suggests a view of mimesis in early encounter as a way of relating to the unknown other by becoming an experiential analogue of him, at least temporarily, at the same time persisting in observation of one's interaction with him as participant in it. This by no means excludes—indeed, the possibility of continuous reflexivity positively includes—the kind of playful and ironic behavior we observed on the part of the woman who sang after M. Bellefin, expanding the occasion to include byplay with her peers, of which he was the apparent target.

Imitation seems to have been a readily available modality of establishing engagement, some commonality of an immediate sort. It created a bridge between oneself and another in the "copying," embodying the other in a way that was noticed. To the extent that it was noticed, imitation was a means of relating self and other, among other things, in the mutual realization of the imitative behavior itself. By miming and reproducing what the other does, one can literally feel oneself to be building a collaborative activity. Thus, to elaborate on Taussig's formulation, this is a production of the self-other dialectic, with potentials for both identification and differentiation with and from others. It seems crucial that imitative behavior be recognized as such by one's interlocutor. Indeed, given the extent of attention paid to the phenomenon in European explorers' journals, it seems that indigenous people's acts were regularly recognized as imitative. And in such moments of recognition, some of the questions about the instability and indeterminacy of relationship that were so salient in early encounters (but not only then) were, at least temporarily, deferred.

This enactment of mutual identification, then, coexisted with refusal as an early type of response. In the next chapter we will expand our view of the range of other kinds of mediations in early and later relationships and in so doing attempt to locate some principal differences between indigenous and nonindigenous forms of action that become heightened in their intersection.

Imitation is another aspect of power relations unfolding in asymmetrical performance, as was the one-sidedness of refusal of sensory uptake on encounter. These early moments in which those in encounter had little experience of each other and came to it from quite different points of view were characterized, as the discussion has shown, by lability and instability, as well as attentiveness of outsiders and locals to emotional states of joy, anger, and so on that they imputed to each other. Imitative behavior of a more affective rather than reflective kind was deployed in the unstable and uncertain contexts of early encounter, often characterized by great intensity and reciprocal attention on the part of outsiders and indigenes to each other's emotional states. At the same time, we have seen in a number of examples indigenous people's turning imitative action initiated with Europeans as their focus toward their own audience, often for comic effect, exemplified by the woman who sang for/in relation to Bellefin.

Attending to others requires complementarity—a relation "between," unfolding in time and space—which can exist as a matter of degree and quality and thus imply questions of power and influence. Sometimes in the first instance indigenous people acted the other, creating a recognized ground of commonality. The indigenous people seem to have been more prepared to do this and habitually more at home with imitative action than the outsiders. Yet while we need to recognize imitative capacity as cultivated culturally in indigenous practices, it should not be taken as evidence of fundamental difference of human civilizational kinds, a property of a kind of society or kind of person. Imitation as in these examples is much better understood as grounded in honed cultural capabilities, relational and inevitably transitional between and dependent upon other modes of action.

To refute the interpretation of early imitative behavior as evidence of primitivity is perhaps not difficult to do, as few admit nowadays to ideas of others as "primitives." We nevertheless have to remember how it was interpreted then, as by Darwin; and we must remember that it continues, in altered ways, to be so interpreted to this day—more in the guise of persisting otherness. Even the Benjaminian orientation of Taussig, toward an understanding of the ways in which outsiders and locals become mutually entangled, assumes an original degree of otherness in terms of which imitation is linked with naturalistic powers of copying, rather than as a basic and culturally highly developed framework for sociability. Otherness there is, no doubt; but sociability tends to get overlooked.

I return here to the suggestion made earlier that a more appropriate understanding of imitative behavior is as both generically human and a specific, culturally developed capacity, and that the interaction between these levels and its changing character need to be couched in a wider view that acknowledges kinds of person as social categories continually reconstituted—though partially rather than entirely—as social circumstances change. The persistence of the conventional interpretation of imitative behavior as primitive is part of the historical imbalance shaped by preconceptions, lived in the encounters themselves, and surviving them in some of the ways that these encounters have been subsequently understood.

CHAPTER 3

Mediations

In no Australian indigenous language that I know or know of is there a word that can be readily translated by the multipurpose English word "thing"; nor is there a word that readily translates as "work." While one always has to exercise caution in reading from language to culture, in this chapter I aim to show how this observation relates to historically deeply entrenched differences between indigenous social and cultural formations and those that have come to Australia with its colonization.[1] I return to amplify this observation in the conclusion of this chapter, which I hope will have shown how the evidence of indigenous-nonindigenous relations over time must unsettle some of our taken-for-granted assumptions concerning valuation of "things" and how indigenous interests in the bodiliness of outsiders were an extension of their orientation to the social potentials of relationship.

There was, to begin with, considerable difference between outsiders and indigenous people in the extent of their intentional orientation toward meeting previously unknown people. Arriving outsiders actively looked for indigenous people; while the latter were often overtaken by surprise and moved away from or sought to evade the outsiders, for which they were often considered timid (see Davenport, Johnson, and Yuwali 2005). This chapter examines these differences in interest and approach under three headings: the matching of emotions, the alignment of attention, and the sharing (or not sharing) of intentions. Many of the stories here are about "things": objects and what was made of them by indigenous and nonindigenous people in encounter, since these were so much a part of the European approach. To begin with, we consider an early observation of indigenous Australians that represented them as people with few if any wants.

"All Things Necessary for Life"

Captain Cook was sent from Britain in 1769 to carry a party of scientists from the Royal Society to the Pacific Ocean to witness the transit of Venus. Government instruction to him included secret orders (opened at sea) to look for the long-suspected but as-yet-elusive Terra Australis—the supposed southern continent; this was a matter of intense interest to him. Cook was also "to observe the Genius, Temper, Disposition and Number of the Natives if there be any" everywhere he went (as well as to take note of the geography, plant and animal life, and other aspects of the continent). He was, further, to "endeavour by all proper means to cultivate a Friendship and Alliance with them, making them presents of such Trifles as they may Value inviting them to Traffick, and Shewing them every kind of Civility and Regard; taking Care however not to suffer yourself to be surprized by them, but to be always upon your guard against any Accidents" (NLA MS 2).

Presents were to be given for the purposes of showing civility and inaugurating exchange. Official instructions were often liberal sounding in recommending good treatment of natives, but they were also always oriented to fulfillment of the expedition's aims. The colonizing instruction to Cook was preeminent: "You are also with the Consent of the Natives to take Possession of Convenient Situations in the Country in the Name of the King of Great Britain: Or: if you find the Country uninhabited take Possession for his Majesty by setting up Proper Marks and Inscriptions, as first discoverers and possessors" (NLA MS 2).

Cook's stated view of the "natives" is often cited for its appreciative tone:

From what I have said of the Natives of New-Holland they may appear to some to be the most wretched people upon Earth, but in reality they are far more happier than we Europeans; being wholy unacquainted not only with the superfluous but the necessary Conveniencies so much sought after in Europe, they are happy in not knowing the use of them. They live in a Tranquillity which is not disturb'd by the Inequality of Condition: The Earth and sea of their own accord furnishes them with all things necessary for life, they covet not Magnificent Houses, Houshold-stuff &c., they live in a warm and fine Climate and enjoy a very wholsome Air. . . . In short they seem'd to set no Value upon any thing we gave them, nor would they ever part with anything of their own for any one article we could offer them; this in my opinion

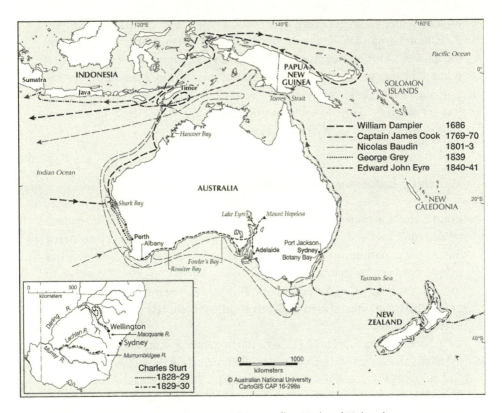

Figure 3. Explorers' routes. CartoGIS, Australian National University.

argues that they think themselves provided with all the necessarys of Life and that they have no superfluities. (Cook 1955: vol. 1, p. 399)

Cook's experiences led him to see the natives' setting "no value" on anything, nor parting with anything.

In subsequent exploration, by others, interest in the natives was subordinate in the range of purposes with which the outsiders came; they were a lower priority than we might expect from our present perspectives. They were to be placated, kept on good terms, and made useful where possible. They might usefully supply information about the country, such as availability of water and information concerning terrain. Once they set about colonizing the continent, outsiders largely had exploration of the country on their minds and explicit instructions to find arable and usable country (Wolfe 1999). Journals of continental explorers (such as Baudin, Péron, Grey, Sturt, Edward John Eyre, John Lort Stokes, and many others) contain sections such as "Visited by the natives," "Our intercourse with them," "Description of their weapons and other implements." Though the basic plot of their writings is one of exploration, their stories of encounters with natives are a hazardous and emotionally fraught subplot—far removed from Cook's calm echoes of the Enlightenment and his Rousseauian view of a people without wants.

Watching Emotions for Trouble

Emotion is often understood as intersubjectively and interactively constructed (Wilce 2009:481) and emotions as forms of expressive response to our shared life. In many outbursts in unexpected encounter on the part of indigenous people, however, we mainly see surges of overpowered surprise and alarm, to some extent couched in culturally conventional form (dancing in place, singly or together), but often also in evidently unintentional, raw physical reactions (trembling, shaking).

Charles Napier Sturt (1795–1869), starting from Sydney and later on from Adelaide, traced several of the westward-flowing rivers, hoping to find an "inland sea." He determined that these rivers all merged into the Murray River. His third expedition in 1844 from Adelaide northward never reached the center of the continent as he had intended; he returned to Adelaide in poor health with the expedition under another's command. On that final expedition into uncharted territory, he encountered indigenous people who had seemingly had no prior contact with outsiders. He and his men "saw a party of natives assembled on a sand hill, to the number of fourteen. As we advanced towards them they retreated, but at length made a stand as if to await our approach. They were armed with spears, and on Mr. Browne dismounting to walk towards them, formed themselves into a circle, in the centre of which were two old men, round whom they danced" (Sturt 1849: vol. 1, pp. 340–41). Regarding his party's approach to an old man who had become aware of the Europeans advancing on him (they were on horseback), Sturt reports: "In order to allay his fears Mr. Browne dismounted and walked up to him, whilst I kept back. On this the poor fellow began to dance, and to call out most vehemently, but finding that all he could was to no purpose, he sat down and began to cry" (ibid., 1:339). Sturt goes on to report of this old man, however, that within a short time: "We managed to pacify him, so much that he mustered courage to follow us, with his two companions to our halting place" (ibid.).

On coming upon some natives at a river, Sturt observed that several of them "trembled greatly" (ibid., 1:110); and of another man whom the outsiders interrupted in collecting wood, that he expressed "horror and amazement—down went his branches—out went his hands—and trembling head to foot, he began to shout as loud as he could bawl" (ibid., 2:63).

It was once believed and fervently hoped that a great river entered the Indian Ocean on the northwest of Australia, and that the country it drained might be suitable for colonization. In 1837 and 1839 George Grey (1812–98) led hardship-plagued expeditions, the first an ill-prepared exploration of northwest Australia from Cape Town—only one man of his party had seen northern Australia before. Wrecked, almost drowned, and completely lost, Grey was wounded in a skirmish with Aborigines. The party traced the course of the Glenelg River, in the Kimberley region of Western Australia, before retreating to Mauritius to recover. Two years later, Grey returned and was again wrecked with his party in Western Australia. Though they were the first Europeans to see the Gascoyne River, they had survived the subsequent near-waterless journey on foot to the present location of Perth only with the help of Kaiber, a Whadjuk Nyungar man mentioned in Chapter 1 as Grey's guide. Grey (1841: vol. 1, pp. 362–63) records that first-contacted natives he approached began singing in an effort to "sing them away."

Péron (2006:177) describes a young man who sighted the Baudin party of exploration (in Tasmania) from a promontory and was apparently so excited by this unexpected appearance and so encouraged by "our signs of friendship" (what those may have been, is not recorded), that he "jumped rather than climbed down the rock and was with us in the blink of an eye. . . . There was nothing stern or wild in his features; his glance was keen and lively, and his air expressed both goodwill and surprise. M. Freycinet embraced him, and so I did the same; but from the indifference with which he received this demonstration of our interest, it was easy to see it held no significance for him." These outsiders were warily attentive to the natives' emotional states. Their journals evince a continuing concern and running interpretation of this, largely in the interests of their own security. However, they seem to have been inclined to read a great deal into situations, perhaps without verifiable basis for their interpretations. This often resulted in misapprehensions, sometimes perilous ones, as the following episode illustrates.

A few days after some men of the Baudin expedition had made their

presence known to a local group of Bruny Islanders (Tasmanians), a M. Maurouard engaged in what he thought was a sporting round of arm wrestling
with an indigenous man, forcing him to give ground in a way that apparently
seemed to everyone to clearly spell victory for the Frenchman. The French
thought the indigenous men had accepted what they saw as "defeat" at this
"sport." But a few minutes later a spear came flying back at them, thrown by
one of the natives who had seemingly left a few minutes earlier, and pierced
Maurouard's shoulder. Baudin wrote of earlier minutes of this episode: "It
seems that the best possible relations existed constantly between the two parties. A quarter of an hour before the departure, the natives had indeed all
disappeared, but as they had been loaded with presents and were in excellent
spirits, the men were far from distrusting them" (1974:304).

It seems the Aborigines' disappearance a quarter of an hour earlier may
have meant more than the visitors thought. It may have provided an occasion
for some who were negatively inclined toward the French to talk among
themselves. This constant concern with emotional states in these early, face-
to-face encounters is gradually transformed, with extension of colonization
and the proliferation of settlers and their institutions, into ever more stereo-
typic characterizations of indigenous people (see Chapter 4).

Music and Materiality

There was a repertoire of early encounter methods that voyagers brought
with them to try to channel early contacts. Some of these involved music,
dance, and greeting behavior, and a considerable range of material offerings
that, it was hoped, would engage indigenous people and create good feeling.
In a letter of 1788 Arthur Phillip wrote, linking music and imitation:
"They . . . are fond of any very soft Musick, and will attend to singing any of
the Words which they very readily repeat" (Clendinnen 2005:26). Captain-
Lieutenant Watkin Tench (an officer of the First Fleet) reported in his journal
that one of his party "whistled the air of Malbrooke" at which the natives
appeared "highly charmed" (see Tench 2009:43; also Clendinnen 2005:9–10).
The singing was not all one way. William Dawes (1825) reports a lively young
Aboriginal girl rising to sing for an English company—though the effort to
charm with song is more often reported of themselves by diarists than of
natives.

Clearly music was not only thought to be engaging and soothing; it also stood out as a mode of contact far different from trying to make propositional content understood. It was meant to launch something between arrivals and natives that the latter could attend to directly, and the fact that natives sometimes took up the tune and sang back was an additional, but perhaps unexpected, benefit.

Two recent historical works have focused on other elements of the colonial repertoire: dancing (Clendinnen 2005) and shaking hands (Shellam 2009). At Sydney Cove, 29 January 1788, three days after landfall, Lieutenant William Bradley "had his first meeting with the Australians. It was a remarkably friendly encounter, the British party being welcomed ashore by unarmed men who pointed out a good landing place 'in the most cheerful manner, shouting and dancing'" (Clendinnen 2005:8). Then, Bradley says, "'these people mixed with ours and all hands danced together.' The next day at Spring Cove there was another impromptu dance party when about a dozen of the local men came paddling in soon after the British landed, left their spears in their canoes as a sign of friendship, and all proceeded to more 'dancing and otherwise amusing themselves'" (ibid., 8).

With reference to this dancing reproduced on the cover of her book *Dancing with Strangers*, Inga Clendinnen (2005:9) comments: "What [Bradley] shows us is the British and the Australians dancing hand in hand like children at a picnic: that is, dancing in the British style. . . . Furthermore, the pairs are scattered over the whole foreground, with none of the local preference for formation dancing, which reinforces my suspicion that it was the British who took the initiative." I share Clendinnen's suspicion: that the English took the initiative in this combined English-Aboriginal dancing, as they did in producing music. (There is evidence of Aborigines dancing by themselves and at a distance, perhaps not in welcome but self-protectively or to induce outsiders to approach; see, e.g., Bradley 1969:66; Baudin 1974:322.)

So seemingly did the French take initiative in collective dancing. Baudin reports a fairly trouble-free, even care-free, meeting of some of his sailors, who had been fishing with a small party of natives to whom, to their great delight, the French had offered two bottles (for more on glass and shiny objects, see below). "After this first present the friendliness between them and our men became so great, and confidence on either side so firmly established, that they all started dancing together. But as they found this exercise too tiring or not very interesting, they had soon had enough of it and preferred to occupy themselves in something more to their liking" (Baudin 1974:318). We recognize this as an exclusive or selective "they"—they the natives, not the sailors. Again, we sense a difference in role: the French, the likely proponents of the dance; the natives, willing participants, for a time.

With twenty troops and twenty-three convicts, led by Edmund Lockyer, the British established an outpost on the western side of the continent, at King George's Sound (on the south coast of Western Australia) on 25 December 1826. On 21 January 1827, as instructed by the Secretary of State for War and the Colonies Earl Bathurst, the Union Jack was raised and a *feu de joie* fired by the troops, formally annexing the territory, in assertion of the first official claim by the imperial government to British possession over the whole continent of Australia. As Tiffany Shellam writes in *Shaking Hands on the Fringe: Negotiating the Aboriginal World at King George's Sound*, shaking hands became widespread: "It is not clear how or when the practice of handshaking began . . . but by the time Lockyer arrived in December 1826, it was an action that the King Ya-nup [her name for the local people] instigated in their first meeting with him" (2009:70).

Whether hand shaking was indigenous or introduced practice, it proliferated, becoming a new ritual, constructed jointly by both Aborigines and newcomers. It looked friendly but probably a variety of feelings and intentions were underlying (ibid., 71). The same is true for Australia generally. It is possible, but not certain, that forms of hand shaking, or at least hand holding, may have been conventional prior to colonization. Certainly holding parts of the other's body in greeting, including the male genitalia, was customary in parts of Australia. It is not at all clear that hand shaking such as that practiced at King George's Sound had the same meaning for Aborigines as for the soldiers; but it is clear that it came to be understood as a form of greeting and could signify welcome, thanks, gratitude, and generally a peaceable attitude.

These modes of creating collaborative interaction contrast with avoidance; and they overlap with forms of identification, modalities (Introduction, Chapters 1 and 2) that seem to have originated in an indigenous repertoire. The outsiders came prepared with musical instruments; there is no evidence in any documents of indigenous people playing music of their own accord in early encounter. The handshake is inherently reciprocal, highly generalizable, and seemingly relatively egalitarian. There is always the question of who extends his hand first—but there is a relative equality and a physical touch, but a limited one. The embrace mentioned of the young man by Péron seems not to have met with recognition. All of these activities—music, dancing, and probably also hand shaking—likely to have been European led, were aimed at directing the flow of early encounter. In slightly stronger terms, they were regulatory of it.

Recent attention to such activities as dancing in the literature has been by an ethically motivated search for points in colonial history where things might have gone differently, where contacts might be seen as having been more mutual than they are usually shown to be. There is even, perhaps, a suggestion of what Tim Rowse (2003:256) has called the Australian counterfactual: the imagination of Aborigines never dispossessed; even Australia not colonized. Clendinnen and Shellam illuminate early contact as part of informed national reflection upon alternative paths that might have been followed in indigenous-nonindigenous relations.

Reluctance to Receive

In many places in the Pacific, early European ships arrived in need of water, food, and other basics of subsistence, and the Europeans rapidly engaged with locals to try to acquire these. They also brought supplies of what they regarded as tradables with them—everything from beads to knives and hatchets—and, especially in some places, found great differences in indigenous appreciation of them. Those who had had experience elsewhere in the Pacific, or knew of it, generally found rather puzzling the Australian indigenous reactions to items that had proved of interest in other colonial settings and that they hoped to use to engage the indigenes or to begin trading with them. Some European representations appear more representative of Western presumptions about the appeal of material items than of actual Aboriginal response.

Mirrors, glass beads, snuffboxes, hatchets, and knives did not necessarily prove attractive. While it was often the case in Australia that explorers sought information from locals about water and other supplies, there seemed to be much less in the way of food for which they could barter, as they regularly did in other parts of the Pacific. For their part, not only did Aborigines initially show little interest in European food; there is evidence that they positively avoided it.

On first encounter with the Baudin expedition, Tasmanians took no interest in European food (bread, biscuit) and drink (including arrack) (Baudin 1974:302), and for the most part they refused it even when urged (but see Shellam 2009:185 on King Ya-nup developing a liking for ship's biscuit). On other occasions, the Bruny Islanders ate shellfish in front of the French (ibid., 318, 347). They seemed unconcerned about eating in the presence of outsiders, but they were not interested in sharing French food, even fish that was obviously locally caught and offered to them. Nor would they take liquor (though over the longer term drinking spirits and alcohol everywhere became problematic; see Beckett 1965; Brady 2002, 2007; Hunter 1993; McKnight 2002). It is quite possible, but remains speculative, that reluctance to eat and drink unknown foods and liquids may have to do with very widespread concern about poisons or harmful substances being transferred in that medium (cf. Sansom 1980). At any rate, Baudin's party met with quite steady refusals on both scores. Captain Cook observed the same reluctance on the part of Aborigines encountered at Sydney. From a very different part of the continent—the Kimberley region of Western Australia—and considerably later, we have the information that indigenous people given rations for the first time buried them for fear of *kardiya* (whitefella) magic (P. A. Smith 2000:81).

Early reserve in parts of the continent concerning food stands in contrast to what later unfolded everywhere in Australia as indigenous people began to depend upon rations around points of settlement. Sometimes they were under coercion (in which their labor was coopted); other times much less so, but in which there was some external supply of food. One crucial factor in this was dislocation from country they knew, whether they were forced off it by settlers or themselves decided to go in to points of colonial settlement and social intensity as other Aborigines had done (Stanner 1958; Hamilton 1979). In the Kimberley, stations began to issue rations within ten years of pastoral settlement (which did not begin there until the 1880s) to entice or coerce Aborigines to "sit down" (P. A. Smith 2000:80).

However, in some circumstances food continued to be treated very selectively by indigenous people in their relations with developing stations or other outposts as settlement proceeded. Where indigenous people managed to maintain their numbers, health, and mobility, they could treat rationed supplies as a novelty rather than a necessity, so rations had little coercive effect (Foster 1989:65). In South Australia (Foster 1989) and elsewhere as landed regimes gained a foothold, distribution of food rations effectively became a form of compensation to indigenous people for loss of their lands and their resulting inability to hunt and forage and feed themselves. With time and changing circumstances, and sometimes desperation on the part of Aborigines whose numbers were reduced and who had been forced away from water

Figure 4. Louis Auguste de Sainson, *Port du Roi Georges (Nouvelle Hollande): Un naturel montre à ses Compagnons les Cadeaux qu'il a recus à bord de l'Astrolabe*. Plate 23 from Jules Dumont d'Urville, *Voyage de la corvette l'Astrolabe: Atlas historique* (Paris: Tastu, 1833).

and food sources, the availability of food and the establishment of rationing regimes became the basis of colonial management (Rowse 1998). Rationing was a method of exercising control, providing an alternative for indigenous people to their killing pastoral animals, for which many pastoralists felt themselves entitled to kill Aborigines (Giles 1928; see Chapter 5). Rationing was both an element in a regime of rewards to control behavior and a way of assuring a concentration of cheap labor (P. A. Smith 2000).

There are numerous early instances in diaries and journals of Aborigines displaying interest in European technology: Arthur Phillip in the first days at Sydney noticed an old man peering into a pot in which sailors were boiling meat, apparently interested in both the pot's contents and the novel method of cooking. Indigenous people sometimes absconded with numerous small items, perhaps, Baudin (1974:305) thought, more out of curiosity than with a purpose of use. It seems likely that it required time and experience for Aborigines to see or find any use in many objects (though axes and knives were an exception). Baudin (1974:350) remarks that people did not "attach the slightest importance to the nails that we wanted to give them and returned them to us as serving no purpose." The attention they paid to gear and equipment interested Europeans, who probably found it warranted, but perhaps were ambivalent about crediting Aborigines with the requisite curiosity and cognition. Péron (2006:178) says of one young man who rushed to encounter them after he had examined their bodies and clothes for a time:

> Our long-boat, however, appeared to interest him even more than our persons, and after studying us for a few moments, he jumped into her. There, without worrying in the least about the sailors in her, he seemed to be absorbed in his new examination. The thickness of the knees and ribs, the solidity of the construction, the rudder, the oars, masts and sails—he looked at everything in that silence and with that close attention which are the least ambiguous indications of interest and thoughtful admiration. . . . He tried several times to push the long-boat out to sea, but the painter holding her defeated all his efforts; and so he was obliged to abandon her and return to us, having given the most striking demonstration that we had ever had of concentration and thought amongst uncivilized peoples.

That curiosity may have been a large factor and that indigenous people may have desired to examine items without oversight on the part of outsiders are suggested by the following:

> Approaching the shore, we found a very big fire—undoubtedly lit during the night—which was still burning. Around it, scattered at random, lay almost all the objects that we had given the natives or that the latter had stolen from us, even at the risk of their lives. We had earlier discovered several others here and there in the woods; and we remained persuaded that, after satisfying a childish curiosity, these ignorant men, encumbered (as it were) by our kindnesses, abandoned the objects as soon as they had ceased to please or amuse them. (Péron 2006:202)

Visitors saw clothes as self-evidently useful, but indigenous people saw them quite differently at first. Baudin and his men noted Tasmanians cursorily examining clothes as a matter of curiosity and then discarding them. This ran counter to European common sense that clothes should be quickly perceived as advantageous, offering warmth and bodily protection for people who wore little (Baudin 1974:303; though he reports women's often wearing kangaroo cloaks [330, 344]).

A different indigenous preference is shown by the following:

> One of our sailors exchanged his jacket for a kangaroo-skin. The native tied it around his neck and went off a little way. His principal concern was to remove all the buttons, and then he abandoned the jacket, which the sailor took back again when he got into the boat. Another native, who had been dressed in some long canvas breeches, found himself so encumbered by them that he had all the difficulty in the world to reach a tree about twenty-five paces from him. There, he very quickly got rid of this uncomfortable attire and would not even take the buttons from it. Of these, they all appear to be very fond. (Baudin 1974:305)

Baudin (1974:345) reports that jackets given as gifts were later found discarded at the foot of a tree (see also Shellam 2009:188 on the indigenous return of "gifts"). Only the buttons, which were of blackened bone and not metal, had disappeared. Shirts, trousers, and other items, were initially appreciated mainly as button bearers, and clothes provoked curiosity as to whether or how they were part of the person.

Clothes came to be appreciated by indigenous people after a time and in many places became expected for (and by) Aboriginal people as part of a "civilizing" process, as Europeans saw it (Barwick 1974). But this may have had a quite different significance among Aborigines: early mentions of the adoption of clothes suggest that Aboriginal people valued them as a new way of producing forms of difference and distinction among themselves. It may be that possibilities presented by items of apparel resonated with indigenous feeling for interpersonal differentiation. Perhaps certain items were more valued in this way than others (for remarks on hats and scarves, see Barratt 1981:65; Laracy 1980:179; McBryde 1989). This opens a wider question of whether and how differential access to Europeans and their resources may have contributed to changing, temporarily or permanently, the nature of social relations among people within indigenous groups.

The navigator Phillip Parker King (1827: vol. 2, pp. 125, 133, 136) while surveying the Australian coastline and looking for rivers to access the interior, took on board an Aboriginal man whom they named "Jack." It seems likely that Jack and others mentioned in this episode had been visited the previous year, 1820, by another brig, and thus that these were not "first contacts." Jack and other men appeared confident and unafraid to go on board, were demanding of goods, and it was difficult for King to persuade them to disembark (2:120–21). After Jack had spent some time consorting with the English, King observed that he separated himself from other Aborigines and was overtly somewhat disdainful of them. He surmised that Jack now felt himself to be in possession of superior knowledge, due to his association with the English. He gloried in wearing items of European clothing, as Shellam (2009:187–89) also reports of some people near the military post at Albany in southern Western Australia in the early nineteenth century. Besides hats and scarves, military jackets and handkerchiefs came to be valued as distinguishing items.

A note by Baldwin Spencer of 1894 from Oodnadatta, South Australia, suggests that there, too, possessing clothes quickly became a mark of distinction for the few who did. He observed: "It was often a marvel how boys, who owned any, managed to keep their remnants of clothes hanging on, but they were very proud of them; the more tattered they became, the greater was the ingenuity shown to preserve and make the most of them" (Spencer 1928:384).

Baudin's (1974:347) observations suggest some variation among people in how quickly they recognized that mirrors reflected their image; some glanced briefly at them and passed them on, while others displayed greater interest (178). There was keener interest in other shiny objects. Buttons, bottles, and sometimes beads seem to have had the self-evident appeal on first encounter that the French were expecting, perhaps more of other objects. "Of the various objects that we distributed amongst them, glass beads, smallwares etc., the buttons off our clothes appeared to give them most pleasure," noted Baudin (345). Small, compact, concentrated, and shiny, their appeal is reported here and continent-wide.

About bottles and buttons, there was little equivocation or difference of opinion among the natives, the French found. They were invariably eager to strip the buttons off clothes that they would then dispose of: "With everyone sitting down again, they turned their attention to pockets and the metal buttons on some of the men's waistcoats. Several did not ask before searching through them for things they might fancy, while others indicated by unambiguous signs how pleased they would be to own the buttons. Some were cut off and distributed amongst them to their great satisfaction" (Baudin 1974:318).

Next to buttons, bottles were immediately and universally prized (Baudin 1974:318, 345). The "theft" of bottles of arrack was evidently to obtain the bottles, not the content (ibid., 330). On one occasion, a glass's sparkle at first made a young man "cry out in astonishment," but, curiously, after he had taken the bottle and studied it for a moment or two, he threw it into the sea (Péron 2006:178). Sparkling beads also were objects of interest and desire (Baudin 1974:319–20), though not always. Illustrating a range of the preferences so far discussed, this passage from Baudin shows the attitudes to food and the regard for bottles: "We all dined ashore, sitting with the natives, but were unable to persuade them to eat anything. However, they gladly accepted all the empty bottles that we gave them. I do not know if they were afraid that we might ask for them back when we left, but as soon as a bottle was given to them, they passed it over to their wives, who went and hid it in the woods and then came back to resume their places amongst us" (347).

Bottles were shiny and at least partly translucent, and the French recognized this as attractive to the Bruny Islanders. They could also serve as containers, though it is not clear from Baudin or Péron that they were valued or, to their knowledge, used for that reason. The buttons were condensed, compact, and decorated, perhaps sometimes incised. They may have resembled or suggested known special, even sacred, objects.

Luminescent objects were appreciated wherever they could be acquired along trade routes in continental Australia, and they seem to have been among items regularly invested with special regard, even sacredness, by Aborigines. In the Kimberley (McCarthy 1939; Akerman 1979), pearl shell was used for personal adornment and was highly valued for its shimmering quality. It was traded along with some other objects of high value and ceremonial use (bullroarers, shell beads, hair girdles). In many parts of northern Australia, a mythological snakelike beast commonly called the Rainbow Serpent is associated with pearl shell and luminosity (H. Morphy 1989). In many parts of Australia, once glass was available, Aborigines started making spear points and knapped glass items from it. Probably more relevant to its high valuation are many indications of an association of sharp and dense objects (both wood and stone) with (sacred) power, and their capacity to magically pierce the human body (Elkin 1945). In Central Australia, sacred objects (*churinga*, in Spencer and Gillen's early spelling) were usually made of stone or hard wood, ovoid in shape, extremely dense, ranging from a few centimeters to three meters or so in length (Batty 2006). Paul S. C. Taçon (1991) has written about "the power of stone," the association of stones with preternatural power, in western Arnhem Land. It is tempting to see the enduring, dense quality of many kinds of what Aborigines consider special, perhaps sacred, objects, and the luminosity of others, as relevant to the preferences recorded in Tasmania by Baudin, and elsewhere in Australia, for objects of glass, stone, luminosity, compactness, and density.

There was evidently a considerable dimension of prior, culturally shaped appreciation that the Aborigines exercised with respect to the objects Europeans offered them. Items early seen as of transcendent value seem to be comparable across many parts of the continent.

Indigenous Reactions and Offerings

What do early sources tell us about preferences and forms of action regularly initiated by indigenous people? To answer this question, it may be useful to distinguish "interaffectivity," "interattentionality," and "interintentionality." Originally proposed by psychologist Daniel Stern (1985) to characterize human developmental capacities, these terms help us to distinguish types of relationality.

"Interaffectivity" is the simultaneous matching of affects and emotions to the affects and emotions displayed by another or others in overt behavior: how do we feel in relation to each other, and by what means do we signal this to each other? Nonrecognition, described in earlier chapters, is a refusal to allow interaffectivity to emerge in any obvious form and is a restriction of affect and response within the actor. Imitative behavior is an enactment of matching that channels some affects and emotions but may leave a remainder unexpressed. Some other forms of immediate response to "critical situations" (cf. Giddens 1979:123ff., 228–30 on routine and "critical" situations) involve overt and obvious discharge of emotion but are not explicitly other oriented.

"Interattentionality" is the alignment of attention to the attention displayed overtly by others. Such attentional states are themselves an instance of attentiveness and also signal interest and readiness or potential to attend further relative to a context. Outsiders came prepared with a repertoire to try to align attention of the indigenous people on particular objects and actions, but the latter often focused their attention differently.

"Interintentionality" is the sharing of information with others about one's intentions and beliefs concerning oneself and them. This sharing often occurs by verbal means, but also by (other) bodily based ones, particularly where verbal channels are difficult or blocked. While bodily imitative behavior may render a certain kind of information, it seems inherently context bound. It rests upon mutuality in the present action and context; it is therefore unable to support the development of shared foci that depend upon complex understandings of intentions and possible forms of action. Bodily imitative behavior seems to pose limits to the development of intention-guided behavior insofar as it creates a defining image of mutuality.

Interintentionality is complex in another related way. Sharing of information may draw upon reserves of understanding—concerning persons, objects, institutions—that are not common and may not be easily shared. And insofar as interintentionality may converge on particular objects and events within a short time frame, there may result a situation of unintelligibility or incomprehension about what intentions and beliefs of others are or what present interaction may imply. Sharing of information about intentions and beliefs is entwined with affectivity, attentionality. Under conditions of limited mutuality it may result in misunderstandings or misconceptions.

While all of these capacities are enormously important in human interaction, these dimensions of relationship are/were often abortive or simply had little chance of being fostered in circumstances of colonial-indigenous imbalance.

Skin and Sex

Much of what interested the indigenous people seems not to have been part of the visitors' intended "repertoire" of interattentionality and interaffectivity, but arose from indigenous interests and questions about difference and identity. Where conditions for face-to-face encounter were established, the most intense foci of immediate attention for indigenous people were the skins and sex organs of the outsiders. Raising questions of similarity and difference, and potentially charged with great affect, these indigenous investigations challenged the outsiders to interact in ways for which they were not prepared.

The question "Were we dead?" in Chapter 1 is related to the observation that, all over the continent, indigenous people—where this was possible and relations had not turned hostile—displayed interest in the (skin) color of the outsiders. Apparently they were not always certain at first about the distinction between skin and clothes and sometimes marveled at the realization or revelation of fairly consistent skin color all over the body beneath the clothes, so different from their own coloring.

Often on first acquaintance some indigenous people clearly thought that clothes, hats, and gloves worn by outsiders were part of the person and were amazed when they saw them separated. An instance of fright at the removal of apparel comes from Péron (2006:179):

> One of our sailors was wearing a pair of fur gloves which, upon approaching the fire, he took off and put in his pocket. Seeing this, the young woman began to cry out so loudly, that we were alarmed at first; however, we soon realized the cause of her fright, and her expressions and gestures left us in no doubt that she had taken these gloves for actual hands, or at least for a kind of living skin that one could, at will, remove in this way, place in one's pocket and put back on again.

Once the Aborigines had some experience of clothes, it seems to have become clearer that there might be more similarity between indigenous and nonindigenous people that had not been as apparent when the latter were fully clothed. Aborigines then tested their own methods of producing similarity and interaffectivity.

For some women Baudin's party encountered (an incident mentioned in Chapter 2), attentiveness to difference involved the women's painting their own faces with charcoal and other daubs and then doing the same to the French. The French followed some women for a time, and when they caught up to them, "everyone sat down, and the beauties, obviously wanting to please the new company with them, smeared their faces with charcoal moistened with saliva. They then made so many entreaties to their admirers, that the latter allowed themselves to be daubed in the same way" (Baudin 1974:324).

Following his giving a small mirror to a woman whose face, like those of the others, was smeared with either ground charcoal or with red ochre, Baudin (1974:347) says: "They painted in the same way several of the scientists, who good-naturedly tolerated this whim of theirs. The ceremony greatly amused the spectators and brought loud bursts of laughter from the natives."

Why would the women do this? And why would it be considered funny? These actions seem to have been undertaken to create commonality and good feeling—positive interaffectivity—between people who knew each other relatively little. In this case, the women applied to the scientists something that the natives regularly did to themselves. Against the background of the strangers' novelty, here is something that creates a ground of similarity between them and at the same time heightens the paradox of their being both different from the natives and acquiescing in becoming like them in at least this playful way.

Also repeatedly recorded in journals from across the continent and related to questions of skin and clothes was indigenous interest in "sexing" the outsiders: were they or were they not formed as were indigenous people themselves? Were they recognizably male or female? And what if they were? William Bradley (1969:60) reported this as the chief curiosity of the Aborigines upon their encounter at Botany Bay. The Aborigines brought some of their women to the shore and, all being naked, repeatedly pointed alternately to their own genitalia and the women's; they were understood by the English to be questioning which the outsiders might be. Initially clothes impeded satisfaction of this curiosity, but "they were immediately satisfied in this particular by one person in the boat" (ibid.; see also P. P. King 1827: vol. 1, entry of 2 July 1819 in north Queensland).

Indeed, the persons of the outsiders were themselves perhaps the greatest objects of indigenous attention and potentially great generative sources of positive interaffectivity. But the outsiders were not prepared for this exactly and had little protocol established for themselves as the focus of interattentionality—they had brought things for the purpose. They therefore improvised, usually offering limited views of that which the natives most wanted to see.

To satisfy this, probably the greatest of their curiosities, the Bruny Islanders, for instance, took opportunities to inspect the outsiders when they could. That one of Baudin's sailors had his son with him presented such an opportunity, for the Europeans were more prepared to offer up the younger among them for inspection than the older: "They forcibly carried off the son of the *Naturaliste*'s master-carpenter, but contented themselves with examining him from head to foot without doing him any harm. After satisfying their curiosity, they left him free to rejoin his companions. This young man was carrying a large hatchet which did not tempt them in the least, although they had watched very closely how he used it" (Baudin 1974:350).

On another occasion, Baudin recounts their meeting some native men whom they had seen and given things to in the morning. The natives got them to put aside their guns, then they sat together, and the men examined the Frenchmen, insofar as they would permit. The hairless chest of the doctor "caused great exclamations and even greater shouts of laughter. After satisfying themselves in this region, they passed on to our legs, and several were obliging enough to give in to this whim. They would have liked very much to see something else, but we did not think it advisable to show them" (Baudin 1974:320).

A similar curiosity was, however, requited by Philip Gidley King's party.

When it became obvious that the Aborigines were curious, King made one of his men unbutton to "undecieve [*sic*] them in this particular," at which sight the locals made "a great shout of admiration" (P. G. King 1980:35; cf. Baudin 1974:220). Indicating approaching young women, they "made us understand their persons were at our service" (P. G. King 1980:35); however, says King, "I declined this mark of their hospitality." As this suggests, the discovery that their visitors were males sometimes led Aboriginal men to make it clear that their wives or other women were sexually available to them, within a very short time. This was often (but not always) linked to what the natives took to have been some prior expression of friendliness, or gift, from the outsiders.

Sturt (1849: vol. 1, p. 296), for example, says: "I gave the elder native a blanket, and to the other a knife, with both of which they seemed highly delighted, and in return I suppose paid us the compliment of sending their wives to us as soon as it became dusk, but as we did not encourage their advances they left us after a short visit." He recounts other incidents of women being sent to his camp in numbers (entry for Friday, 14 March 1845; Sturt 2002:168).

This must be understood as part of a larger order of things, in which it was men who made such offers of women. Clendinnen (2005:152) generalizes: "The offering of women for sexual use to cement friendship or political or economic alliance was standard practice among Australians" (cf. Hiatt 1996:55; McGrath 1990:192–93). Historian Charles Rowley (1970:30) observes how great was the resulting indigenous vulnerability.

From early journals it becomes clear that women did not begin by acting freely with outsiders but at least initially remained at some distance. Men made sure they stayed out of sight. Eyre (1964: vol. 1, p. 223) comments on the appearance of some women: "These few women were the first we had seen for some time, as the men appeared to keep them studiously out of our way." (Bradley [1969:141] observes that on encounter in New South Wales, Aboriginal men were "very jealous of their women being among us"; but some occasions were more relaxed [Baudin 1974:304].)

So, it seems women were presented in the first instance at men's behest (McGrath 1987:74–75, 1990:193; Berndt 1987:189–90; Elkin 1938:161–62). The Australians thought to attend to the visitors' inclinations in terms of priorities that they themselves recognized. Either experimentally or in terms of conviction that the visitors, in this respect, were similar to themselves, they offered women and thus relationship on an assumption of commonality, rather than of unbridgeable difference. This involves presumptions concerning the perspectives and wants of others and is both interaffective and interintentional.

There is another, gendered side of normative male control and initiative in the sexual deployment of women that makes an early appearance in the journals: women choosing to go directly to the outsiders where this was possible or occasion could be made for it. This is a specific exercise of agency still within the bounds of a normative but gender-differentiated set of understandings, rather than unfettered freedom. Thus we learn from Baudin (1974:305) of such an early initiative by Tasmanian women, on the occasion of the wrestling match initiated by M. Maurouard, the cause of later stone and spear throwing by the indigenous men. What were the women doing while that was going on? "If several of the [French] men are to be believed, the women used various ways and means to draw some of them aside, and the signs that they made were too expressive for anyone to mistake their intentions. Some of the oarsmen from the *Naturaliste* even affirmed that upon their following them, the women had entirely voluntarily satisfied their curiosity, but not their desire" (Baudin 1974:305; see also p. 324).

In other words, the women were as curious as the men. They were going about their own explorations, which, as Baudin (1974:324) also makes clear, may shortly have led to one or more of them leading a compliant Frenchman away into the forest for further investigation. This suggests a particular female orientation toward sexual curiosity and experimentation, rather than the frequently attested male one toward establishing a bond with visitors through the medium of women (McGrath 1987; Merlan 1992).

On this very important embodied modality of interrelationship, sexuality, Clendinnen shows how rapidly the character of sexual interaction changed. In locations of considerable scale such as Sydney (the First Fleet of 1788 was carrying 1,023 people, including 751 convicts and their children), offering of women by indigenous men was rapidly transformed under many circumstances into sales of sexual favors.

Erhard Eylmann (1908) was a German researcher who traveled in parts of the Northern Territory in the late nineteenth century and spent time in towns such as Darwin where a considerable number of European and Chinese men had been present for a decade or more. He notes the regularity of interactions in that time period involving an indigenous husband and wife approaching newcomers like himself to negotiate terms for sexual use of the wife for a short period in return for some item (often tobacco or money). Eylmann (1908:459) also reports an incident in which a woman became indignant when he refused such an offer, asserting that he really wanted to do it, but he simply had no shilling! In other words, she did not want her desirability to be impugned, a remainder of female agency and interest that went beyond the terms of trade.

Organizations of practice are complex and sometimes lasting. The sexual offering of women in friendship and alliance was a fairly commonplace understanding among the few older indigenous men I came to know well enough for them to refer to such matters, when I first began research in the Northern Territory in the late 1970s. Men who had lent a wife to a visitor, usually but not always indigenous, for a shorter or longer period, were not ashamed of it nor reluctant to talk about it when it was relevant. They did not think of this as a diminution of their own prerogatives in the situation, nor of their standing in others' eyes. But things have changed a great deal in this regard, and I think it is quite uncommon now for men (and women) to be able to talk about such exchanges except in awareness of how much they are seen as salacious or perverse by many other Australians.

Clearly, the transformation of relational sexual offering into exploitative and market relations happened in interaction with European mores, forms of behavior, and great inequality of access to desired resources and goods. The offer of women increasingly took place under circumstances in which indigenous men had much less control over them and little influence with nonindigenous men. Competition over women, as well as indigenous men's resentment, was a leading cause of deadly violence (McGrath [1990:196] comments on such developments near Sydney in the early nineteenth century). As the frontier and settlement expanded, these incidents of violence often occurred in complex circumstances in which Aborigines had been in contact with European posts, ration stores, and cattle stations. Indigenous women sometimes assumed a certain independence of action, but, in general, all over the continent they were subjected to what historian Patrick Wolfe (1999) has called "sexual bombardment," producing in his view a great contradiction to the colonial "logic of elimination" and settler expectation of indigenous demise: an expanding "half-caste," then "part-caste" population.

Interintentionality: Mixed Signals

In European strategies of "first contact," as we have seen, their estimations of value and interest were not borne out in many cases. Sometimes the natives did not linger long over even the flashiest mirror, and they piled clothes given to them under trees. This frustrated the Europeans' own acquisitive desires: to obtain something from *them* was a complex operation, requiring development of some practical understanding of how values may be negotiated. They could give out things they thought the natives wanted; but how to get things that they wanted? To engage in exchange requires some degree of interintentionality, but how could each side develop it, and how long might this take?

Interintentionality involves the ever-present human problematic of intuiting the other's perspective upon interaction so far and being able to recalibrate one's stance and response in relation to an intuition of how things are shaping up. Normally, this happens fluidly and relatively unproblematically, although of course the surfacing of problems and misunderstandings for one reason or another is also routine. In situations of early encounter, we constantly see moments in which recalibration—the estimation of the other's perspective on objects of common attention and of disposition—stalls and becomes instead a moment in which, on one side or both, difficulty surfaces. One example, again from an early account, can illustrate the issues.

Baudin's men quickly saw that the Tasmanians valued their own tools and especially their spears. Baudin (1974:350) reports that the natives showed them to the French and demonstrated techniques of edging and polishing them. There was an exchange of such demonstrations: "Firstly, they use a stone, as we would a piece of glass, and then, for polishing them, they employ an oyster shell that they have sharpened on one side. Our gardener gave one of them a pruning knife and demonstrated its use to him. He used it for the same purpose as his stone and then gave it back when he was ready to perfect his work with his oyster shell. These people appear to have no knowledge of iron and its usefulness."

Baudin ends by commenting on the absence of iron as a deficiency of native technology. Clearly, one of Baudin's thoughts is, with our (iron) tools these processes could be improved. On this and other occasions the journals make it clear that the French made many approaches to local men to collect their spears. Perhaps they wished that the men would have sometimes offered spears in the way they themselves offered buttons or beads. But the Tasmanians did not do so. They probably had their own understandings of what spears are for and why one would want them.

The French sought to collect spears, we presume, as interesting objects of "primitive" but ingenious technology. It was hunting technology; spears were mainstays of Aboriginal men's lifeworld. Conceptions underpinning the French desire for spears—as evidence of primordial lifeways and men's role in them—were outside the thoughts of the Tasmanians who were (with some difficulty) persuaded to give them up for items they clearly valued:

> Captain Hamelin wanted to exchange something for one of their spears. He proposed the deal by signs that were well understood, and it was agreed that they would hand over a spear in return for a uniform button. The agreement concluded, one of them went and fetched the weapon and relinquished it upon receiving the settled price. The two others did the same, taking care not to let go of their spears until they had already been paid. As one had brought two, we tried to see if he would agree to part with the second by not paying him until after we had received it. But he was on his guard against this and did not even want to give it up after being paid for it. However, the practice had grown up of holding one end of the spear as the button changed hands, so he was obliged to let it go and this did not appear to please him.
>
> The negotiations finished, the natives stood off a little from us, as if afraid that we might use against them the arms that they had just sold us. However, upon seeing that we were heading back to our boats, they followed us again. (Baudin 1974:321)

We can imagine why the natives harbored this fear. They could not have remotely guessed why the French were collecting their spears. They may have imputed to them an intention to use them. They did know that at this transfer, they would be left without the spears, and the French would have appropriated them. That may be a reason why one man brought two spears: not to give over both but to be able to retain one.

Shortly after this exchange one of the natives attempted to snatch a drawing that had been done of him; and some natives picked up stones and began throwing them, several reaching as far as the boat. Why the drawing offended was never clear to the French. Baudin was hit and aimed his gun at the perpetrator, who "ran for his life" (ibid.)—an indication that these people understood the possible range of gunfire. The French returned to their boat, expecting that a large number of men might soon follow. Some dozen or more did appear on the beach, but when they saw that the French were keeping close watch on their movements, they disappeared into the forest.

This description indicates that some practices of exchange had begun to take shape. In the absence of standardized negotiations, they involved a value equivalence established at least temporarily (button for spear), along with practices that suggest an absence of trust or spirit of reciprocity—the holding onto one thing until the other has been given over, signaling a reservation that otherwise the transfer will not be completed. That these practices seemed ungenerous or unbalanced to the natives is suggested by their anger after the transaction and also by the attempt to retrieve the picture that was being sketched. The Tasmanians seem to see themselves as being treated unfairly, things being appropriated from them. On the other hand, to the Frenchmen it may not have been obvious at all that the Aborigines had any kind of right to the picture being drawn by one of themselves. In another passage Baudin (1974:350) refers to his men as having "bought" some large spears from the natives, presumably on similar terms.

To obtain these spears was not a simple matter of offering something to the natives that they could accept or reject. It was about getting something from them that required some idea of their perspective upon the thing sought and the transaction more broadly. That the spears had great value to the locals seemed clear: they were exchanged against the coveted buttons. But even then, the exchange was made with difficulty, and with some apparent reluctance on the Tasmanians' part. The exchange was scarcely regularized to "this for that"; there was no accepted equivalence. The matter of spear exchange produced vital—and negative—emotional response, partly managed by the French stratagem of letting the men maintain physical contact with the spear until the button had been transferred. The French seem to be setting the terms; the Tasmanians, acceding to but not fully accepting them.

Little trust is evident between parties. What was at stake? Also, did the Aboriginal man recognize in the picture an image of himself? That he snatched the pictures drawn of him suggests a sense of indignation, his resisting having something taken from him that he does not want to reduce to equivalence with anything, including the spears.

The French were clearly aware of disquiet in these transactions but persisted with them and, in doing this, shaped the context of exchange—not exactly to their liking—but they pressed on with their purpose.

The French tendency was to cast these exchanges as purchase, but though that may have made the exchanges intelligible to them, it is clear that no such reduction had been achieved. The existence of a shared understanding of a general equivalence between the two items did not amount to a "purchase" of spears. There was a remainder about which the French were not certain. No attempt to "add" another spear to the pile for another button was simply taken as unproblematic by the Tasmanians. The French and the Tasmanians had only very approximately matched intentions and expectations. The obvious dissatisfaction and aggression the locals exhibited about spears and drawing were an indication of a considerable disparity between perspectives about the objects of transaction, accompanying affect, the gauging of intentions and how matters between them might go forward. In such mismatching, uncomprehended and unaddressed, we have one of the foundations of violence, about which more lies ahead.

Relational dimensions of affect, attention, and intention involve a good deal of unpredictability in social action and openings toward new possibilities for action. They are inherently matters of engagement and process and not simply of any existing repertoire.

Ethics and Violence

Violence runs through indigenous-nonindigenous relations. Explorers and colonists had a view of themselves within a frame of reference that included ideas of world history and civilizational differences. High-minded outsiders did, at least on some occasions, explicitly think of their treatment of indigenous people as moral tests of their own selves and ill treatment of them as a "stain" on British government (Barta 2008:533).

Some explorers whose journals have figured so far (from the late seventeenth to mid-nineteenth centuries) wrote of the importance of peaceable interaction. George Grey (1841: vol. 2, p. 64), in dire straits as usual (he had many misadventures) on his trek northward, says of his considerations about whether to ransack a native store of nuts for his hungry men: "I was reluctant to mark the first approach of civilized man to this country of a savage race, by an unprovoked act of pillage and robbery." Reluctant, yes, but he seems to have gone ahead with this.

Sturt, Eyre, and Grey (all explorers making early contacts across the continent) are noteworthy for their expressions of concern and recognition of the moral qualities and potential civilizability of the natives, and of (fellow) ethical beings in them. All repeatedly remark on their essential human worth, their kindness, and the absence of wanton cruelty, but they also foresee with regret the deleterious effects of their exposure to European society, which they were helping to advance (Grey 1841: vol. 2, pp. 222–24, 373, 377). The tone of these earlier journals of exploration in eighteenth- and early nineteenth-century Australia is different from the hard-edged tenor of many later journals; with the extension of colonization, the stereotyping of Aboriginal character envisioned their being eliminable.

The Australian colonies rapidly moved from being a penal outpost of the empire, under military authority, to full-fledged colonizing ventures. The colonial occupation of the continent was never in doubt. Wolfe (1999) writes that the logic of settler colonialism is that the elimination of indigenous groups, by one means or another, is inevitable. The lesser valuation of indigenous life is inherent in the project, not incidental to it. However, the clarity of the fundamental logic of replacement—taking over the land, eliminating the indigenous people, in order to found land-based economic activity—does not mean that its implications are equally realized in all situations or for all people. There was always varied opinion on Aborigines among the Australian public: some saw them as fellow humans, others did not (Reynolds 1974). There were people of humane, remedialist, benevolent, and Christian sentiment who sought to do what they could for Aborigines and no doubt kept some from destruction, but such efforts did not change the overall tide of events. Historians, musicologists, and others have been able to show some of the detail of indigenous response to colonial incursion in song, dance, and interaction with local settlers and have noted that events differed regionally depending on a variety of factors; even, hopefully (but retrospectively) that there was "nothing inevitable about the course black/white relations would take" (McDonald 1996:182, concerning New England). Of course it is always possible to see differences in complex events. Yet, with some variation, throughout the continent these events were consistent with marginalization and elimination, especially when viewed at the large scale of political-economic transformation: the "wool rush" of the 1830s in the south and east, the northern pastoral rush in the 1880s and 1890s, and a series of rushes for valued minerals.

Governments, too, understood the violence and damage that was being done to indigenous people and whole social orders. A select committee reporting to the British Parliament in 1837 recognized "every element of the process of destruction" even as it was being instituted across southern Australia (Barta 2008:535). Outright violence and massive retaliation against Aboriginal people who got in the way of pastoral development took a significant toll, but so did disease, alcohol addiction, malnutrition, sexual predation, and consequent social fragmentation. Those who found themselves presiding over indigenous removal in one part of the country often later did so elsewhere (for example, George Augustus Robinson, a major figure in the rounding up of Tasmanians, was later involved in management of indigenous people—protection to them if nomadic, but with encouragement to sedentarize—under the Port Philip Protectorate in Victoria).

Recently Australian academics waged what were called "history wars" (so labeled by Macintyre and Clark 2004), offering another instance of the prominence of indigenous issues in Australia. These involved contestation over whether the extent of colonial violence was major or minor; if the former, whether terms including "invasion," "warfare," "guerrilla warfare," "conquest," or "genocide" apply; and if violence were minor, whether colonization was generally marked instead by humane intent on the part of government authorities, with damage to indigenous people largely attributable to unintended factors (such as the spread of new diseases) rather than to malicious policies or consistent eliminatory intent. These "wars," considered important to national reputation, were taken up by academics, political figures (including, prominently, two prime ministers, Keating [1991–96] and Howard [1996–2007] on opposite sides of the issue), and public institutions. Major conservative figures in the debate (notoriously, historian Keith Windschuttle [2002]) skeptically demanded precise body counts of Aborigines allegedly killed, along with other similarly vexatious nonsense on the part of those insistent on minimizing the scale of violence.

There have been debates between those who have argued that the term "genocide" should be used only where there is an avowed policy (Reynolds 2001); and others who believe the term can apply to a "logic" of elimination even if, as in Australia, most official government pronouncements were outwardly protectionist (see Moses 2004:28). All such debates are conducted in uneasiness concerning comparison with Nazi policy toward the Jews. It seems obvious there was a different configuration in Australia than in Nazi Germany. Government policy outwardly stated its duty to protect, combined with government awareness of the destructiveness of colonization and completely inadequate action to prevent any of this. There was enormous disparity between government policy pronouncements and settler *and* official practice. For example, appointed protectors and justices of the peace were often also pastoralists and fully aligned with settler interests to the detriment of Aborigines.

Dirk Moses (2004:33) writes of the need to understand the "dynamic process" by which the potential for violence inherent in the colonial project was turned into genocidal intention and perpetration. He identifies this moment in Aboriginal hostility and resistance, any evidence of which was rapidly branded an "outrage" and allowed the radicalization of policy and practice into an overtly declared or enacted intent to kill. Such radicalization, though, whatever the actions of Aborigines, seems to me to have been most directly the result of successful lobbying by settlers persuading other settlers and any officials that an exterminatory course was necessary in order to secure colonization itself (Roberts 1969:329). Any of the usual governmental injunctions to deal moderately with the natives simply failed to gain any traction.

It is entirely consistent with the assumption of the right to explore and colonize that, from the very beginning, outsiders demonstrated their superior firepower to Aboriginal people. Furthermore, not only were such displays reported; it is clear that outsiders used such disproportionate power not only to protect themselves and to show what they could do, but also to "repel" and "punish" aggression (see, e.g., Reid 1990:30).

Baudin and his party were asked on a number of occasions to lay down their guns, and he recorded that he only had to shift his gun to see how much people feared it (Baudin 1974:323). "At the slightest move from us, they were on their feet, especially if somebody touched the gun, for they certainly knew what effect it had and stood in great fear of it. I have no doubt that at some other time some of them must have had unpleasant experience of one" (320–21). Can this be an innocent remark? Such experience was most likely with his own crew (it is unlikely these Tasmanians could have had encounters with any other Europeans). While diarists felt little difficulty in committing to paper accounts of their display of firepower to intimidate and impress, they were much more reserved about committing to paper reports of their use of firepower on indigenous people. Over decades, reference to such episodes is cloaked in coded language, treated allusively, or passed over in silence.

Aborigines to whom guns were shown, of course, saw uses of their own for them. Baudin (1974:341) found them not reticent in asking the French to use their guns to procure game for them that they would otherwise have hunted. They also saw in guns a way to easily overpower their enemies. Working through a local interpreter, Nyungar people in the Swan River area told George Grey that he should kill nobody until he had passed a certain place on his trek north, after which, he reports, they advised him "indiscriminately to shoot everybody I saw" (Grey 1841: vol. 1, p. 293). Likewise Sturt (1849: vol.

1, p. 111) reports that a guide he took along with him was so enraged when they encountered a party of bush Aborigines that he told Sturt to shoot them, "pushed his blanket into his mouth, and bit it violently in his anger." This is evidence of the regional differences and enmities that existed among Aboriginal people across the continent. Anthropologists have long seen Australian social formations as of small scale, with network-like, tensile capacity to stretch out, in which differences were significant and constantly negotiated (Myers 1986; Sansom 1982). The Nyungar approach to Grey belongs to a time when recruitment of outsiders to ongoing struggles was a resource that Aboriginal people attempted to gain for themselves, before the extension of colonization and crystallization of a fuller sense of black-white opposition. While hostility and self-defense were common indigenous early responses to outsiders, and indigenous leaders and defenders did emerge in conditions where defense was possible (Pedersen and Woorunmurra 1995), the technological and numerical disparities were overpowering, and dislocations of indigenous people became the almost inevitable consequence, mitigated only by the creation of remote-area reserves such as Arnhem Land (declared, after some failed efforts at pastoralism there, in 1933).

Corroborees and Footballers: Producing Aborigines

What, in general, happened to indigenous people dislocated in whole or in part from their way of life as the tide of colonization moved across the continent? The rearrangements were differentiated and regionally specific: the last ill-fated Tasmanians and many others were removed to settlements and missions; these and other institutions began to gather children, usually of "part caste," in order to educate and separate them from their families and people. From these and other locations many indigenous people attempted to remake a land-based existence working as pastoral labor or to farm themselves, but often under conditions of enormous difficulty of access to land and credit; like those who succumbed in England to enclosure movements, they became indigent laborers (Goodall 1996; Haebich 1988, 2000, 2004; Scrimgeour 2006). Some historians offer narrative interpretations of resilience and survival over the long term (Goodall and Cadzow 2009).

However, that is a vast field that cannot be treated in detail here. Rather, the aim of this chapter is to illustrate from contact material some fundamental differences in approach of indigenous and nonindigenous people to each other in order to illuminate some deep-seated differences between them. This section aims to show these differences interwoven in the intercultural form known as the "corroboree." On the one hand, the corroboree realized European logics of conversion of relational forms into products for display; on the other hand, it became for indigenous people a livelihood and the basis for new relationships among themselves and with settlers.

The Tjapukai Aboriginal Dance Theatre in Kuranda, north Queensland, has been performing daily since May 1987 and has been called Australia's most successful Aboriginal tourist product (M. Parsons 2000:564; Henry 2012). It is also Australia's largest private employer of indigenous people. It presents contemporary examples of the corroboree, which Darwin called the Australian "dance-party."[2]

"Corroboree" apparently derives from a word (*garaabara*) from the Dharuk language of Sydney that originally referred to a style of dance and came to be applied to public dance events staged by Aboriginal people for settler audiences. Of course, such displays had their origins in internal indigenous settings and were performed and traded there. Originally some were restricted as part of sacred ceremonies; others were for entertainment, performed around themes, topical events, and stories, and these probably were the predecessors of tourist displays. Clearly, Aboriginal people adapted corroborees, sometimes incorporating Christian among other sacred elements, and continued to perform them in contexts we would regard as religious and with "cosmological" purpose (Swain 1993). Explorers and settlers observed many performances at large and small gatherings (see Bushman 1841; Calley 1959; Bennett 1928; Petrie 1992; among many other sources). Increasingly performances came to be staged for, or at the request of, European owners and managers of pastoral properties and for special occasions as display and what was taken by audiences to be entertainment. In 1946, the Duke and Duchess of Gloucester visited Elsey Station, Northern Territory, and were treated to a corroboree, as well as displays of fish and turtle catching by local Aborigines. Everywhere, this was a taste of alterity. At the same time, the manners, movements, and lives of outsiders became the material that indigenous performers wove into new performances for both inside and settler audiences (Casey 2011).

Corroborees have fascinated European audiences in the past and into the present. Of urban areas where corroborees were performed in the past, this has been particularly well documented for Adelaide (M. Parsons 1997, 2000). Aborigines living near this growing city in the early nineteenth century first turned their hand to supplying settlers with firewood, but they were prevented from continuing by authorities who noted the depletion of trees and discouraged any success that might bring more Aborigines into town. Although government and administrative effort was generally dedicated to keeping them out, the "Sunday corroboree" had become standard in Adelaide by 1845, despite being considered a nuisance by many white residents (Parsons 1997:49). Small payments became customary, and at least some of this went to Aborigines. Corroborees were advertised in the local papers, seemingly sometimes at the behest of indigenous performers (ibid.). They increasingly emerged as commercial entertainment, and "joint venture" arrangements (Parsons 1997) were established in which there was substantial nonindigenous organization and promotion, fee collection, and redistribution of some portion of profits, needed gear, fishing equipment or the like, to indigenous performers. Independent performance groups also arose, some managed by indigenous people and others by whites dealing with them.

Later, versions of corroborees were staged in theaters, and series of "joint venturers" (Parsons 1997) sponsored corroborees, including hoteliers, who thereby assured themselves of lively trade, and organizers of football and cricket matches. Some of these events attracted audiences of thousands and became public features over the nineteenth and well into the twentieth century. Sunday evening performances on the banks of the Yarra River in Melbourne grew so large that Governor La Trobe banned them in 1840 (Parsons 2000:564). An estimated crowd of twenty thousand, a sixth of the city's population, turned out to watch what was called the Grand Corroboree at the Adelaide Oval in 1885 (Parsons 1997; Whimpress 2000; Casey 2011). Large crowds at these events had long attracted disapproval from missionary and benevolent societies and others, who thought they encouraged indigenous people in what they judged unseemly, profane, and disruptive performances, and who, in any case, frowned on their visiting centers of population. Nonetheless, this later resulted in another kind of joint venture, the fund-raising corroboree under missionary sponsorship. Corroborees continued all over the continent, and in some places (like Kuranda) have emerged, transformed into polished tourist performances, as well as cosmopolitan urban dance performances of national and international renown. In many, perhaps most, of these performances over time indigenous people have set content, exercised artistic license, and cannot be simply seen as having been completely manipulated by nonindigenous organizers (Casey 2011).

The corroboree is of interattentional significance. There are several other interesting, perhaps puzzling, aspects of the history of corroboree that merit comment and that relate to both interaffectivity and interintentionality.

Some performances took on the character of display for settler audiences, in towns, cities, as well as on pastoral properties for special occasions. As they did so, nonindigenous publics and organizers took on the authority to judge their quality, not simply as "barbaric," immodest, and indecent (Parsons 1997:59), as missionaries and others often did, but also as sham and inauthentic, and the Aborigines as having lost their culture and become "tamed" (Casey 2011). Second, in view of that reaction it is also interesting that one of the most persistent corroboree fascinations was the staging of warfare and mock battles (Collins 1802:543; Bellingshausen 1945:85–90; Casey 2011) with spears and woomeras—performances that audiences regarded as "thrilling." Spear-throwing demonstrations, at least, remain standard today at places like the Tjapukai Dance Theatre—but often members of the audience are also invited to try their hand (and to dance) in what appears to be a leveling maneuver. Third, in the large performances of the nineteenth and early twentieth centuries, it is noteworthy that occasionally audiences invaded the performance space. This was partly because much greater than expected spectator numbers sometimes attempted to enter the grounds, an interesting fact in itself; but also because on some occasions audience-performer demarcation was simply not observed by spectators once they were inside. Casey (2011) suggests this be seen as "performance of white entitlement" and, like judgmental evaluation, the claiming of an all-knowing subject position. Last, accounts indicate that indigenous performers were enthusiastically cheered at the end of performances for singing the national anthem of the time (Parsons 1997:58).

The corroboree is a performance, distinct from real life, but there can be little doubt that, as an event, these features of corroboree tell us something about the ambivalent and unresolved desires of the wider public and at least the accommodations, if not the closer considerations, of Aborigines involved. The public took pleasure from seeing indigenous people contained, while fantasizing them as genuinely warlike. Enjoying the spectacle of a performance in an "indigenous space," the audience demonstrated by its behavior the fragility of such a space. The public could approve indigenous demonstrations of allegiance to national being and identity. These shows clearly represented, for audiences, an objectification (Myers 2001:20) of the social process of interrelation with indigenous people, reducing their essence to a few items and revaluing them as interesting, possibly thrilling, display. Writing of the cultural logic of nation building, Amanda Nettelbeck (2008:15) has dubbed this sort of display-making a "trophy moment." David Cahir and Ian Clark (2010), on the other hand, have emphasized the emergence of what they call a certain "business acumen" among indigenous performers on the Victorian goldfields or their commodification of culture.[3]

These ambivalences resonate with events that have recently swirled around (former) professional Australian rules footballer Adam Goodes. A sportsperson of Scots-Irish and physiognomically obvious indigenous ancestry, he played for the Sydney Swans in the Australian Football League (AFL). The winner of prestigious sporting medals, Goodes was designated Australian of the Year in 2013. During his term he attracted criticism for speaking of the hurt and pain felt by many indigenous people on Australia Day, the annual celebration on 26 January of the arrival of the First Fleet and raising of the British flag (and countered by indigenous commemorations of the occasion, from the first occasion in 1938, as a "day of mourning"). Running close to the boundary line in the opening game of the annual Indigenous Round between Collingwood and the Sydney Swans, Goodes heard a girl, a Collingwood fan, calling him an "ape." Goodes stopped and told the security guards to escort her away. She later apologized, claiming she did not know this was a racial slur.

This incident attracted significant public attention and developed into a wider debate about racism in Australia and the nature of its relationship with indigenous people. Over the following years, and particularly in 2015, Goodes was repeatedly and loudly booed by opposition fans at most matches. While so-called "slagging" of this sort is a feature of football competitions,[4] the relentless nature of this harrying led to Goodes's taking stress leave from the game in August of the 2015 season. Many clubs and players in the AFL supported Goodes in the first week of his leave by wearing indigenous-themed guernseys (jerseys) or armbands, and a video was prepared by the eighteen club captains to discourage the crowd from booing. Debate continued on his role in drawing attention to racial discrimination and promoting indigenous causes.

However, relating to indigenous display: another cause of controversy was Goodes's demonstration of his indigeneity on the football field during the annual Indigenous Round in May 2015. He celebrated a goal with an indigenous themed dance and threw an (imaginary) spear at Carlton fans, describing this as an opportunity to "show that passion and pride about being a warrior and representing my people" (ABC).[5] Some commentators saw the act as aggressive and threatening, with conservative commentator Andrew Bolt describing it as a "challenge to race war."[6] The suggestions that Adam Goodes "stop the war dance, and take it like an Aussie and harden up" came from nonindigenous footballer Jason Akermanis. In this new period, the "war dance" was interpreted as rebellious and oppositional, display out of control.

The history of corroboree provides evidence of commercial and public pressures toward reduction of "cultural" displays to thinglike, marketable status and their containment. Meanwhile, indigenous people even in earlier remote areas have steadily entered into new intensity of contact with market products, with resulting tensions.

A Contemporary Coda: The Excluded Middle

By the latter 1960s, where they had not been occupationally sidelined before, many indigenous people were let go from pastoral work throughout the north. They had typically received very modest wages, if any; much of what they earned was expended or "booked down" at the local store, and they might receive the rest, often for special occasions such as "race days," when any available money would rapidly be spent. In the late 1960s many station-dwelling Aborigines became unemployed and were also widely regarded as unemployable elsewhere in the economy. From the 1970s onward, where it had not happened previously, indigenous people in even remote areas and communities became more fully enrolled to receive cash welfare payments. In communities where I lived in the early period of my research in Katherine, at Barunga (then called Bamyili) and Elsey Station, I saw officers arrive, sign people up, and the categories of welfare payments expand from aged and widows' pensions to UB (unemployment benefit) and a range of other categories. As recipients of modest cash incomes, indigenous people began to purchase commodities of their own choosing (rather than having to select from limited stores as previously available to them on pastoral stations, for instance, usually directly deducted from whatever wages they notionally received).

Welfare cash income did not enable the accumulation of wealth; it was immediate, disposable income for people who lived in relatively poor conditions. Indigenous people had no accumulations[7] and (especially in the northern pastoral and mining area I know) had largely lived completely on the poorest fringes of the economic circuitry of wider Australian society, outside the political and economic mainstream. Access to cash, together with (for many) greater geographical distance from their country, represented for many a considerable change. Austin-Broos (2009) refers to these as grounds of "ontological shift." In these transformations, undoubtedly one item of highest value was the truck, or car, or means of transport, among locales over which networks of kin were distributed. New transport not only brought people together, it allowed new ways to disperse, as an Australianist literature shows (Nash 1986; Myers 1988; Gerrard 1989; Young 2001; Fogarty 2005). Administrators and governments sometimes evaluate uses of vehicles as profligate and as enabling intractable indigenous uses of housing in numbers and networks of users (Heppell 1979; Memmott 1988, 2003, 2007; Sanders 1990; Read 2000; Lea 2008b; Lea and Pholeros 2010).

Indigenous people in remote communities began to consume items well outside the range that station stores had stocked and beyond immediate food needs. Choices may be limited in remote areas, but people take opportunity to shop in major centers. From local stores or larger centers, items in demand include vehicles, TVs, video and tape players, washing machines and stoves, mobile phones, refrigerators, clothing and shoes, bed frames, suitcases, blankets, brooms, flatware, dishes and cooking implements, toys, guitars, photo albums, foods, and a few decorative items (mostly for graves, plastic flowers). Most houses of indigenous families I know who live in camps in the vicinity of Katherine do not decorate internally. Camp households range widely in their equipment and furnishing, some with little or no furniture, others with at least mattresses, stoves, and refrigerators, perhaps a few plastic chairs, and a minimum of kitchen utensils that usually need to be replaced regularly, given their use by numbers of people and irregular household schedules. Rental apartments or houses in town may have some furniture, tables, chairs, couches, and mattresses on the floor to sleep on. Plastic flowers as grave decoration have become standard; and in the early 1990s I began to see occasional photographs of the deceased on graves, contra the continental public stereotype that indigenous people do not like to see images of the dead. While that has been true, this new (and still occasional) practice reflects the taking up of a new opening that has appeared, perhaps on the model of European and Torres Strait Islander grave marking.[8]

Though indigenous people have been acquiring many of the ordinary market consumables, their relationship to them is variable, and regular patterns of difference from "standard" usages, as above, are noticeable. Especially in the kind of communities I know, which have recently transited to a much fuller spectrum of consumption, people still relate to consumer goods in distinctive ways. For example, in the Elsey Station community, I once noticed two little boys scrapping over where and how to play with a medium-sized plastic car bought the day before. Their father watched in growing annoyance as tension between them grew. At one point the children moved away for a moment from the car. He wordlessly went over, picked it up, and smashed it a few times against a tree until it was no longer usable, dropped it, and sat back down. He and the children said nothing.

Such an incident indicates a shift and tension in progress (see similar episodes in Burbank 2011:47; also Blakeman 2013:191–93, who writes of the physical destruction of "things" that are, in Yolngu terms, *napungga'ngura* "in the middle," disruptive of relations between people). Some of the feeling involved was epitomized for me by a remark of Jimmy Daniels, one of the older men with family near whom I lived in the Elsey Station camp. Jimmy had one of the sole functioning vehicles in camp at that time. He was constantly being asked to give people rides, as was anyone (including me) who had a functioning vehicle. Everyone with a vehicle knows that this will be their fate and largely accommodates to it and seeks acceptable ways of limiting demand. (Mine was to hold firm to not transporting alcohol, which cut down some of the most vexatious trips.) One morning Jimmy awoke and went to his car to begin the day's struggle with its various impaired systems. After an unsuccessful stretch of attempted bush mechanics, he said, not angrily but neutrally, in English: "I'm glad the bastard's dead." In other words, the tension that we experienced daily in managing transport had been transcended, at least for the moment, by elimination of the "thing" in the middle (cf. Myers 1988:23).

Much literature has emphasized fundamental indigenous orientation to interpersonal relatedness. Myers (1988:24), deliberately adopting an economistic idiom to make contrast with its grounds clear, writes of indigenous "investment" in people rather than things. When "things," often new portable ones but also, as indicated, large ones like vehicles, become a source of conflict and heighten tensions in relation to others, the resolution is sometimes to obliterate, often wordlessly and definitively, what is separative. This can occur even in the case of what seem to others to be very economically "valuable" assets, such as cars (Myers [1988:26–27] writes of people setting fire to vehicles as a resolution of continual demand). Although most people want to be able to access a car and have things, this is not the only imperative. It can be a relief to get rid of alien elements, making this an anthropological and not a pathological issue.

But what is the issue? Here something like civilizational difference mentioned early in the chapter, as well as interpretation of it, becomes important.

Myers (1988) has cogently argued that the idiom of "property" is misleading and inexact for Aboriginal contexts in which relations to materiality continue to be at least partly constituted in action as a matter of shared identification. This continues the continental modality of people with few movable goods for whom human relation to land has been a key value and form of objectification (Munn 1970) and contrasts with notions of property ownership in Western terms. In the former mode, both material things and land are key platforms for the negotiation of identification of people with others via those sources of value. How things may be constituted in interaction as extensible to others (including and even mainly by those who claim some authority in relation to them) is significant; it is a basis of shared identification. Those who study indigenous child socialization involving this mode, for instance (Hamilton 1981; Eickelkamp 2011), observe how early and strenuously children are enjoined to share with others as a way of constituting relationships of self and other; and how children who are offered treats or sweets will call other children to share in what is being offered rather than try to keep it for themselves. The injunction to share is one of the more strenuous forms of socialization, contrasting with permissiveness accorded to children to do what they want in many other ways. Social relations expressed principally in the vocabulary of kinship are inherently extensible and never fully given as a defining structure (see Chapter 5); thus a key issue is how relationship to any given items, place, or even person, is negotiable and a possible basis of shared identity. This produces an orientation to materiality and many things as replaceable rather than as inherently valuable in themselves. (There are clearly exceptions to this, as when people favor a particular cup or other item and may take pains to retain it about them.) Things and places are bearers of human identity and of the effort that goes into constituting them in those terms; they are not "things" as such. This is the sense of destroying things when they appear conflictual in the identification of people with others. Mortuary practices ban houses and even vehicles upon the death of people chiefly associated with them, ending existing identifications, forged in the person's lifetime, and limiting the capacity to carry such identifications into the future.

Women were seen as yet another modality in which identifications could be forged, particularly and most directly between and among men, and gender relations to some extent complied with these terms. This is a kind of value of women that did not reduce them to ownable property but aligned them with other forms through which identification could be negotiated and in which they, too, participated as both willful and socially constrained subjects.

Conclusion: Things and People

Early European encounter strategies centered on offers of things that were meant to appeal. However, an account of interactions cannot be based on any taken-for-granted notion of "thing." Indeed, there was no word of the kind we know for "thing" in Australian languages. Early European encounters also urged people into particular routines, even if only short-lived. However, in no Australian language is there a word for "work," a generic term for the routinization of daily effort. These linguistic observations remind us that it has been a historically variable social practice to constitute value in mutual identification through the material objects and mundane practices of frontier situations.

The indigenous people encountered by the colonists were everywhere interested in and curious about difference—when they had the peace, space, and outsiders' cooperation to be so—and what difference might imply. Europeans in early encounter, we saw, were ill at ease when their own bodiliness became the focus of interattentionality; they were keenly attuned to indigenous affect as they saw this as a matter of their own security. At first, however, the indigenous people were most intensely interested precisely in bodiliness of the outsiders, in skin (and clothes as perhaps part of the person), in establishing their sexual nature. Once they triumphantly confirmed sexual recognizability of outsiders, indigenous men went on—early and then persistently—to offer their women in mediation of relationship. We have also seen that this was not simple domination of women; women, too, were interested in these matters. But deployment of women in sexual mediation did involve a conventional indigenous hegemony: men's persuasion and coercion of women. Then, increasingly, this form of relationality was largely transformed into domination of both indigenous men and women by outsiders, to the point of "sexual bombardment." Sexual exchange was converted into dominated exchange.

Concerning the "things" offered by Europeans in mediation: indigenous attitudes to many "things" were a matter of puzzlement, and sometimes frustration, to Europeans. To varying degrees they have remained so. Many "things" were only glanced at early on, and clothes were discarded (yet, later, treated as markers of distinction and identity, and worn to tatters). Food was initially avoided and suspected; then, rationing became a necessary basis of a sedentized life. Today, cash is regularly asked for and given for its relational value in many indigenous settings, rather than calculatedly in terms of its value as currency (Merlan 1991b).

Captain Cook's resounding statement that the natives were "wholly unacquainted" with not only "the superfluous but the necessary Conveniences so much sought after in Europe" is echoed in the words of Archdeacon Broughton in the Report of the Select Committee of 1837: "they are a quick, intelligent people; but they have, I may say, no wants: you find it impossible to excite in them any want which you can gratify, and therefore they have no inducement to remain under a state of restraint, nor are they ever willing to leave their children" (in Barta 2008:522).

The archdeacon linked evident lack of interest in things to form of life—not unreasonably. However, this did not take into account other indigenous sensibilities concerning materiality. We saw that Aborigines sensed transcendence in beads, bottles, and buttons; that they valued their finely crafted spears—and, as we know from across the continent, many other such things besides. The archdeacon went on to connect lack of interest in things with what he saw as a problem: Aborigines would not settle down; which was often (willfully or interestedly) misunderstood as their having no attachments or belonging to place. The archdeacon's mention of unwillingness to leave their children rings ominously, as we now know that outsiders were soon to harvest young indigenous and especially "part-caste" children from their families to educate and "civilize" them (Scrimgeour 2006).

Materialities—the qualities of objectness (Myers 2001:88)—have continued to be a pivot of differentiation and contestation between many indigenous and nonindigenous Australians. Though there are different materialities at issue today in indigenous-nonindigenous relations, nonindigenous Australians continue to attempt interattentionality by relying upon things with little concept of or concern for indigenous valuation of them (see Chapter 8). This is not only because of great cultural difference, which this chapter has explored, but also because of the embedding of that difference in the subsequent historical experience of relative poverty, marginalization, and administrative management through which many indigenous people have lived.

Paul Kockelman (2016:120) has recently observed that what passes as a local cultural order may have its origins in colonial imposition. His own ethnography examines ongoing transformation in a Mayan Guatemalan highland community from the emphasis, in local economy, on concepts of the equivalence of people (as labor) and things (for use), toward commensuration, or making people and things differentially evaluable and rewardable in the market terms of a nongovernmental organization (NGO)–led ecotourism project. His observation relates to the longer-term hypothesis (developed in Wilk 1991) that labor pooling—the locally most extensive form of man-power replacement, a man-day of work for a man-day of work—may have originated when the subsistence economy was subject to unprecedented colonial stress. In short, seemingly culturally ingrained communal labor organization may be the product of predatory capitalism.

The indigenous Australian uses of material and personal resources give a different value to things and capacities of persons than is common in the wider society. These differences originated in the long-term past and are not any simple consequences of colonialism. But they have changed through their collision with other values. For instance, Aborigines used to have few portable things. Now, while they often exercise what is often for administrators a frustrating degree of mobility among people and camps (see J. Taylor 1996; Warchivker, Tjapangati, and Wakerman 2000; Taylor and Bell 2004; among many others), they have longer-term fixity in particular places, with an accompanying, growing material repertoire (houses, swags, dishes, vehicles that are both hugely desired and can pose problems in contemporary terms, and so on). Both Austin-Broos (2009) and Kockelman (2016) speak in terms of ontological incommensurabilities and shifts. My discussion in this chapter has ranged over large spans of time, not in the interest of establishing unbroken continuity but to show that there has been consistency in some apparently fundamental indigenous-nonindigenous difference at times and in particular circumstances of this interrelation. Austin-Broos (2009) has written about the kinds of suffering involved for indigenous people at Hermannsburg (a former Lutheran mission in Central Australia) in constantly having to redefine themselves and their forms of value. The evidence of intersecting difference has allowed me to range over time periods to cast light on it.

This chapter also sought to bring to light certain persistent tendencies in indigenous concerns and ethics. Recent theorization of relationality as central to indigenous social orders has helped to create openings for more ethically inflected approaches to history and social relations, and, importantly, helped to elucidate indigenous ethical positions. Anthropologist Deborah Bird Rose first conducted research from 1980 to 1982 in the Victoria River District of the western Northern Territory (Rose 1992). Colonial invasion of this area began much later than in the south—in 1883 with the taking up of vast tracts of land for raising cattle. Intense frontier violence lasted for some decades (see Lewis 2005, 2012). Aboriginal survivors eventually settled on cattle stations as cheap labor, sustaining those operations until minimum wage and technological change forced most of these people from pastoral work and even off pastoral properties.[9] Rose and some others[10] have made a concerted effort to render indigenous voices hearable and to project their viewpoints on these events. One of Rose's (1989) key informants was an elderly Northern Territorian indigenous man named Hobbles Danayarri. In some of his eloquent stories, we hear Hobbles's strong moral sensibility concerning the injustice of colonization and its consequences; he expresses himself partly in terms of common Australian parlance, the "fair go" that Aborigines should have.

Hobbles Danayarri also had thoughts concerning accommodation in the context of a brutal colonial history. Expressing an acceptance of the past as the basis from which we will build our future, he suggested means of transforming the wrongs of the past into more equitable relationships. Chief among these, he saw "cross-ways marriage"—in other words, intermarriage—as a way forward, to be "friends," because "we own Australia" today. He evidently accepts that both blacks and whites are here to stay. Offers of bodily relationality in this poetic mode of Hobbles—as well as sometimes more exploitative, vernacular ones—retain some strength across gulfs of difference and long spans of brutal treatment (Rose 1989; see also Grant 2016).

Ethical concerns continue on both indigenous and nonindigenous sides, and they change over time, as we will explore in subsequent chapters. This chapter brought to light a different, very contemporary ethical preoccupation on the part of intellectuals of dominant Australian society concerned with indigenous people and their situations: that is, the attempt to cast them as agents, rather than victims, as in the books by Clendinnen (2005) and Shellam (2009). To my mind, however, we cannot simply argue in any meaningful way for "agency" imagined as a distinctive, persistent social force (cf. Merlan 2016b). In the case of overwhelming societal asymmetry such as we see between indigenous and nonindigenous people in the processes of colonization and their aftermath, we must adapt Wolfe's words and reflect that, like colonization, accommodation to domination is not simply an event but a drawn-out process of somewhat indeterminate structure and fragmenting nature. This prioritizes the need to understand the tenor of relationships, forms of consciousness, and action in ongoing circumstances of interaction, rather than withdrawal from attempts at such understanding (see Introduction).

CHAPTER 4

Treachery and Boundary Demarcation

Treachery as Idiom of Domination

One of the ways that whites saw Aborigines as different, in their very nature, was their "treachery." "Treachery" was a powerful idiom of domination, nurtured by a settler assumption of entitlement; to consider Aborigines "treacherous" legitimized action during a certain period of colonial exploration and settlement.

I do not argue that Aborigines lacked a capacity for treachery. Spencer and Gillen (1927:444–45) refer to it when describing visiting between groups: someone would be invited into camp as a visitor, lulled into security, and then attacked. There is credible testimony that Aborigines were often filled with suspicion of not only people seen as more unfamiliar and distant but even of kin and countrymen. However, in this chapter I will deal with "treachery" as a specific intercultural product, generated within asymmetric structures of colonization. The "we" of this relationship was constituted by the colonists' intentionality, not by interintentionality. The settlers presumed that the activities of colonizers were worthy and that indigenous people should be committed to them. When colonists' kindness was returned with ingratitude, the colonists attributed a "treacherous" disposition.

Records of earliest colonial encounters include the idea of "treachery." This characterization appears to evolve and become more general as part of the constitution of a substantial settler public. This chapter explores the discourse of treachery and the shaping of a generalizing stereotype in a settler colonial context. "Treachery" implies betrayal, and it also anticipates the nature of future action and relationship. To grasp this forward-facing aspect of treachery, it is important to consider what we mean by "interintentionality," one of the three concepts that I introduced in the previous chapter.[1] Intentionality is a dimension of action, the sharing of which would seem to imply knowledge concerning both self and other. Intentionality relates not only to immediate context but also to future possibilities; it is a projection beyond immediacy. Interintentionality, the sharing of intentions to some degree, maximally including sharing of information, is more complex still. To attribute to others a "treacherous" nature is to reassess what one thought of as (at least potential) commonality (however asymmetrically constituted) in order to block or set limits to it.

Explorers and early settlers were worried about the emotional temper and inclinations of the "natives," and they made efforts to interest, amuse, and engage them. The newcomers arrived with a sense of civilizational difference, however, as European views of "savages" had been shaped by reports of encounters with other Pacific Islanders. When Abel Tasman sailed in 1644, on behalf of the Dutch East India Company, from southeast of New Guinea along the Australian coast, his instructions were influenced by reports from the earlier landing in 1606 of Willem Janszoon, who had warned of "wild, cruel, black savages" (in Sutton 2008:40; Tasman 1642:107). Tasman was always to be on his guard and armed because "in all countries of the globe experience has taught us no savages are to be trusted, by reason they always suppose people who appear so unexpectedly and strangely to them, are only come to invade their country; all which is proved in the discovery of America and the Indies, by the surprise and murdering many careless and unwary discoverers, many times to the ruin of their voyages" (Tasman 1642:114). These instructions recognized that mistrust was generated by the enterprise in which Tasman was engaged, which "the savages" correctly gauged as intrusive. The instructions considered the people to be encountered from the point of view of their expected contribution to the company's success. The assumption of civilizational superiority on the part of Europeans, and hence entitlement, is a fundamental presumption of most explorers, colonizers, and settlers.

Outsiders could be blind to the limits of their efforts to "conciliate" the natives. Baudin's party had presented gifts to the Tasmanians on at least two occasions, and Baudin thought that "trust and friendship" had developed between the French and Tasmanians, so that it was "impossible to harbor the least suspicion of them" (Péron 2006:188). Nonetheless, Péron reported "cowardly and ferocious treachery" toward M. Maurouard following his defeat of a local at arm wrestling (Chapter 3). Maurouard was suddenly hit on the shoulder by a long spear "thrown from behind the nearby rocks" (ibid.). The Tasmanians disappeared and the French did not give chase. The outsiders had thought they knew what the natives thought, based on their own view that they had treated them well, but they found that they did not know the natives. The natives' violent action not only showed the French that they did not grasp native intentions, it strengthened what seems to have been ongoing tension among the explorers concerning the difficulty of *really* judging how the natives felt. The lesson was that they had to live continually with uncertainty and fear.

Treachery as a characterization of indigenous action is also to be seen in the record of the killing on the Adelaide River in 1869 of J. W. O. Bennett, a draftsman for an early survey party in the upper part of the Northern Territory. The original memorial stone erected to mark the spot of his death near the Adelaide River includes: "Mr Bennett placed implicit confidence in the blacks and treated them with familiar kindness. They requited his kindness and confidence by treacherously spearing him when off his guard."[2] This implies that the indigenous people who speared him had a relationship with Bennett. He is said to have treated them with kindness—but they betrayed him. Was there really a relationship, at least a reciprocal understanding of kindness, or is this just a facile assumption? Or an assumption that allows a posture of victimization on the part of the betrayed?

Another description of the relationship was offered at the time. The leader of the survey party, George Goyder, refusing to retaliate for Bennett's death, explained: "We were in what to them appeared unauthorized and unwarranted occupation of their country. . . . Territorial rights are strictly observed by natives . . . it is scarcely to be wondered at if, when opportunity is allowed them, they should resent such acts by violence upon its perpetrators" (Reid 1990:35). Goyder's understanding was not unique; it was found among many explorers and settlers of educated or otherwise enlightened views, as indicated by further examples below.[3]

To attribute "treachery" is thus an interpretive choice; it implies that a relationship exists with another, and that the other has broken this compact. That is, it implies beliefs about human subjects, or a degree of interintentionality. How do those on the other side think about relationships and the situation the presence of outsiders placed them in? Why could outsiders think that other and prior relationships in which indigenous people were enmeshed would be of lesser significance and not play a part in shaping their actions?

Even where contact began with curiosity on both sides and included friendly encounters and exchanges (see, e.g., Lewis 2005 on the lower Victoria River, Northern Territory), the increasing presence of settlers and especially the large-scale introduction of animal herds (Reid 1990:85–112) generated Aboriginal resistance and hostility and resulted in desperation and larger-scale attacks by Aboriginal people upon encroaching parties and large-scale uninhibited killings of Aboriginal people. Understandings of Aborigines as treacherous came to constitute part of a thickened and ever less permeable boundary between them and settlers.

However variably and even sometimes amicably they may have developed, the deeply asymmetrical relations between indigenous people and others were basic to these encounters. One set of actors was knowingly moving into the space of another, without any prior knowledge or agreement on the part of the latter. There was no such movement, or any possibility of it, in the opposite direction. Outsiders arrived with particular, varied, but well-established logics of exploration for a variety of purposes, all of which included in their minds possibilities of discovery, settlement, land usage, and forms of economic activity.

The extent of divergent orientations toward each other and differing orientations toward the existence of relationship is revealed in diarists' accounts of the minutiae of the everyday. The activities and thoughts of explorer and settler Edward John Eyre enable insight into the kinds of imaginings—and perhaps delusions—that he entertained in close encounter.

Colonialism at Close Quarters: Eyre

Born in Bedfordshire, England, in 1815, Eyre migrated to Sydney upon completing grammar school and became a large-scale pastoral holder before his eighteenth birthday. In addition to exploring inland South Australia and New South Wales, Eyre was instrumental in attempting to maintain peace between white settlers and Aborigines along the Murray River. In 1840–41, together with his Aboriginal companion Wylie, Eyre undertook exploration into parts of Australia still unknown to colonists. He became the first European to traverse the coastline of the Great Australian Bight and the Nullarbor Plain by land, making an almost 2,000-mile trip to Albany, Western Australia. His *Journals of Expeditions of Discovery* demonstrate his ability, like Goyder's, to imagine the Aborigines' perspective on the circumstances of the time. In what amounts to a plea of mitigation of Aborigines' violent responses to colonial incursions, he considers it natural that Aborigines would see explorers and colonials as unwarranted intruders. While Eyre seems relatively enlightened in presenting Aborigines as provoked and transgressed against, he was still fully engaged in the processes of colonization.

Among Eyre's aims was to open a route between South Australia and Western Australia along which cattle and sheep could be overlanded. This, he must have realized, would bring great change to Aborigines' lives. He volunteered to lead an expedition and pay half the costs. The party that set out from Adelaide in 1840 was made up of six white men, including John Baxter, his station manager, an Aboriginal retainer called Wylie, and two other Aborigines. They took with them thirteen horses, forty sheep, and supplies to last three months. They arranged to be met at Spencer Gulf (the westernmost of two large inlets on the southern coast in the present state of South Australia) by a government ship with more supplies.

Eyre traveled westward across what is now known as Eyre Peninsula and along the coast. The harsh conditions and lack of water forced him to send all of the members of his party back to Adelaide, except for Baxter, Wylie, and two other Aborigines. The men left with some packhorses and sheep to travel over 1,300 kilometers through harsh, desolate country, including the scorching Nullarbor Plain. There was little water and there were very few ways to reach the sea because of the huge cliffs that lined the coast. Their experiences were harrowing; Eyre and Wylie survived, but with difficulty, after a journey of four and a half months. The two other Aborigines traveling with them killed Baxter and decamped with supplies. Eyre and explorers like him were objectively dependent upon their Aboriginal workers and guides. Though richly resourced and supported in institutional terms, Eyre and Wylie were not equipped to survive in a vast, inhospitable environment.

Under these difficult conditions, Eyre (1964: vol. 2, pp. 57–58) notes that Wylie caught two opossums. Eyre decided to wait and see what Wylie would do, as a test of their relationship. He writes:

> I was curious, moreover, to see how far I could rely upon his kindness and generosity, should circumstances ever compel me to depend upon him for a share of what he might procure. At night, therefore, I sat philosophically watching him whilst he proceeded to get supper ready, as yet ignorant whether I was to partake of it or not. After selecting the largest of the two animals, he prepared and cooked it, and then put away the other where he intended to sleep. I now saw that he had not

the remotest intention of giving any to me. . . . [I] asked him what he
intended to do with the other one. He replied that he should be hungry
in the morning, and meant to keep it until then. Upon hearing this I
told him that his arrangements were very good, and that for the future
I would follow the same system also; and that each should depend
upon his own exertions in procuring food; hinting to him that as he
was so much more skilful than I was, and as we had so very little flour
left, I should be obliged to reserve this entirely for myself, but that I
hoped he would have no difficulty in procuring as much food as he
required. I was then about to open the flour-bag and take a little out
for my supper, when he became alarmed at the idea of getting no
more, and stopped me, offering the other opossum, and volunteering
to cook it properly for me. Trifling as this little occurrence was, it read
me a lesson of caution, and taught me what value was to be placed
upon the assistance or kindness of my companion, should circumstances ever place me in a situation to be dependent upon him; I felt a
little hurt too, at experiencing so little consideration from one whom
I had treated with the greatest kindness, and who had been clothed
and fed upon my bounty, for the last fifteen months.

Notice that Eyre does not imagine himself to be in a general situation of interdependence with Wylie, let alone dependence upon him. Rather, he won-
ders what might happen if he ever *were* dependent upon him; he clearly sees
himself as the benefactor in their relationship, giving more to Wylie than
Wylie gave to him. His kindnesses to Wylie were not requited or returned in
the case of the opossums. Wylie, on the other hand, is (at first) openly self-
absorbed. He simply keeps the opossums for himself. When Eyre implicitly
threatens him, he moves to avoid the consequences, thus making it apparent
that he is doing so at the same time that he tries to seem solicitous in his offer
of some food to Eyre. Were the matter more significant than a meal when one
is not in especial need, were it a matter of Wylie's defending him before others
or against contrary native opinion, or were starvation the issue, we can imagine Eyre might think of this in the sharper terms of treachery or relationship
betrayed.

The key to Eyre's story of this incident is his understanding that he had
extended trust and care; he was now questioning his supposition of mutuality
and loyalty. He does not attribute to Wylie any unprompted effort to imagine
himself in Eyre's place. He does not act in a way that Eyre would take to

conform to Eyre's expectations of relationship. In circumstances in which Eyre trusts him to share food, Wylie does not recognize or prioritize his relation to Eyre. Eyre, as we note, sees Wylie's eventual handing over of the other opossum not as a positive expression of relationship between them but as something he does because he apprehends Eyre's threat to cut him off from the flour supply. Wylie's offer to share does not arise from an internalized sense of obligation or gratitude.

Eyre's family background (he was a son of an English clergyman), education, his position in developing colonies, and experiences with native people are all relevant to understanding the ethical positions he took. He was exemplary of a colonial who could sympathetically imagine an indigenous point of view in general terms. Eyre does not call Wylie "treacherous." However, Eyre feels disappointed. He had assumed a "We," and it was not there, at least not in the form he had assumed.

"It is said . . . that the Australian is an irreclaimable, unteachable being; that he is cruel, blood-thirsty, revengeful, and treacherous" (Eyre 1964: vol. 2, p. 153). Eyre cited this view in order to question it for the benefit of a settler readership and quite probably political authorities—emergent publics for this sort of writing by a man of some experience. Thus Eyre wrote how one might view the murder by Aborigines of a young boy who had been left at home in his homestead near the Murray River in Victoria while his parents and others had temporarily left the premises. The boy's older brother, he notes, had previously fired at Aborigines approaching the homestead. Why, then, should the Aborigines not see even these youngsters as linked to those by whom their existence was threatened? Despite the brutality of the attack, and though the young boy personally had not harmed anyone, Eyre says it is necessary to consider how the natives see this boy, his relatives, and the entire situation. Though Eyre does not put it this way, we may conclude that, in general, he resists the notion of any preexisting understanding with the settlers that the natives are breaching; on the contrary, he aims to show how the settlers fail to consider indigenous concerns. He roundly denied that they offered unprovoked violence. On the contrary, "the character of the Australian natives is frank, open, and confiding. In a short intercourse they are easily made friends, and when such terms are once established, they associate with strangers with a freedom and fearlessness, that would give little countenance to the impression so generally entertained of their treachery" (ibid., 211).

Eyre never uses the word "treachery" except as a conception commonly held, which he finds unjustified. His frank exposition of the unevenness of the playing field distinguishes Eyre from the majority of colonists and must have made him highly unpopular in some quarters. On the basis of these remarks alone, we might consider him progressive. However, his writing about Wylie conveys expectations—of native gratitude, reciprocity—that were second nature to the outsiders and the basis of their common indictment of Aborigines as "treacherous." He seems to have had little sense of his and Wylie's practical interdependence. Instead, he studies Wylie, regards his disposition of the opossums as a test of character, and finds him wanting in loyalty. Eyre is confident of his power to retaliate by cutting Wylie off from the prized supply of flour and apparently applies no character test to himself for thinking that way. Eyre's fuller history allows us to identify him, at least later in his career and in increasingly demanding positions, as a champion of colonial order and not averse to its establishment and maintenance through violence.[4]

Colonialism at Close Quarters: Sturt

Most explorers recorded their unease about the motives of indigenous people around them, wondering how different were their aims, motivations, and intentions from their own. Sturt (1849: vol. 1, p. 133) says on one occasion that "the circumstance of the women and children venturing to us" could be taken as indicative of "no present hostile movement being contemplated by the men." But of this same encounter he says that notwithstanding a "seeming friendly feeling towards us, there was a suspicious manner about them, which placed me doubly on my guard" (134) and "a certain restlessness amongst the men that satisfied me they would not have hesitated in the gratification of revenge if they could have mustered sufficiently strong, or could have caught us unprepared" (1849, vol. 1, pp. 137–38).

Sturt is intuiting something about which he has limited direct evidence. He is not simply incorporating what he sees the other doing into his own conduct, but inferring motivations and intentions that have no transparent behavioral counterpart.

What does treachery look like in Sturt's interpersonal, everyday interactions? Sturt (1849: vol. 1, chap. 4) recounts that his young Aboriginal guide, Topar, knew the country of his expedition to Central Australia. As Topar evidently understood, his hope was to find inland waters. Sturt was continually straining to chart the party's forward course. He was concerned with mapping the country, ruminating on where to go, how to work his way inland, trying to discover water as a matter of immediate need.

Due to flooding of the lake on which they found themselves, they were cut off from the natives on the Darling River. Sturt determined to make an excursion into the interior to examine the ranges that had been seen by Mr. Poole of his party and to ascertain if there were a body of water to the west of them. He and three others of the expedition, plus Topar, who knew this area and named some of its places, took off with a light cart and some provisions. A blanket that Sturt had given to Topar, the latter gave to his mother, before setting off "as naked as he was born" (Sturt 1849: vol. 1, p. 149). After about thirty miles of proceeding generally northward, Topar called out for them to stop at a native well (150). He also directed them forward toward another, which, however, turned out to be dry. After a day or two, when they stopped to breakfast, Topar caught sight of smoke rising from the creek ahead of them. He excitedly urged following the smoke and directed the crossing of the creek at various places, apparently desiring to find the other natives, rather than having any clear plan to lead the expedition to waters. After a couple of days of this Sturt himself took charge of setting the course, generally pursuing a plan of attempting to penetrate the ranges by finding a gap through them. He also had in mind attempting to follow a major creek. They arrived at one place where some natives had recently been, but "none were there when we arrived" (159). Topar, in short, led the expedition into the range, failed to lead them to adequate water in country that he knew, and may, Sturt surmised, also have wanted to deter them from heading into the interior. The very idea of heading into ranges as they did was against the apparent sense of other Aborigines whom they had left back at camp, who had shown alarm at the idea.

At several points Topar suggests changes of direction because he sees native smokes rising and wants to catch up with those groups. At one point at which Topar had promised to take them to water so abundant they could swim in it, Sturt writes:

Down this gully Topar now led us, and at a short distance, crossing over to its northern side, he stopped at a little green puddle of water that was not more than three inches deep. Its surface was covered with slime and filth, and our horses altogether rejected it. Some natives had recently been at the place, but none were there when we arrived. I was exceedingly provoked at Topar's treachery, and have always been at a

loss to account for it. At the time, both Mr. Browne and myself attributed it to the machinations of our friend Nadbuck; but his alarm
at invading the hilly country was too genuine to have been counter-
feited. It might have been that Nadbuck and Toonda expected that
they would benefit more by our presents and provisions than if we left
them for the interior, and therefore tried by every means to deter us
from going: they certainly had long conversations with Topar before
he left the camp to accompany us. (ibid., 159)

Sturt expected Topar to do his best for the expedition, and Topar violated this
expectation. Sturt imagines that this may be because Topar wants to meet up
with other Aborigines with whom he has plans. Topar clearly has other concerns, which he discusses at length with his countryman, leaving Sturt unable
to understand. Sturt is aware of all this, and tries to ascertain what Topar's
concerns may be. Sturt expects his commitment, and his failure to demonstrate it amounts to treachery.

The natives on Sturt's expedition were both marginal to it and essential for
it to succeed. Their names are not in Sturt's final list of the members of the
expedition (1849, vol. 1, p. 46), though they were physically present. Leader,
assistant, surgeon, draftsman, storekeeper, servants, stockman, shepherd,
bullock drivers, and even the boats, bullocks, carts, drays, and dogs are enumerated, but not Aborigines.[5] Sturt obviously did not think of them as regular
members of the party in the same way he thought of other members of it.
Aborigines are nevertheless described and characterized—what Sturt thought
of their character and temperament is prominent in the text, as he seems to
look for dependable people. For example, he writes of two men who had previously worked for Eyre and with whom Sturt also had to do, in hyperbolic
terms:

These two natives, Camboli and Nadbuck, were men superior to their
fellows, both in intellect and in authority. They were in truth two fine
specimens of Australian aborigines, stern, impetuous, and determined, active, muscular, and energetic. Camboli was the younger of
the two . . . active, light-hearted and confiding, and even for the short
time he remained with us gained the hearts of all the party.

Nadbuck was a man of different temperament, but with many
good qualities, and capable of strong attachments. . . . He had somewhat sedate habits, was restless, and exceedingly fond of the *fair* sex.

He was a perfect politician in his way, and of essential service to us. I am quite sure, that so long as he remained with the party, he would have sacrificed his life rather than an individual should have been injured.(ibid., 44–45)

Topar, the lad Sturt took along with him to find inland waters, is less fully characterized, but Sturt describes him in terms of his deeds—his "treachery" and "deception," as Sturt calls it. Topar bypassed potable waters that he allegedly knew about and ultimately led the party to inferior waters for reasons that left Sturt guessing: Was he trying to forestall the party's heading inland? Was he proposing movements in order to catch up with other Aborigines, rather than treating Sturt's party's interests as primary? In any case, Sturt's characterization of Topar's actions as "treachery" arises from an expectation of commitment. Topar must have understood that his actions forced Sturt to recognize his dependence upon him. What Sturt could not see and divine was important to him. Topar knew that Sturt wanted to find large inland waters, and he in fact promised him waters deep enough to swim in. Sturt came to see Topar as neither acting in the party's interests nor actually producing desired results. Topar, in turn, identified with Sturt to the extent of having a good idea of what Sturt wanted him to do and outwardly acting as if he were doing it.

When explorers were dealing with indigenous people face-to-face and at small scale, as were Eyre and Sturt, they tended to take one or a small number of close assistants, whom they entrusted to secure the cooperation of other indigenous people—that is, of bringing their fellows into conformity with outsiders' expectations—doubtless a task of some difficulty. White explorer or person in command expected their compliance, loyalty, and commitment to his own person and perspectives. Take the example of the "boocolo" (chief, elder) of the Cawndilla tribe of the Williorara, with whom Sturt clearly formed a relation of particular intimacy of this kind, with lavish praise to suit:

Of all the race with whom I have communicated, his manners were the most pleasing. There was a polish in them, a freedom and grace that would have befitted a drawing-room. It was his wont to visit my tent every day at noon, and to sleep during the heat; but he invariably asked permission to do this before he composed himself to rest, and generally laid [sic] down at my feet. . . . He was a man, I should say, in intellect and feeling greatly in advance of his fellows. We all became exceedingly partial to this old man, and placed every confidence in him. (ibid, pp. 145–46).

Thus the boocolo was seen as deferential and compliant; but also as in command of himself.

The boocolo's character was tested when some flags, left behind while Sturt's men were out surveying, went missing. Sturt accused the natives but they denied the theft. He then directed his assistant Mr. Poole to stop all issue of presents and provisions to them. To unblock supply the boocolo tried but failed at first to get the flag back. Sturt angrily asked him why the natives had stolen from him, when he did not steal from them. This clearly positioned the boocolo as in between. The boocolo then held talks with several natives, which ended by their heading from the Darling and, the following day, bringing back the flag and staff. The boocolo was a guarantor for the behavior of others—insofar as he was at pains to maintain the relationship he had with Sturt. Treatment of people as pivots in this way probably had great effects upon internal relations, for example, making it possible for some indigenes to have relatively little or no personal contact with outsiders, while others had a great deal.

Some early explorers and colonists, like Eyre and Sturt, showed understanding of indigenous positions concerning trespass, colonial violence, infringement upon their movements, and usurpation of their resources. Some, like Eyre, wrote explicitly on these topics, in the face of widespread colonial inclination to dispossess Aborigines by any means necessary. But all, sympathetic or not, were very much on the lookout for trouble from indigenous people and also on the lookout for trustworthy types who would assist them with their projects. They valued such people and came to feel strongly about them. Even the most liberal-minded, like Eyre, despite his recognition of indigenous perspectives, aimed to advance colonization, overland animals, take up pastoral country, and the like. Above, we see that Sturt, while busy surveying indigenous land, had no hesitation in accusing Aborigines of theft—but did not see himself in such terms. The average settler was practically self-interested and ideologically less charitable than Eyre. Most had preconceived ideas about how Aborigines should behave in the face of occupation of their lands. They should make way, find some form of accommodation—or be removed. Most colonists conceded few grounds for grievance, and certainly they were not prepared to tolerate hostility. Hostilities on the part of Aborigines became "outrages" to be avenged.

Although explorers and indigenes watched each other and began to be able to recognize and typify forms of response, a widening sphere of the taken-for-granted involves increasing complexity and reflexivity concerning the extent to which commonality of motives and forms of action cannot be taken for granted. Some aims and actions are schismogenic, division producing, from the outset, but become more systemically so.

Consolidating Settler Consensus and Community

"Treachery" is an idiom that arises and consolidates in an enormous blindspot: complete unwillingness to entertain or follow through on seeing the colonizing situation in structural terms as fundamentally altering the situation of indigenous people and to recognize their invadedness (Wolfe 1994). With firmer establishment of nonindigenous Australians one aspect of developing settler community was consolidation of consensus about what indigenous people were like, how they were to be regarded and treated. In this phase of firming establishment there emerged, even more strongly than before, a view of indigenous people as "treacherous" in general and as not living up to expectations: one could not trust them, because one could not know what they were thinking or liable to do. The idea of treacherousness became widely established as an entrenched characterization in settler publics, many of whose members had limited or no experience of indigenous people as personalities, but saw them as belonging to a type. Settlers were not entirely confident of their control, but imagining indigenous others as "treacherous" did not build their confidence, either. Diarists devoted special praise to the trustworthy and stalwart.

The thickening of boundaries between indigenous and nonindigenous is directly related to the emergence of new public spaces in which indigenous people had little direct role or representation.[6] A public (M. Warner 2002) requires constant imagining and involves a dimension of strangerhood or impersonality—a coming into range, people addressing each other about what concerns them, that goes beyond the scale of interpersonal networking and takes on greater fixity of representational variants, points of view, and debates, as circulation proceeds. Interpersonal experience and relationship with indigenous people became less common with the growth of post-frontier settlement. The relevant audience largely became that of like-minded colonists thinking and communicating *about* Aborigines; increasingly, among people only some of whom have any direct experience with them.

The tendency for stereotypes to "thicken" is evident as early as when Philip Gidley King was captain-general and governor-in-chief of the colony of New South Wales (1800–1806).

> When King took up office in 1800 he was by profession a member of the kindness and amity school. In June 1802 he received instructions from Lord Hobart to pardon the five Europeans who had been found guilty by the criminal court on 18 October 1799 of wantonly killing two aborigines. Hobart added the rider [cutting across this lenience slightly] that every means should be used to cultivate the goodwill of the natives. At that time King had not lost faith in the policy of amity and kindness. In a proclamation [on 30 June 1802] he announced that any future injustice or wanton cruelty against the natives would be punished as if it had been committed against the persons and estates of any of His Majesty's subjects. He went on to forbid any act of injustice or wanton cruelty against the natives. At the same time he pointed out that the settler was not to suffer his property to be invaded, or his existence to be endangered by the natives. (Clark 1962: vol. 1, pp. 166–67)

He committed to humane means of resisting such attacks. His proclamation implied recognition of Aborigines' invaded situation.

> He ended by recommending a great degree of forbearance and plain dealing as the only means to avoid future attacks and to continue the present good understanding. . . .
>
> By 1805 King had joined the ever-growing chorus of settlers who accused the aborigines of ungrateful and treacherous conduct. A native, while . . . eating with one of the settlers and his labouring man, had scarce ended his meal before he took an opportunity of seizing the settler's musket and powder, and by a yell summoned his companions, who instantly put the unfortunate settler to death and left his servant, as they thought, in that state. On the same day, about three miles from where the first murder was committed, a house belonging to a settler was set on fire by the same band of natives. After a search the mangled and burned limbs of the settler and his man were found, some in the ashes and others scattered. This finished King's faith in amity and

kindness. To stop such barbarities he directed a party of soldiers to drive the natives from the area. (Clark 1962: vol. 1, p. 167)

How could "treachery" seize the public imagination so fully? Were not explicitly formulated governmental instructions largely protective and cautionary in tone, urging consideration for the interests of the Aborigines? Gaps between governmental/bureaucratic instructions (to explorers as to almost all others officially commissioned) and practice were great. They existed between the home government in England and governments of the colonies; between the latter, their operatives on the ground, and settlers; and sometimes at other levels in between. Relations between colonial oversight from England and office and institutions in the colonies illustrate gulfs at these various levels.

In England, Charles Grant (later Lord Glenelg) was appointed secretary of state for the colonies in 1835.[7] Only the year before, the British Parliament had passed the South Australia Colonisation Act 1834 enabling formation of the colony. The new lands were declared "waste and unoccupied," with no mention of native occupants (Reid 1990:9). However, the originator of the theory on which colonization policy was based, Edward Wakefield, asserted that South Australian settlement would be a "Colonization, organized and salutary" (Reid 1990:2), and therefore would allow for the protection of natives. Glenelg asked the Board of Colonization Commissioners in Australia to give early attention to "conciliation" of the Aborigines, and to advise them of the "advantages of British civilization, morality and religion" (ibid.)—in order to avoid the evils of colonization elsewhere (e.g., in New South Wales and Van Diemen's Land, examples in everyone's consciousness). Glenelg, a member of the general committee of the Church Missionary Society, demanded the appointment of a protector and review of the board's arrangements for purchase of land. Glenelg was among those who considered Christianization essential and a legitimation of colonization (Scrimgeour 2006). Robert Torrens, the chairman of the Board of Colonization Commissioners,[8] openly declared that he wished to avoid the interference of any protector. The board shortly passed an order declaring *all* lands of the colony open to public sale, yielding, however, notionally to Glenelg's insistence on "protection."

The proclamation read by the first governor, Captain John Hindmarsh, to colonists arriving at Holdfast Bay (an area now within the southern suburbs of the city of Adelaide) in December 1836, which had been approved by Glenelg, was substantially concerned with Aboriginal affairs:

> It is also, at this time especially, my duty to apprise the Colonists of my resolution to take every lawful means for extending the same protection to the NATIVE POPULATION as to the rest of His Majesty's subjects, and of my firm determination to punish with exemplary severity all acts of violence or injustice which may in any manner be practiced or attempted against the NATIVES, who are to be considered as much under the Safeguard of the law as the Colonists themselves, and equally entitled to the privileges of British Subjects. I trust, therefore, with confidence to the exercise of moderation and forebearance by all Classes in their intercourse with the NATIVE INHABITANTS, and that they will omit no opportunity of assisting me to fulfil His Majesty's most gracious and benevolent intentions towards them by promoting their advancement in civilization, and ultimately, under the blessing of Divine Providence, their conversion to the Christian Faith. (Hindmarsh's Proclamation, Library of South Australia, quoted in Reid 1990:3)

Despite appointment of a protector, but without any clear implementation of indigenous "privileges" as British subjects, again in South Australia some familiar things began to happen: instead of absorbing Christianity and civilizational advancement, the Aborigines demanded and took some rations (biscuits) and refused others (oatmeal); stole things from government supply and from settlers; were punished, sometimes by death and at the location of their violence against settlers, while Aborigines' evidence was held to be inadmissible in cases regarding them as well as Europeans. Settlers became restive, began to take matters into their own hands, demanded protection and an "effective" police force and the right to bear arms in Adelaide and elsewhere. In 1841, Aborigines attacked a party overlanding sheep, which ended in large-scale reprisals—murders—perpetrated against Aborigines on the Murray River. The party that set out to deal with the Aborigines included a force of sixty-eight police, volunteers, and Matthew Moorhouse, the protector appointed in 1839. The latter's efforts to deal with matters lawfully was overridden by the size and mood of the European party, who found themselves confronted by a large party of Aborigines in an equally hostile mood. The deaths of not less than thirty Aborigines in a few minutes ushered in a period in which Aboriginal attacks on settlers diminished. Aboriginal displacement rapidly followed, their institutionalization in a "Native Location" (a camp established by the government), indigenous indigence, drunkenness, sexual predation upon Aboriginal women, and implementation of ideas—part of an acceptably Christian package—of separating Aboriginal children from their parents and putting them in schools and similar civilizing institutions.

Talk and writing of "treacherous natives" became a commonplace presumption that licensed all kinds of violence. Frontier attitudes and interests early began to reshape and dissolve enlightened (but unimplemented) government ideology; the coming of settlers with their herds in many places (Reid 1990) and the entanglements between colonists and Aborigines over women, rations, and resources impelled the latter to more desperate acts and attacks. This continued apace in a notorious "outrage" of expanding settlement in the Northern Territory.

During 1870 some three thousand sheep from the Lake Hope area in South Australia were overlanded to the Northern Territory to supply the men working on the telegraph line on the Roper River in the upper central northeast. One of the group's leaders, John Milner, was killed by the Aborigines. Eventually his brother Ralph arrived at the northern destination on the Roper River with only one thousand sheep. In February 1874 a mounted constable was posted to Barrow Creek and a police station was also opened. Eight days later a group of Kaytetye men attacked the station resulting in the death of two white men, and the wounding of a third.

Some believe the attack was retaliation for the white men's treatment of Kaytetye women. Others say it occurred because the white men had fenced off a major waterhole and refused the Kaytetye access to water and rations during a time of drought. Both are plausible grounds for the attack. A few years earlier, the Kaytetye had allowed the first parties of telegraph workers to pass through their country. They had subsequently developed some dependence on the Barrow Creek station for rations and supplies, and the issue of women would be unsurprising with this degree of engagement.

Following the killings at Barrow Creek, Frank Gillen (later postmaster at Alice Springs and collaborator of ethnologist Baldwin Spencer), along with many others, was vehement in his support of the vigilante squad of men from the stations up and down the line who rode out and slaughtered an uncertain but probably large number of Aboriginal men, women, and children.[9] There was no investigation and no attempt to restrain subsequent revenge attacks.

Disproportionate death-dealing violence was accepted as the just reward of "treachery" once this had become a common understanding.[10]

The Treachery of the Native American

Parallels are easily found in North America across similar gulfs of difference and purpose. Karen Ordahl Kupperman (1977:264) writes that while colonists in North America found much to praise in Indian character, there "was even greater agreement on the Indians' bad qualities. Virtually every writer wrote of their treachery." The sense of having been betrayed springs largely from feelings of violation based on an assumption of relationship seen through the lens of settler purposes. Relatedly, Richard Drinnon (1980:51) quotes the New England Saints (Puritans) as imposing on every newcomer to their midst in the early seventeenth century the view that "the Savages are a dangerous people, subtill, secreat, and mischeivous" (see also p. 130).

Robert Berkhofer (1978:522) begins his consideration of "white conceptions of Indians" by asking why whites stuck with the general term "Indians," applying it to all and sundry natives, when they realized that Indians themselves made much finer distinctions among groups. His answer is that they dealt with Indians in terms of broad generalizations that suited their understandings and purposes of colonization and did not enter into complexities of relations that did not. There existed, more or less prevalent at different periods, images of Indians both as "good"—noble, proud, dignified—and "bad"—indolent, fiendish, lecherous—and these images were applied largely in relation to settler concerns. In some contexts the imagery of Indians as "good" was useful or welcome; in others, that of "bad" Indians was drawn upon. Perceptions of Indians were shaped to some extent by experiences with them but also indirectly and by prior conceptions of Indian character.

Conclusions: Emotion and Self-Deception

Treachery was not the only concept within colonial discourses; it competed with recognition of indigenous belonging and entitlement. However, the demands of a certain phase of settlement subordinated such notions to the shared concept of indigenous "treachery." This chapter has examined the

Aboriginal reputation for "treachery" as an instance of the processing of new relationships and, in particular, of interintentionality.

This chapter has presented "treachery" as arising in self-deception, or, at least, faulty evaluation of frontier situations. It arises from a sense of betrayal of relationship; but the cases presented in this chapter encourage our doubts that the relationship was felt to exist in the same way from the indigenous side. Eyre's relationship with Wylie developed in the context of his project of exploration. Eyre came to wonder—for the future, he thought, when he should perhaps be in an extreme situation—whether the relationship he attributed to himself and Wylie, which in his view ought to involve loyalty and a willingness to share, was reciprocated. He was disturbed to notice that Wylie did not act toward him with what he took to be appropriate levels of commitment and loyalty. Once confronted, Wylie quickly divined Eyre's punitive intent and amended his outward behavior. We see here what may be a universal human capacity for reciprocal monitoring, even across differences of culture and language. At least, it is common for people to believe that they can do so. Wylie's actions became calculated; while Wylie understood Eyre's immediate strategy, it seems less likely that he fathomed Eyre's understandings about persons, loyalty, and more. Eyre questioned Wylie's character and remained skeptical about Wylie's disposition. Testing him only produced more uncertainty and no apparent recognition on Eyre's part of their interdependence. One may say of him what Drinnon (1980:53) observes of Roger Williams, the founder of the Rhode Island colony in North America: "A belief in the brotherhood of man could share psychic space, in the same man, with a belief in its negation."

Treachery as a characterization of Aboriginal action by settlers is found from earliest exploration. Treacherousness as a stereotype of Aborigines becomes widespread in a certain period of colonization. This might be called a "middle" period, approximately a time in which an expanding settler public, with communications circulating among themselves, continues to feel uncertain whether Aborigines in their otherness pose a threat to them. This uncertainty arises from three presentiments not universally but widely shared: first, that indigenous people have grounds for grievance against settlers expecting their loyalty; second, that their motives and calculations are often unknown; third, that they have other meaningful relationships that may claim them. Settler concern regarding Aborigines, widely regarded as lesser beings in any case, is to pacify them, remove them if they present any obstacle to colonial intentions and certainly if they offer hostility. Liberal intimations on the part of some colonists that Aborigines have grounds for grievance are not matched by steps to fundamentally question or turn aside the unleashed forces of colonization.

Eyre tested what he thought was Wylie's loyalty and became convinced that he was not loyal in the sense of unquestioningly taking Eyre's side and preferring him in the terms of a special relationship (Keller 2007:21). Was Eyre's self-regard wounded by this? Why should he care? He justifies his experiment by saying he is testing Wylie for a future extreme circumstance; but he clearly has some emotional investment in being recognized as a benefactor. Does he assume Wylie is endowed with ordinary emotions as he understands them? Eyre had run afoul of forms of behavior that came easily to Wylie: he was not about to "give" without being asked; but he was sensitive to demand and clearly able to understand the threat concerning the flour. But what sort of demand was this? Wylie also probably realized that demand from Eyre, couched indirectly as it was—go ahead, have your opossums, and I will keep the flour that I have so little of—was not to be equated with demand from any of his countrymen. Wylie was probably sensitive to the power and resource differential in his relationship with Eyre and Eyre's undoubtedly limiting the room for negotiation between the two. Eyre's immediate consideration was: Let me test what would happen if I were really in dire straits. His conclusion, from this episode, seems to be that he did not really know. Wylie did not display loyalty as Eyre conceived it. What went on in Wylie's head was not completely clear to him.

In Sturt's reflections on Topar, in the context of exploring difficult terrain, we see a question much more clearly developed: what was Topar really up to? He knew the country; he could see evidence of other Aborigines; he knew what Sturt wanted and had promised to find it; but was he leading the party astray? And if so, why? The accusation of treachery was fueled by Sturt's sense of Topar's having other, unknown motivations that were his real object; he was apparently not fully engaged in Sturt's project and was more fully engaged in others—hence the sense of betrayal.

King's change of heart—from the school of amity and kindness, to that of exterminatory rage—was also fueled by that which was invisible—the real motivations of the attacking Aborigines, which led to gruesome violence, another "outrage" in the colonial vocabulary. King had, after all, spoken of cultivating goodwill, nipping violence in the bud by "plain dealing." What could that be? In what respects could it have satisfied Aborigines aggravated to the point that they were apparently bent on driving the settlers they dealt with away? King had made public his hopes and expectations, and Aborigines were egregiously flouting them—another betrayal, and one that had wider implications, given King's position.

These episodes show different levels of expectations betrayed and all on the settlers' side: what they expected and the kind of beliefs they had about the relationships that existed or that they wanted to exist between them and indigenous people. Though a few colonists did, in common with Eyre, sympathetically articulate an indigenous position of "invadedness," even the most liberal thinkers did not doubt the worth of colonizing the continent. They allowed for little sense of grievance on Aborigines' part. Most colonials, including those who dealt daily and closely with some Aborigines, saw themselves as benefactors and managers of them. They were sometimes disappointed by Aborigines' lack of "loyalty," which implied terms of unconditionality and asymmetry of relationship to specific outsiders, rather than interdependence. Many Aborigines were caught between relations with outsiders and their own people. But some relationships of the more singular kind that Eyre desired were apparently formed (possibly as in the case of Sturt's old man who came daily and slept at his feet).

Settlers became even more concerned with what they could not know for certain, what indigenous people were thinking, that burst forth occasionally in what they called "outrages," licensing (they thought) even more extreme eliminatory action. When "outrages" occurred—a term applied whenever Aborigines offered violence—there followed the usual policies of intimidation and lesson teaching, designed to show them that any breach would be followed by massive retaliation: shock and awe, as George W. Bush more recently put this idea. A "We"-"Them" boundary becomes more solid, based on the difference settlers already felt. There is ever more distance—physical, occupational, social—between Aborigines and most settlers. The understanding of indigenous people as treacherous and untrustworthy becomes a standard element of a series of negative attitudes that structure settler relations to Aborigines over at least a significant period of settlement history.

CHAPTER 5

Cruelty and a Different Recognition

Northern Territory Aborigines have developed a vocabulary for describing people at their worst. Let me contrast two terms: "cruel" and "cheeky." A persistent indigenous characterization of settler action, a trope of indigenous accounts of the past, is that whites were "cruel." The speakers known to me used the English (or English-derived) word "cruel" (*gruwel*) even when they were otherwise talking in their own language. For English speakers and in indigenous usage "cruelty" is the needless, unjustified, gratuitous, and intentional infliction of pain and suffering. It implies suffering without reason. Thus cruelty may be a puzzle, behavior with no obvious explanation.

"Cheeky" (a Kriol term)[1] has a different meaning, something more like "dangerous," "aggressive," "unpredictably prone to anger." In Jawoyn, spoken in Katherine camps and at Barunga, the word for this is *baranggu*. The same word is used for an aggressive personality and for toxins and poisons in plants and vegetable matter. In Mangarrayi (Elsey Station), the corresponding term *larrganda* is applied only to persons. The comparable Wardaman term is (*yi*) *menjen* (*yi-* is an animate prefix). This is typically a characterization of persons, and not entirely a negative one, but one understood to be grounded and justifiable in circumstances. "Cheeky" may be nonevaluative, referring to the natural tendency of a person or thing. For example, Phyllis Wiynjorrotj (whom I describe below) approvingly described her brother as *baranggu* when referring to his fully and explosively maintaining avoidance practices, which customarily demand violence toward women (sisters) who do not keep proper distance and demeanor. For Phyllis, her brother's adherence to proper behavior was a matter of pride.

I asked myself: did "cruel" enter these language communities as a loanword because it renders more fully the sense of the gratuitousness of certain aggression? Unlike "treachery," "cruel" does not presuppose an entitled "We" or a relationship breached, but it is nonetheless a moral evaluation expressed by indigenous people when their expectations of relationship are aggressively transgressed. It is a judgment concerning matters of relationship and not simply one of objective facts of aggression.

This chapter is about some indigenous ways of recognizing and evaluating persons and making relationships. Those remarking cruelty in certain white settler actions did not generalize that white settlers were, as a category, cruel. Stories relating to those times show that indigenous people remained open to the possibility of viable relationships with outsiders even in the face of appalling violence and rough treatment, rather than drawing a definitive, impermeable indigenous-nonindigenous boundary. While they recognized "whiteness" as a difference, they did not see whites as a different human type. Not only did they remain open to relationships with outsiders in general, but they maintained relationships with particular outsiders, some of whose actions were notoriously aggressive and even murderous. They were thus forming relationships in indigenous terms—kin- and place-based and network-like in their extensibility.

There is another way to think about difference, characteristic of nonindigenous actors but increasingly common among indigenous actors: the categorical bounding of people as belonging to certain human types, linked to a modern capitalist rationality. The aim of this chapter is, first, to show the utility to indigenous people colonized by pastoralists of their older openness to relatedness and, second, to illustrate the rise of a more categorical approach as nonindigenous actors established or expanded mining and pastoral ventures, permanent points of settlement, and thus worked their way, in domestic and work circumstances, into indigenous social circuitry. The clash between these two relationship modalities—or ontologies, ways of being—continues in the Northern Territory, especially among middle-aged and older indigenous people who were shaped in those indigenous terms I have described. Aboriginal women are especially vulnerable to the interplay of these different ways of being.

I will first say more about indigenous use of the term "cruelty" and illustrate its sense as a relative term, its application mitigated or palliated by relatedness. Then I will discuss two women I came to know well, from two different zones of the Katherine region, whose accounts of the "cruelty" of settlement shed light on the phenomenon from their somewhat different experiences and perspectives.

Relativizing Cruelty

The lives of many older Aboriginal people I came to know from the late 1970s had overlapped with those of seniors who had lived through acts of violence, even murderous violence, upon indigenous people in the late nineteenth and early twentieth centuries. The things they referred to as "cruel" in the colonial establishment period were part of personal memory, though the most extreme kinds, typically not of their own personal experience. The region where I heard these stories includes Elsey Station, Bulman, Barunga, Roper River Mission, and Katherine; most of these are settlements in a southern and central Arnhem Land social field composed of related and intermarried kindreds, with differing intensities of connection to other such fields resident elsewhere in the wider region. Though a majority of people at Bulman have, over time, been of socioterritorial groupings known as Rembarrnga and Dalabon with attachments to country at Bulman and farther north, there is no social boundary that separates them from others (for instance, at Barunga) with whom they are networked by kinship including marriage. Aboriginal people of these communities shared memories of white pastoralists and stock workers who managed the work regimes in which they participated. They point to massacre sites of Aboriginal people as pastoral settlement and Europeans penetrated the region.

Edna Ponto, who was already in her seventies in the late 1970s, told me what she had heard of the whites from whom the Aborigines were being saved by the formation of Roper River Mission in 1908. These pre-mission whites were "very cruel, killim, shootim. Hit baby on the ground and leave their dead body."

Deborah Costello, Edna's older campmate, described how the cruel times ended with the arrival of police and the mission:

> In old days proper bush. Scared for cruel white man. We would just see white man, get our things, and off. Scared for cruel white man. They had rifle more powerful than horses. Wreck on other side of river.[2] They get some white men there, speared them by night. Painted themselves with white paint and rushed them with spear. Killed a good lot of men. Some on this side of river. Some they didn't kill. Went to Roper, some to Pine Creek.[3] They wanted young girls from the natives, they said no. They started to fight. They ran away through the hills. They had rifle. We [our] parents used to be tell us—cruel things used

to be happening to them. They [whites] used to go back for more horses. They been doing that long time, then police station put up. They defended the black people. First police and then missionary came. All over the place people used to tell us. Good missionary came. They teach girls and boys. Tell them to go to school. Native parents they brought us down to the missionary. Some died away from whooping cough and influenza. This river was covered with native people. All the billabongs everything here shut [filled] with natives.[4]

Deborah recalls that the missionaries drew many people to the mission and that parents put their children into missionary care. This may be partly retrospective reconstruction, as Deborah comes from a family that accepted the missionaries and became committed Christians. While Deborah narrates the police as defending black people, other, older and middle-aged people present the police as unaccountable and often terrifying. Whether or not this new regime was so benign, it certainly contrasted with the preceding unfettered exterminatory aggression against Aborigines. Howard and Frances Morphy have suggested that Aboriginal people of this area see their history through the lens of a "golden age," the relative peace that followed the murderous period of exploration and pastoral incursion (Morphy and Morphy 1984). Deborah's story has this shape: contrasting the whites of the earlier period and the whites of the later period. Without typifying whites as "treacherous," she contrasts whites whose actions were unfathomably cruel with whites (police, missionaries) whose violence was more accountable.

One of the region's white pastoralists was Billy Farrar, whose grandson told Gillian Cowlishaw (1999:69): "I grew up gotta [with] my old grandpa old Billy Farrar. He was married to my sister-in-law Mrs Farrar, Judy.[5] Billy Farrar used to have pistol revolver. He's Queensland man. He was riding along. Well, he was tracking another lot of blackfella you see. They chased those cattle. Then bush blackfella way, [the others] come along behind and BANG with shovel spear. Bang at that man. They got shot. Two or three men might be, or six or seven. That's why we shifted out [from] there." Cowlishaw (2007) also quotes Judy Farrar as talking "of her long deceased husband as 'that old man' with pride in the toughness he had shown to 'myalls,'[6] or 'bush blackfellas,' who killed cattle. It was said that 'No-one could creep up on Uncle Billy.'"

My long-term coworker and friend at Barunga, Phyllis Wiynjorrotj, lived her life within a range of connections to people and places at Beswick Station, Bulman, Pine Creek, Mataranka, and Elsey Station, as well as Barunga itself.[7]

Her childhood experience was focused on two points of white settlement: the Maranboy tin mine, and Mataranka.[8] Phyllis told stories of the white pastoralists, storekeepers, and market gardeners who took up properties in the vicinity of the present Barunga community in the early twentieth century, followed by those mining for tin at Maranboy from 1913. One cattleman, Mick Madrill, established a homestead at Alligator Hole (Nimarranyin). Madrill established a mail run and was a regular visitor at the enormous station (pastoral property) Victoria River Downs near the West Australian border. His station at Alligator Hole was visited by Aborigines seeking tobacco, which Madrill supplied sparingly only to his "working boys." Madrill was known to keep a sharp eye out for others who did not belong to his group of workers and was said to have shot some Aboriginal men. Another pastoralist who arrived in 1925, E. J. (Ted, or "Cowboy") Collins, became a partner in Beswick Station with Madrill months before the latter's death in 1942. When I interviewed Collins in 1977, he told me that it had been necessary for Madrill to kill Aboriginal men who were preying on his cattle. Phyllis always said of him that he was *baranggu*, "dangerous." In contrast, Phyllis described white farmer Jack Gill at another nearby location, Garndayluk, as good and peaceful, and she referred to Dan Gillen, the storekeeper for whom her parents worked at Maranboy baking bread and making beer, as "grandfather." Some miners on the Maranboy minefield established long-term relationships with Aboriginal people who worked on the field and also domestically; some had personal relations with one or more Aboriginal women. Some miners allowed the larger kindreds of these workers to camp nearby and to ask for tobacco and other goods.

Even whites known as "dangerous" were understood in their particularity in this settler context of small-scale enterprises, farms, and stations. Indigenous people had relationships with them, making arrangements regarding work and keep. Mick Madrill engaged in acts of extreme violence, yet in Phyllis's and her contemporaries' imagination he exists in a space between "dangerous" and "cruel." He was known in his particularity; he had "working boys"; he was some people's "boss." Yet because he was unbiddable and not susceptible to acting in appropriately relational terms, Barunga people of Phyllis's age killed him "blackfella way," according to senior man Peter Marneberru:

Mick Madrill, he hated the old people. In the old days people had a dog, he had a lot of cattle, that's why he didn't like them. Mick Madrill,

him say, "We don't want this fucking myall blackfella around this area."
Then him shoot around, try and shoot the people. Cheeky bastard, too,
that head stockman for him. They bin kill him, that Mick Madrill. One
clever man, old man.[9] One of the stockmen, old Dick, bin kill him,
him own boss, because him bin cruel all day to the old people. Blackfella rule, they been base that ironwood tree, they put in everything
longa there, then close him up, and put wax [over that hole] and then
him bin finish. (C. Smith 2004:45)[10]

Although characterized as 'dangerous' and known to have killed people, people such as Billy Farrar remain in memory in terms of their particularity, ad-
mired for their energy and toughness; it is significant that Farrar has
descendants in the region. However, extreme violence perpetrated without
reason and outside a framework of knowability was often described to me as
"cruel," that is, as beyond recognizability, as generalized and abstract. Mick
Madrill was both cruel and known to an extent: he had clearly established work
relationships with some people and could undoubtedly have commanded
some allegiance in the way that Farrar and many others like him did had his
attachments not been too remote and unaccountable, his actions "cruel."[11]

One might argue that indigenous people could not act on the evaluation
of outsiders as "cruel." From a position of weakness, they could not draw clear
boundaries between themselves and powerful outsiders. I suggest that the
combination we have identified—maintenance of a recognizable persona even
if a "dangerous" one—should not be explained only as a product of such weakness; it also reflects distinctly indigenous ways of making relationships, arising under specific social conditions, in which people did not necessarily treat
differences as unbridgeable boundaries. Recall the Aboriginal man near Perth
who asked George Grey "Were we dead?" and the woman who proceeded to
identify him as her departed son (Chapter 1). She saw Grey's skin color, but
its significance was not a given. Such differences were open to interpretation;
they could be bridges to relatedness and recognizability. Older Aboriginal
people in northern Australia do not treat "color" as a self-evident "racial"
boundary. Rather, they continue to foreground, or at least trial, the particularities of association and relationships with others. That tendency to openness has often made them vulnerable to outsiders such as Farrar and Madrill
who did not think and act in such a potential, inclusive way. In the clash between less and more categorical ways of understanding difference the racialization of difference can intensify.

In the remainder of this chapter and the next, I will suggest that indigenous people have gradually adopted "racial" distinctions between self and nonindigenous others. We could say that, in this respect, they have been assimilated, becoming more European in ways. Assimilated from what? Here I turn to a brief account of relatedness, indigenous style.

Terms of Relationship

The story of Phyllis Wiynjorrotj illustrates what I mean by Aboriginal terms of relationship. Phyllis was born probably between 1926 and 1930. Her father, Charlie Lamjorrotj, was recognized as an important man in the Aboriginal social order focused on Maranboy, the tin mining site, and Beswick Station. The University of Sydney professor of anthropology Adolphus Peter Elkin, after recording Arnhem Land music at Mainoru Station in 1949 (Elkin 1961) and at Beswick in 1952, referred to Lamjorrotj[12] as the "Djauan [Jawoyn] headman," a renowned singer and ceremony man with connections further west (through his father). Lamjorrotj was certainly by then recognized as a leading personality,[13] but Phyllis and her siblings knew that his father, Bamjuga, had begun to live in this area only a couple of decades earlier (perhaps in the 1920s?), having worked as, or for, a "mailman."[14] Coming in from outside and "emplaced" in the region relatively recently, Phyllis's family on her father's side became completely accepted by others as the locally most notable kindred of the socioterritorial Jawoyn identity that is associated with the Katherine and Waterhouse Rivers.[15] Phyllis always referred to Melkjarlumbu (Beswick Falls, the magnificent Arnhem rock pool on Beswick Station) as her "father country," and to its totem, crocodile, as her principal dreaming. The Maranboy-Barunga-Beswick region was, as she explained, within country identified as Jawoyn. In her later years she mourned changes that she perceived at Melkjarlumbu: "My father is burying the water here," she would say, meaning that the sandbank was growing and the water pool becoming smaller. She interpreted this as her father and brother having come back here as spirits, covering over the water. From her father and her father's father, Phyllis retained a network of kin relations in Pine Creek, the smaller mining town ninety kilometers northwest of Katherine, whom she visited occasionally.

Phyllis's mother, Laurie, came from the Chambers River area south-east of Barunga, where her Worawurri clan was associated with the long-nosed sugarbag (honeybee) dreaming, and within the larger region considered Jawoyn and neighboring another socioterritorial identity, Yangman. A principal place in this area for Laurie and her clan is Jurlkbarrambumun, a river crossing featuring submerged rocks in the water, the manifestation of the sugarbag bees. To tend this place, people used to clean it. Laurie spoke Jawoyn and Yangman, the latter originary to the drier country extending to (and south of) the Roper River.[16] From her mother and mother's father, Phyllis had family ties to people residing at Elsey Station and at Mataranka, the two postcontact gathering places of the socioterritorial groupings Yangman and Mangarrayi. Raised partly at Mataranka where her father served for some years as police tracker, Phyllis used to visit camps at Mataranka and Elsey during the years I knew her (from 1976 until her death in 2005), giving gifts to relations there.

Phyllis had around her a large immediate as well as slightly more distant kindred and countrymen. She had one son from an early relationship in Pine Creek, and then five children from her marriage (arranged by her father) to a Dalabon man from the Bulman area. She had two full ("same father, same mother") brothers and three sisters, and she was related to their nieces and nephews, most of whom reside/d at Barunga and Beswick Station. Phyllis's way of telling the "finding" (Kriol) of each of her children followed a cultural formula: in a named place, the child's father (or other close paternal relative) espies or recognizes the child through some unusual event and shows the child its mother, whom it enters. Thus, Phyllis's oldest daughter, Lynnette, was identified as a bullock that her father attempted to shoot. When the animal failed to fall after several attempts, Phyllis's husband recognized it for what it was: a child. This daughter, Lynnette, later married a Yangman man, Frank, who had lived at Elsey Station with his family before he ceased station work and moved with his wife to Barunga. Phyllis and her son-in-law treated each other with the greatest respect; so there were also his relatives to keep up with whenever she visited Elsey. Lynnette, her husband, and their three children, when younger, always lived with Phyllis, as did—eventually—a number of their children.

Phyllis's father Lamjorrotj had a second wife, Violet, of the Rembarrnga socioterritorial identity from Central Arnhem Land. From that marriage Phyllis had a set of paternal siblings that she also kept up with, some at Barunga, some at Beswick, and others farther afield in Arnhem Land.

When I first visited Barunga in 1976, Phyllis's brother Gordon was chairman of the Bamyili Town Council. She always observed the appropriate brother-sister avoidance expected of opposite-sex siblings but lived in daily close relationship with her sister-in-law and their children. When Gordon died Phyllis became the understood principal custodian and go-to person of Barunga and Beswick, supported ceremonially and in many other ways by "business" (ceremony) men of Central and Southern Arnhem Land, resident in both communities who had previously supported her brother. As principal custodian and now recognized head of her (paternal) clan, Bagala, with its acknowledged territorial and social focus at Barunga and Beswick, Phyllis was called upon for all kinds of participation and consent with respect to Town Council matters, development and service delivery, maintenance and formal guardianship of ceremonial and burial grounds at Barunga, the conduct of land claims, as these began to preoccupy people in the 1980s and 1990s. She was a member of numerous boards including Nitmiluk National Park Committee.[17] She sometimes complained she would not go to another meeting. Clans such as Bagala are formally patrifiliative (children are members of their father's clan). Phyllis's children, though known as members of their father's clan, are in practice oriented to their mother's side as a result of the position of Phyllis's family at Barunga over decades. Though her relatives bear a number of different surnames, local people are aware of the family connections underlying them. Her bilateral kindred now functions quasi-corporately in a number of environmental, developmental, and commercial proposals in the community and region; the genealogical and marriage ties of Phyllis's family are relevant to these purposes. Her nieces at Beswick have now largely taken over her focal role.

Phyllis's life was emplaced and kin based. Katie Glaskin (2012) has proposed that Aboriginal personhood be understood as having "embodied relationality" at its core. That is, people are regarded as consubstantial with other persons, including ancestors, with other living people, with creator creatures (totems, such as the crocodile), and with places. In daily interactions people regard and call each other by terms of kinship and appropriate social category (in the Barunga area these include moieties and subsections, or eight-term social category sets),[18] as well as by personal name or nickname (often reflecting some perceived characteristic or commemorating a particular event).

In all these ways identities offer particularistic, multifaceted, and multiple intersecting openings to relationship. Everybody is not related to everybody else in the same way, of course, nor at equal intensity (a fact that emphases on "relatedness," citing Myers 1986, have somewhat tended to underemphasize). In most indigenous communities I know, within the network of kin are those whom one might, or may, marry; affinity is always an extremely important boundary of difference within overarching kinship. But people who live within this framework are able to follow up one or more specific pathways structuring people's understandings of themselves and others that enable meaningful relationships (and also meaningful sources of disagreement and fractiousness). This was the system with which the Mick Madrills, the Jack Gills, the Billy Farrars, and all the other outsiders collided. Some, like Madrill, were repelled, regarding the old "myalls" as an unbiddable and inseparable welter who insisted on crowding in on his "working boys" for a bit of tobacco: he could only keep his "boys" sorted with a gun. Others, like Billy Farrar, lived out some of the possibilities of relatedness on partly indigenous terms, with a particular woman, fathering children, and sometimes extending forms of recognition and material support to some of those who formed a kindred and an entourage around such relationships.

They could do so partly because, when encountering outsiders and finding few or none of these modalities of relating, indigenous people are inclined to confer relationship, or at least to test it. Thus the visitor who expresses a desire to get to know people—the intending anthropologist, for instance—is typically given a kin designation relative to his or her first hosts, and, known as this identity, the visitor has potential for furthering relationships. To enact this potential, however, typically requires a degree of give and take that outsiders are unprepared for, and so we have relatively few documentary sources about colonial settlers gaining practical insight into the relational practices of indigenous people. Eyre's story about his relationship with Wylie (Chapter 4) offers rare insights into intimate circumstance: Eyre's apprehension of complexity in Wylie's character, his consternation at realizing that he does not know Wylie's mind, his intuition that Wylie has other considerations, very likely tied up with his relationships to others. Eyre does not let the reader forget that he can withhold from Wylie, and that, in the end, he has the whip hand. More generally, outsiders—bolstered by enormous power differential and by the conviction of civilizational inferiority of indigenous people—acted with anonymous "cruelty," in which the outsiders saw none of the human possibilities we have seen to cluster in Phyllis. Instead, indigenous lives as they were lived were unrecognizable, and they were effaced in great numbers.

The old indigenous way of making relationships, when it collides with overriding outsider ways, makes people vulnerable. Anonymous "cruelty" and the particularities of indigenous relationality contrast dramatically in the story told to me by a woman with whom I spent much time from my arrival in 1976 until her death in 1997. Elsie Raymond, a Wardaman woman, was born at Delamere Station, probably in the early to mid-1930s, in a region in which Aborigines had been exposed to intense frontier assault (see Rose 1991; Lewis 2012), as W. J. Browne established three pastoral stations: Delamere, Willeroo, and Price's Creek (see Figure 1) in 1880 (stocked in 1881).[19] None was profitable, and Browne sold them to Alfred Giles, Browne's manager, who was living with his wife at Springvale, the property seven miles from the growing settlement at Katherine. Giles kept a diary while managing for Browne from Springvale, and he wrote an account of his earliest exploration in the territory between 1870 and 1872, while he was leader of the party sent to establish a route for the Overland Telegraph (Giles 1928). The latter reveals episodes of violence along the Overland Telegraph party's route and in the wider Katherine region, particularly on the Roper River (the home area of Edna Ponto and Deborah Costello, mentioned above).

Giles overlanded sheep to Delamere in 1882 and was growing cotton there.[20] He undertook pastoral operations at Willeroo from the mid-1880s,[21] and between 1885 and the turn of the century he fought guerrilla warfare in the area of Willeroo and Delamere against the Wardaman (Lewis 2012:204–19). After the spearing of the Willeroo manager Sid Scott in 1892, parties of settlers that set out from Katherine killed large numbers of Aborigines (ibid., 208). Giles was at the time justice of the peace in Katherine, and his support for reprisals illustrates the alignment of government with settler interests. Newspaper reports of the time referred to the country being "infested" with "wild blacks" who were "committing outrages." They represented the reprisal party leader Lindsay Crawford, together with his "half-caste" assistant, as having "dealt out white man's justice with their Winchesters," when avenging Scott's spearing. When the police arrived at Willeroo from Pine Creek, "they found plenty of employment burying the sons of darkness" (cited in Lewis 2012:208). Nevertheless, Wardaman could attack from the relative safety of high country, and so persistent were their efforts to drive pastoralists out that Willeroo was abandoned in 1895 and again in 1900.

Paddy Cahill and his brother Matt were involved in violent events at Willeroo in the mid-1880s. Together with his brothers Tom and Matt, and with the legendary Nat Buchanan,[22] Cahill had overlanded twenty thousand cattle to developing Wave Hill Station (on the Victoria River) in 1883. He subsequently managed Delamere and later tried buffalo hunting and pearling in (what was later designated) Arnhem Land. In 1912 he developed a homestead at Oenpelli and was soon visited by W. Baldwin Spencer, then chief protector of Aboriginals in the Northern Territory. Spencer thought well enough of him to appoint him "protector" and manager of an Aboriginal reserve; he and his family also built up gardens and grew fruit, cotton, and other crops at Oenpelli Reserve. He died in Sydney in 1923.

Elsie Raymond showed me a cave, Yiwangarlangarlay, on Delamere (known as Paddy's Spring in English), in which, according to her grandparents and other seniors, Paddy Cahill had "yarded up" and then dynamited a large number of "old people." Young Elsie had spent time with her father's mother, Wuluwari, who showed her places and told her stories of this tumultuous time (Merlan 1992). Elsie also showed me the massacres site Monborrom, in Elsie's "father country"; it was the Aboriginal name of "Old Willeroo" (the first Willeroo homestead, at the base of the Moray Range). One of the most poignant stories Elsie told was of the shooting of Aborigines at Yererdbay, or Double Rockhole as it is called in English, on Delamere. A large slick-sided rock hole surrounded by stands of lancewood, this was the scene of an attack upon Aboriginal people by white stockmen, who are said to have forced some off the cliff and to have shot others. Elsie told the story that her father's father, Yiwarlidagarl, came upon this place at night (perhaps news of the killings had traveled). He found that his younger brother's wife, Lanyinga, had been shot, but her baby was still alive at her breast. He took the child home to his wife, Wuluwari, and she was said to have suckled him[23] and raised him, before she had her own child, Elsie's father, Yidorr.[24] This is the Wuluwari with whom Elsie walked the countryside as a child. Elsie remembered this event as a moment that defined her relationship to a senior man of mixed Wardaman and white parentage, Bill Harney, whom Elsie regarded as a close relative.[25] The baby raised by Wuluwari later had a daughter who eventually became Bill's mother; that is, Elsie's father's father's (younger brother's) son, the rescued baby, was eventually Bill's mother's father. Elsie's telling of this story always concluded with something her father told her about what his father Yiwarlidagarl did, an image that had stayed in her mind ever since. It played in both our minds when we visited remote Double Rockhole together, the first time she had been there in many years because of restrictions placed on access to pastoral areas by the station management. What she remembered hearing was that the morning after the massacre, Yiwarlidagarl came back and looked down from the top of steep-sided Double Rockhole and saw the stockmen down below gathering the bodies together and burning them before they went back home to Elsie's father's country at Old Willeroo.

Elsie told me this story a number of times, mostly in her language, Wardaman, and usually with very little comment. But once she paused and, looking at me searchingly, said (in Kriol): "What for cruel like that?" I understood the question to be about the wantonness and the gratuitousness of these killings. Maybe it was also a question specifically to me, an outsider but also one of her regular companions: could *I* explain the inflicting of this reasonless suffering? Whether she thought I might have some special insight into this extreme and shameless cruelty, I cannot be sure.

Many older Wardaman people were aware of not only the "cruelty" but also of their people's fight, and they took some pride in that. However, from the early 1900s Wardaman people began to camp near homesteads on their territory and to abide by the station's demands and impositions. Elsie grew up in the Delamere camp, in very spartan conditions, in which the able-bodied were "paid" in keep and rations for work and were "let go" during the wet season (the monsoon lasts roughly from November to March) to provide for themselves, since little stock work could be done. These conditions, which had the effect of keeping Wardaman people closely engaged with their country, lasted until the wartime internment of Aboriginal people in native labor camps ("compounds"), mainly around Katherine. After the Second World War, many returned to the station stock camps and thus to their country, in some measure. When Wardaman people came into Katherine, they were viewed as among the "bushiest," least acculturated indigenous people, who continued intense sociality among themselves and with others of the region with similar orientations.

Elsie was raised in the kind of understandings of emplacement and relatedness that were illustrated in discussion of Phyllis's life. In the 1960s, Elsie and her husband Kaiser, a Mudbura man from the Victoria River who had been a stockman on Willeroo and elsewhere, moved to Katherine. Afflicted by lung weakness, he was glad to find a job as a groundsman at the hospital, and together they raised a large family, sometimes living in Katherine and sometimes on Manbulloo Station to the south of town. Their sons and others of the family continued to work at Willeroo, Delamere, and other stations in the region south of Katherine. But the implementation of "equal wages," 1966 –68, meant that fewer workers were hired, and from then on the camp at Willeroo was only seasonally and sparsely occupied. The community and social intensity of Willeroo was gone, and its material disadvantages—no running water, electricity, or school and extremely hot corrugated iron sheds as accommodation—contributed to indigenous people's move into Katherine. Elsie and Kaiser, their large family of six children, and other relatives (Elsie's father, aunt, and mother often among them) became a focal point for other Wardaman and "southerners" around the town. For Elsie—gregarious, stable,

Figure 5. Elsie Raymond at Yerrerdbay. Photo by author.

organized, a nondrinker—this meant an almost continuous flow of people through her household. She was open-handed, known and respected well beyond her immediate kin for her generosity. She became known to white townspeople and would talk cordially with many. Storemen, businessmen around town, managers at the abattoir, all came to know Elsie and Kaiser and allowed them to collect offal and other surplus goods. Well-meaning church groups from Darwin and Katherine, always interested in recruiting Aborigines to their congregations, contacted her, and she sometimes went to church, but her heart was not in it. She was happiest when fishing, foraging, and mixing with her kin and countrymen and passionate in arguments with them.

Judged acceptable tenants, Elsie and her family were among the first allocated a town house (one of six houses in town set aside by the Department of Aboriginal Affairs in the 1970s). Elsie and her "mob" and another household of close relatives on her father's side formed a large assemblage of kin and countrymen that was criticized as breaching rental conditions for its size, its tolerance of visitors, drunk or sober, its rows, noise, and many critical moments. (Elsie had her sons seek out her father and bring him home in any condition, in preference to leaving him to the fortune of Katherine streets and riverside.) When the "Wardaman mob" was evicted from the houses, Elsie's "second mother" declared that she was going to pull up all the plants with which she had beautified the grounds. They moved to a camp called Bunjarri on Manbulloo Station south of Katherine, at first living in sheds and later in solid housing.

Elsie had a magisterial knowledge of the region south of Katherine (just as Phyllis did of the east and north of town). Her knowledge took in not only Wardaman but also neighboring and intermarried socioterritorial groupings: the Mudbura (her husband was such), Yangman, Dagoman, Alawa (one of her daughters-in-law came from Hodgson Downs, a key Alawa location), and others. She had appropriately decorous relationships with other indigenous people around Katherine town, who came from a different regional population pool (such as the Mayali and Jawoyn who lived in the fringe camps on the river and to the north of town, contrasting with Elsie's social focus to the south). She participated in young men's initiations, central to her large kindred. Elsie was the crux, in short, of a large set of human resources in terms of which she lived. Her story, through the emplaced knowledge she gained from her elders, allows us to traverse colonial and postcolonial history, from the "deathspace" (Taussig 1987) of the frontier, which she recounted in many stories, to the race-based divisions of living space and work that affected her life and that of all around her at Willeroo and in town, even while she and her countrymen preserved some of their own ways of living among themselves and, partially and more tentatively, with outsiders. However, her emplaced, kin-based relational modality left her vulnerable not only to the impositions of her own countrymen (of which there were many) but also to outsiders.

Elsie was among those particularly disposed, throughout her life, to take up the challenge of dealing with outsiders. After Elsie's husband died, she had a number of long-term relationships with white men (most of whom had done stock work and drank fairly heavily). She slowly regained her vivacity and continued to look after her children and grandchildren and many other related children, grandchildren, and great-grandchildren besides. But the male partners were sometimes abusive and even inveigled some of her younger charges into sexual relations. This angered Elsie, but she did not have a clear-cut way of dealing with this kind of imposition. Did she recognize something of her younger adventurous self in these liaisons? Her main outward emotion seemed to be jealous rage. Her last years of domestic life had some of the enjoyments of family in them, but they were also turbulent. Friendly, intelligent, quick-witted, an engager and experimenter and not a theorist of people or her times, Elsie never became racist, nor was her outreach distorted by racism. She experienced all the differences that thinking and acting in terms of race had made during her lifetime (see Chapter 6), from dalliances with stockmen in her youth that we may see as exploitative but that were also intensely absorbing to family crises arising from these liaisons. She suffered the removal of children, and she learned to fear police and similar authorities. Her life in a town where racism was commonplace had tragic consequences. Maintaining an indigenous perspective on the possibilities of relationships, she continued to look for openness among, as they say in the territory, "black, white, and brindle."

I met a number of people like Elsie, in her age cohort, as well as other indigenous people who had more fully adapted, not very surprisingly, to the racialization of human types so fully manifested in the dominant social order to which they were exposed. People like Elsie retained a keen sense of the "cruelty" of colonial incursion. But she and many others who grew up in those times between personal memory of the frontier and what they took to be better conditions, remained oriented to the kind of feeling given expression by a Mudbura community leader Hobbles Danayarri, whom Rose (1989, 1991) cites as a historian of the neighboring Victoria River area (see Chapter 3). He concluded: "You know before, Captain Cook been making a lot of cruel, you know. Now these days, these days we'll be friendly, we'll be love mijelb [each other], we'll be mates. That be better" (Rose 1989:142–43). Elsie would never have put it in general terms—that was not her way. But she lived according to a feeling that what Hobbles said was possible.

Cruel Clashes and the Birth of a Dependent Station Order

I lived in the Aboriginal camp on another cattle property, Elsey Station, for a year in 1978–79. During that year of continual residence I spent much time sociably in camp. This was the beginning of a relationship that intensified from the 1980s into the 2000s, during a period of land claims[26] and that persists to this day. One of my fellow campers in 1978–79 was Kitty, whom I called *yilambura*, "Auntie," in the local language, Mangarrayi.[27] Calling me "niece" (brother's daughter), Kitty displayed that lack of absolutism about "racial" difference; like Elsie Raymond, she related to whites (at least ones who shared her life space) as different but along pathways of recognition and access.

Kitty was highly regarded as one of the "old people." Her time (decades) living on Elsey had overlapped with that of indigenous people who were on Elsey around the turn of the twentieth century and into its early decades. Kitty was a member of a large kindred, some of whom now looked after her needs. A granddaughter was committed to her daily care. Hannah, then in her late twenties (and to whom I was a classificatory auntie, she my niece), married with children but often living quite independently of her much older husband, camped with Kitty, prepared her food and tea and her bedroll at night, kept her belongings in order, went fishing and foraging on the river with her, and helped her with shopping and managing her pension money. All this Hannah did with great patience and little grumbling—truly the best living situation that old people may expect. Following Hannah's lead in her treatment of her grandmother Kitty, I tried to behave as I thought a good niece and attentive junior person would. I "heard" Kitty's demands about what she needed, ful-filled many of her minor requests to do this and that, spending much time with her close relatives and countrymen, especially in groups of younger and older women. In this mode, my outsiderness became less important. We walked around, fished, sat a great deal, in company with others—we lived the life she knew. She began to tell me stories about early times at Elsey, about her youth, places on the river, important events and ceremonies at Elsey, and through this detail filled my head with a sense of Elsey's history and people.

Before turning to some of Kitty's stories, let us put Elsey Station in per-spective. Exploration on behalf of the Overland Telegraph Line had taken parties of surveyors through wetlands (now called Warlock Ponds) south of present Elsey, within its current boundaries (Red Lily Lagoon), and onto the Roper River in the early 1870s. There were skirmishes with resistant Aborig-ines, but more were soon to come. Elsey was the third pastoral station to be established in the Northern Territory, the lease taken up in 1879 by Abraham Wallace and stocked personally by him with almost three thousand head of cattle overlanded from New South Wales in the following year. The head sta-tion was first located at Garlyag (Warlock Ponds, fifty kilometers south of the Roper River); in 1904 it was relocated to Ngarrmirn.gan (Red Lily, a wetland), which indigenous people of Elsey describe as having been impossibly mosquito-infested as a homestead. The homestead was moved to its present location upstream on the Roper River at Guyanggan (McMinn's Bar).[28]

Elsey has been the subject of two novels and of an early example of the "as told to" Aboriginal memoir. *The Little Black Princess* and *We of the Never-Never* were written by Jeannie Gunn, the wife of station manager Aeneas

Gunn; they were at Elsey in 1902–3 until Aeneas died prematurely.[29] Widely read in Australia and made into feature film in 1982, *We of the Never-Never* presents the joint use of land and waters by Aborigines and pastoralists. Gunn sympathetically acknowledges that the colonists occupied Aborigines' land. If not compensated, their "cattle killing" and "even man killing" should not be seen as offenses against the whites (1907:185). Yet it is clear from her description of preparations for a "nigger hunt" along the river on the part of Aeneas and station hands that they were prepared to remove Aborigines by force from waters needed by cattle. While it is likely that some of what went on was withheld from her by the station men, it is hard to believe she had no sense of the violent conflict. Indigenous stories (Merlan 1978, 1996) indicate that such deadly violence continued until at least the late 1930s (Larbalestier 1990:80). But then something nearly providential happened: a long term of fairly benevolent, hands-on station management by Harold Giles from 1926 for nearly three decades. He worked for H. E. Thonemann, who was the (largely nonresident) part owner of the Elsey property and an adjacent run, Hodgson Downs, from 1914 into the 1950s.

Harold Stanage Giles was the third of four children of Mary Augusta Giles and Alfred Giles, pioneers of Willeroo and Delamere. Born in 1890 at Springvale near Katherine—the property from which his father largely removed Aborigines by one means or another—Harold moved with his family to Bonrook Station near Pine Creek when he was four. Schooled in Adelaide, later a policeman and soldier in World War I, Harold met and married a young nurse from the Maranboy Inland Mission Hospital, in Phyllis Wiynjorrotj's home area, in 1924. With his family, Giles managed Elsey Station for almost three decades, getting to know all the indigenous families. They called him "Kayku," the source of which remains unknown to me. While Giles was firm, he was judicious and nonviolent, a stabilizing regime. This was the foundation for the third Elsey book, *Tell the White Man: The Life Story of an Aboriginal Lubra*, written in 1949 by H. E. Thonemann, with an introduction by A. P. Elkin.

Tell the White Man attempted to represent the perspective of Buludja, a young indigenous woman at Elsey who was found to be a leper and sent to a lazaretto near Darwin. More broadly, the book provided perspective on life at Elsey, including Giles's effort to maintain and restore his workforce. Because he found that women were having (or keeping) few children—probably killing many they bore—he offered a "baby bonus," a steer to the camp for each baby born and nurtured. The children born from the 1930s onward were the adults of the period of my research, who had grown up during "Kayku Giles time," as they called it, a cohort of which Buludja was an early member. Thonemann's account of a visit by the Duke of Gloucester, marked by an Aboriginal corroboree suggests that the station had acquired a good reputation. Thonemann provides insight into leadership and organization of the Aboriginal camp, most of the details of which can easily be linked to people and families at Elsey in the present. Compared to the first decades of the twentieth century, this was a "golden age" indeed (Morphy and Morphy 1984). But Kitty's memory, to whose stories we return shortly, reached back before Giles's time.

In a 1951 paper, Elkin took Elsey Station as exemplary of a positive "reaction and interaction" between Aborigines and settlers—a community of people, emplaced in their own country (on two neighboring stations, Elsey and Hodgson Downs), observing marriage and other regulations among themselves, speaking their own language (Mangarrayi), with no missionary activity and few (but consistently present) whites, and good relations between indigenous and white leadership. Under such conditions, Elkin maintained, the pauperization and disintegration evident among Aborigines elsewhere could be avoided. With appropriate and "intelligently appreciative" attention to their health, education, and training Aborigines could come to an "intelligent appreciation" of a new form of life in which they would learn to be "responsible individuals," shed their "parasitism," and take their place as "self-dependent" members of the broader community. Elkin does not make clear the relation between such growing individuation and assumption of "responsibility" and the communalism that he approvingly observed.

In 1951, Thonemann put Elsey up for sale, receiving extremely low offers that reflected the state of the cattle industry. He sold the property to an absentee overseas owner, and after Giles's departure in 1954, managers with much less local knowledge and reason to remain in the long term came and went. The introduction of the "award wage" in 1966–68 had the effect that pastoral managers had less reason to welcome Aboriginal communities on properties. During the 1967 annual show weekend, camp residents who were piled on a cattle truck (as happened every year) and taken to the show in Mataranka were told to stay there. Although Mataranka was not foreign to them, it was a terrible blow: there were no facilities, people had only the swags (bedrolls) they had come with. A member of a leading family who had been educated at Roper River (or Ngukurr, the ex-mission of Edna Ponto and Deborah Costello), who had taken community advisory training in Darwin, and worked for the Department of Aboriginal Affairs, led efforts for some years to gain a small living area on Elsey.[30] Many of the Elsey camp were thus able to return in the 1970s, after several years adrift and after numerous community tragedies occasioned by the increased availability of alcohol and privately owned motor cars. The community leader died in a car wreck, and his two sisters took over the effective leadership of the community at Jembere (the name later changed to Jilgmirn.gan, usually spelled Jilkminggan).[31] All this and more Kitty and her age-mates lived through.

In 1978–79, Kitty told me that in "Gunn time" (the manager Gunn's era) Elsey Station gathered some Aboriginal people to it. This was a phase in the pastoral trajectory: widespread extermination, followed by the decision of some indigenous people to camp close to the station, enabling the differentiation of these insiders from "outsiders." Kitty said that insiders, led and armed by "Miglinin"—undoubtedly John McLennan (1869–1932), the "Sanguine Scot" of Jeannie Gunn's *We of the Never-Never*—drove Aborigines from significant waters, exterminating outsiders (Merlan 1978). While others felt unable to talk about insider complicity, Kitty and her age-mates did not appear to feel shame about Aboriginal men having participated in exterminations. These were known men, working for the station, whose families remained significant and close relatives and campmates.

At first I thought I had not understood Kitty's stories, but as she repeated them and similar stories, I realized that the men and women of her age cohort, and those of Kayku Giles's time (some of whom had more reserve about this kind of content), shared this understanding of Elsey's history.[32] Jimmy Daniels, "full Yangman," whose country at Warlock Ponds was the first station homestead, told me of his father, one of the insider stockmen, a man in his prime in the early twentieth century. The son of another then-prominent man, hearing Jimmy's stories, volunteered that his father too had worked for "Miglinin." It became clear to me what kind of achievement the "community" appreciated by Thonemann and Elkin had been: the aftermath of collective violence, collectively "forgotten"—the colonial refashioning of a local cultural order (cf. Kockelman 2016:120).

The indigenous impulse to recruit whites to their concerns is reminiscent of explorer George Grey's being told by indigenous people to shoot everyone beyond a certain point on his travels. Although Kitty described McLennan as *larrganda*, "cheeky," she attributed not only responsibility but desire to the Aboriginal men who carried out Elsey's founding expeditions. Aborigines' concerns evidently overlapped with settler purposes. For example, a stock-boy named Dujgarri was enraged by the attempts of one of his own brothers, War-rayanbuwa, living away from the station, to steal Bagurrngiya, one of his wives. When Dujgarri reported this to McLennan, according to Kitty, McLen-nan and his stock-boys then rode to Warrayanbuwa's camp and shot people. Kitty gestured, illustrating how the rifles were greased and loaded, and how the expedition set off; where it found its victims was a place she and I had often visited. She told how some tried to get away by crossing the river. This all happened when she was little, she explained, with no evaluation. "Today nothing," she concluded, meaning that nothing like that happens now. Her saying so was similar to Deborah Costello's telescoping of Roper history, from the bad times when "cruel" things happened to the arrival of the missionaries marking a new period when parents took their children to the missionaries to be schooled. One of the constants I dimly saw in all these distilled perspec-tives on the past was an accommodation to a present situation, legitimated by a sense that violent action had given way to new and more hopeful relation-ships. Although extreme frontier violence had occurred everywhere in the region, leaving massacre sites, bones, and stories widely known, the younger people—as far as I could see—were neither asking nor being spontaneously told much about them. Frontier stories and knowledge of massacre sites were fading in the latter decades of the twentieth century as older people died with-out, as far as I know, having relayed those stories or locations to their families.

Accommodations with Relative Strangers: Bounding and Bridging Difference

With few exceptions, the people telling me these stories had not shared their lives closely with whites. Whites were constantly in their lives, a persistent presence felt to be different, judgmental, and often authoritarian. On cattle stations they maintained this presence with distance: the station homestead and the Aboriginal camp remained socially distinct. Aborigines lived in very poor shelters with no facilities and were routinely seen as "the blacks" who lived in the "blacks' camp." They were known to whites and managers on the station as personalities and in terms of their family situations and histories. They had most to do with whites in the context of work, and children were offered some (but minimal) schooling at some stations in the postwar period.

At some stations (like Willeroo and Delamere), there had never come a "golden" period of smooth relations between the stations and the large Aboriginal communities living on them (Morphy and Morphy 1984): people and families worked, were given some rations and supplies, and were "sent bush" (made to go away) in the rainy season. They had some life on their own, away from the station and even at it, and continued to organize annual ceremonies. But there was no evident period of mutual regard between indigenous people and management. At stations such as Elsey, there did come a period of calm and relative stability between station management and Aboriginal camp, mainly in the long period indigenous people knew as "Kayku Giles time." Giles's departure gave way to a series of much shorter management regimes, followed by the removal of station residents triggered by the equalization of wages. New government programs in the 1970s, 1980s and 1990s, including land excision and rights claims, enabled some people to return to a small living area excised from the station.

When I stayed at Elsey for the entire year (1978–79), I lived in the Aboriginal camp. The station manager and his wife and family lived at the gracious homestead, some two and a half kilometers away. The Aboriginal camp was independent of the station as a living area, but the manager interacted with its principal personalities as his workers. He picked people up and dropped them off, sometimes bringing meat for the camp. Only limited mutuality was possible or desired. At that time older people were still attempting to organize ceremony, to store sacred objects used in ceremony, to move about the station for these and other purposes. The station manager declared that he wanted to know as little as possible about this; he required only that they lock gates and not allow stock to wander. Every Saturday, the manager's wife took to town the women she called "old girls," the Aboriginal women (including my aunt Kitty, my grandmother Amy, my daughter Lulu, my first cousin Maudie, my mother Daisy, sometimes my mothers-in-law Jessie and Sheila, and others) who had formerly worked for the station. While some of these women were managing their own households, others, like Kitty, were looked after by the more able-bodied. Back then, transport amounted to one community pickup truck, if it was in working order, and a few private cars, mostly unreliable. Management recognized that as the least able to access transport for weekly shopping (the nearest store was forty kilometers away), the "old girls" were vulnerable to those who could offer to shop for them: their money might be spent on alcohol. The manager's wife would help them pay and take some money home, perhaps leaving some at the store for future purchases. Early on

Saturday mornings these women would wash and wet-comb their hair and put on a fresh dress. They knew her expectations of cleanliness and neatness; after all, they had done the laundry, ironing, and housecleaning for years, and they knew that camp conditions were far from those expectations. The manager's wife would pick up only the "old girls"—nobody else allowed—not the way Aboriginal people would have handled matters. While her guardianship relieved the women from the pressures of shopping with close family, they would still have to share what they bought with hungry relatives.

In the regime that had evolved by the time I visited, people shared a generalized sense of past injustice, especially on such subjects as station work and whites' inadequate recognition of Aborigines belonging to the country, but most young Aboriginal people did not express curiosity about the past. Their relations with white people were limited and instrumental. Whites' attention to members of the Aboriginal community was based mainly on present and former work relations, which management had circumscribed to prevent their becoming more intensive and multifaceted. The need to fix broken-down vehicles, to share one public telephone in the Aboriginal community (often out of service), to access medical care, to settle domestic and camp violence were not met by such distant and instrumental management. Many members of the Aboriginal community satisfied some of these needs through relationships with other whites of importance in the small town forty kilometers away: with the storekeeper and his family, with the clinic worker, and with some other long-term residents of the town. Camp residents had ties to whites who visited the station regularly. All these relationships, while usually friendly, were circumscribed by their specific purposes. While whites and Aboriginal people claimed knowledge of each other, and even some familiarity, they accepted boundaries: these ordered relationships would not become more full; they remained specific to purpose.

Daily relationships with whites centered not on cruelty or violence but on alcohol, money, the management of the alcohol-abusive behavior of Aborigines in town, food, medical care, camp management, water supply, housing, and schooling. Nights and sometimes days in the camp were punctuated by news of drunken conflicts, motor vehicle breakdowns, and, all too frequently, road accidents. Even by the friendliest of teachers, Aboriginal people were disciplined to keep their interactions largely to school matters. These interactions sometimes expanded a little: a particularly committed pair of teachers, feeling that children would benefit from knowing more about the wider world, took a busload of students and two adults to Sydney. Small local business operators who wanted to bring in tourists or fishermen or to fish themselves, cultivated closer relationships with some community members, often of a hail-fellow-well-met kind. This gained them access to the station, but it did not spare them from critical evaluation: some were thought of as good, friendly, others as dismissive. When camp violence was exacerbated by the growing availability of alcohol, camp residents would call in station people and police, but often they would not reveal particulars or press charges, as police thought they would and should do.

Senior people in the Aboriginal camp saw a need to cultivate decent relations with whites whom they saw as not allowing Aborigines to push familiarity too far and thus as closed to their own heartfelt concerns. The community would sometimes discuss asking the station to allow use of the telephone or to help with repairing something, to donate a "killer" (freshly killed bullock for meat). People arguing in favor—the recognized camp leadership—would be tasked to make the request. Knowing station management and being able to negotiate with them were valued skills.

White people were and are therefore not seen as all of a kind—some were biddable, others were referred to as "nother kind whitefella," which meant unapproachable, ungenerous, maybe volatile. Aboriginal people had a sense of whites as people who typically remained somewhat aloof, whose dispositions were variable, and from whom one mostly kept some distance. There was clearly much reserve on the part of Aboriginal people about dealing with whites. Talk about them was situational rather than constant. But there seemed to be an assumption, especially on the part of indigenous people more practiced in dealing with them, that whitefellas do vary and that it is an empirical matter: see how they act. The polarity blackfella-whitefella had come to be a matter of common sense to both Aborigines and other Australians.[33]

Difference: Categorical and Permeable

In Chapter 4 I showed how a colonial sense of entitlement and of civilizational superiority contributed to colonists' accusations of indigenous "treachery" when Aborigines refused the allegiance they expected. For example, the *Northern Territory Times* reported an incident in which some Aborigines gathered and were yelling to be let in before the house of a Mrs. Niemann living at the Daly River mission station. "Possibly their object was nothing more serious than to frighten some tobacco out of a lonely woman, but the incident emphasizes the untrustworthy and treacherous character of the aboriginals" (*Northern Territory Times*, 13 July 1900; in Larbalestier 1990:73). Through such reportage, a categorical view of Aborigines as treacherous consolidated.

This chapter has explored indigenous evaluation of settler action by inquiring into the meaning, to Aborigines, of "cruel." "Cruelty," like "treachery," comes close to being a boundary-marking category, but its application to whites and their actions is selective. My examination of this selectivity reveals a modality of relationships that is not fundamentally categorical but permeable. I have found that people apply the notion "cruelty" to whites who were relatively unknown, or at least socially distant. Incoming "whitefellas" who forged personal relations with at least some indigenous people were considered "dangerous," "aggressive" (or "cheeky"); but even if murderous, they were not completely beyond the pale of interaction and coexistence. By forming sexual and de facto marital relationships with indigenous women, they came into contact with a wider kindred that they tolerated, thus living within a "middle ground" (White 1991). In establishing work relations, incomers such as Mick Madrill showed little tolerance for connections with additional indigenous people beyond his "boys," and he murderously prohibited circulation of desired goods to "myalls" beyond his work regime. Indigenous acceptance of such people was personal—based on direct contact and the way in which they had established their place in the indigenous social order, however partial this was.

There was thus an indigenous way of making relationships with outsiders that did not categorize them in racial terms but drew on intra-indigenous terms of recognition. We have seen in earlier chapters that indigenous people considered skin color an interesting difference and investigated it closely when they could. However, the indigenous people in the far north that I know use these ostensibly color-based terms—such as "whitefella" and "yellafella"— without necessarily demarcating a distinct racial type. Terms denoting color leave open the particular relationships that one might have. In that sense, indigenous behavior remains relatively unassimilated to patterns of racial categorization that can be found, for example, in the northern New South Wales town studied by Gillian Cowlishaw (2004).

While Aborigines have certainly been made to suffer the exclusions, injustices, and injuries of the ways that Australian laws and institutions have deployed "race" (Cowlishaw 2004; Grant 2016), their own failure to adopt racial thinking as a matter of common sense and practice is a reminder that racial thinking is a historical product. The indigenous-nonindigenous clash was determined not only by great differences of technology and power but also by different modalities of relating to difference, which I will call "categorical" and "permeable."

Indigenous social orders gave rise to what I am calling the "permeable" approach to relatedness. Indigenous society was and is fundamentally structured in terms of kin relations. As a basic recognition mechanism for knowing and relating to others, kin relations provide a template for recognition of commonality of kind. Aboriginal people do not understand kinship as biological. Though they know that procreation involves parental relations of a biological kind (similar to those recognized by most members of European societies for understanding their own social life), their idea of filiation also includes other generative processes. For example, impregnation by "child spirits" grounds the born child's attachment to places and to the symbolic order of totemism; people inherit essences in names borne both by creator figures and by humans. There are also customs of nurture and adoption.[34] Indigenous modalities of kinship extend further than "genealogy" as narrowly construed. Kinship is not inherently confined to any type of structure that we may attempt to impose upon it using what we assume to be a cross-cultural vocabulary ("family"); or inherently limited to any specific domain of activity. Aboriginal practices of kinship generate networks of connection which, more or less directly, link persons with others organized in particular kinds of kin ties (e.g., between mothers and children, mothers' brothers and sisters' children, and so on); anthropologists refer to them as "kin types." Kin relationships have moral valence and each kin type is understood to have a specific expressive character, such as the mutually nurturant and protective relation between mother and child. Within overarching notions of kinship people consider whom they might marry; the possibility or promise of marriage is an extremely important differentiator within regional populations.

However, relations of kinship have implications for all domains—economic, political, religious. Being someone's mother is not simply a matter of domestic import. The social significance of relationships, in sociologist Talcott Parsons's (1951) terminology, is diffuse rather than specific, relevant in every kind of interaction. Their significance is also personal, linking individuals with others understood as whole persons embodying a particular set of social characteristics. Relationship is not impersonal or narrowed to some particular activity, domain, or purpose. Precolonially people could apply their kinship system to all with whom they had significant contact.[35]

The postcolonial possibilities of relationality based on kinship are illus-trated by Phyllis. Not only was she member of a particular clan, linked to particular places and dreamings via her father, and a daughter of a mother with specific ties to place, language, and kindred, and of a "second mother" with other personal and social symbolic connections, and a specific history of upbringing that implicated all of these. She was also an agent within social networks that came to include nonindigenous people who did things, over significant periods of time, in her country. The affective urge associated with this way of being in the world is, as we saw in the case of the woman near Perth who saw George Grey as her son (Chapter 1), to make people part of this network-like system where possible; even where it comes with difficulties, and perhaps also with benefits, as with outsiders such as Billy Farrar. Social networks link persons who likewise have a multiplicity of links with others: relations of kinship are ramifying. There is no inherent mechanism of bound-ing or closure cutting off people who belong from those who do not; poten-tially, relationship continues to ramify but is in practice given specific character by propinquity and kinds of engagement. The continent-wide ten-dency observed in Chapter 3 to offer women to outsiders was one key way of attempting to make relationship, induce reciprocity, and make of even relative strangers "strange relatives" (Redmond 2005). These offerings, however, could lead straight to the heart of indigenous social order and relationship and con-stituted, as Rowley (1970:30) observed, one of its key vulnerabilities in en-counter with settler Australia.

There were limits to the openness of this ramifying kinship system: some mechanisms of "closure." For example, people of some categories were obliged to marry only people of certain other categories, and they cannot or should not marry into others lest they enter into a "wrong marriage." A second exam-ple is that in northeast Arnhem Land and parts of the Katherine region, but not in the Western Desert, one inherits membership of a clan from one's father.

However, notwithstanding such structures of closure, kinship as the basic generative ordering device is not bounded and does not by itself produce bounded categories. The practice of kinship produces clusterings of kindreds, differing from each other in terms of greater and lesser intensities of interac-tion, the latter strongly correlated with propinquity.[36] Interaction is organized according to requirements of daily life, but there are possibilities for wider interaction in special events. In the organization of knowledge, value is at-tributed to the extension of ties across space. Such extension encounters difference, and kinship relations have been able to make "kin" of persons who speak a different language and originate in a different country. In communities mentioned in this chapter, it was common for people to be multilingual, such that language difference constituted not a social boundary but a social difference. People such as Elsie Raymond and Phyllis Wiynjorrotj have sweeping regional knowledge of people as kinsmen across socioterritorial differences represented by what some nonindigenous people call "tribal" designations such as "Wardaman," "Yangman," "Jawoyn." Such designations apply to sections of country defined in many regions by the understood inherence of a particular language in them (Merlan 1981; Rumsey 1993), by their being the area of a particular assemblage of totemic geographies (featuring tracks that typically extend into other similarly distinguished sections of country, and some stationary "dreamings" or main sites that contribute a distinctive character to the area), and by the forms of personal origin of people in those sections (by being born at a certain place, "conceived" as a child spirit, having lived at a place, and so forth).

The personal, multiaspectual system of diffuse significance that I have described differs markedly from ways of living relationships that are strongly categorical, with specific boundary criteria (such as "race"), limiting extensibility. The categorical relationality that outsiders brought with them considered persons in terms of their specific utility. Indigenous women were wanted for sex, domesticity, and kinds of work, but often not as the whole persons that they were, with all that implied. "Working boys" were wanted for the extraction of their surplus labor time, not as agents within an economy of subsistence that was part of a whole life. They were to help produce goods (minerals, cattle), some of which were part of local settler economies, but many of which were also destined for regional, national, and global markets. Indigenous workers were evaluated in market terms (as performing well or badly, worth having on some basis or not), but they were never welcome in terms of the form of life they lived. Thus, Miglinin's stock-boys at Elsey were valuable just insofar as they could help clear the country of human impediments to pastoralism and work cattle. Indigenous pastoral workers like Elsie's kin were generally retained into the recent past as long as they were not too costly; they were removed once their cost rose. Professor Elkin, despite urging governments to respect "group life," looked forward to a time when Mangarrayi people at Elsey would be responsible individuals, separable from their social matrix, or their practice of kinship at least narrowed down to something manageable in terms of rational work-related criteria. Madrill retained stock-boys at Beswick and Alligator Hole as long as they worked to his rule and did not bring the complications and demands of their wider social relationships into their expectations of him; when they did, he threatened or practiced violence. It is in the context of indigenous ways of making relationships that we can understand the baffling indigenous acceptance, however partial, of violent outsiders as "strange relatives."

While categorical relationality, manifesting as racial absolutism, was largely absent from the response of Aboriginal people to colonial instruction, their history has led to Aboriginal people's applying color distinctions in ways that approximate Australian norms. For those indigenous people whose usage remains nonstandard, to be a "whitefella" is not inherently a bad thing (though it may imply social distance from Aborigines, and it certainly implies difference); nor is it necessarily stigmatizing to refer to someone as a "yellafella." For cosmopolitan sensitivities, however, to call someone by a color term can be offensive, precisely because the social presuppositions informing such usage carry the weight of association with exclusion, discrimination, and boundary marking, categorical difference; and because such associations are a widespread and expanding majoritarian form of common sense.

CHAPTER 6

Race, Recognition, State, and Society

How, in their historical and contemporary situations, can indigenous people be people of value to themselves and others? Australians have answered this question at two levels considered in this chapter: in laws, policies, and administrative practices (including enumeration) and in their interpersonal dealings with indigenous people. I will move back and forth by examining a topic that links these two levels and illustrates their discordance as much as their concordance.

See No Evil: A Northern Idyll

I will start with the story of Bett-Bett of Elsey Station. This large pastoral property on the home country of people who call themselves Mangarrayi also became the main base of Yangman survivors of early exploration and pastoral incursion, whose home country had included the original Elsey homestead site, Warlock Ponds, fifty kilometers to the southwest of the present one. Jeannie Gunn, a Melbournian who came to Australia's north as the wife of Elsey Station's manager Aeneas Gunn in 1902, wrote two books about her experiences on Elsey: *We of the Never-Never* (1907) and (for child readers) *The Little Black Princess: A True Tale of Life in the Never-Never Land* (published in 1905 and revised in 1909). Bett-Bett is the "little black princess." In Gunn's fairytale trope, Bett-Bett's realm is the open bush: she has neither scepter nor devoted subjects, but a natural "palace" extends around her. The book tells how Jeannie and her husband and a Scots stock worker, "Big Mac" (probably the leader of the "nigger hunts" mentioned in *We of the Never-Never*, John

McLennan), came upon the girl by herself by the riverside, with only her faithful dog Sue. This finding is represented as fortuitous. They took the girl—described as "black," a "nigger, every bit of her," skinny and lithe—home with them, and she happily agreed to stay with Mrs. Gunn. Bett-Bett could speak some pidgin English: "Me plenty savey Engliss, Missus!" she said on encounter with the Gunns and Big Mac—contrasting with the fact that, to Jeannie, "she looked such a wild little nigger" (1909:3). It turns out she had learned some English from Aborigines at the homestead, and she was thoroughly connected to them: she was promised in marriage to an influential Aboriginal man Gunn calls "Billy Muck."

The book continues as an idyll of Jeannie's experiences with Bett-Bett at home and on rambles through the bush on washing days; accounts of the peculiarities and habits of the Aborigines around the homestead, their constant scheming to get "chewbac" (tobacco); mutual avoidance among indigenous in-laws (which Gunn at first did not understand), as between Bett-Bett and her "little bit father," local "king" Goggle Eye; Aborigines' fear of their enemies from Willeroo Station; Bett-Bett's caring for small animals; her hunting and bush skills—and, in dramatic final sections, the death of Goggle Eye from being "sung" (ensorcelled), and Bett-Bett's leaving the homestead (in 1902) to go back to the bush for a time with her people. Applying to Bett-Bett a commonplace trope of the wistful displaced Aborigine, Gunn describes her as having become "bush-hungry."

When the Gunns picked Bett-Bett up in 1902, she was about eight years old, they estimated. Sixty-seven years later, in 1969, a woman of Aboriginal and European parentage named Dolly Bonson, living in Darwin, was baptized into the Seventh Day Adventist Church, which she had long attended. On that occasion she revealed publicly that she was Bett-Bett. Her biographer Alan Holman casts a very different light on her presence at Elsey Station than Jeannie Gunn's story of her finding. When Dolly, alias Bett-Bett, was born, her mother, Gmurdi, recognized the newborn's light skin color and hysterically opted to leave her on an ant bed rather than suffer having a "half-caste" girl-child. The baby was rescued by her aunt "Djoodi" (probably "Judy," with "aboriginalized" spelling), who looked after her. The biography revealed that Dolly's father was Louis Cummings, a worker on the Overland Telegraph Line. It was not unusual for such workers to have sexual relations with Aboriginal women and dealings with other members of their kindred.

When Jeannie Gunn left the Northern Territory in 1903 after her husband's sudden death, Dolly was sent to Darwin, and, unusual for that time, she got to know her father. In 1924 Dolly married an Englishman named Joe Bonson. They had a family, and I met one of their grandsons in the 1990s when he worked for the Northern Land Council in Darwin. Knowing that I had done a great deal of recording of the life histories of Jawoyn people, John approached me to see if we could discover more about his grandmother's background. Notwithstanding the help given by Phyllis Wiynjorrotj, her family, and others, all that we could discover was that Bett-Bett's—Dolly's—mother may have been Jawoyn (but there is little certainty) and that Dolly had been born near Katherine and from there was sent south to live at Elsey Station. Her kin links among Aboriginal people may have favored this, while Cummings himself seems to have been the one who arranged this with the Gunns.

Nothing in Gunn's book suggests that the "little princess" was of mixed race, even though this was obvious to Dolly's mother and to any observer of Dolly or of her photograph. Dolly Bonson appears in numerous Northern Territory records as "half-caste." In 1937, thirty-two years after the book's original publication, Jeannie Gunn acknowledged that "there was a definite white strain in my little Bett-Bett, which exactly was why we brought her into the homestead and cared for her as we did, the poor little helpless waif. And that is why all through the years she has been so cared for and sheltered by all who knew her story. It was only for the sake of my little child readers that I left just that one thing untold" (*Northern Standard*, 12 February 1937, quoted in Larbestier 1990:75).[1]

Jeannie Gunn had helped to smooth over—indeed, partly as a matter of literary conceit, to conceal—Bett-Bett's background. Her approach in the book was to treat Bett-Bett as an Aborigine—in the first edition she repeatedly refers to her in the language of the time as a "nigger"—and to describe her in ways that emphasized her continuity with an Aboriginal heritage and way of being. But it seems that Bett-Bett's presence in that protected Elsey location was the result of relationships and arrangements over which she and other Aborigines had had little say. She was removed to Darwin on Gunn's departure because Jeannie Gunn and others thought that a half-caste girl-child in the care of an Aboriginal camp would be treated as a sexual object by white and black. Removed to Darwin, beyond the reach of Elsey Aborigines and her erstwhile promised husband Billy Muck (presumably an arrangement made in the Aboriginal camp without Jeannie's approval), young Dolly nevertheless experienced many forms of unequal and prejudicial treatment as a person of mixed Aboriginal-white ancestry. However, she became the wife of an Englishman, a staunch Christian, and the matriarch of a large Darwin family some of whose scions came to be preoccupied by the question of who she really was and where she had really come from. Her relatives felt a need to make her historically more transparent to themselves in terms that they were, by then, able to value.

Questions of mixed parentage, more particularly mixed sexual relations, have played a significant role in indigenous lives at Elsey as elsewhere. However, Australians, indigenous and nonindigenous, in different ways, have found it difficult to "see," recognize, and articulate interaction as reciprocity of perspectives and being. The issue of racial mixture has been especially problematic. Thus, there was a gap between what Gunn could clearly see and her representation of it. In her time Gunn could not say what was evident: Dolly did not occupy an unproblematic location that Gunn could easily narrate. She was part of a larger order of things in motion that Jeannie did not wish to deal with. Instead, Bett-Bett as an Aborigine, a "wild little nigger," became part of Jeannie's post-frontier life as a writer, supplying to a reading public something of what it wanted to imagine. The parable of Bett-Bett raises the wider question of the lenses of "recognition" and the extent to which it implicates not only the interlocutor as "other"—it certainly does—but also as "self." As Dolly's story also shows, though Aborigines were generally more accepting of mixed race, it presented problems for them too.

Bett-Bett's story brings to light some of the issues that this chapter deals with regarding the situation of colonized, now postcolonial, indigenous minorities. The question confronts them, but it also confronts the societies in which they live: How to be people of value? What values? Who is the arbiter? How different must we, or they, be to be people of value? And if not completely different, what then?

Racial Policy and the Varying Significance of Mixed Race

When the six British colonies—Western Australia, South Australia, Tasmania, Victoria, New South Wales, and Queensland—agreed in the 1890s to federate as "Australia," the national ideology represented "the people" as racially homogeneous, what Etienne Balibar (1990) calls a "fictive ethnicity"—British Australians. That is, the national type was demarcated not by its separation from Britain (as was American national identity in an early period), but by delimiting and specifying who one was by who was excluded: peoples of Asia, the Pacific, and Aborigines. The Australian national type was also not defined internally by a strong racial polarity in the way that occurred in the United States, with its large slave population, continual debates in the U.S. Congress about the future of slavery in the expanding nation, and the social and economic implications of manumitting a large population initially concentrated in and defining the character of a particular region of the country. In the Australian colonies, the threat of nonwhite, unfree labor was to be dealt with by immigration policy: known as the "White Australia" policy.

How could a nation with an indigenous black minority hope to have a "White Australia" policy? As "racial purity" became a, if not *the*, symbolic organizer of the fledgling national imagined community (Markus 1979), Aborigines were stereotyped as archaic relics of the Stone Age, and—wherever colonization had reduced them to misery and marginality—as, at best, a population to care for humanely until they died out. As Wolfe (1999, 2016) has pointed out, Aborigines were much less present as a comparator or competitor population than were American blacks. In Australia's imagined community, the black-white binary has been of different significance. Not only have Australian "blacks" always been a smaller proportion of the population, they have not been enslaved (and emancipated) peoples without land but colonized, dispossessed, and in some regions displaced. Of course, no national myth of Australia could completely erase the black, indigenous presence, and a politically potent and morally laden black-white binary has been evident in the relatively great presence of indigenous issues in public space of the last several decades, compared to a previous "great Australian silence" (Stanner [1968]1991).

Australia was founded on a series of exclusions and inclusions, based on the commitment to a British identity. The Australian government's "White Australia" policy was concerned to keep unwelcome (racially "other") kinds of foreigners out, or to repatriate them, as with the Chinese and cane-working Pacific Islanders ("kanakas") in north Queensland. The Immigration Restriction Act of 1901 mandated the limitation of non-European migration, effectively allowing immigration to Australia only from the United Kingdom and some other European countries. John Curtin, Labor prime minister (1942–44), in the wartime context restated the ideal to Parliament: "This country shall remain forever the home of the sons of Britishers who came here in peace in order to establish in the South Seas an outpost of the British race"[2] (cf. Stratton and Ang 1994).

Australia was in this respect like other Anglo colonies whose restrictive immigration aimed at maintaining a "white" population: South Africa and the United States (the U.S. federal Chinese Exclusion Act of 1882). They shared some of the mechanisms (such as literacy tests) and underlying sentiments brought to restrictive state management of nation building. In South Africa, between 1895 and 1903, restrictive immigration laws were introduced to minimize the entry of free Indians into Natal. The Natal formula was shortly applied in the rest of South Africa. A South African law of 1897, replaced by one of 1903, devised a literacy test to be applied in a European language to the disembarking immigrant. This law in fact provided the model for Australia's literacy test. Australia's act originally required a dictation test, obliging a person seeking entry to Australia to write out a passage of fifty words dictated to them in any European language, not necessarily English, at the discretion of an immigration officer. This test was sometimes circumvented, and certainly often discredited for its arbitrariness and misuse, but it remained formally in place until 1958, alongside the main legislation and its intention: to ensure the predominance in Australia of immigration from favored countries and the persistence of Australia as a fundamentally British nation.

Aborigines, though sometimes sequestered on reserves managed for their "protection," could not be excluded from Australia: they were residents of the continent and acknowledged as originary, though "primitive" (comparable in this respect to Native Americans). The prediction that Aborigines were a "doomed race" had to contend with the rise, evident in the colonial census from the late nineteenth century, of a mixed race population. They were most noticeable and numerous where colonization and settlement had been early and expropriation relatively completed. The first "protection" law—Victoria's Aborigines Protection Act 1869—defined "an aboriginal" (to be admitted to missions and reserves) as "every aboriginal native of Australia and every aboriginal half-caste or child of a half-caste, such half-caste or child habitually associating and living with aboriginals" (section 8)—a broad definition reflecting humanitarian factions on the Board for the Protection Aborigines. But amendments to the act, in 1886, effectively mandated the exclusion from reserves of many "half-castes," in the expectation that they could and should assimilate to the wider colonial society. This change empowered the board to break up Aboriginal families and communities on racial criteria that they themselves did not observe in their life together. Because of economic depression and popular white racism, this experiment in forced assimilation was not successful, and Victoria and other Australian colonies (which became states in 1901) developed "protection" laws that gave local officials (including police) much discretion about whether a person of mixed descent was an Aboriginal whose life was to be administered under each state's statutes and institutions of protection. The Victorian experiment was nonetheless the early expression of an abiding official expectation that persons of mixed descent had a genetic endowment that favored their absorption, in the long term, into Australian society. One way that governments would promote this process would be to remove "half-caste" children from "Aboriginal" domestic settings so that they could be raised in white families and/or in residential institutions. Bett-Bett's removal from Elsey to Darwin—under the authority of the South Australian legislation that applied to the Northern Territory until 1920—was but one of many instances of this process.

In the Australian federal pact sealed in 1901, the six states reserved to themselves the right to make laws about Aborigines: the constitution specifically forbade the national government to do so, until a constitutional referendum amended the relevant section—51(26)—in 1967. However, in 1911, the national government acquired responsibility for administering the Northern Territory, a region consisting mostly (at that time) of Aboriginal people. Thus the Australian government became one of the seven governments in Australia that legislated the "protection" of those classed as "Aboriginal."[3] Their laws included the prohibition of sexual relations between Aborigines and others, as well as (in some of Western Australia, Queensland, and the Northern Territory) empowering public servants to approve (or disallow) marriages between Aborigines and others. In Western Australia, for example, Commissioner A. O. Neville was officially entitled to manage legal guardianship of the children of people of Aboriginal descent, define appropriate limits of their socializing (and limit contacts with dark and unacculturated kin), and to authorize or disallow Aboriginal women's choices of marriage partners (Haebich 1988:348–51; Jacobs 1986; McGregor 2011:5–6).[4] Government officials and the public anticipated (and some hoped) that sexual unions between whites and blacks (whether authorized or not) would have the effect of "breeding out the color." A marriage like Bett-Bett's (to a white Englishman) was likely to be viewed favorably, if the official empowered to make a decision judged the husband a respectable, nonexploitative man. So one widely understood and endorsed version of "assimilation" was racial absorption to create a racially homogeneous population at the national level. Cecil Cook (the Northern Territory's chief protector, 1927–39) was one of the more articulate exponents of this vision, using his authority over marriage to enable a hybrid population to form, adapted to the Northern Territory's demanding tropical climate.[5]

Other elements of the policies and practices of protection included subsidies to missions established in the remote homelands of the dark, phenotypically unmixed populations in Western Australia, Queensland, South Australia, and the Northern Territory. Governments up until the Second World War hoped that vast reserves (such as Arnhem Land, chartered in 1933) would continue to be inviolable homelands for Aborigines who remained racially distinct and less acculturated. To preserve them in this way, it was thought necessary to keep them away from white population centers. As adviser to the Commonwealth in 1912, Baldwin Spencer had noted that Aborigines from "remote" areas had tended to travel to centers such as Darwin, where they developed health, behavioral, and moral problems, particularly if they came into contact with Asians (who continued to be a minority population in northern Australia, notwithstanding the "White Australia" policy).

The institutionalization of children recognized as "half-caste" was practiced by governments in Queensland, Western Australia, South Australia, New South Wales, and the Commonwealth, though these jurisdictions differed as to their policies and practices about allowing continuing contact between the child and an Aboriginal parent (nearly always, the mother). The Australian government has apologized (in February 2008) to the so-called "Stolen Generations"[6] after receiving a report documenting the painful effects of these practices, *Bringing Them Home* (Wilkie 1997).[7]

Throughout the period in which child removal was practiced opinion on the education of part-Aboriginal children was divided: some bureaucrats and experts held that they were ineducable beyond early grades, while others (including Cecil Cook; see Austin 1990) believed that they should receive an education equivalent to that of white children and, importantly, that they would be fully capable of competing in the labor market if educated. Cook's and others' ideas about education were linked to fear that part-Aborigines were susceptible to communist agitators, were they to be both educated and unemployed.[8]

Until the 1940s, Australian governments focused their schemes of racial absorption and "improvement" on people of mixed descent, assuming that "full-bloods" were unassimilable and that they were likely, in any case, to die out. After World War II, they began to reexamine and to root out concepts and policies explicitly framed in terms of "race," and the policy shifted to the "sociocultural" assimilation of both "full-blood" and "half-caste" Aborigines, with a "premium on civic qualities as the basis of national unity" (McGregor 2011:17). The Australia government signaled this shift from "race" to "culture" in the terminology of a new welfare ordinance in the Northern Territory in 1953. All people who had been under the Aboriginals Ordinance were exempted from the new welfare ordinance except those who, because of special needs, came under its jurisdiction as "wards." There was to be no mention of race. A "ward" was someone who, "by reason of his manner of living, his inability to manage his own affairs, his standard of social habit and behaviour, his personal associations . . . stands in need of special care." The director of welfare became the guardian of all wards. Under the new policy, Aboriginal people would be committed to the care of the state solely because they were in need of special care and assistance. The new register of wards was almost entirely consistent with the list of "full-blood" Aboriginals under the old ordinance. The principle of wardship only lasted for a few years. In 1964 the Welfare Ordinance of 1953 was replaced by the Social Welfare Ordinance 1964. The new ordinance was to provide for the welfare of Aboriginal people in the same manner as other members of the community, and the register of wards was abandoned for an even more explicitly mainstreaming approach that, however, practically applied in large part to Aborigines. In 1972 an incoming Labor government established a Department of Aboriginal Affairs, taking over the programs of the Welfare Branch of the Northern Territory Administration, whose staff became responsible to a minister for aboriginal affairs.

When I first came to live in the Northern Territory, in the late 1970s, these assimilatory efforts were continuing, all thoroughly imbued with an ideology of equalization and remediation. My first experiences of organized Aboriginal communities such as Bamyili (now renamed Barunga) near Katherine were that programs aimed at sociocultural assimilation and that recognized great differences in manner of living between camp-dwelling Aborigines and the "mainstream" were still very much the order of the day. Classes in Katherine and Barunga were provided, and voluntarily attended by women, on household management, food and dietary practices, and child rearing; homemaker services came to houses in Katherine such as the one Elsie and her kin had been allotted. Some men attended classes at Barunga in banking, money and its management, and a variety of practical crafts, gardening, animal husbandry, and other skills. The oldest men had typically had extensive experience as stock workers and had helped to train young men, but demand for their skill had declined until it was almost obsolete. Such Aborigines had been made to labor under regionally specific conditions, let go (as in the Katherine pastoral region) as an aspect of technological and economic change, and have generally been treated as somewhat peripheral to labor requirements. As Wolfe (1999, 2016) has long observed, colonial interest was principally in the appropriation of land and replacement of the originary population in its relation to land, not in that population as labor.

These men and women, increasingly without work, had recently been fully included in the welfare state through their access to unemployment benefits. At this time, late 1970s, the government was also refashioning government institutionally and ideologically to include Aborigines and to recognize forms of indigenous difference. The Aboriginal people of the Northern Territory had also been granted land rights. In *Milirrpum v. Nabalco Pty Ltd* (1971) 17 FLR 141 (the "Gove land rights case"), Justice Richard Blackburn had decided against Aboriginal claimants in northeast Arnhem Land who were contesting the federal government's right to lease land to the Swiss company Nabalco. Blackburn found that although the Yolngu people had a developed system of relations to land, it was not "proprietary" (they could neither alienate the land, nor exclude nonowners) and was therefore not recognizable.[9] The Yolngu plaintiffs' loss of Milirrpum prompted development of a federal statute, recognizing indigenous relationship to land. Under the Aboriginal Land Rights (Northern Territory) Act 1976 nearly 50 percent of the territory has been placed under inalienable Aboriginal title.

The people with whom I was beginning to work in the late 1970s had been through two regulatory phases, "protection" and "assimilation," and they were now entering a third, "self-determination." We can understand "protection" and "assimilation" as encouraging and requiring certain ways of seeing Aborigines. The early ("protection") vision was of Aborigines as primitive and probably doomed; protectionism was one response to that perception, and though it had some humanitarian proponents, it overlapped and in many instances was continuous with colonial incursion. It certainly served as an ostensible basis of colonial regulation of indigenous people. "Protection" was part of that "White Australia" phase of nation building that had formulated a national identity in explicitly racial terms. This was partly calqued on the British tradition (as well as being partly oppositional to it; cf. Kapferer 1988) and was given specific continental definition by exclusion of unwelcome foreign "races," especially Chinese (who largely worked for themselves) and Pacific Islanders (some of whom had been kidnapped, some induced into long-term indenture).

With assumptions of a "White Australia" prevalent around federation, some people of indigenous background, namely, the racially mixed, were seen as destined for absorption, preferably without trace, into a population that was normatively "white." While "half-castes" were not "Aboriginal natives" from the perspective of constitutional law, they could be administered as "Aborigines" under the Aboriginals Ordinance, even if they were known as (and identified as) "half-caste," of "mixed aboriginal blood," and so on. As an effect of a 1936 change in the Aboriginals Ordinance, individuals could apply for exemption and be subjected to evaluative measures concerning their fitness to pass into the wider society. Such "passing" was a legal and administrative ideal; the social reality was that "half-castes"—whether officially exempt or not—were viewed as a distinct section of Northern Territory society, and from the 1930s many began to view and comport themselves as distinct from Aborigines who were unmixed and unacculturated (Merlan 1998:189–90).[10]

Whether "absorption" of the half-caste enacted or contradicted the "White Australia" policy was debatable. The white/half-caste difference was patent in visual terms, but it was also supposed to be transitory, and I suggest that this may have made the process of absorption tolerable. After all, such "blacks" were not a threat: they had been expropriated. There is no reason to assume that difference understood in this way compels a salient or politically potent black-white polarity. Such polarities take shape in particular conditions. The numerical and economic conditions for polarity of the United States did not then exist in Australia. However, the social and political position of people of mixed descent changed when government policy, in the transition from "assimilation" to "self-determination," revised its perspective on "unmixed" indigenous people. In the "protection" era, the "unmixed" had been seen to fall outside any immediate possibility of absorption. The remote inviolable reserves were intended to give them space to live in their originary condition and for the value of their originary qualities.[11] The secretary of the federal Department of the Interior Joseph Carrodus observed to the first state and federal conference on Aboriginal policy of 1937 regarding the desirability of first planning for people of "mixed blood": "Ultimately, if history is repeated, the full-bloods will become half-castes" (Commonwealth of Australia 1937:21). History was not repeated, but nonetheless the policy of assimilation sought from the mid-twentieth century to reach out even to "full-bloods" and to offer them training in citizenship.[12] When the Australian government conceded land rights to the residents of remote reserves in the Northern Territory in the 1970s, the people of mixed descent—formerly marching in the front ranks toward assimilation—found themselves marginal to a policy that now valorized Aborigines' cultural continuity. As the more "assimilated," they were less able to demonstrate the continuing adherence to territorial customs that would warrant recognition of land rights. Many, however, had some education and kinds of skills that the unacculturated (and typically darker) had not acquired. The claim of the more assimilated to "Aboriginal identity" was more clearly secured under a new census policy introduced between the 1966 and 1971 censuses, but the entailments of being recognized as "Aboriginal" were, for these "mixed" people, limited.

We will soon return to these policy phases in Australia's census and enumeration practices, part of a technology of exclusion and inclusion. First, I want to examine how assimilation policy affected those people who were middle-aged when I got to know them in the late twentieth century. Most of these are women, and their stories illustrate the varied character of sexual colonization that has been their lot.

Sex, Children, and What Comes Naturally

Upon first contact, indigenous people showed interest in "sexing" outsiders by inspecting their genitalia. We recall the report of "a great shout of admiration" when P. G. King (1980:35) made "one of his men unbutton and publish his privates" (Clendinnen 2005:11) to meet indigenous demand. For indigenous people, it was one of the forms of understanding of the outsiders that made them not only human, but also potentially open to extending to them the kinds of approaches they might make among themselves. Establishing that early arrivals were male, the indigenous men could offer them sexual hospitality, the use of their own wives and female relatives. Nor were indigenous women without this curiosity. As we saw, they pursued the question of the sexed nature of outsiders themselves, when they could.

Clearly, outsiders came into a context of indigenous sexualities that were not prudish. Gender relations raised issues of interpersonal and societal control and status—both personal and political. Men made claims to the deployment of women while continuing to reserve their own interests in those women as primary. Sexual and marital relations were aspects of wider networking. Everywhere, gender relations were key in a certain continental organization of marriage as male achievement, with famously intense obligation of men to their in-laws (Hiatt 1996); as well as in the organization and symbolism of sacred ceremonial practice (Hiatt 1971). In these arrangements women's sexuality was deployable at times as a male-controlled resource, often in men's interest in bonding with other men. Women, too, took the opportunity to deploy their own sexuality in ways complementary and sometimes resistant, rather than completely opposed, to marital political norms (see Collier and Rosaldo 1981; Merlan 1988, 1992).

To outsiders, indigenous men's deploying the sexuality of their own wives and daughters to others was confusing and even depraved. Outsiders wondered about the degree of women's autonomy in sexual matters; outsiders could also be opportunist, attempting to discount the men's interest.[13] Indigenous men sought to secure their control. Early colonial arrivals commented on indigenous men's directing women's movements in order to prevent direct contact of outsiders with their women and thus to control the sexual offer of women. As indigenous-nonindigenous interaction became more constant, and less open to constructions of interpersonal reciprocity and bonding, such offers became more directly a means to acquire desired goods that outsiders controlled. Though both indigenous men and women often seem to have agreed on this stratagem, the men took a leading role in offering indigenous women to outsiders for money, tobacco, opium, alcohol, and food.[14] This represented, in short, a shift from a focus on relational possibility to material transaction in which indigenous women seem to have often been the more-or-less compliant medium.[15] With this shift, however, the social relations involved became much less controllable, both those between men, and between men and their women. If outsiders ignored the claims of indigenous men, refusing to return women to their husbands, for example, deadly friction ensued. Indigenous women sometimes remained with their indigenous partners but sometimes went with the outsiders.

Aboriginal people were exposed to massive sexual colonization and predation. As Charles Rowley (1970:30) wrote, "The Aboriginal tradition of using sexual relationships to cement social ties rendered them especially vulnerable." Much of what took place was brutal, exceeding any arrangements as indigenous people might have envisioned them. Force and violence were visited upon indigenous people without consent; or, if sometimes with consent, so thoroughly grounded in enormous social inequalities and radically different practices and understandings of the consequences (for instance, the deployment of alcohol and opium to lure indigenous women, and/or their husbands and kin) that we cannot help but ethically judge this as repugnant.[16] Perhaps women sometimes chose to remain with outsiders rather than return to their husbands and kin, often a response to enormous imbalances of power and command of resources. We can never know, for instance, whether Aboriginal women captured by sealers in southern Australia for sex and other kinds of work (Ryan 1981; Clarke 1996) were making "choices." Missionaries acted on their certainty that indigenous practices of gender, sex, and ceremonial were repugnant.

Across the pastoral north, indigenous women were sought out as temporary and more permanent sexual partners. Again, in some cases, these relationships became domestic partnerships of various kinds, in a few cases even leading to the recognition of offspring as family and inheritors of positions in pastoral operations and possessors of property. However, no doubt the majority of white male–indigenous female relations over time were temporary (if not always completely unconsensual), and without doubt the majority of so-called "half-caste" offspring of such relations remained unacknowledged by their fathers and subject to policies of removal and institutionalization. In colonial times, the reverse, black male access to white women, was probably vanishingly rare. There were many more white and Chinese men than women, to begin with. Some Chinese came as indentured laborers from the mid-nineteenth century. The 1850s and 1860s saw the largest pre-federation migration of Chinese to Australia, with numbers peaking around forty thousand. As settlement proceeded and more families became settled in remote parts of the continent, the main thrusts of economic development were based on industries (mainly pastoralism and mining) that were powered by men, so settler societies were numerically and socially masculinist—with European women eventually welcomed to bring refinement and stabilization, as in other settler colonial contexts.

From the lives of indigenous people I have known relatively well, and in the lives being lived around me, I know of violent, predatory, and exploitative actions. However, each generation has also been genuinely interested in sex with other kinds of people. For age-mates of people such as Elsie Raymond, growing up on cattle stations, white stockmen had the allure of the outsider, the illicit, and the powerful. For white men in outback occupations that brought contact with indigenous camps, Aboriginal girls and women were persons of (prurient) interest, whether one could gain their attentions by fair means or foul. Many Aboriginal women in Elsie's parental generation had sexual experience with outsiders. Elsie's birth mother was herself of part-Afghan[17] background on her father's side. Some adult women I knew who had lived in the mining camps south of the Arnhem escarpment had no children probably because venereal infection had rendered them infertile. Eylmann (1898) reports a fairly harrowing scene of access to alcohol, opium, and sexual use of women at Pine Creek, which became the settler epicenter of these people's lives from the 1880s. Half-caste children resulted, and almost all the indigenous women who were born in the first third or half of the twentieth century that I met in Australia's north said that they had part-Aboriginal siblings or children whom the authorities had removed to mission or government institutions for "half-castes."

Two prominent women at Elsey Station had a half sister, the daughter of their mother and a white stock worker from "Kayku Giles time." This girl, like Bett-Bett, was removed from Elsey by a Native Affairs patrol officer, disregarding protests of her mother and others. Institutionalized in Darwin, during the war she was sent south to Adelaide, attended schools in South Australia and New South Wales, became a staunch Jehovah's Witness, married a European man in Sydney, and years later finally made a return trip to be reunited with her sisters at Elsey Station, where she lived with her own family, husband, and daughters, until her death (see her story in Merlan 1996 in her own words). She took a strong role in the affairs of the indigenous people on Elsey who had, in the interim, moved away from the station homestead and established themselves as an independent community. Like Bett-Bett, she built a position of strength through family, education, and religion; she came to help them and improve their situation according to her acquired standards and values—with a strong sense of the differences that had developed between them but a determination to work across them. Her children continue to live and be involved in the community and to take greater interest in its historical and cultural character than do many other residents, who take this more for granted.

Elsie Raymond was a bit less able to turn her situation into one of outward-facing relative strength, though she did so to a degree, especially in her older age. Much of her strength resided in family and community. As a young girl on Willeroo and Delamere, Elsie was reared by her grandmothers and mother, and they intended her to follow a marital course they planned. Her father promised her to a much older man and delivered her to him; this would have probably been a few years prior to World War II. But young and attractive Aboriginal girls also ventured to flirt and more with the stockmen—often the cause of much domestic uproar. They did not think in terms of sexual exploitation, which it no doubt also was. This was the girls' fun and adventure (as it was that of the stockmen), and in middle age when I met her, Elsie recounted all this in those girlish terms. And so it happened that Elsie had two half-caste kids—first a boy, then a girl. The outsider father took no responsibility. In fact, he was at that time breaking the law by consorting, as the Northern Territory Aboriginals Ordinance 1918 made illegal Aboriginals' drinking alcohol, supply to them, whites' proximity to Aboriginal living areas, and interracial sex.

Elsie sometimes called her two children "yellafella." Aboriginal people of Elsie's age used such "color" terms without implying demeaning characteristics or other (social, moral) presuppositions. For many European/Australians and southern indigenous people, such color designations have become taboo. However, the fact of a mixed-race child *was* linked for such people as Elsie's mother with the knowledge of her daughter's carrying on, outside of the course set for her and with outsiders. And so, as Elsie and her mother told me (in the presence of that boy-child, by then an adult), when her mother saw the child, and realizing his father was a stockman, her mother said that she was going to smother him. Pleading, Elsie managed to slip away with the child until her mother's rage cooled. The "child" they were talking about sat with us impassively, listening, no comment, and I thought (at the time), that he might have been amused, embarrassed, and possibly both. A smaller storm also arose over the second such child. Elsie raised them both, as much as she could. Both were taken away from her as small children by a patrol officer from Native Affairs, a cause of extreme grief to her, and they were institutionalized for some years in Darwin, several hundred kilometers away—the assimilation policy in action.[18]

Elsie had a (somewhat lighter-skinned) half brother (from an "Afghan" father and Elsie's mother, described above). He took the route followed by some talented and aspiring boys in his circumstances and became an expert stock worker and station manager, eventually taking over management at Manbulloo Station, just south of Katherine town. Their mother lived in the Aboriginal camp there at that time with Elsie's father, Ngamunugarri (generally known by his given English name, "Tarpot"). This brother had married a white woman, a nursing sister. The pair aspired to respectability, kept a standard Australian household regime, and their children did not play with children in the Aboriginal camp at Manbulloo—camp conditions or behavior was not allowed. The couple refused to allow any of his camp-dwelling relatives (including Elsie and her mother) into the station house. Any discussions among them were held outside, under the trees. Elsie was more comfortable camping by a river with minimal equipment and foraging for bush foods than sitting in a house. That balance between ways of being was not to be repro-duced to the same degree in the younger generation—though they have an interest in working in indigenous affairs.

Elsie married an indigenous man and had a large family. Their children lived close by, so they had the joys of grandchildren. Elsie was not able to protect them from the many harms of a Northern Territory town: alcoholism, ill health. One of her sons was killed in a road tragedy involving alcohol. One by one we watched these beloved children disappear. Elsie herself was active in attempting to win back living situations in Wardaman country for herself and family and came to be held in high regard not only in Katherine's Aborig-inal communities but also by people in organizations and government.[19]

Two siblings of another woman, Julie Williams, also a close companion of mine for years, had been taken to Darwin and institutionalized, as had two siblings of another indigenous friend who still lives at Barunga. Their situa-tions arose from the native labor camps of the Second World War, where the army employed Aboriginal people in wood cutting, carting, road work, laun-dry and kitchen duties, sanitary work, loading and unloading stores. Aborig-inal camps were located at least five miles from soldiers' camps, to minimize contact. This seems to have been ineffective. Whatever the original source of the infection, 56 of 120 soldiers in a commando unit on the upper Roper River (i.e., in the region of Maranboy and Elsey Station) were diagnosed with vene-real disease (Forrest 1985). In May 1943 all Aboriginal women in the Maran-boy area were taken to a compound known as "Joe's Garden," at the farm of Joe Israelson, twelve kilometers from Maranboy. A significant number of women brought together in this and other such internment camps in "army time" already had one or more children by white fathers, some of them sol-diers who were only temporarily in the north. A woman friend whose mother had two children, recounted their removal in harrowing terms. She never saw them again, though she has visited their graves in Adelaide.

In most cases I knew of, the women (mothers, siblings) were able to gain some information concerning the children who were removed and made ef-forts to reestablish contact with them. Elsie made occasional trips to Darwin and waited outside the compound to see her children when they were young. In later life, one returned to Katherine to live; the other lived farther away but visited periodically. Many but not all other women had such contacts with their removed children. While these contacts did not have the continuity of daily life lived together, they were nonetheless very important in many ways for mothers and children. For all of them, reconnecting with lost children and keeping up connections with them were signal moments in their lives. In some cases, however, separations were relatively complete. In the case of Julie and others, the children in question lived on, but different lives, for most practical purposes separate from their Aboriginal kin at home, with only intermittent contacts or news.[20]

All these stories were part of a nationwide social machinery of regulating the indigenous population to preserve the racial purity of the national population. Yet, governmental practices of classification and ordering always exist in the context of assumptions and practices that are outside of any directives that flow from the state. In these circumstances, many practices were imbued with other forms of taken-for-granted settler ascendancy. Wolfe (1999:29–30) has said that when white men sexually exploited indigenous women, they flouted the "White Australia" policy and thus "contradicted the logic of elimination." There was in fact little contradiction to the "White Australia" policy of a broadly political or structural kind—at that time. However, children resulted from miscegenation; they were anomalous, so they had to be absorbed.

While state policies made much miscegenation illicit, popular norms tolerated and even encouraged it. At Elsey Station in 1968[21] there occurred a murder (perpetrated by an Aboriginal man called Larry-Boy) and subsequent manhunt for him that were sources of activity and media reporting for weeks. A young indigenous woman who worked at the homestead was found axed to death and in a nearby shed was found a much less severely wounded white stockman with whom she had been consorting. When asked about his part in all of this, the white stockman said he could not understand why he had been attacked, since "sleeping with Aboriginal women was going on all the time" (Harvey 1983; Bowditch [1968]2014).

Demographic Visibility and Exclusions

In a colonial situation, the colonized are visible in some respects and not in others. We saw in Chapter 4 that Sturt did not record as individuals the Aborigines on his trip of exploration: he wrote out a list of participants from which the Aborigines were omitted. They were nevertheless present, important to the expedition as pathfinders and known to him by name.

Can we imagine that this was merely a simple omission? Or due to explorers' lack of familiarity with indigenous people? Or is this nullity evidence of something more profound about the relationship between settlers and indigenous people? I suggest that the exclusion relates to a larger-scale question of invisibility perpetrated systematically if sometimes unwittingly (cf. Cohn 1987:237, on underestimation of women in early Indian censuses). The question of demographic exclusion and inclusion can be fruitfully examined over time.[22]

Len Smith (1980) has conducted painstaking historical research on the Aboriginal population of Australia. The question is often asked: What was the precolonial population? How radically was it reduced by colonization? Smith considers all the evidence (and speculation) concerning this question and concludes that the sources do not allow one to say precisely how large was the precolonial population.[23] The present indigenous population (at the 2011 census, an enumerated 576,000, of whom 10 percent would claim Torres Strait Islander origins; J. Taylor 2011:286) is returning to this magnitude, but it is a population very different in character from the precolonial one. This section is concerned with changes in the official classification of the Australian indigenous population and their implications.

Early attempts by the colonies (later states) to enumerate the Australian population were seemingly guided by a principle that those nonparticipant in Australian society should not be included (L. R. Smith 1980).[24] This meant that this category of "aboriginal natives" had a particular (administrative) meaning. Only those "natives" (the usual generic term then) were to be included who were visibly taking part in the everyday settler life. Other natives not participant, identified as "aboriginal natives," were not censused. This arrangement maintained for a time an approximate equivalence between those considered "full-bloods" in the explicitly racializing terms of "blood" and those "natives" who were considered "aboriginal natives." There was seen to be little value in enumerating or registering them. While this may have also allowed the government not to expend money on such activities, this was not simply a matter of economy. Another factor was the relative position of political constituencies (generally favorable to protection as well as Christianization of the Aborigines) that wanted such accounting to be done (cf. McCombie 1859). The lack of accounting was part of a larger social order.

As mentioned above, as disastrous and obvious population decline (due to disease and violence) became evident, protection regimes were established in the various Australian states—including rationing stations, missions, sometimes schools—which increasingly delimited Aborigines' places of residence. People placed under such forms of administration were "aboriginal natives," and it would have been technically possible to enumerate them. Aboriginal women in these locations began, however, to have more and more "half-caste" children. Thus their being "outside" of the dominant settler society was a euphemizing fiction of separateness, consistent with their managed and powerless condition.

Official claims that "aboriginal natives" were difficult to count because of a mobile lifestyle sometimes entered into the picture: that they were seemingly only temporary in a given location was given as a reason for not considering them countable. Their relegation to stations and reserves objectively removed some of these grounds, though this did no doubt present difficulties. In any case, early demonstrations that one *could* enumerate such people did not change official tendency in the matter (Smith et al. 2008). Indigenous people who were seen as integrated into settler life, even if of full Aboriginal descent, were enumerated, but they were very few. There was variation from one state regime to another, but the overall initial tendency—generation of a category of "aboriginal natives" excluded from enumeration—was common across states until federation (1901). The states enumerated fed their counts to the Commonwealth, which attempted to distinguish "full-bloods" and "half-castes." Notably, and consonant with practice rather than "White Australia" policy *sensu strictu* around the time of federation, the first Commonwealth statistician, George Handley Knibbs, obtained a legal opinion that "persons of the half blood" or less are not "aboriginal natives" within the meaning of section 127 of the constitution (which stated that these would not be censused), but both policy and census practice remained confused (Smith 1980:29).

Over the longer term and in changing conditions of the expanding "mixed" population, of concern was to keep at minimum levels the population that might be designated "Aboriginal" in the above sense: people visible to the governmental system as such. As recounted above concerning changes in Victorian protection acts from 1869 to the 1886 Half-Caste Act (so called for its exclusion of this category), "half-castes" were to be merged into the general population of the colony (Smith et al. 2008:539). In this state, whiteness was partly to be achieved by mixing in those who were (often visibly and socially) nonwhite. In many cases such people were living under shared or similar burdens of disadvantage to the "Aboriginal" population (ibid., 540). People excluded in this way were not to "consort" with the "Aboriginal" population, official goals being to keep people of "mixed race" from proliferating and to prevent those who might adopt the mores and manners of the wider society from falling back into association with the unacculturated. This designation of a fairly exclusive "aboriginal native" ("full-blood") category and forcing others of "half-caste" or less off stations and reserves and notionally into the wider population, "set the pattern for the solution of the 'half-caste problem' throughout Australia for the next eighty years" (ibid.). Despite variability across state regimes, according to this "political arithmetic" (ibid.), in the main only people who had a proportional background calculable as less than one-quarter white were to be deemed "Aboriginal." The first Commonwealth census, taken in 1901, was only a compilation of colonies' data. At the first Australian census of 1911 only those "aboriginal natives" living near white settlements were enumerated, and the main population tables included only those of "half or less" Aboriginal descent. Over the longer term, the question of how to define "Aboriginal population" remained indeterminate until the 1970s between inclusion of "full-bloods" only, on the one hand, and the latter plus "half-castes," on the other, whose increase was administratively visible from the second decade of the twentieth century (Rowse 2017; see L. Smith 1980:10–54 for detailed discussion of policy and practice in this regard).

The first half of the twentieth century at least saw routine state-by-state institutionalization and child removal, against a background of negative societal and governmental evaluations of Aboriginal descent and social environment. In parts of Australia a growing "colored" population[25] was subject to policies that allowed official exemptions from social exclusionary measures (e.g., from restrictions on the purchase and consumption of alcohol) by official permit. Although the "colored" population was intermediate in the manner of mestizos (as in many parts of Latin America), mixture was not directly associated with positive social qualities, but rather with possible mobility toward a "whitened" social status and manner of life. The discriminatory implications of "colored" status provided the impetus for members of that population to act in exclusionary fashion toward "Aborigines" or "full-bloods," in some cases even toward close relatives.

I encountered this occasionally in Katherine in my early research there. There were "colored" people (as they, and others, called them) who lived within the town, while at that time "full-bloods" largely did not but were almost all camped in humpies[26] on the town fringes without access to important resources (water, power) and initially without tenure.[27] Many of the "colored" town population were in continuing employment (in government services, railways, post office, or in rural work). While some originated from other places than Katherine, or from interstate, and had few or no prior local connections, others were related to local "full-blood" people. Some older members of the "colored" families were highly sensitive, after years of policy interventions, to identification of them with "full-blood" relatives. A senior woman of a large "colored" family, when visited by a full-blood woman who was her biological niece,[28] refused to admit us to the house. A full-blood man who attempted to initiate conversation with his biological father's sister, a "colored" woman (who had the same mother as his father, but a white father), when he called her "Auntie" in a shop, was loudly and publicly shamed: "I'm not your fuckin auntie." Such encounters were fraught, not simply because of the histories of categorization differentiating them, but also because there had been some socioeconomic differentiation along the lines of such categorization between those who adhered to more open-handed practices of sharing with kin and the "colored" who tended to husband resources differently. On encounter with resource-poor, camp-dwelling relatives, members of "colored" families knew from experience they would be asked for money and resources—there being between them and many "full-bloods" a degree of socioeconomic difference more like that prevailing between whites and full-bloods. In other words, the situation of "colored" was socioeconomically more like that of the white Australian working class.

By the late mid-twentieth century, "tribal," "full-blood" people largely lived in communities or settlements and were more fully enumerated and demographically visible.[29] However, the manner of life of such people, who persisted in greater numbers in the far north and west where white settlement had been proportionally less than in southern and eastern Australia, had not become that of the wider Australian community. In the southern and eastern regions of proportionally higher settler numbers, Aboriginal people of mixed descent responded to the challenges of enumeration in at least two ways. Some had, over years, been excluded from, or left, the now more fully enumerated "Aboriginal" population as then defined. Others responded by refusing to describe themselves fractionally and responded to the census as "Aboriginal" (L. R. Smith 1980). By as early as 1950, the Commonwealth Bureau of Census and Statistics realized it could not achieve enumerations to the standard of accuracy it aspired to in the terms it was deploying.

The situation changed in the context of two structural transformations that can be considered moments of the transition to a federal policy of "self-determination." First, as a result of the referendum of 1967, the Australian Commonwealth assumed the responsibility to make laws on behalf of Aborigines,[30] and the removal of a section of the constitution changed the way in which enumeration was reported and used.[31] The section removed read: "in reckoning the numbers of the people of the Commonwealth, or of a State, or other part of the Commonwealth, Aboriginal natives shall not be counted."[32] In a related move, the Commonwealth of Australia promulgated a broad, social, subjective and self-identificational definition of racial belonging and officially abandoned quantified notions of "caste" categories.

In removing fractional or other restrictive identification, the new Commonwealth definition allowed for self-identification in a way that had never happened before. This move is clearly associated with enormous change in censused populations of Aborigines. From 1971 to 2011, the number of individuals identifying in the census as Aboriginal or Torres Strait Islander increased by almost 300 percent. This is well beyond anything that can be accounted for by natural increase (as John Taylor [2011:289ff.] shows in detail). Len Smith (1980:55) cites as behind this "the movement of large numbers of 'part-Aboriginal' people previously excluded from the Aboriginal population moving back into it." This is a significant part of the return of indigenous numbers to the rough order of magnitude of the time of colonization.[33] It is associated with considerable change in a number of ways.

First, it enabled people to be censused as Aboriginal for whom this had not been possible. Prior to 1967, a race question was included in the census to establish the number of "full-blood" Aborigines, the term "full-blood" here referring to people with an Aboriginal blood quantum of over 50 percent. After the 1967 referendum, the wording of the census question used "race" but did not ask for blood fractions of race. Second, by the same token it also allowed the grouping together as "Aboriginal" of people whose lives are characterized by a diversity of socioeconomic, locational, and other circumstances (as is also true, for example, of "whites" and other census categories). This is dealt with in a variety of ways in supplementary research, including by promulgation of cross-cutting "location" categories (urban, regional town, remote, and so on) and by other differentiating dimensions, many of which have some degree of coincidence with older "racial" categories, but only inexactly. ("Full-blood," for instance, though no longer an official category, is proportionally much more closely associated for indigenous people with remoteness of location.)

Explicitly racial, educational, and many other characteristics are not randomly distributed over this new "Aboriginal" category. This intersects with recent demographics of urbanization and the related issue of indigenous-nonindigenous intermarriage.

Over the period from revision of the Commonwealth definition to the present, the proportion of Aboriginal people living in urban locations has risen from 44 percent (1971) to 79 percent by 2013.[34] Just over 21 percent resided in locations described as remote or very remote; sites at which the accessibility of "goods, services and opportunities for interaction" were deemed by the state to be "very restricted." A subset of this group, about 90,000 strong, resided at very small residential sites mainly in central or northern Australia, in desert, coastal or island locales.[35]

The prevalence in Australia of intermarriage with nonindigenous partners for both indigenous men and women is strongly evident in national census data and occurs more frequently in urban than remote Australia. As long ago as the 1991 census, national aggregate census data indicated that one-half of all Aboriginal marriages (i.e., in which one spouse identified as Aboriginal), involved a non-Aboriginal spouse, with 83 percent of resulting children identifying as Aboriginal. This identification was a major factor responsible for a very considerable increase in proportion of Aboriginal population living in major urban areas and in certain states (O'Reilly 1994). At first this looks like the phenomenon of so-called hypodescent: the automatic assignment of children of a mixed union between members of different socioeconomic or ethnic groups to the subordinate group. Yet it is clearly to be understood as a matter not of subordination but rather of apparent claim to identity by one of the partners and on behalf of the children, even very likely by people for whom the "proportion" of indigenous heritage may be only one smaller component among others. In any case, the association of urban location and indigenous identification is relevant to the large increases over the last four decades in indigenous censused population. There is a strong tendency for those in this category who identify as Aboriginal to identify as only Aboriginal (as in the above figure of 83 percent identification among children of Aboriginal-non-Aboriginal intermarriages).[36]

What census questions are people answering? The two latest Australian censuses of 2011 and 2016 had a yes-no question of the following form: Is the person of Aboriginal or Torres Strait Islander origin? The answer could be varied only by choosing both, if applicable. The inclusiveness of the current "Aboriginal" category means that many are so categorized who make up the increasing urban proportion of indigenous people censused, and within this sector are the largest proportion who are intermarried with nonindigenous partners. In other words, there is strong association of urban location, lesser proportion of solely indigenous biological heritage and intermarriage with nonindigenous people.

The large-scale inclusion of indigenous people within a single category has produced what demographer John Taylor (2011:286) has dubbed a "postcolonial demography." What does he mean by this? He characterizes the post-referendum acquisition of official population data involving the construction of indigenous population as constituting the "minority half of a statistical binary" (ibid.). With the combination of a single, national methodology of enumeration has emerged a (new) indigenous-nonindigenous polarity.

Taylor places this in the context of the recent governmental policy aim to reduce the differences in health and other outcomes as between indigenous people and others, what has been called "closing the gap":[37]

> Postcolonial logic requires that the representation of Indigenous sociality be relational because the aim is not to give expression and substance to Indigenous difference *per se* but rather to compare it. . . . The focus then is on information that defines the "other" based on a legal/analytical definition of Indigenous peoples as opposed to self-definitions that are more practical/strategic. . . . This produces frustration for Indigenous peoples because of their historical and social diversity and because the question of definition now pits [quantitative?] analysis against [qualitative?] identity. (J. Taylor 2011:288)

An indigenous-nonindigenous binary constructed for purposes of equalization with a broad comparator, adds Taylor (ibid., 287), "presumes a degree of homogeneity and sense of collective identity that simply does not match Indigenous people's actual sociality and spatiality." The outcome is a demography that "exists solely to service constitutional and legislative requirements" with scant regard to the nature of Indigenous social and economic relations, and certainly not one reflective of "Indigenous world views and practice" (ibid.).

One can certainly take Taylor's point that the aggregate census picture is not useful for many purposes (service delivery, for example, which, to be effective, requires different and supplementary information).[38] It ignores major geographically distributed differences (Biddle 2011). To exemplify from an issue referred to above, although intermarriage between indigenous and non-indigenous partners is now high in aggregate terms, it is very different in different parts of the continent. Highest levels of intermarriage between indigenous men and nonindigenous women, for instance, are found in Tasmania—an area of the country with minimal phenotypic distinction between indigenous and nonindigenous people, within a context of often fiercely defended indigenous presence and continuity. The implications of intermarriage are different there than, say, in parts of the Northern Territory, where intermarriage is much rarer.[39]

The large-scale reidentification of people of some indigenous ancestry as Aboriginal is a demand for recognition of a continuing presence, albeit much changed (L. R. Smith 1980; Smith et al. 2008); a celebration of survival, especially hard won under settler colonial conditions (Moses 2010).[40] Beyond the census, there are other ways in which people of indigenous heritage identify themselves that show concern for these aspects of the situation, rather than (merely) with personal or individual identity, to which the census is most closely geared (see F. Morphy 2007).

Consider for instance the descendant of Bett-Bett, referred to at the beginning of this chapter. Like many others, he wanted to know something more concrete about his and his family's background that perhaps could have provided a wider opening into community and location. I have known many other people like him, on similar quests, ones of personal but also wider identity, imagination, and belonging.

In its breadth, this new kind of visibility to the Commonwealth does not satisfy either the demographer's desire (J. Taylor 2011) for a more defined meaning of an "indigenous" category; nor does it give full expression to indigenous people's interests in conveying and making persuasive the terms of their continuous presence and claims to survival (Grieves and Whitton 2013; cf. Rowse 2012 on the distinction between "population" and "people"). It also did not satisfy many indigenous people for another, related reason: some say that the Commonwealth definition is too vague, making it possible for people to claim indigenous connection without demonstration of communal or collective attachment. Evidence of community recognition is sometimes absent, some complain. The broad definition makes possible a kind of visibility of the individual that some other indigenous-identifying people find unsupported at a collective level. But it does reconstitute a potentially more potent political category.

This postcolonial demography began to take shape from the time the Commonwealth assumed responsibility for indigenous affairs. The apotheosis of this third phase has been the turn to visibility based on self-identification and rejection of older forms of identification and differentiation. This distinction was informed by new sensibilities for liberalization; it also plays a role in the equalizing and remediationist effort to "close the gap" (Kowal 2008).

Expectably, this redefinition has been the basis for enlarged Commonwealth administrative oversight of indigenous affairs, but not in ways that have been associated with continuing development of indigenous political bodies. The beginnings of "self-determination" from around 1970 saw the shaping of an indigenous political body, the Aboriginal and Torres Strait Islander Commission (ATSIC), established in 1990 under the Labor government of Prime Minister Bob Hawke (who figures in events of Chapter 7). From around 2000, ATSIC's functions were largely mainstreamed at Commonwealth level into existing portfolios (for housing, welfare, and so on), and ATSIC was disbanded by a conservative government in 2004.

Conclusion: Recognition and Misrecognition

Parts of this book have illustrated visibility as a physical but also a social and, in this chapter, governmental classificatory optic. Unlike the first chapter, which involved not seeing in physical presence, this chapter has had a great deal to do with (not) seeing (and counting) as social and regulatory exclusion and inclusion.

This chapter's material endorses the usefulness of Foucauldian insights regarding government as a set of practices of classification and ordering. It has however also illustrated the historicity of the state and inconsistencies and changes in its rationalities and practices, rather than its pervasive power and consistency. The chapter began with an illustration of the nature of a state-recognized moral hazard at the turn of the twentieth century and onward: miscegenation, widespread sexual interaction, and exploitation. Protectionism involved a combination of humanitarian and conserving strands that intersected with the technocratic and overlapped more and less with the eliminatory. Assimilationism aimed to reduce numbers and/or to erase the difference represented by indigenous people and in the process evacuated large numbers from indigenous status whose very being represented a complication of administrative categories as well as perceived moral hazard. The turn to self-determination and ideological liberality allowed for community- and self-designation, among other forms of recognition.

The personal consequences of the longest span of the twentieth century and its assimilatory practices are significant aspects of indigenous life histories. The elimination of administrative person fractions came about as an element of liberalization. A Foucauldian would nevertheless remind us that self-designation is still largely in received terms, but with a (deceptively?) enlarged space of freedom. John Taylor's identification of the indigenous-nonindigenous "binary" above is suffused with a demographer's dissatisfaction: to what uses can this large and diverse "indigenous" category be put? Its greater political potential is clearer, partly because it includes the urbanized, educated, and politically informed and is linked with increasing public awareness (see Chapter 3 on "history wars") of colonial history. Australia hardly ever faced a derailing challenge to its colonial takeover but now clearly faces forms of moral hazard—both national and international condemnation, for example—more than ever before.

This chapter briefly addressed a difficult and contentious issue concerning the relations of indigenous and nonindigenous people, closely bound up with visual recognition, but not that alone. This chapter has introduced the question of mixed race. It is geographically differentially distributed in indigenous bodies; but physiognomically unmixed indigenous bodies are now mainly found in the peripheries of the nation—the remoter areas—and are unusual and evocative when invited into the center—into urban areas, major spectacles such as the Olympics, and so on. The strong empirical visuo-racial referent of indigenous-nonindigenous difference has become limited to a small proportion of the enlarged indigenous category. But it is politically contentious to say this. That is not hard to understand, given the eliminatory history in Australia: expectations of racial doom, regulatory efforts to separate dark Aborigines from others. But obviously racial mixture continues to be a noticed difference of social significance.

Early colonial organization of population was marked by consideration of "aboriginal natives" as outside normal societal boundaries, in terms of manner of living and racial identity in combination. Categories were created, partly aimed at both limiting and focusing the liability of the state, especially toward increasing indigenous people of mixed ancestry. Despite the developing state's drive toward a white nation and replacement of the indigenous population, some people of mixed descent were declared "inside" national social boundaries, in terms of social disparagement. Eventually, onerous fractional reckoning was abandoned.

Thus was physical "vision" subordinated in various ways to the power of state building. This might be seen, in some respects at least, to parallel first contact subordination of physical vision by indigenous people to their contemporary social imaginary (Chapter 1). But Australian state action was bureaucratic and regulatory, not fundamentally the deployment of deeply sedimented practice but attempts to regulate in sociopolitical terms. The incipient Australian state excluded "aboriginal natives" in their racial distinctiveness as long as this was firmly bound up with social distinctiveness. The status of people of mixed race was contentious governmentally until fairly recently. Australian yearbooks from 1900 to the 1960s contain table after table of people designated "half-caste." The state continued to try to measure this category until 1966; but there had been variations along the way. The 1953 change to the Aboriginals Ordinance in the Northern Territory, mentioned above, had accepted the demand by "half-castes," first made in 1936, to be exempt from it en masse. In assimilationist theory, such persons were to be merged into the wider community, and the power of absorption was to make them part of the whole, to the extent possible, physically (Rosaldo 1989).

"Race" as vernacularly understood, however, has strong material, discursive, and practical dimensions (Moore, Pandian, and Kosek 2003:42). Bodies are racialized in terms of them. Phenotype can play variable roles in racial assemblages but in most it is important, one of the immediate dimensions in terms of which people apprehend others, and the chains of material and ideational associations connected with phenotype. (Saldanha 2006 refers to this kind of clustering as "viscosity" of race.) Race is not simply a label or a discourse; and the way that such assemblages work is a process that social actors are constantly in the middle of, pulling together its many elements as part of what it means for them to take account of their situation, implications of its various elements, and possible forms of action.

We may wish that people would be able to transcend the social meanings of racial assemblages. But across a range of settler colonial cases are evident forms of denial and repression of what we can now, given previous clarifications, call "racial mixing"—that is, kinds of embodied mixing across differences as locally experienced with consequences for the way in which people identify and treat others. These denials and repressions take a variety of forms, from the sort of reaction we saw in Elsie's mother—the desire to put an obviously "mixed" infant to death, given her considerations concerning her daughter and their shared life—to regulatory ones on the part of governments, up to and including efforts to make sure that sexual and social mixing are constrained and that, when they do occur, they are appropriately dealt with, penalized, and ideally transformed.

Today, a large majority of the censused indigenous population of Australia is publicly apprehended by selves and others as mixed race, but in the national public sphere the topic is an uneasy one. Sometimes phenotypically unmixed northern Aborigines look at southern ones and wonder what they have in common with them, to the extent that embodied ways of understanding self and other are salient. Southerners sometimes look at such northern Aborigines and feel they cannot measure up to them (Cowlishaw 2004:221–22). A nonindigenous Australian populace often looks at mixed-race Aborigines and thinks of them as inauthentic, or less authentic, than the physically Aboriginal type. When such people as sportsmen insist on publicly identifying themselves as Aboriginal, another underlying stereotype has it that Aborigines naturally have some kind of physical advantage, but they are also resented if they celebrate their Aboriginality.[41]

But one thing may be repeated in conclusion: the "White Australia" policy had its beginnings at a time when there was no politically potent indigenous-nonindigenous polarity. By this I mean that notions of the homogeneous, British-descended white nation were dominant, its advocates convinced of the promise and rightness of this. There had been colonization, expropriation, and assimilation was the plan. But a revised indigenous-nonindigenous polarity of some potency was building. The next chapter recounts and analyzes an episode as an instance of how it began to count and the clashes inherent in the process.

CHAPTER 7

The Postcolony: Sacred Sites and Saddles

Introduction: Australia as Mine Site and Sacred Site

In February 1991, the Australian prime minister Bob Hawke announced that his government would not allow a heavy-metals mine at Coronation Hill, in the upper Northern Territory, because Coronation Hill was a "sacred site" for Aboriginal people.

In fact, mining of uranium and other heavy metals had occurred in this area in the 1950s (around the time a major prominence there was named "Coronation Hill," in honor of the coronation of Queen Elizabeth II in 1953). Kin of Aboriginal people who became involved in the later Coronation Hill dispute (1985–91) were in the area in the 1950s, living on stations and around uranium mining camps. Some who were also living farther afield by then, in Katherine, made representations to sympathetic (white) employers about the customary significance of the region, but there was no public debate in the 1950s about whether these deposits should be mined. From the late 1970s, however, the Australian government policy of "land rights" had made it necessary for governments to consult traditional owners about the customary significance of sites of new mining activity in the Northern Territory. As well as conferring title on traditional owners, the land rights regime highlighted what became known as "sacred sites."

Disputes about sacred sites were the product of changing indigenous-nonindigenous relationships in the final quarter of the twentieth century in Australia. The first nationally prominent sacred site dispute occurred at the Aboriginal-owned Noonkanbah Station, Western Australia, where the Western Australian state government, in 1979–80, allowed exploration company

AMAX to drill for oil in what the resident Yungngora people said was a sacred site. Western Australia's premier, Charles Court, insisted that exploration go ahead, and a convoy of forty-five nonunion drilling rigs and trucks left Perth protected by hundreds of police on 7 August 1980. Violent confrontations between police and Noonkanbah protesters ensued, as the drilling rigs forced their way through picket lines. The site turned out not to be prospective. The Coronation Hill issue, 1985–91, was the second sacred site dispute to seize national attention. In the Northern Territory, the dispute was framed by leg-islation that compelled more respect, by governments and mining companies, for the perspective of customary owners, even though the indigenous people concerned did not formally have title to the area at that time.

This more effective representation of the indigenous interest was possible because of the terms on which the Australian government granted the North-ern Territory "self-government" in 1978. The nascent Northern Territory gov-ernment was obliged to pass laws complementary to the Australian government's Aboriginal Land Rights (Northern Territory) Act 1976. One such law was the Aboriginal Sacred Sites (NT) Act 1978. Coming into effect in November 1978, this statute established the Aboriginal Sacred Sites Protec-tion Authority (ASSPA) in 1979 (reconstituted in 1989 as the Aboriginal Areas Protection Authority, AAPA). The ASSPA employed anthropologists (and engaged them as consultants) to document the customary significance of sites whose law the customary owners cared to reveal; documented sites could then be registered and protected from intrusion or destruction, whether or not the sites were on land under Aboriginal title. Many Northern Territory politicians and much of the Northern Territory public resented this law as Canberra's imposed restraint on their sovereign right to develop the Northern Territory. However, while the law was sometimes disrespected, it enabled the respectful representation of Aboriginal perspectives on land use, through the ASSPA's advocacy.

Under these new circumstances, the question of indigenous connection to Coronation Hill had to be publicly debated once mining was proposed on that site. However, as this chapter will show, it was not a simple matter to represent the "indigenous connection" with Coronation Hill. Not only was the Austra-lian public divided in its perspective on Aboriginal custom, but Aboriginal custom had been affected by colonial history. Changes in indigenous people's lives had attenuated, or at least generationally differentiated, the beliefs and relations to land of the communities relevant to any consideration of Corona-tion Hill. This chapter will illuminate the relationship between the terms of

Australia's belated recognition of customary perspectives on a "sacred site" and the historically dynamic perspectives of those deemed to be its customary owners/custodians. For indigenous participants in the Coronation Hill issue, the site had a different order of value from anything that others could fathom, and that order of value was itself changing, as one generation succeeded another.

Coronation Hill: Background to Indigenous Belonging and Recent Events

Coronation Hill is a feature of the South Alligator River Valley, north of Katherine and about ninety kilometers by secondary road from the smaller town of Pine Creek. The area across which the older generation of people that I came to know had moved, regarding others within it as their (close and more distant) "countrymen," extended from around Oenpelli approximately 350 kilometers to the north (by road) in Arnhem Land from Katherine. One of their main arteries of movement by foot was along the Katherine River (and sometimes by hopping cars on the railway, which had reached Katherine from Pine Creek in 1917). Coronation Hill is within the former boundaries of an economically marginal pastoral property called Gimbat Station, first occupied by a pastoralist in the 1880s, intensively worked from about 1935, and extinguished as a pastoral lease in 1987.

Gimbat's rocky uplands are filled with art and bone deposit sites, evidence of the life led by Aboriginal people before colonization. Near the station, where Aboriginal people were concentrated periodically as workers from the early twentieth century, sites and natural formations were markers of continuing indigenous presence and practices. During World War II, some Aboriginal people from Gimbat and from other neighboring stations such as Goodparla were interned in the army's native labor camps farther south and at Katherine. One objective was to keep them away from the coasts where they might be tempted to collaborate with the Japanese; another was to harness their labor power. Some absconded from the camps and made their way back; others returned to Gimbat at the end of the war, with the closing of the camps.

At Gimbat, pastoral work was seasonal, and people also lived or were employed at regional farms, mines, and around Pine Creek and Katherine towns. The Gimbat and adjacent Goodparla pastoral leases did not flourish as pastoral properties. For some time from the 1980s, the lessee of Gimbat, of German origin, operated a fly-in tourist venture, bringing visitors (largely from Germany) who came to shoot buffalo in remote areas on the Katherine River. The rather run-down, buffalo-infested properties were resumed by the federal government in stages, mainly over the years 1987–89.[1]

Many of those for whom Gimbat was home were people of the socioterritorial grouping known as Jawoyn. This large-scale identity also applied to people whose places of origin were the river systems farther east, who likewise regarded themselves as Jawoyn. After World War II, the eastern Jawoyn largely regarded Barunga (formerly called Bamyili), the largest Aboriginal community in the Katherine region, as their home base. This included such people as Phyllis Wiynjorrotj and her countrymen (see Chapter 5). Jawoyn was an inclusive identity at a broad level, but there were different social subsystems among people who identified themselves as such. There had clearly been dialect differences within the Jawoyn language, which were partly standardized in coresidence at places like Barunga; some dialect differences persisted nevertheless. Social histories, orientations to locality and to other indigenous sets of people differed among subgroups. The people who oriented to Gimbat and Goodparla and the Jawoyn of more easterly origin, like Phyllis Wiynjorrotj, knew each other to be different in these respects, despite their common Jawoyn identity. Those Jawoyn people who worked and lived around Gimbat did so on the basis that a particular subset of Jawoyn people regarded this as (part of) their home territory. Those people could be identified in terms of the clans of which they were members and/or were recognizable as bearers of certain family names, as well as in terms of their patterns of intermarriage and regional association. Some people from another large-scale socioterritorial grouping from farther north, known as Mayali, had lived and worked with them on Gimbat and other pastoral stations of the region. People of these regional combined subgroupings—the northern Jawoyn-Mayali, or "northern Jawoyn," as I shall call them—had the longest-term relationship to and knowledge of the Gimbat area. These northern Jawoyn recognized Gimbat as part of the wider Jawoyn area, and the special, more localized, clan-level attachments of a subset of Jawoyn people to the area were also recognized.

After the Second World War, a few northern Jawoyn continued to live at Barunga and at Eva Valley, a former pastoral station, and at the pastoral training station of Beswick. They and many Arnhem Landers, eastern Jawoyn, and others had come to these communities during the war. From then until the 1970s Barunga had been a focus of sociality—marriages, a vibrant ceremonial life. But the personal and historical center of gravity of northern Jawoyn had been around Gimbat, the upper Katherine River, in Katherine and its outlying fringe camps, and in Pine Creek rather than Barunga. When in Katherine or its camps some of the northerners accessed its town facilities (including its alcohol outlets). I became more aware of the internal structure of the Jawoyn through my work on two land claims. The Northern Land Council asked me in 1980 to write the claim book for the Katherine Area Land Claim, which began to be heard in 1982; the Katherine Land Claim presented "all Jawoyn" as claimants, and it gave rise in 1985 to the Jawoyn Association. Later, in 1987, a claim to portions of Gimbat Station became possible, when 65 percent of the Gimbat lease was incorporated into Kakadu National Park as its "Stage 3." The Kakadu Stage 3 claim, on which I was the senior anthropologist, presented a distinct northern subset of the Jawoyn as claimants, commencing in 1992.

The proposal by the Coronation Hill Joint Venture (CHJV) in 1985 to mine heavy metals at Coronation Hill implicated these northern "Gimbat" people, rather than the larger "all Jawoyn" entity that the Katherine Area Land Claim was then mobilizing. The Katherine claim was proving to be fraught because it included Katherine Gorge (eventually renamed Nitmiluk National Park), the region's principal tourist attraction. The Katherine Area Land Claim was finalized, in the claimants' favor, in 1988. Prominent among the claimants were people with connections to Gimbat. The claim process revealed them to have the best knowledge of the broader area, including Katherine Gorge and northward, as the Katherine River was the northern corridor for those who had moved through this region since before World War II, from northern stations and mines to concentrations of related indigenous people mainly around the towns of Pine Creek and Katherine.

Thus CHJV, from 1985, found itself addressing Jawoyn people with a lively sense of their customary rights to land in the Katherine region well north of the township. Working with residents of communities in and near Katherine and at Barunga, CHJV was interested in anybody who was Jawoyn, but especially in those who were known to have connections with the Coronation Hill area. As a result, a dozen or so young men, some of them Jawoyn, were hired to work on the exploration effort. One middle-aged Jawoyn man (of eastern Jawoyn family), with some background in community organization and training, was hired as CHJV's Aboriginal liaison officer, working from an office on Katherine's main street. Thus the company sought to persuade the relevant community of people of the benefits of the mining development.[2]

Unannounced exploration, including road building on Gimbat in the late 1970s and early 1980s, had already caused anxiety among several Aboriginal families linked to Coronation Hill and to Gimbat. Some of these families lived in town, others at Barunga and Eva Valley, a pastoral property with near access to the Katherine River. Residents of both communities included people who knew this country and expected to continue their hunting and foraging in it. I had first met these people in 1976. After a period of research in Katherine town, I moved to Bamyili sixty kilometers east, living and working with Jawoyn people whose key senior man at that time was Sandy Barraway; he called me "daughter." Later that year I met his brother, Peter, and gradually their extended "Gimbat kindred," then living at Bamyili, at Beswick Station twenty-five kilometers northeast of it, at Pine Creek, Jabiru, and fringe camps of other regional towns. During the period I worked with them on the Katherine Land Claim I heard not only of their experiences of living on Gimbat but also their concerns about road building, disturbance of sites, and the possibility of mining on their country. I became aware of their understanding that sites in the Coronation Hill area were those of an apocalyptic creator figure—Bula—who, if disturbed, would set in train a cataclysm of flood, fire, and destruction of human, animal, and plant life. Senior people constantly repeated that this calamity would affect not only the immediate area but the whole world.

Thus, it was no surprise to me that in March 1986 the Jawoyn Association announced that it was opposed to exploration at Coronation Hill. However, when a later meeting of Jawoyn people at Barunga resolved to approve exploration, the ASSPA issued permission for exploration. This was quickly revoked by the Jawoyn Association and later restored by the ASSPA. CHJV staff regarded all these changes as vexatious.

Each of these decisions was made by organized groups of indigenous people, differently constituted and authorized, but overlapping in membership. Up to the end of the 1980s the principal actors in the Jawoyn Association—men from the Jawoyn and associated communities in and around Katherine—regarded the views of the Gimbat-connected senior people as very important. However, since those people were themselves being approached and pressured by a variety of actors, paying attention to what they thought did not always lead to a collectively agreed upon view on such matters as permission to explore and paid work for Jawoyn. For example, when CHJV hired the son of a prominent Gimbat man, long dead, the surviving Gimbat-connected seniors objected that the son was working against his family's and his own nature. Listening to these Gimbat-connected seniors increased public understanding of Coronation Hill as an apocalyptic site. However, some younger people such as the Jawoyn liaison officer for the CHJV regarded all this as "fairy tales," superfluous to his people's need for jobs and a living. This man had been trained as a community development officer at Bagot, an Aboriginal living area in Darwin; his outlook departed from that of many in the generation above him, to which senior people knowledgeable about Gimbat belonged. His mother was a knowledgeable woman in indigenous terms of eastern Jawoyn background (and a close friend and "sister" of Phyllis Wiynjorrotj). She sometimes held Coronation Hill to be sacred and inviolable, but as the dispute continued she supported the views of CHJV workers, including her son. Urged on by him, some Jawoyn families petitioned in support of the mine, with natural advantage to the more literate, informed, and larger families.

Indigenous people associated with Coronation Hill, especially the "elders," were being asked to make definitive determinations about matters about which they had never been asked before. At first, such people thought it dangerous to discuss this apocalyptic tradition publicly; they had previously not spoken of it or had spoken only in a whisper. Older women, responsibly and respectfully, in their terms, emphasized that men's knowledge and responsibility was far greater than their own: the whole tradition, to the knowledge of the Gimbat insiders, had been associated with secret-sacred, dangerous ceremony. These insiders were protecting a very important collective tradition. But it had been collective under conditions very different from those that now prevailed, with rising demand for more revelation, more detail, more specification of what this tradition would and would not be compatible with, in relation to mining development.

From 1985 CHJV consulted with three senior Aboriginal men variously called "custodians," "traditional owners" of area: brothers Sandy Barraway and Peter Jatbula and their "father" Nipper Daypilama Brown (see Figure 6). Sandy and Peter were close "brothers" in Aboriginal terms by virtue of their two different fathers being sons of the same man (in English terms, "first cousins," but this does not satisfactorily render the Jawoyn sense of them as brothers). Nipper Brown was their "father," junior to their own fathers in that set of siblings. CHJV's attempts to win their trust included giving Sandy a saddle (which, it later turned out, he gave away). Consultations, meetings, and eventually governmental inquiries proceeded until 1991, when the federal cabinet prohibited mining at Coronation Hill. These were also the years in which the Kakadu Stage 3 Land Claim (including much of the old Gimbat lease) began to come into focus. A land claim was lodged in June 1987, and

Figure 6. Peter Jatbula, Nipper Brown, and Sandy Barraway, 1989. Photo by David Cooper (1989).

preparation of the claim proceeded until the Aboriginal Land Commissioner began hearings in 1992. About 35 percent of Gimbat was not eligible to be claimed under the Land Rights Act, as it had not been included in Kakadu National Park (as Stage 3). Considered mineralogically prospective, this portion, including Coronation Hill, had been proclaimed a "conservation zone" on 5 June 1987.

We can thus delimit the Coronation Hill dispute as occurring between 1985 and 1991 and concerning a land portion ("conservation zone") that was not under claim. However, it is important to understand that from the point of view of clans associated with the former Gimbat lease, there were three concurrent opportunities to assert ownership and custody of their country: the Katherine Land Claim, the Kakadu Stage 3 Land Claim, and the consultations over CHJV's mining proposal, so politicized that it became a matter for the Hawke government to consider. Assessments of the likely environmental impact of mine operations, including archaeological and heritage surveys of the mine area, also solicited testimony from those identified as Coronation Hill's custodians.

Commonwealth and Northern Territory laws created an indigenous impediment to mining, and questions to the men sought to define how much of an impediment this was. CHJV asked them what kinds, how much, at what level exploration could take place. For the key men, given the apocalyptic nature of the region, almost any disturbance was difficult to countenance. Yet under pressure they often gave ground, in ways that only led to accusations of their inconsistency. They were asked: Is blasting OK? If so, within what perimeter? Their answers had to consider how much disturbance such actions would cause and to weigh this against their feeling about the region. How were they to answer such questions, even for themselves? How much was too much, given the prospect of an apocalypse?

A land-based tradition is linked to places. These were named, and the location of some was clear. Mining exploration pushed the issue of locating all of them exactly and also, from the miners' point of view, delimiting their scope. To the extent that the miners worked with indigenous organizations and people and examined matters with their concerns in mind, they wanted to know: Where exactly were these places? How far did you have to be from a dangerous place to conduct exploration? Even about the roster of repeatedly named dangerous places there were uncertainties. Where exactly were certain sites located? The men with whom I worked spent considerable time trying to be more certain of the location of some sites. Sometimes places identified by a particular name were at some kilometers' distance from previous identifications. Such inexactitude was intolerable from the miners' point of view.

The pressure to give definite and positive answers included free and luxurious accommodation during meetings and employment or offers of employment for relatives. Realizing that their views were important and that pressures for answers would continue, those consulted had to come up with a consistent position. This was not easy. In 1987 the Commonwealth Senate Inquiry into the Potential of the Kakadu Region was held at Barunga near Katherine—its title indicates what was at stake. During those hearings, two of the three principal men, under questioning by federal senators, alleged that there was "nothing there" at Coronation Hill. On other occasions, and indeed with increasing frequency, they said that the minerals and the gold were the "blood" of Bula, and they spoke of the influence of Bula over a wide area. Or were they at times simply hopeful of getting over all the questioning? The men were aware of public disapproval and incredulity about the apocalyptic tradition that it was their responsibility to present. Some public commentary denied that it had existed prior to the mining proposal; other skeptics asserted that it was focused on a different place, not on the proposed mine site. The men were at risk of exposure for not knowing much, and certainly for not knowing what their elders had known. The three men were differentially susceptible to and aware of such opinion.

Referring to some Jawoyn people's support for the mine, conservative columnist Andrew Bolt looked back in 2011 on Hawke's disallowance of it as "one of the most shameful surrenders to unreason of his time in power" and "the end of his government's intellectual rigor"; "Green pagans beat black rationalists," costing "us billions" and "local Aborigines jobs." Economic assessments of the project by Broken Hill Proprietary Company (BHP) contended with environmental perspectives. After spending $9 million exploring the site, BHP said that Coronation Hill contained a proven 650,000 ounces of gold, 100,000 ounces of palladium, and 30,000 ounces of platinum, making it the only mine in the world where all three metals exist in commercial quantities. Conservationists drew attention to the risk to Kakadu National Park of mining on a slope bordering the South Alligator River, the main water artery of Kakadu. "The chances of water pollution from the mine or the tailings dam are just too high," said David Cooper of the Aboriginal Sacred Sites Protection Authority (Woodward 1990). The Protection Authority's sacred sites surveys contributed to the designation of Coronation Hill as "Sickness Country." On 3 October 1985 the ASSPA registered an extensive Upper South Alligator Bula Complex, comprising about 250 square kilometers, including Coronation Hill. Declaration of this complex of sites ran completely counter to the miners' demand for delimitation; it brought initial exploration by the CHJV to a halt for a time. Having wedged the proceedings in this way, in 1986 the ASSPA took a considerable role in negotiations between the mining consortium and Aboriginal people, the Jawoyn Association, and other organizations.

The men identified as custodians thus had to work with a variety of personnel from organizations of all kinds—the CHJV and its investigative teams, the Aboriginal Sacred Sites Protection Authority, the Land Council, the Jawoyn Association, environmental groups, and others—to create a documentary basis for claims about the area relevant to the mining proposal. They had to be definite about locations of places, especially those said to be key dangerous sites. Some of these places were well known and consistently located, including both "natural-looking" and (to outsiders) apparently man-made (ceremonial) sites. Other places, while known to the men by name and approximate vicinity, had not been visited by the men since their childhood or were known only from conversations long ago. Among these less identifiable sites were some they held to be important and apocalyptic. Continuing investigation brought to light the men's uncertainties and the differences in the nature and particulars of their knowledge. Historical transition was made very plain in all these exercises. Some Jawoyn assumed that somebody must know the country's important details; and surely it was the three principal men. Positioned as the "right people," as intrinsic embodiments of the dangerous region, they were consistently asked for extrinsic proofs. Their decreasing familiarity, since their youth, with the area made proof strangely difficult. The process demanded consistent evidence of a kind they had never previously encountered. Their experience of themselves and the region as consubstantial, however, went beyond the kinds of concreteness that were continually being demanded of them.

Nonetheless, the public had access to evidence of a history of indigenous concern with the area's apocalyptic character. A Jawoyn man from Gimbat, Soupy Marrapunyah (who had died in 1975) had worked with the agronomist Walter Arndt during Arndt's time (from 1947 to 1956) at the Commonwealth Scientific and Industrial Research Organization (CSIRO) experimental farm, near Katherine. Closely related (first maternal cousin) to the principals later concerned with the Coronation Hill dispute, Soupy had married a local woman from the Katherine-area social network that had found a way to live near and in the town, working on the CSIRO farm and at Manbulloo Station just south of it. He managed this interloping without drastic consequences (and his family has grown up around Katherine with limited contact to the region farther north). When associated with Arndt, Soupy had expressed his concerns about mining around Coronation Hill and nearby sites; he had told Arndt of the apocalyptic tradition and had taken Arndt to Gimbat to see the area. Arndt's written articles, of generally documentary character, supported the senior men's evidence in the 1980s.[3]

By 1989 the heat of controversy was such that Prime Minister Bob Hawke appointed a federal Resource Assessment Commission (RAC). The RAC was led by Judge Donald Stuart, a Royal Commissioner and the founding chairman (1984) of the National Crime Authority of Australia. The RAC sought expert advice from, among others, anthropologist Ian Keen and myself (Keen and Merlan 1990).

The RAC reported on Coronation Hill in 1990. The cabinet decision of 1991 to prohibit mining apparently largely reflected the view of the prime minister, who described himself as usually "pro-mining." In this case, as he later explained, he took the view that "belief" of indigenous people should not be treated with contempt. "I was in an absolute minority," Hawke later said of his position within his cabinet (Allam 2010). In keeping with a Westminster political convention, prime ministerial opinion prevailed in a divided cabinet.

Gimbat's Bases of Knowledge and Certainty: The Law of the Father

According to Gareth Evans, minister for minerals and resources (1984–87), Gimbat was the "clapped out buffalo country" of two pastoral leases (Eccleston 1986). According to geologists from the Bureau of Mineral Resources, it was potentially one of the most valuable mineral deposits in the country. According to the Environment Centre NT, the area was home to the greatest variety of animal species in all of Kakadu. According to the Australian Conservation Foundation, mining was incompatible with Gimbat's national park status in any case, and mining in Stage 3 would threaten wetlands in other parts of the national park. Environmentalists also referred to Aboriginal views that the area was the "result of the actions of spiritual beings during the creation era" (ibid.). However, mining was not new to the area. Uranium was discovered along the headwaters of the South Alligator River Valley in 1953. Thirteen small but rich uranium mines operated in the following decade, employing over 150 workers at their peak in 1957. No Aboriginal people were directly employed at any of these mines. There were some concentrations of Aboriginal people camping near them, including some I came to know in the late 1970s and 1980s, by then elderly. From their accounts of these mines it seems that there was regular sexual demand upon Aboriginal women (Chapter 6). According to many detractors of the apocalyptic tradition (including some indigenous people), previous mining in the area demonstrated that it was not dangerous.

Gimbat had been the home or part of the home country of a large number of middle-aged and older Jawoyn and Mayali people whom I met in the late 1970s. As a modest cattle operation, Gimbat served a kind of holding function for indigenous people who were closely associated with this area by family ties and whose possible points of entry into other local subsistence systems had not become defined in ways that kept them elsewhere. They made periodic (mostly walking) trips to the peanut farms on the Katherine River and north to mission communities in (what was, in 1933) to become the Arnhem Land

Aboriginal Reserve, but they returned to Gimbat and neighboring Goodparla. Gimbat people were taken to army camps following the Japanese bombing raid on the town (and Darwin) of 19 February 1942. A group of them evaded army camp management and went bush, up the Katherine River, back into the Gimbat area, for a time, then came back to Katherine. Of those who later became involved in the Coronation Hill dispute, this wartime experience in Gimbat would have refreshed their knowledge of the area. Some Jawoyn and Mayali people have had longer associations with Gimbat than others. Some of resettled background have continued some association with waterholes and fishing places near Gimbat, but these tend to be the best-known and most widely used of waterholes. They have not retained more intimate relations with that northern country. The people who continued to relate most strongly to Gimbat were those who had lived in it and walked it in their youth.

Each of the three indigenous "principals" of the Coronation Hill dispute— Nipper Brown, Peter Jatbula, and Sandy Barraway—had a different way of dealing with the problem of intercultural recognition of a source of authority on which they could build their positions. None had in mind a horizon of political autonomy, but the course of events led to some opening out of their situation into a sense of what kinds of arguments about Coronation Hill were being made and how they might best deal with them. In the end, for each man, those responses settled into a slightly more coherent pattern than at the beginning.

Nipper Brown had lived and worked at Gimbat and been "made young man" (initiated) there. He always portrayed this as having been encouraged by Joe Callanan, the white owner/manager of the prewar period. Joe was a rugged, second-generation cattleman (his father was known to Aborigines as "Old Joe," he as "Young Joe") who worked closely with Aboriginal people, learned their language, treated them a bit rough but was respected, and had a part-Aboriginal daughter (who grew up at distance from the Aboriginal camp). It is quite possible that Old Joe, perhaps urged by older Aboriginal men to provide time and some resources, effectively put the initiatory cycle into motion.

Peter Jatbula was named after his birthplace in Gimbat. His name incorporated the name of the apocalyptic being (Bula, or Bulardemo) that indigenous people associated with the area. His name means "leg-Bula," and while "Jatbula" is first and foremost a placename, it also alludes to ways in which people incorporated the sacred tradition into their bodies. Peter had a deep sense of his connections to this area as part of his being. But he had lived in

Gimbat as a young person, and he was frustrated because he was not entirely sure exactly where the place Jatbula was. On several occasions he and I walked around the base of hills and scarps looking to match the image he had in his mind. We never succeeded in a certain identification of that place. What he as an individual remembered was now critical because there were few others who had the personal history and incentives to seek this place out.

Like Peter, Sandy Barraway, too, had grown up at Gimbat. Both men had been secluded in middle Gimbat for their "young man" initiations and had been shown some of the features of named, important areas by older men at that time.

For Peter, Sandy, and Nipper, upper Gimbat was an area of very important places. In these men's minds, there was always a web of dangerous sites, interconnected. As the Coronation Hill dispute went on, the set of sites they named as belonging to this network became more constant, but the idea of a network and the ability of places to "feel" disturbance in others was there from the beginning of my hearing stories of Gimbat.

In some parts of the area Bula was said to have been hunting and at one place encountered something that caused him to fall. At some others, Bula was underground. Mining would surely rouse him. Though it was cold down below where he was, disturbance would cause something like volcanoes, and everything—Sandy was the most articulate on this score—birds, people, ground, trees, animals—would be blown up, thrown about, and floods would cover the land, reaching "Sydney, Melbourne, overseas," as he would say. All of the Gimbat-linked people of Peter and Sandy's age and above were imaginatively seized by the power of this story. When I first began to learn of it in the late 1970s from Sandy—because he wanted me to take him to Gimbat to check if exploration was taking place there as he had heard—certain placenames and other names associated with this story (Bula himself, his wives, and others) were only ever mentioned in whispers, no matter where the discussion took place. Whispering was an evocation of power and of its regulating force on human action. By the end of the Coronation Hill dispute, some of these names had become household names, regularly printed and mentioned in the media.

As well as being given this unprecedented currency, the knowledge of the three principal men was repeatedly held up to scorn in the tribunals of public commentary, including by a purported expert, Steven Davis (see Davis and Prescott 1992), who asserted that the area was not Jawoyn in the first place, invoking a hypothetical history of their having taken over this country from others, who were conveniently not there to tell the tale. Davis also said that the beliefs concerning apocalypse were as "fresh as today's newspaper," and this was widely repeated. Still others branded the Bula tradition "archaic." Such interventions must be understood as regular features of the "sacred sites" issues of the period and the collision between indigenous and nonindigenous relations to country, not as isolated incidents.

The difficulty of publicly discussing mining's disturbing activities can be illustrated by focusing on one of the clearly located places in the vicinity of Gimbat. Called Nirlaynjurrung in Jawoyn, it is a towering hill marked on cartographic maps as "Big Sunday," a clear indication that its character as a sacred-dangerous place had made its way to the mapmakers. Peter, Sandy, and their age-mates could say a great deal about how they and their families had conducted themselves around this place in the past. They moved slowly through the area near its base; they did not talk, or they only whispered; they refrained from gathering or hunting. Older men had carefully climbed the hill because there was a large cavity near its peak. Animal movement could dislodge stones into it, and men had feared in their youth that these could rattle down inside the hill and cause disturbance. An old man (one of Peter and Sandy's grandfathers) named Berrakgolotok (literally, "Pigeon Hand"; he was a leper), accompanied by some others at a distance, had worked carefully to install wire netting over the cavity to prevent this. These were the ways of treating the dangerous places, critical experiences of caution and care that the three men had absorbed from their seniors. But mining? Blasting? Who could say? Except that the idea was alarming.

In the vicinity of Gimbat there were ancient paintings that Aboriginal people associated with the Bula story. But they were not nearly as vivid a focus of concern for them as some of the hills, "natural" locales, in the South Alligator Valley; and a particular place with stone paths and formations in middle Gimbat that the men knew to have been the location of Bula ceremony in the past. None of the three men had attended such a ceremony; its performance had been discontinued before their time. But they had had contact with an older generation of men that had attended performances, still knew songs, and they knew how the ritual was performed. This had now become a carefully guarded kind of knowledge and, even more, an imago of respect. In brief, as one might expect, ceremony involved the enactment of extreme danger and possible catastrophe played out in embodied form.

Keen (1993) has written of how the Bula tradition was rigidified throughout these processes and made into "beliefs" that necessarily had to be unchanging to be valid, thus insisting on an embalmed version of Aboriginal culture. To some extent this was an unwitting collaboration, in that the principal men were driven to regularize their statements, and public opinion demanded a much more fixed main account of the Bula story. I want to take a step back from these events and make several points about principal men's differing relations to the entire affair.

I would argue that Gimbat's apocalyptic tradition is likely to have been a "contact" phenomenon; in no way would this impugn its authenticity, its grounding in an order of value and experience. That the Bula ceremony and tradition were a product of colonial-era encounter cannot be proven, but it is a productive perspective. All of the Aboriginal people of this region were caught up in the vortex of mining around Pine Creek from the 1880s, as sources from ten years or so later make clear (Eylmann 1908, written from his field trips of the late 1890s). The attraction and impact of a large foreign population there (largely Chinese) of opium, alcohol, work, and sexual relations would have been considerable. It is clear that a large indigenous population originally of the Pine Creek area faded away, probably with high mortality and morbidity from diseases among the causes. The Pine Creek area was not Jawoyn; it was one to which they were outsiders, the in-migrants and survivors of that vortex of colonial activity. They would have been circulating back and forth to their homeland on the Katherine River and its lower reaches in the Gimbat area. Here near the Katherine River the ceremonial complex in mid-Gimbat was partly man-made, woven imaginatively together in myth and ritual practice with the features of landscape at the ceremonial site. Mid-Gimbat would have been a retreat from the swirling dynamics of Pine Creek and for Aborigines who knew that the country was not difficult to reach in a few days' walk.

One of the things that suggests the Bula story's connection to early colonial contact is its apocalyptic nature. Dangerous sites are not unusual in indigenous Australian cosmologies.[4] Yet this complex was handed down in tradition as unusually dangerous and as affecting everybody—as Sandy Barraway always said, Sydney, Melbourne, overseas, the immediate world and the known world beyond. They were claiming importance for this place. The ceremonial complex constituted as men of high degree (Elkin 1951) those who could avert catastrophe from their persons, blending this with some elements common to other regional ritual performances. The tradition may parallel contact disruption, focusing relations to danger and responsibility for managing it in specific places and forms of ritual action. This concentrating of effects made of the Bula area a kind of colonial-era black hole, as important (and dangerous) as the colonial upheavals confronting indigenous people practically and psychically. The high point of ceremonial performance was certainly in the early decades of the twentieth century, so that the three principals overlapped with a few elder men who had participated in its last performances. By the time I got to know them, older men spoke of old men they had known as the last to have attended ritual performances, though songs were preserved as part of the repertoire of accomplished singers. Though this must remain speculative, Bula may be a ritual projection of colonial cataclysm (cf. Petri 1950 on Kurangara, a cult of the Kimberley region in Western Australia). Like most things sacred in indigenous cosmology, it was dangerous to talk of it.

The fact that the force of Bula was largely preserved as a matter of nondiscursive behavior is important. Its significance in the time of Coronation Hill, however, was lived out in interaction with a range of people and institutions of Australian society who demanded that it be talked about to be validated— and be accurately mapped and measured besides. Its main purpose in the unfolding dominant mining scenario was to be revealed as something perhaps interesting but archaic and static and not an impediment.

The three principal men were dragged into speech about Bula, over and over, and each gradually became somewhat more constant in what he said regardless of audience. There is truth in what some detractors said, that the complex was in some ways "archaic"; and one comprehends CHJV's complaining about inconsistencies of location of sites. But in all of these negative positions there was something more fundamental, basically an exterminatory intent: to get rid of the problem by annihilating the Bula tradition. CHJV and others all did this in different ways by seizing upon and supporting claims that the Jawoyn were interlopers and should therefore have no influence on the mining decision; by heaping scorn on the inadequacy of indigenous knowledge and claiming its absolute recency; and in other ways. All were too far removed from concern with the Gimbat-linked people to understand (or care) what they were dealing with, and so instead they accused them of fabrications and inconsistencies.[5]

Bula had not been transmitted as a value-bearing psychic burden to people of younger generations in the same embodied way it had been transmitted to the Gimbat-linked people of Peter and Sandy's. Many younger people did not know, could not "believe," as some said, in the same way. CHJV liaison officer Andy Andrews put the entire matter into discursive terms when he dismissed it as "a lot of fairy tales." People who saw things that way inclined to the rationalism of saying: the area was mined before and didn't explode; Bula isn't true. But such rationalism did not find anchor in the deep-seated sense of Bula's significance for the three men personally. Nor did it appeal to others whose relationship to the surrounding world had been mediated by their lived experience in Bula country and by continuing reverence for the kinds of awareness and circumspection this required.

Nowhere was this kind of relationship to the world to be replicated among these people and their descendants, even for those who continue to be custodians of the area on changed ontological bases. The Bula business was indeed a primary site of struggle, derided as such by many of the involved outside parties in an era of recognitions. Its forms and the human bearers of its meanings were not familiar.

Given that there was no discursive meta-tradition for talking about Bula, no way that the men could sense to relativize the significances that they had absorbed, each of the three principals was pushed to come up with a way of dealing with the extreme pressures they were placed under. To my mind each came up with a rather different way of handling things, the clash of different orders of value explored above as each lived this.

Nipper, the oldest, told very brief versions of the basic Bula story: the significance of Bula sites and their apocalyptic nature if disturbed. He gave few other details. In person he confidently located only those Bula sites that the other two could also confidently locate, and he was not concerned to locate others (as the other two were). He knew what he knew. He had lived to be a young man in the area and had explicit memories of many minor features of place and event that could only be learned by living through them: where he was initiated; where bone packets of his mother and other particular people were located on top of nearby scarps; where fights took place among stockmen; his countrymen and companions, who had camped where; and the like. From his imposing, handsome physique and his being somewhat older, outsiders often expected him to be very knowledgeable and even more philosophical than the others, but he was not so oriented. He lived (as married man, later widower) on a can-do basis in the Aboriginal camp style of his early life and that of his contemporaries, a style that most outsiders would not be able to adapt to because of its physical hardship. He was known to his family and campmates by a range of humorous nicknames they tagged him with, commemorating episodes in their collective life in which he was typically the butt of events: "Burned Grass" (for a time when he and his wife Queenie nearly burned up in their swag [bedroll] in a grass fire because he was too drunk to notice); "Gun Fighter" (because when drunk he sometimes got into a threatening mood); "Rubbish Dump" (for a camp location); and so on. Especially in early years, when asked pointed questions by outsiders, Nipper tended to be conciliatory or inscrutable, as many outsiders found him.

On one occasion (Merlan 1991a) Nipper was interviewed by a CHJV employee attempting to gain his consent, shown a papier-mâché model of Coronation Hill, and told what would happen to the hill at each phase of exploration and mining, until at last it would be flattened. At the end of the display, asked what he thought about this, Nipper quietly replied: "Good one." In short, Nipper was being asked what he would think were this to happen. Completely unaccustomed to this kind of interrogation of his assumed interiority and unequipped to enter into it, probably also not at all thinking he was being treated as authoritative and asked for "permission," Nipper answered, as he often did, in a placatory way, giving the pleasing, short, completely unrevealing—also impersonal and often meaningless—answer.

Sandy was almost always the most fluent narrator of an "outside" version of the Bula story—that is, one that can be told to an audience. Its basics were very much like Nipper's but more prolix: there were dangerous places inhabited by Bulardemo, and disturbance of them would cause volcanoes and floods, destroying everybody and the world we know. He also told other versions that were more explicit about how people came into being, and the hunting that Bula did, leading young men adepts (in ways that verged on content that could not be publicly revealed, probably part of what he had absorbed as a young initiate). When challenged on details about particular places or overall significance, especially in the first few years of conflict, Sandy often tended to give ground and agree that there was "nothing" in places that would impede mining. Since Sandy had been the one to push me for worried trips to Gimbat from the time I first knew him (and I had a functioning vehicle), I knew that this was a concession to the moment. Sandy began to see that nothing he could say would keep all parties at bay, but he did show tendencies to be conciliatory toward the particular views of those he was presently with. However, Sandy never minded telling the story of the power of Bula sites and did not appear to think such telling would be taken as a sign that he was a "myall," or ignorant blackfella. He rather had an image of himself as someone who might be faulted by outsiders for not knowing "blackfella" things. Perhaps relevantly, he had continued to attend ritual longer in his life than Peter had; none of the three had done so for some time.

Peter Jatbula eventually developed a way of responding to approaches that seemed to satisfy outer demands and his inner needs and feelings. In the first years of conflict, he too was sometimes conciliatory. In the 1987 Senate hearing he agreed with Sandy that Coronation Hill had "nothing there." But as with the others, this did not seem to me an adequate expression of what he felt. He always referred to his father as an expert on the countryside, especially around Pine Creek, Gimbat, and the mineral fields of the wider area. His father had been a traveling man, a footwalker,[6] and had worked at many mines. Peter actually harbored some desire himself to discover minerals and had me get soils assayed in a couple of places near Katherine. But, according to Peter, his father had been very concerned about Bula and had not allowed whitefellas to "humbug" Bula places. This was the strongest line of resistance that Peter put up about Coronation Hill. Coronation Hill was called Guratba, "kurrajong rope" (a bush vine), and Peter alleged that Bula had gotten rope there. He also said his "father's law" would not allow Coronation Hill to be disturbed and that he "followed" his father's law. This became a staunch answer after the first more fragmented two or three years.

Different from Nipper and also largely from Sandy, Peter's "double consciousness" concerning most whites—his view of himself from their perspective—was that they were derisive of Aborigines and their beliefs.[7] He rarely recounted the Bula story, or indeed any "dreaming story," the way Sandy and Nipper did. When he did, it was usually to people he regarded as sympathetic and not scornful. But when the controversy began to rage, Peter did speak forcefully on some occasions, especially to the white audiences whose importance he had come to understand.

Peter had worked as a stockman and on work gangs with white laborers and had what seemed to me a fairly realistic view of the sorts of things they would think. In fact, Peter was a gifted raconteur of many kinds of stories (as represented in Merlan 2016a). But these were picaresque conventional tales of devils, hunters, trickster figures—his own repertoire consisted in a great number of these from older Mayali and Jawoyn men—as well as stories from life of hunting and walking trips, incidents and episodes of all kinds, from wartime to recent times. Of all three men, he was the most inclined to narrate his own life, using many Aboriginal narrative resources, but his repertoire was partly bounded by the limits of judgment that he had gained in his interaction with whites. His view of himself and his situation was ironic, every contretemps and difficulty that he met with expected, almost invited—a pull toward an abyss that was reflected in his drinking (but he also had periods of chosen sobriety). His view of whites in general was imbued with cynicism, that everybody wanted something and was out for himself. He was in fact capable both of racial hatred when he saw himself demeaned in a way he thought racially motivated[8] and of acceptance and approval of people's action when he saw them treat him as an equal. He had good memories of white bosses who invited their Aboriginal workers to table instead of making them eat outside, as so many did. He also had memories of himself and Nipper "belting up" a white stock worker with a stirrup who had expressed contempt for him as a "black bastard." In short, Peter had as a basic part of his personal makeup a view of himself in events from whitefella perspectives in a way Nipper never did. That meant that he had traveled some kind of distance from the quiet self-sufficient acceptance that Nipper had of the meaning of Bula. But he bridged that distance by embracing his father's law as authority. For him there was no other meaningful authority. There were people who could force you to do things, but to his "father's law" he gave the measure of consent he was capable of.

On one important occasion in 1986, he spoke to an audience brought together by the Aboriginal Sacred Sites Protection Authority in the following terms:

I don't think white people understand this rule but
We understand their rule, white man law
Our rule, they reckon we might be myall or something, we not myall
We got ceremony and we understand for European side
We understand what they got law
Not go their property
But this business long time long time ago before white man came
We don't know but father been, when we been grownup little bit
Then we been understand, we know
Because we gotim business we gotim 'nother place business
They understand this
Bulardemo business from all around
Whitefellas make a hole and they say that's bullshit
But that's not bullshit, we telling true
We true, tellim true God in Heaven, he mightn't believe in that
God but that's the white man law
When I been go school, missionary
I was gota missionary but

War been come bang! I went bush
My father been take me to mining, wolfram, tin, gold
My father been savvy gold there langa Guratba
He said don't takeim any white man, that's the law
Bulardemo by and by him rockim you and me
Shakeim that ground, you and me can't alive
Buji [if] him burn tree him burn city you and me gone
We can't stopim, no hope
Never look country
Even Bulardemo might be stopim some things but him go forever
Can't look country, finish.

A free translation: Peter doubts that whites understand Aboriginal "rule" (law, usually with special reference to ceremony).

> But we understand their law. They think we are ignorant, but we understand European law: not to go on their property. But this business [Bula] has been here since long before white man.[9] When we were small we didn't know [about it], but we grew up and came to understand. [Aboriginal] people from all around know this business. Whitefellas dig a hole, and they say [our business] is bullshit [made up], but it's not. We are telling the truth, God in Heaven. The whites may not believe in that [our] god, but that's the white man law. I was in missionary school but the war came and I went bush. My father took me to mines. He knew there was gold at Guratba [Coronation Hill], and he said, "Don't take any white man there, that's the law. Bulardemo will rock you and me, shake the ground, we can't survive. If he burns up trees, cities, we'll be gone. We can't stop it, no hope. We'll never see the country again. Bulardemo may be able to stop some things, but this will go on forever. We can't see the country, finished."

Peter's "double consciousness" is most clearly expressed in words when he reflects on whites' skepticism: The whites think we are lying. But no, we are not, we are telling truth (by) God in Heaven. The whites may not believe in our law, but that (God in Heaven) is *their* law. Implicit is a comparison between their law (which we Aborigines know) and our law (which they do not know). Though the English expression is unrefined, he implicitly proposes that whites should think in Aborigines' terms to realize that *we* (Aborigines) are telling truth as serious as white man's god in heaven.

Thereafter Peter brings in his personal history: he started school, barely, in Katherine, before the Japanese bombing occurred and he and his family went bush. That's when he went to mining camps, and his father explicitly warned him not to let whites near Coronation Hill. The consequences are dire: Bulardemo will be unstoppable, not even able to stop himself. He will rock the country, burn, and destroy. The country will no longer exist, we will not see it again.

All of the men's ways of dealing with the situation were culturally and historically inflected. But beyond fundamental shared understandings among them, their approaches to the Coronation Hill situation differed. May we not assume that responses to Captain Cook's and other early arrivals (Chapter 1) would have exhibited the same range of diversity, were we able to know more?

Coronation Hill and Political Representation

How was a resolution to be reached in all this fracas and disquiet over Coronation Hill? In this northern Australian postcolony these Aboriginal people had no stable polity as such and no confidence of being able to enact the relation they felt to country in decisive terms. So, much depended on the quality of nonindigenous recognition.

Characteristic of the "postcoloniality" of the latter twentieth century has been the evolution of greater public awareness of indigenous issues and perspectives and the felt need, and often regulatory requirement, to be seen to take them into account. There remains nevertheless a good measure of incommensurability between some elements of indigenous (and organized, indigenist) thinking and action that plays a part in such episodes as sacred sites disputes. I find useful here Povinelli's (2001) suggestion of a larger project of critique of a "rational" political economy view of the world in terms of "incommensurability." As mentioned in the Introduction, it seems to me her central emphasis is on how incommensurate worlds emerge in encounter and how they are sustained in their incommensurability. One question this chapter raises is whether these worlds are sustainable in their incommensurability. How does their contention, in power-unequal situations, change them? I think that history will force incommensurable worlds to become entangled and to partake of materials in common. This chapter demonstrates that the difference was not articulable or resolvable in the terms of political economy, the "value" of the mine economically and to nation and society, in the terms that miners, government representatives, and others suggested should reasonably be the case. Other dimensions of incommensurability touched on in this chapter include particular indigenous ways of regarding and transmitting information and modalities of response to pressured demands to reveal interiority of thinking in a consistent manner that lead to repeated misunderstandings and to a perception by nonindigenous people that indigenous interlocutors elude them. The story I have told also shows that there are generational differences among indigenous people—between those who had absorbed this area in their youth and their children and grandchildren. As well, we cannot ignore the problems and weaknesses in institutional and personal attempts to present and sustain an "indigenous position," as if there were a unified indigenous value field and a united voice.

Despite "land rights"—the Jawoyn success in claiming Katherine Gorge National Park in 1989 and portions of Gimbat Station in 1996—they have not developed a strong collective sociopolitical vehicle, notwithstanding efforts of the Jawoyn Association, for example, in this direction.

Social cohesion among people as "Jawoyn" was fragile (and this dispersed and attenuated sociality was not new). With any intensity it tended to be limited in scope to smaller subsets of relatives and associates. Cohesion was tested beyond the limit by this vexing Coronation Hill situation. Their everyday affairs were distributed over a range of places and institutions (welfare offices, health centers, community councils and associations, the National Park Board, land councils, Jawoyn Association, and many others) that constituted an array to be dealt with, asked for resources, avoided, or confronted (e.g., for nonpayment of benefits). Social intensity existed in households and fluid domestic arrangements to which, in the era of recognition, such recently fortified, larger-scale identities as Jawoyn had limited direct relevance, except for the possible resource streams that organizations might offer. There had never been any weight-bearing, overarching tribal structures, and they were not to be established easily by recognition measures. The sacred significance and renown that Peter refers to in the case of Coronation Hill was indeed region-wide, including more than Jawoyn people; but the renown of Bula was greater among people whose origins were in the Gimbat region than among Jawoyn or others from elsewhere. And because of the secret-sacred nature of the Bula complex, its locations, absence of people from the area for some decades, and other forms of social change rapidly progressing through indigenous communities over the postwar decades, Bula in the embodied, emplaced form that Nipper, Peter, and Sandy internalized was generation-bound.

Notwithstanding that the Aboriginal people had no strong determinative power—a national interest existed that could always override their views—from the late 1970s there was the new set of political conditions that mining companies were starting to get used to.[10] There would be consultation with appropriate Aboriginal parties, and there would be some effort to come up with cooperative solutions that recognized their involvement.

One powerful form of representation, common in Northern Territory and federal government and corporate circles, was the imaginative account of the great economic potential that would be forgone if Coronation Hill did not proceed. In order to make this representation more potent, some account was taken of indigenous job possibilities, so here the CHJV liaison activity was important. The representation of Coronation Hill as a source of prosperity undermined indigenous solidarity and revealed some genuine differences in perspective and values among indigenous people.

Another nationally fairly powerful form of representation was environmentalist: the mine would pollute important waterways (as had allegedly other mines in the area, also a disputed issue); it was destructive in a region of high animal diversity; it was inconsistent with the natural and societal conservation and heritage values of a national park. Just as CHJV partly advanced the case for mining through its indigenous liaison, so also did environmentalists seek to advance their views through identification of environmental with indigenous concerns.

Each of these powerful representations claimed that indigenous interests coincided or overlapped with their own. To that extent any position of the identified Gimbat principal men was marginal. And indigenous views were not unitary. So, was there a separate indigenous space in any sense?

That is debatable. There were many indigenous-chartered organizations that worked closely and for the most part sympathetically with the men, in what were presumed to be their interests: the Aboriginal Sacred Sites Protection Authority, the Land Council, the Jawoyn Association. Through their efforts, there emerged to public view an area designated "Sickness Country" because of the Bula presence. However, every specific aspect of that representation was disputed publicly. There were many efforts to deny the authenticity of the Bula tradition; to dispute indigenous attachment to the area; to question that the three principals were the appropriate indigenous people to speak for the area, for one reason or another;[11] to counter the "truth" of the danger attributed to the area in terms of the Bula tradition; and to claim that the Bula business was "archaic." All organizations that worked with the three men were aware of weaknesses in their statements, problems of consistency and of limitations on personal capacities (due to alcohol consumption, and poor health). There was no untrammeled view of indigenous concerns on grounds of sociocultural continuity. However, as the dispute proceeded, a more unified Jawoyn voice declared that the Jawoyn wanted to "close 'em up, forget about it": no mining. Perhaps the most forceful articulation of this view came from a member of the Northern Territory Parliament, John Ah Kit.[12] Ah Kit accompanied the three men a number of times to Canberra to lobby federal parliamentarians.

Given the issues, the forms of representation and the power of some, versus marginality of the men's position, no resolution of this issue of a pluralist sort was possible. Everybody could not have some of what they wanted, given the way issues had unfolded. It was mining (exploration) or not.

Speaking later of his difficulty in persuading the cabinet to prohibit mining at Coronation Hill, Prime Minister Bob Hawke said that he found "nauseatingly hypocritical" the attitudes of his colleagues in the cabinet who could accept the virgin birth, the Holy Trinity, and other pieces of belief, but treat Aboriginal people as "idiots not to be respected." Though admitting that he was in an "absolute minority" in the cabinet decision, he strongly argued that one "has to respect the beliefs" of these people: "it was a question of the expressed beliefs of the Jawoyn" (Allam 2010).

From his powerful position as prime minister, Hawke justified his decision to prohibit mining by publicly acknowledging Bula as a domain of ultimate value. In belief of a religious kind, he identified what Susan Star and James Griesemer (1989) have called a "boundary object." Star and Griesemer (1989) have written of the need to manage tensions that arise in scientific work in complex institutional settings, so that all concerned can agree on generalizable findings. Their ideas apply not only to natural science objects in museums but to any collision of "different social worlds" that cannot simply be managed by allowing pluralism or laissez-faire solutions. Collaborative solutions, they argue, require the constitution of boundary objects.

Boundary objects are objects that are both plastic enough to adapt to local needs and the constraints of the several parties employing them and robust enough to maintain a common identity across sites. They are weakly structured in common use and become strongly structured in individual-site use. These objects may be abstract or concrete. They have different meanings in different social worlds, but their structure is common enough to more than one world to make them recognizable, a means of translation. The creation and management of boundary objects is a key process in developing and maintaining coherence across intersecting social worlds (Star and Griesemer 1989:393).

Hawke constituted a boundary object by recognizing belief, in particular *religious* belief, as a domain of ultimate value. He was operating comparatively and at a high level that flew over the many conflicting and unclear matters of fact and representation in the men's account that the years of interrogation had turned up. We may not accept as true some of the kinds of things that their beliefs involve, he said, and he acknowledged he could not. But in respecting that domain, we all may have to give up other things of value. Hawke said that he would normally be pro-mining. He did not refer to the imaginary of economic potential in the 1991 public statement, nor did he propose (as pro-mining positions typically did) that economic benefits were some kind of common denominator that everybody should be able to agree on. Instead he referred to common respect for religious belief. In the strident controversy, the question of Bula was represented in confrontational terms as either completely valid (but in this case as an unchanging legacy from the past) or as "archaic" and therefore without current relevance. It was neither, for it was "belief."

This was not the first use of high-level "translation" to try to deal with the asymmetry of boundaries between concerns defined as indigenous and non-indigenous. Earlier in the twentieth century, in the first professional ethnography of an Aboriginal regional group, the American anthropologist William Lloyd Warner (1937) deliberately used the word "civilization." In the 1930s, supporters of Aboriginal people's cause, such as anthropologist A. P. Elkin (1938), based their appeal to the public for widened understanding of Aboriginal people on the basis of the equivalence of their institutions with those of the dominant society, hence their worth. From fieldwork conducted in the 1930s, W. E. H. Stanner (1966) later published as a treatise on ritual of the Daly River region a work deliberately entitled *On Aboriginal Religion*, an assertion that what they were practicing was recognizably a form of religion (not magic, something lesser and more primitive) and not reducible in

Durkheimian fashion to a sociological role. It was an expression of ultimate value.

In his own way during the controversy, Peter Jatbula also arrived at boundary object–producing comparison, as can be seen in his speech quoted above. Peter lived his everyday life in awareness of white views of Aborigines. In speeches about Coronation Hill to audiences he knew he had to convince, he also showed an awareness of the views of white Australia (you don't believe us or know our law, and so on). In this speech he developed a comparative framework in which he attempted to place Aborigines and whites on par: your god in heaven, our law; your property law, our legacy of relationship to country. Words expressing underlying and emergent boundary objects include "rule," "law," "believe"—like Hawke's "belief." Some words Peter used, like "business," have special significance in Aboriginal Kriol that white audiences would not automatically understand and might, in fact, misunderstand, given its formal identity with an English word (see note 9), and that he expected to be heard as terms of ultimate value. In fact, to white audiences Peter's words were almost always translated into Standard English. In the end, an ABC Radio National commentator concluded a 2010 program on Coronation Hill with the observation that this was the only mining project in Australia to have been stopped on "Aboriginal religious grounds" (Allam 2010).

Peter produced boundary objects he understood as meaningful. The men had to rely more upon such objects in a public dimension of their relation to the area and the contest over it. Boundary objects are collaboratively constructed. In Coronation Hill, however, and other postcolonial cases, boundaries are asymmetrically constructed. The kind of ontological attunement of the men to Gimbat was not publicly understood but construed as a matter of "beliefs" about dreamings, which some Australian audiences took to be genuine, others found "unbelieveable." The public position of the Gimbat men was made possible by recent shifts favoring forms of recognition of indigenous concerns in Australian society; their older relatives had had little success in attracting support some years earlier, except on the part of an interested person and amateur ethnologist. To shape what he understood to be a needed public position, Peter produced some of the strongest terms he could—"law," "business"— deliberately placing them in relation to notions of God and religion. The Gimbat men were continually set upon by those, including some Jawoyn, who argued for a political economy view of the situation as the desirable way forward and who generally impugned their position.

Hawke's intervention—constituting the object "belief"—enacted his power to frame. But even someone in his position could not sustain an imposition that silenced issues of economy. He shortly lost the leadership of the party and the prime ministership, making him the only serving Labor prime minister to that point to have been removed by his party while in office. In his view, he later said, the decision he took regarding Coronation Hill was a decisive element in his loss of the prime ministership of Australia six months later (Allam 2010).

CHAPTER 8

Recognition: A Space of Difference?

Recognition Reconsidered

I aim to accomplish two tasks in this final chapter. First, I want to return to the matter of the Introduction by placing Recognise in a series of what I regard as similar, government-led or approved projects concerned with indigenous-nonindigenous relations in Australia. This requires discussion of some events of recent history, but what is most important is to derive a sense of the series to which the initiative belongs and the changing terms and meanings involved. We move away from the local scenes of my ethnographic experience to the national level of indigenous-nonindigenous relations, its actors and institutions. At that level, apology, reparation, and a range of related concepts (see Chapter 6), including "recognition," signal acknowledgment of the less powerful. Once having contextualized recognition in the recent period and the specific governmental project Recognise, our consideration will be: what does "recognition" mean? Also, what has it meant in the view of Australianist anthropological authors?

Second, I return to an anthropological question set out explicitly in Chapter 1 (but considered in chapter content throughout the book). This has to do with the nature of culture over time, particularly under the conditions of settler colonialism and postcolonialism. I referred to "sedimentation" of practices, dimensions of social and cultural orientation that perfuse a range of practices and may, in and of themselves, be persistent but not easily identifiable. What perspectives does the material of this book give us on culture, temporality, and change—the dynamics of difference—under such conditions?

Reprise: Recognise

Recognise is the most recent of a series of proposals to repair indigenous-nonindigenous relations at the level of the nation-state. The first was the constitutional referendum of 1967. The referendum made no change in the citizenship rights of indigenous Australians. Rather it achieved two changes invested with symbolic importance. First, by removing section 127, the referendum allowed the Australian government to include the numbers of "aboriginal natives" when using a population base to make allocative decisions. For example, the agency empowered to administer national elections could take into account the numbers of "aboriginal natives" when determining the boundaries of House of Representatives electorates. This change had become necessary in 1962, when the Australian Parliament changed the franchise in order to permit (but not compel) those classed as "aboriginal natives" to enroll to vote in national elections. Second, the referendum removed a restriction on the powers of national government on which the colonies had insisted when writing the original constitution: they had barred the national government from legislating with respect to "aboriginal natives" within any state. This had not prevented the Australian government from exercising authority over "aboriginal natives." The Australian government took over the administration of the Northern Territory in 1911, and its legislation included the Aboriginal ordinances to which I have referred throughout this book. In addition, the Australian government administered the national social security system, and its reforms of that system had gradually rendered indigenous Australians eligible for welfare payments on the same basis as all other Australians. The effect of the 1967 referendum was to enable the Australian government to legislate about "aboriginal natives" in any part of Australia, even if that meant overriding the laws of a particular state. Those who campaigned for this change did not predict or advocate any particular use of this additional power, and the national government, since 1967, has rarely exercised it, wary of the strong sentiment of "states rights" in Australian political culture.

That is, while the referendum enabled the Commonwealth to make "special laws" about indigenous Australians living in any of the six states, it did not require use of that power and in fact did not specify that the Commonwealth must take a greater role in indigenous affairs. According to Bain Attwood and Andrew Markus (2007), the campaign for the referendum generated high expectations of major reform in indigenous affairs that were not met. In the campaign to change the constitution, no one promoted "land rights" as a likely or desirable exercise of the proposed added national government powers. When public opinion supported "land rights," the Australian government legislated only in the Northern Territory, where its power did not derive from the change made to the constitution in 1967. The referendum was represented to the public as a vote *for* Aborigines, saying "yes" to their inclusion and giving them parity in the Australian polity.

I see the referendum vote as having been consistent with public and governmental commitment to procedural fairness and natural justice, rectifying previous disadvantage and exclusion. Much of the legislative reform that effected equality and inclusion—mandated by the bipartisan postwar policy philosophy of "assimilation"—had been the work of state legislatures, and this reform agenda had largely been completed, by state and Commonwealth governments, before the 1967 referendum. The referendum was not seen as creating new or special rights, but as righting wrongs and equalizing unequal statuses. Any questions of "difference," a major concern in this book, were muted in the campaign for constitutional change.

When it became clear in the late 1970s that the Australian government was not willing to use its newly acquired powers to uphold land rights in Western Australia and Queensland, a group of private citizens (calling themselves the Aboriginal Treaty Committee, ATC) proposed that the Australian government enter into a "treaty" with indigenous Australians. Their treaty campaign (1979–83) was thus an attempt to reinvigorate the idea—strongly but unspecifically expressed in 1967—that not only the well-being but also the rights of indigenous Australians were a national responsibility, no longer to be left to state governments. By enshrining certain commitments in a treaty, the ATC considered it both possible and necessary to put certain indigenous rights beyond the reach of Parliament and processes subject to the political cycle.

The ATC sought to create an indigenous mandate rather than preempt indigenous views by elaborating treaty content. A key figure in the ATC, H. C. Coombs, thought that indigenous Australians should cede sovereignty and that the Australian government must be willing to pay a high price in this event in the form of a treaty that really would benefit indigenous Australians.[1] These ideas gained some support, especially among an educated, governmental elite. Importantly, there was some resonance with ideas being explored by a small set of politically active indigenous people.[2]

In 1985 poet, critic, environmental, social activist, and founding ATC member Judith Wright and Jean Conochie published a book, *We Call for a*

Treaty. Wright referred to an earlier proposal that had come from an indigenous source. In March 1972, the Larrakia people, whose traditional territories covered the coastal area in which the city of Darwin is located in the Northern Territory (including Belyuen, the site of Povinelli's research), had sent a petition to the prime minister, Billy McMahon, requesting that a treaty process be established. The petition was signed by five men of the Larrakia tribe. The Larrakia worked in collaboration with activist and anthropologist Bill Day, instituting an organization, project, and newsletter under the rubric Gwalwa Daraniki, "Our Land." They prepared a petition to the queen asking for recognition of land rights. This was eventually received and forwarded from Buckingham Palace to the office of the Australian governor-general, Sir Paul Hasluck, in early 1973. From there it was placed on file in the Department of Aboriginal Affairs before being deposited with the National Archives in 1975. Day has said, approximately forty years after its creation, that the petition has renewed significance in the context of the Australian government's expert panel on constitutional recognition of indigenous Australians: "In displaying the petition, the Archives has compelled historians and the Australian public to reassess it in the light of demands for a constitutional amendment that will recognise the Indigenous inhabitants of our nation" (O'Brien 2011).

In that period such a move attracted notice. A report on it was published in the *Northern Territory News* on 30 March 1972. As Judith Wright tells the story: "Little was heard of this petition in the troubled days of 1972 which followed, and it was not until June that Mr McMahon replied. It was not appropriate, he said, to negotiate with British subjects as though they were foreign powers; and the reason that treaties had never been negotiated with Aborigines was partly that of the difficulty of identifying the people and groups with whom negotiations could be conducted" (Langton 2000–2001).

This fundamental issue had come to the surface in a distinct context in 1980, when the attorney general relied on a decision in *Coe v. Commonwealth of Australia*, denying that Aboriginal people of Australia could be considered as a domestic dependent nation or organized as a distinct political society separate from others treated as (belonging to) a state. Relevant institutions of sovereignty were found to be lacking. "As to the claim to land, it was, said the majority judgment, 'fundamental to our legal system' that the Australian colonies became British possessions by settlement and not by conquest'" (ibid.). The whole of the Australian continent became part of the dominions of the Crown by acts of state whose validity could not be challenged.

A National Aboriginal Conference (NAC) was established by the federal government in 1977 to provide a forum for the expression of Aboriginal views. Following this *Coe* case, the National Aboriginal Conference nevertheless supported the idea of a treaty and sought to negotiate solely with the federal government, first for "agreement in principle," possibly to be entrenched in a reformed constitution, and, second, for more detailed agreements for various regions. The proposed deadline for constitutional reform was 1988. The idea of treaty and constitutional reform were simultaneously in play but clearly did not have a firm foothold in government, nor (then) in the courts. In June 1979, the National Aboriginal Conference raised the issue of a treaty between the Commonwealth and Aborigines. Prime Minister Malcolm Fraser and Senator Fred Chaney, then minister for Aboriginal affairs, responded positively to the initiative, seemingly seeing an interlocutor in the NAC. Unlike the ATC, the NAC raised the prospect of a specific form of agreement, called *makarrata* (the name for dispute settlement in northeast Arnhem Land) and put forward some particular points (see Brennan 1991:62; also below). Also at this time, however, a proposal was made by the late indigenous poet and activist Kevin Gilbert. Gilbert, of Wiradjuri and Kamilaroi (New South Wales) background, was also a playwright and journalist; his best-known book is *Living Black: Blacks Talk to Kevin Gilbert* (1977).

Gilbert combined with Tasmanian indigenous activist Michael Mansell, an Australian lawyer and activist who has dedicated his life to social, political, and legal reform to improve the lives and social standing of Tasmanian Aborigines, from whom he descends. Mansell had worked as a qualified barrister and solicitor of the Supreme Court of Tasmania and the High Court of Australia. He had also been both chairman and legal manager of the Tasmanian Aboriginal Centre, which he helped set up in 1972. He is the secretary of the Aboriginal Provisional Government (APG), established in 1990 as a political vehicle for self-determination aspirations. In collaboration with the NAC, Gilbert and Mansell sent a letter to Prime Minister Fraser, after Gilbert established a second Aboriginal Tent Embassy in front of an encampment before Parliament House. Gilbert's approach had little effect on the formulations by the Aboriginal Treaty Committee. Nor did Prime Minister Fraser take up the proposal.

Gilbert and Mansell maintained that distinct Aboriginal nationhood and sovereignty were the nonnegotiable foundation of any treaty or agreement. With Mansell's and Gilbert's guidance, the NAC sought: "International sovereignty, perhaps introduced through a period of trusteeship"; or "The creation of an additional state within the Australian Commonwealth governed by

Aboriginal and Torres Strait Islander people with current constitutional structures"; or "The creation of self-governing regions within the Commonwealth comprised of self-governing communities involving powers of local self-government" (Brennan 1991:62). Gilbert's impassioned arguments, published in several editions from 1987, set out his ideas on an Aboriginal sovereign position and were accompanied by various versions of a draft treaty, which he wrote and circulated, to "be executed between us, the Sovereign People of This Our Land, Australia, and the Non-Aboriginal Peoples who invaded and colonised our lands" (ibid., 76).

The Hawke government (1983–91, heading a Labor government after the National-Liberal prime minister Fraser) tried in its first term (1983–86) to legislate land rights on a national basis. It was opposed by two powerful forces: the mining industry and the Northern Territory Aboriginal Land Councils. Each saw Hawke's legislation—though for different reasons—as a threat to their existing entitlements (and both were right). Hawke abandoned his proposed law in March 1986, pointing to a faltering of public support for land rights. For advocates of indigenous rights, this was further proof that such rights should be entrenched in the constitution or in a treaty, so that they were immune to changes in political will and public opinion. In the late 1980s the High Court began to hear an argument asserting that the Crown had not legally extinguished customary indigenous Australians' land ownership. The *Mabo* case, initiated in 1982, was not concluded until 1992, but Hawke would have been well aware of its possible significance.

Hawke continued to refer to "treaty," but always with careful attention to its possible implications. In a new development the government funded the NAC to consult Aboriginals around Australia on the idea not of a treaty but whether there might be a suitable indigenous term or concept that could be the vehicle for what was intended. Or, perhaps better put, there was ongoing inexactness over what was intended. A Yolngu term, *makarrata* had become known in W. E. H. Stanner's 1968 ABC Boyer Lectures "After the Dreaming." It signified the end of a dispute between communities and the resumption of normal relations. It was summarized by one anthropologist of the region as a form of "ritualized revenge" (see Hiatt 1987); Stanner's description of the dueling ordeal undertaken by disputant parties in the *makarrata* ceremony used phrases such as "blow for blow," "the drawing of blood." The public servant delegated to report back to government on this term probably did not convey all its relevant denotations, Marcia Langton (2000–2001) has suggested (see also Rowse 1999).

In the end it seems that trying to find an indigenous term was almost surely to sidetrack the discussion from the question of broad relationship between national government and an Aboriginal polity. Although Kevin Gilbert collaborated with the NAC, the variety of proposals and their inclusion of some issues of the moment suggest that Aboriginal spokespeople experienced difficulty in finding an appropriate degree of abstraction and forward vision in these approaches to government. Besides, they were directly confronting issues the government of the day regarded as nonnegotiable. Politicians (from McMahon in 1972 to Howard more recently) have always been skeptical that there is a viable national polity. Indeed, the *makarrata* suggestion produced (indigenous) opinion that any term one could come up with might be quite different and have different implications in different indigenous contexts. And, in any case, we might ask given the lengthy temporizing over it, was any rendering of "treaty" adequate? Evidence of trepidation about "treaty" is revealed by the fact that the term "compact" was widely and alternatively used around this time. Although the differing semantics of these two terms were not widely discussed, it seems on the face of it that "compact" suggests "agreement" (close union, joined, conjunction) with lesser emphasis on the dimension of differences to be negotiated or resolved. What differences is "treaty" to conciliate?

The Aboriginal Treaty Committee and the National Aboriginal Conference were wound up (in 1984 and in 1985 respectively). If there was any substantial outcome, it appears in a Senate subcommittee inquiry and report "Two Hundred Years Later" (1983), which recommended establishing effective indigenous representation and a "compact."

In June 1988, the bicentennial year and a time of ferment, many Aboriginal groups gathered at Barunga near Katherine (Phyllis Wiynjorrotj's home community; see Chapter 5), and what became known as the "Barunga statement" of national Aboriginal political objectives was issued to the federal government. It was written on bark (following the model of the Yolngu bark petitions of 1963)[3] and presented to Prime Minister Bob Hawke at that year's Barunga (annual sports) festival. It called for Aboriginal self-management, a national system of land rights, compensation for loss of lands, respect for Aboriginal identity, an end to discrimination, and the granting of full civil, economic, social, and cultural rights. Prime Minister Hawke responded by saying that he still wished to conclude a treaty between Aboriginal and other Australians by 1990. However, nothing of the sort had happened by the time he left office in 1991.[4] The Australian Aboriginal band Yothu Yindi wrote the song "Treaty"[5] to commemorate the statement, and this became a huge success worldwide, popular in its own right beyond any meanings understood to be attached to it in Australia. There was then a hiatus in public treaty talk and another concept, reconciliation, began to take center stage, from beginnings in the 1980s to its apogee in the 1990s. At this point, "treaty" had been an item in public discourse, but not associated with any term recognition at this level. "Land rights" had also been focal, but (as above) Hawke had been unable to legislate land rights at a national level: there was considerable resistance and a consistent current of public opinion that Aborigines were getting too much. There was also divided public opinion on the effects of Australian colonization on indigenous people, which later was fought out in the "history wars" (see Chapters 3, 6). There was, however, some public understanding that many Aborigines lived in deplorable conditions, with divided opinion on the reasons for this. "Reconciliation," then, came in as a term of public discourse that was intended as a bridge between indigenous and nonindigenous spokespersons, viewpoints, and populations.

The federal Council for Aboriginal Reconciliation (CAR) was formally established on 2 September 1991. The term "reconciliation" came to be widely used in the 1990s, especially through the South African Truth and Reconciliation Commission. There, and perhaps everywhere, it has a strong Christian resonance. But CAR was implemented before the South African commission (enacted 1995). It is useful to amplify relevant, specifically Australian conditions.

The Northern Territory land claims regime had been operating since 1976, returning land to Aboriginal people under inalienable freehold title. That did not in itself mark a change in the national status of indigenous issues, since that statutory regime was held to be "beneficial" and did not recognize a distinct indigenous legal regime except indirectly, as the practices of customary land tenure. Governments were aware that the long-running *Mabo* case was shortly to deliver judgment. A positive result for the claimants there would produce a finding that native title existed prior to colonization and was recognized at the common law. This would require a new kind of accommodation. In the event, the government of the day (under the Labor prime minister Paul Keating, who challenged and replaced Hawke) responded to the *Mabo* finding of 1992 by rapidly enacting the federal Native Title Act 1993, which was in large part to assure "certainty" to nonindigenous landholders and (partly to that end) established a regime of native title claimancy. There was some difference and some commonality between major parties on native title.

Both major parties registered views that the judiciary had been activist in relation to the *Mabo* decision. Some key parliamentarians of the Liberal-National coalition registered the view that "native title" unfairly emphasized indigenous "difference," was prejudicial to "other Australians," and would not satisfactorily address indigenous "disadvantage." Keating's legislation of the Native Title Act of 1993 was intended to reassure those opposed; but acceptance of native title only became bipartisan after 1998, when (under the Liberal-National prime minister John Howard) amendments were made to the Native Title Act, which, it was then generally agreed, contained its implications (Silverstein 2013; Fitzmaurice 2007). By then, resource corporations had begun to adjust to its requirements to consult and negotiate with indigenous groups and accepted this to a much greater extent than had been the case in the era of the Coronation Hill dispute (Chapter 7).

Another influential factor was the report of a Royal Commission established to look into black deaths in police and prison custody. The Royal Commission into Aboriginal Deaths in Custody (RCIADIC) (1987–91) was appointed by the Australian government in October 1987 to study and report upon the underlying social, cultural, and legal issues behind the concern-causing deaths in custody of Aboriginal people and Torres Strait Islanders, after an arrest or conviction, whether by suicide, natural causes, medical conditions, or injuries caused by police. The final report of 1991 concerning ninety-nine deaths in custody concluded that "the immediate causes of the deaths do not include foul play, in the sense of unlawful, deliberate killing of Aboriginal prisoners by police and prison officers. More than one-third of the deaths (37) were from disease; 30 were self-inflicted hangings; 23 were caused by other forms of external trauma, especially head injuries; and 9 were immediately associated with dangerous alcohol and other drug use. Indeed, heavy alcohol use was involved in some way in deaths in each of these categories" (RCIADIC 1991: vol. 1, chap. 3). The report did conclude that glaring deficiencies existed in the standard of care afforded to many of these prisoners. Focus is on the disproportionate incarceration of indigenous people (cf. Weatherburn 2014). This brought more fully than before the evidence of Aboriginal struggle and the extent and nature of social dislocation and disadvantage suffered by Aboriginal people and communities. The commission recommended a process of reconciliation in communities particularly affected; indeed, the entire Australian community.[6]

But what, indeed, was reconciliation to mean? Several meanings can be attributed to the term: the restoration of good relations; the settlement of historical grievance; and the making of conflicting systems consistent or co-existent (de Costa 2002:280). There is some overlap of course, but each in its way has had a place in the reconciliation process in Australia. The stated purpose of CAR was to "achieve recognition and respect for the unique position of Aboriginal and Torres Strait Islander peoples as the Indigenous peoples of Australia through a national document of reconciliation and by acknowledgment within the Australian Constitution" (CAR 2000: chap. 2).

Some indigenous leaders were skeptical of CAR's statement of goals from the outset. Aboriginal and Torres Strait Islander Commission (ATSIC) chairman Gatjil Djerkurra, a Yolngu from northeastern Arnhem Land, opined that indigenous Australians were unlikely to see the draft declaration as representing an accurate reflection of actual indigenous aspirations and entitlements.

Reconciliation proceeded, hailed by CAR (like Recognise) as a "people's movement" characterized by engagement between indigenous and nonindigenous people in local community and other venues. Following the *Bringing Them Home* report on the "Stolen Generations" (Wilkie 1997; see Chapter 6), the popular demand for reconciliation included honoring the recommendation of the Human Rights and Equal Opportunity Commission (HREOC) that Australian governments apologize for their interventions into Aboriginal families. Manifestations of this construction of "reconciliation" included the preparation of what were called "seas of hands" (public art installations, plastic hands planted on stretches of grass), documentation of indigenous histories, and eventually "sorry books," public records in which signers could record their personal feelings about the history of child removals, to be presented to representatives of indigenous communities.[7]

Howard explained his persistent and publicly visible refusal to apologize to the Stolen Generations on three grounds: first, one generation cannot assume the responsibility for the deeds of others; second, removal policy was not uniform, and some children were justifiably removed while others were not; and third, to apologize would set in train a "dangerous" psychological reaction, whereby people might become complacent and think the indigenous box had been ticked. He also made it plain that he thought indigenous people should join the "mainstream," though he thought there was room for regard for the unique place and history of indigenous cultures and people but implied there was not for some kinds of difference. A national apology for the removal of indigenous children was not issued until more than ten years later, in February 2008, by Prime Minister Kevin Rudd. In the interim, however, an unbending Prime Minister Howard (1996–2007) refused to apologize. He expressed sorrow and regret, but refused to make an apology, which had become the expected public expressive term in the representational struggle to which Recognise belongs. Meantime, in the winter of 1997, every parliament in Australia moved some kind of resolution of "apology," producing a variety of expressions.

Toward the end of the reconciliation decade, in the Australian Constitutional Convention of February 1998, a decision was reached to formulate a new constitutional preamble, as a marker of social change. It was to include recognition "that Aboriginal and Torres Strait islanders have continuing rights by virtue of their status as Australia's indigenous peoples" (Australia Constitutional Convention 1998: vol. 1, p. 47). This was a concise statement of what some Aboriginal (and Torres Strait Islander) Australians had long believed to be true; but what rights?

The force of this statement was completely countered by what immediately followed: "Care should be taken to draft the preamble in such a way that it does not have implications for the interpretation of the Constitution . . . Chapter 3 of the Constitution should state that the preamble not be used to interpret the other provisions of the Constitution" (ibid.).

In short, the force of the new constitutional preamble was to be seen to be contained and to have no consequences for its interpretation. The preamble issue went to referendum along with a second issue (which persists at varying levels in the electorate): whether Australia should become a republic and thus independent governmentally from the United Kingdom. Both referendum items failed. The constitutional preamble debate was acrimonious. There was strong enough public support for the existing Australian system of constitutional monarchy that the alternative republic proposal did not prevail.[8] As to the preamble mention of Australia's indigenous people, in the end it was described by the leader of the federal opposition, the Australian Labor Party's Kim Beazley, as a "no-risk" preamble that "has no legal meaning" (Parliament of Australia, House of Representatives, *Hansard*, 11 August 1999, p. 8435).

In the events summarized above (from the 1970s to about 2004), we might retrospectively see "reconciliation," the predominant national-level term in the 1990s, as having been a bridge between earlier national-level events and debates (pivoting in the 1970s and 1980s on "treaty," questions of land rights, and Aboriginal political representation) and the present period. During the 1990s, contention over indigenous suffering and responsibility for it became the key issues over which reconciliation was sought and constituted the particular semantics of reconciliation. Terms that have since resurfaced more clearly, especially "sovereignty," were not prominent then but have reemerged with the question of (constitutional) "recognition."

Two further government initiatives deserve mention here, bookending "reconciliation" trends. First, in 2004, its eighth year in power, the Howard government abolished the national indigenous political organization, the Aboriginal and Torres Strait Islander Commission (established by the Hawke Labor government in 1990), declaring some of its leadership corrupt and its contribution to indigenous well-being inadequate. Second, in 2007, the last year of its eleven years in power, the Howard government launched what is known as the "Intervention," more fully the Northern Territory Emergency Response (NTER). In this highly controversial move the federal government took control of seventy-three "prescribed" (remote-area) communities in the Northern Territory, to monitor and change conditions seen to be undesirable in them. Parliament enacted changes to welfare payments, indigenous land tenure, community governance, policing, and customary law in relation to concerns about a variety of perceived problems: endemic substance abuse-related violence, mismanagement, and economic stagnation. The Intervention measures included ones aimed at reducing cash going toward substance abuse by controlling welfare payments, expanding alcohol restrictions on Aboriginal land, enforcing school attendance by linking income support to it, increasing policing levels, and banning pornography.

The NTER was the federal government's response to the Northern Territory government's publication of a report on child sex abuse called *Little Children Are Sacred* (Wild and Anderson 2007). The response received bipartisan parliamentary support but has also been widely criticized (Behrendt 2007; Langton 2007; Sorensen et al. 2010). Don Weatherburn (2014:123–25), in a restrained appraisal, observes that no one examining the figures concerning child neglect and abuse can doubt the need for sustained intervention[9] to change conditions but agrees that the manner of its conceptualization, implementation, and its effects are debatable. Most immediately relevant here is that the lack of consultation with which the NTER was imposed places it outside a meaningful framework of recognition of difference.

Most controversial about the NTER, I would argue, is that it recognized the extent of indigenous suffering (see also Sutton 2001, 2009; Merlan 2009) but at the same time withdrew government recognition of indigenous political capacity. Its focus was on the reality of suffering and disadvantage; its mode of implementation, non- or minimally consultative (despite general acknowledgment and much argumentation that change can only be effected with the engagement of the people concerned).

The Emergency Response has since been replaced by the fairly similar Stronger Futures policy. Perhaps the main, continuing focus has been on a policy of "closing the gap" of indigenous disadvantage as measured, for example, by great differences in life expectancy between indigenous and nonindigenous Australians (Zhao and Dempsey 2006). In 2008, the Council of Australian Governments (COAG) agreed to six targets to address the disadvantage faced by indigenous Australians in life expectancy, child mortality, education, and employment. This is in many respects a continuation of the emphases on "practical" reconciliation sounded confrontationally by the Howard government and on a "practical-symbolic" dichotomy associated with the conservative government's stance, as well as with another very long-standing debate in Australian indigenous affairs between competing notions of the appropriate relationship between equality and difference. Separating the latter are values seen to allow space for indigenous difference as against others that take health values, for example, to have priority even if ways of achieving health goals are transformative of indigenous difference (Kowal 2015).

These previous trends and cycles set the stage for the present Recognise (constitutional recognition) initiative. There has always been a question, what is "recognition" to mean? In their focus on suffering and disadvantage, previous key terms had understated, even submerged, what might be seen as the more political side of indigenous-nonindigenous contention; that is, position/s that emphasize indigenous political engagement and capacitation. Terms of recognition constitute a spectrum, some less contentious than others. Among the least contentious, and now publicly most widely accepted, is the issue of "priority of occupation." The Australian public has come to *recognize* this about indigenous Australia, and it is common to hear and read of indigenous occupation on the continent going back forty thousand (some say sixty thousand) years.

Correspondingly, on the Recognise website, indigenous Australia is said to be (the first) part of an Australian, common, national history. Slogans such as "We are the first Australians" configure a continuity between the first Australians and the others. Senator Aden Ridgeway has said, "Constitutional Recognition would allow the first chapter in the Australian story to be acknowledged. Our history is part of the shared story of every Australian and our Indigenous heritage is something that enhances and enriches every one of us."[10]

Ridgeway speaks of "our" history (he is indigenous) as part of the "shared story of every Australian." But a growing number of indigenous spokespeople find such formulations merely anodyne. Perhaps correspondingly, major Australian columnists have suggested that recognition of "more than 60,000 years of indigenous life on this continent and the place of indigenous peoples in our national life has a deep moral and political momentum," with 84 percent of voters in support of indigenous recognition (in these terms) (Kelly 2015).

A second term on the spectrum is one of "race" and the eradication of racial discrimination. This might seem surprising and requires a little more background detail. In 1967, with the referendum (see above), the national government was given powers to legislate on behalf of indigenous people. In 1975, to bring Australia into conformity with international human rights standards, a Racial Discrimination Act was legislated federally (which became an element later in the High Court's justification for the finding of "native title" in 1992; see below). In 1998, the Howard government used these powers to make (native title) law that some considered adverse to indigenous interests, and they litigated. The High Court ruled that there was nothing in the constitution that obliged the Australian government to use its power beneficially. It was just as lawful to use that power adversely. This destroyed what many considered to have been the achievement of 1967 and was perhaps one trigger for return to the question of constitutional recognition. This time the focus would be not on the right of the national government vis-à-vis the states, but on the rights of indigenous people vis-à-vis all governments: a constitutional barrier to adverse racial discrimination.

In 2012 a final report (*Recognising Aboriginal and Torres Strait Islander Peoples in the Constitution*) was delivered by the Expert Panel on Constitutional Recognition of Indigenous Australians, which had been charged with consulting on constitutional recognition.[11] The Expert Panel (Expert Panel 2012) recommended that two sections of the constitution be repealed. One is section 25 of the Australian constitution, titled "Provision as to races disqualified from voting," which states, "For the purposes of the last section, if by the law of any State all persons of any race are disqualified from voting at elections for the more numerous House of the Parliament of the State, then, in reckoning the number of the people of the State or of the Commonwealth, persons of that race resident in that State shall not be counted." A second had been earlier modified. As initially drafted, section 51(26) empowered the Parliament to make laws with respect to "the people of any race, *other than the aboriginal race in any State*, for whom it is deemed necessary to make special laws." The referendum vote of 1967 had resulted in deletion of the words in italics, thus enabling the Commonwealth to make laws in relation to Aboriginal people. The Expert Panel (Expert Panel 2012) further recommended that a new section be added to the constitution that prohibits discrimination on grounds of race, color, ethnic, or national origin. But this should not preclude the making of laws for the purpose of "overcoming disadvantage, ameliorating the effects of past discrimination, or protecting the cultures, languages or heritage of any group."

Following on from this, another proposed constitutional section was to recognize both the national language as English and Aboriginal and Torres Strait Islander languages as the original Australian languages and part of the national heritage. A suggested crucial "recognition" section 51A was proposed to read as follows:

> Recognising that the continent and its islands now known as Australia were first occupied by Aboriginal and Torres Strait Island people;
> Acknowledging the continuing relationship of Aboriginal and Torres Strait Islander peoples with their traditional lands and waters.
> Respecting the continuing cultures, languages and heritage of Aboriginal and Torres Strait Island people,
> Acknowledging the need to secure the advancement of Aboriginal and Torres Strait Islander peoples;
> the Parliament shall, subject to this Constitution have power to make laws for the peace, order and good government of the Commonwealth with respect to Aboriginal and Torres Strait Island peoples.

Thus, prohibition of "racial discrimination" has become one of the terms of constitutional amendment enjoying wide acquiescence. It has however become linked with the also widely supported issues of preservation of and respect for cultures (complexity in this notion unrecognized) and languages.

Affirmation simply of priority of occupation and national community is ever less what indigenous leaders expect from the Recognise process. Its semantic spectrum includes a more contentious array of terms, among them political capacitation and sovereignty (and perhaps also acknowledgment of settler responsibility for indigenous dispossession and thus, to some degree, for present indigenous conditions).

In 2004 nationally known indigenous spokesman Noel Pearson composed a thoughtful long essay, "A Rightful Place: Race, Recognition and a More Complete Commonwealth." In it, he addresses (among other things) the issue of constitutional recognition, generally considering recognition desirable, but envisioning a rather different process and key terms. He endorses conservatism (the ground he feels dominant politics to occupy) as truly respecting cultural specificity and diversity for its inherent value. He then suggests that any moves made now must recognize, within the nation, specifically indigenous rights and interests and the fact that there were "peoples" here before the British came. He paints a picture in which national unity is a good but to be served by the acknowledgment of interests and peoples that were prior to it (and, what remains somewhat implicit, may differ from those of the nation at large): an argument for recognition of indigenous difference, involving not just difference construed as emblematic or "cultural," but different forms of life. He too suggests that existing "race clauses" in the constitution need to be removed (see above), but as only one element of difference. He views the constitution as a "rulebook" that sets out power relationships, such as those between the Commonwealth and the states.[12] It is a practical document, not one for aspirations and symbolism: these can be set out elsewhere. But *if* the constitution is properly seen as a rulebook, then it should make provision for indigenous people to be heard in national affairs. The key phrase here (I suggest) is indigenous political capacitation. To that end, Pearson proposes a mechanism, establishment of a new kind of body, to guarantee an indigenous voice in national affairs. Pearson's focus is much more squarely on difference and, correspondingly, political measures than are many proponents of the Recognise initiative who take priority of occupation, banning of racial discrimination, and respect for cultures and languages as their semantic foci.

Pearson has since made this set of proposals more explicit. It sidesteps the constitution as the place for "recognition," advances the case for a Declaration of Recognition outside of the constitution and proposes an indigenous body that would have a say on affairs of state that affect indigenous people. As Pearson later spelled out elsewhere (Declaration launch speech, 13 April 2015), the proposed body would not have power of veto, and it would defer to parliamentary sovereignty. But the model would require tabling of the indigenous body's advice on any particular piece of legislation.

Pearson started to make this kind of alternative proposal back in 2004. Years have passed since then, and, if anything, moving the constitutional recognition agenda forward has begun to seem more urgent to supporters in government and less desirable to indigenous people. This is precisely, I suggest, because the political issues in the recognition spectrum have come to seem more important, even crucial, to them, while others (such as "priority of occupation") are now more widely accepted. There are divisions among indigenous participants in the debate, and critics never tire of pointing this out. The indigenous chair of the Indigenous Advisory Council, for instance, has declared Pearson's proposal unacceptable and even dangerous.[13] But even more fundamental is the fact of the widening disagreement about the central terms of "recognition." More politically pointed terms of "sovereignty" and "treaty" have come back into the debate.

Other indigenous responses to the Working Party's recommendations have contended that they are inadequate, insufficiently substantive, or not touching on central issues. In mid-2014, Celeste Liddle, an Arrernte woman and National Tertiary Education Union (NTEU) indigenous organizer, declared that the Recognise movement was by no means widely accepted by indigenous people and that rushing it might set back the campaign for a treaty with indigenous Australia. Sounding a key term, she also made it clear that a treaty process involved recognition of "sovereign peoples" of the country. Greens senator and indigenous affairs spokeswoman Rachel Siewert has also called for a treaty process, or multiple treaties, around the "unfinished business" of sovereignty never ceded. Constitutional recognition should not be purely symbolic," the Greens have argued, but would recognize the sovereignty of Aboriginal and Torres Strait Islander peoples.

Both prominent indigenous spokesperson Warren Mundine (see note 13) and the notorious opponent of liberal views on indigenous affairs Andrew Bolt[14] have turned the "race" tables, declaring Noel Pearson's proposal in danger of being "racist": no other "race" of people will have a body set up in the constitution looking after them, Mundine has said.

We can now return to some questions concerning Recognise posed in the Introduction. Why is Recognise said to be a people's movement? One answer has to do with expectations: any move to change the constitution by referendum must have popular support or gain it over time.[15] Why does discussion persistently focus on racial discrimination, rather than what we might see as the more comprehensive diagnosis of indigenous situation, historical structural injustice (which involves, but is not limited to, racial discrimination)?

Dominant conservative political opinion (of which the initiative Recognise is part) has cast constitutional recognition as welcoming Aboriginal and Torres Strait Islanders as the first stage of a national history, adding depth and richness to the national narrative. Framed this way, the absence of mention of indigenous people in the constitution is seen as a gap, a needful thing, a job left undone, a failure to recognize indigenous people as part of the Australian story, indeed the first part. But what of political equivalence, which some indigenous spokespeople (like Kevin Gilbert) had long demanded? And what of the sense articulated by Noel Pearson: a difference within? A set of interests, rights, and concerns now caught up in the Australian nation that might nevertheless continue to differ from those of the others in the nation? This clearly sends up warning flags to government and others; and many of those flags have written on them "race," taken as an inflammatory, inherently discriminatory category that the nation must shrive itself of. The idea that it is racist to insist on distinct indigenous rights and identity has long been a tenet of a certain liberal position that considers notionally "equal" treatment *the* priority regardless of historical circumstance (Merlan 1994b).

Recognise is framed as a people's movement, presented as democratic and alternative to being seen as state-led or imposed. It is to be taken to express the democratic will of the people to include indigenous people as "first Australians." Discussion persistently focuses on "racism" as something that indigenous people may (like others) suffer from. A more explicitly historical focus would come much closer to recognizing "nativeness" as something that can be, and has long been, racialized but comes with distinct presuppositions and histories.

Here some of the distinctions long made by the late Patrick Wolfe are useful. In his work, he refers to the concept of "invadedness" (1994, 1999). Indigenous people were invaded, and in that context and its long-term aftermath, they were racialized: they came to be seen as members of what was initially seen as a primitive, later more simply despised and depreciated, race, scheduled for whitening if not elimination. But as shown in Chapter 6, racialization is not a consistent process, nor one that can be understood independently of its historical context. In 1886, Victorian administrators were quite prepared to adjust the relevant racial boundary so that "half-castes" were not to be considered "aboriginal natives" but sent out into the broader community to find their way. Racialization is clearly a dimension of colonial process. In the case of Australia, racialization cannot be dissociated from bounding differences that have consistently distinguished natives and their descendants from settlers, including some who have little "fraction" (in the old vocabulary) of indigenous blood (Grant 2016). The natives of Australia were made intelligible, but their way of being was eclipsed, as a category of racially distinct people. Only more recently, postwar, have social justice issues come to predominate in indigenous affairs. We saw (in Chapter 6) that many people of indigenous background are no longer completely distinct, either racially or in many other ways, from settlers. But this has not dissolved the difference between those who came to settle and those of native origin who have had to live with the consequences of settlement and their understandings of it and themselves in light of it.

The concept of sovereignty also remains to be considered; it has long been a term of the activist vocabulary. So far in Australia, land rights have been the major medium of attempted reconciliation of the enormous disparities produced in encounter between indigenous and nonindigenous Australians (Merlan 2007). Has this amounted to recognition of sovereignty?

Most indigenist positions considered "radical" (like that of Kevin Gilbert, in the round of treaty discussion years ago) insist on recognition of sovereignty and sovereignty never ceded. Recall, however, the Aboriginal Treaty Committee's position that indigenous Australians might negotiate to give up sovereignty in return for substantial settler concessions. This view did not take preservation of indigenous sovereignty to be nonnegotiable, though some indigenous spokespeople, like Gilbert, did and do. The *Mabo* case recognized a form of precolonial title, but analysts have not seen this as equivalent to recognition of sovereignty (Silverstein 2013; contrast the earlier case brought by Coe challenging Australian sovereignty, in notes 16 and 17). *Mabo* is understood rather as signifying something else: that the indigenous population had a preexisting system of law, which would remain in force under the new sovereign except where specifically modified or extinguished by legislative or executive action. The *Mabo* court did not alter the traditional assumption that the Australian land mass was "settled" rather than "conquered." Instead, the rules for a "settled" colony were said to be assimilated to the rules for a "conquered" colony.

Altogether, the legal finding of native title constructed a partial equivalence with "property": indigenous people can be recognized as native title holders and can avail themselves of native title rights where those rights have not subsequently been validly extinguished.[16]

In all of this it is to the Crown that sovereignty is attributed, whereas to indigenous people is attributed native title, which inheres in customary indigenous laws and traditions and must be demonstrably current to be recognizable at the common law. It is an arguable presumption that if the Crown acquired sovereignty, it acquired it from somebody or some source. It has, however, been an explicit judicial point that the courts cannot challenge the Crown's sovereignty.[17] One can imagine legal argument to the effect that "sovereignty" is acquired by the colonial power essentially in relation to other possible colonial powers, who are thereby excluded from it. Long-standing (if qualified) notions of tribal sovereignty in the U.S. Constitution (Chapter 6; note 11 of the present chapter) remain unmatched in the Australian context, even by the most far-reaching of its cases affirming the source of native title in the traditional connection to and occupation of the land. The *Mabo* case is understood to have rejected the doctrine of *terra nullius*, or "land of no-one." As Andrew Fitzmaurice (2007) has shown, the phrase *terra nullius* was not in use in the eighteenth and nineteenth centuries as justification of dispossession of Aborigines in Australia, but was applied anachronistically by historians in the twentieth and then by the High Court of Australia to describe the legal doctrine that no sovereign and no system of law preceded the law that Britain brought to Australia. *Terra nullius* does approximate the application of the principle of the first taker in natural law and the idea that property is created by use to justify dispossession.

In sum, the *Mabo* decision did not affirm a doctrine of indigenous sovereignty.[18] The *Mabo* case sought, successfully, to persuade the High Court to review critically the way in which the Australian state had exercised its sovereignty (as distinct from the claims of the failed *Coe* case). And that is seemingly because of an extrajudicial, political axiom: it is the right of the colonizer to determine who has sovereignty.

Some indigenous activists have taken a view of sovereignty as a political assertion that they want recognized (cf. Reynolds 1996); Pearson's view is less explicit on this point. Along with critical discussion of "sovereignty" as a mode of governance (Muldoon 2008) has come a variety of recent proposals reinterpreting the concept and setting out less absolute notions of sovereignties at different scales, differing in extension. Thomas Biolsi (2005) and Jessica Cattelino (2008), writing of Native American contexts, have observed that one might think of sovereignty in a variety of forms, and, in the plural, as sovereignties shared with other sovereigns. One might think of sovereignty as enjoying and being able to live a life according to the understandings of one's collectivity and having forms of authority one can bring to bear on doing so. Audra Simpson (2014) has explored a variety of ways in which Mohawk establish their sovereign entitlements by contesting and refusing those of the encapsulating nation-states, the United States and Canada, and seeking to vitalize their own space (and time) of sovereignty (cf. Bruyneel 2007). What interpretations of sovereignty may yet emerge in the Australian situation, if debate proceeds, remains to be seen. In my view, advocates of indigenous sovereignty (taken in the sense of full, untrammeled political authority) have not given clear indications of the practices that would actualize it. How does "sovereignty" become specifiable? Are any concrete measures able to fulfill both indigenous demands and expectations of sovereignty in concept and practice?

Initiatives like Recognise represent activation and reworking in the public sphere of conceptualizations that usually have a long, and often complex, genealogy. The preceding section has, accordingly, been historically detailed and necessarily complex. It is only in light of what has preceded the current Recognise debate that we can understand its current national semantics: its overt and covert acceptations. Discussion has enabled us to see what (now and over the last few decades) has come to be more widely agreed. One such feature is "priority of occupation" (though its implications remain unspecified and potentially contentious). Another is the need to do away with "racial discrimination." To that has become attached, in a particular form, the issue of "recognition" (and positive valuation of) indigenous "cultures and languages." However, the conditions of feasibility for maintenance of these remain only vaguely specified in discussions of Recognise, and forms of "difference" remain largely understood in cultural as opposed to political terms. More problematic, and more contentious, terms of "recognition" include those of political capacitation and its mechanisms and the possible meanings and practices of "sovereignty." Each of these terms sends different signals concerning the kind of indigenous Australia to be recognized. A federally funded convention of indigenous delegates concluded a meeting on 26 May 2017, at Uluru in Central Australia. As expressed by influential delegate Noel Pearson, "The Uluru statement rejects mere symbolic minimalism in favour of practical reform. It calls for a constitutionally enshrined voice in political decision-making that affects our people. And it endorses a Makarrata between us and the commonwealth."[19] Previous "mere" statements of recognition were seen as tinkering. Instead, the delegates' call is for a referendum that would put to the public a proposal for a constitutionally mandated indigenous representative body to its place in Parliament. There would be discussions concerning treaties with indigenous people outside the constitution, in the name of Makarrata: this process of peace-making after conflict has been revived once more in the national debate. I now consider particularly anthropological views of indigenous-nonindigenous relationship that have turned on or broached issues of recognition.

Anthropology of Recognition

In *The Cunning of Recognition* (2002), Elizabeth Povinelli develops an analysis of the way in which Australian settler society and its liberal state have devised institutions that "recognize" indigenous culture. This has only been by making it commensurate with their world: that is liberal cunning. Philosopher Charles Taylor (1994), acknowledging the Hegelian (master-slave) dialectic but taking it in a new direction, argued that collectives have rights to positive freedoms and that the "recognition" and preservation of encapsulated and constrained cultural identities is part of what a good life can be, for which institutional provision should be made. Contra Taylor's optimism concerning this, Povinelli sees an *in*capacity of liberal states to come to grips with alterity. Her own central concern is with a notion of the "otherwise," alternatives to existing arrangements. Each existent, she proposes, brings with it its own otherwise, or possible derangements and rearrangements. Ethics involves commitment to bringing new existents into being, something inherently disruptive of power relations (Povinelli 2014).

Another anthropologist, the Caribbeanist and Australianist Diane Austin-Broos (2009:128), has made two comments relevant, first, to the empirical grounding of one of Povinelli's main detailed critiques of state action, its handling of recognition of "traditional" linkages in land and native title claims; and second, with respect to the broader question of conflictual difference, social transformation, and suffering. First, with respect to cunning (and land claims, which figure in Povinelli 1993, 2002; as well as Merlan 1998), Austin-Broos contends it is hard to imagine that the legal system of a nation-state that has usurped an indigenous people could ever duplicate in its jural forms the preexisting system of man-land relations. State intervention has been complex and not only yields what recipients take as benefits in some ways, but also—Povinelli and others would point out—results in misrecognition, at the same time having considerable authority to impose it. Patchen Markell (2009)

observes, with respect to formations and policies of multiculturalism (or indigeneity), that state institutions play a fundamental role in mediating relations of recognition; these are not only person-to-person relations as in
Hegel's parable. Indigenous peoples face situations in which industrialized,
bureaucratized formations are addressing colonized subjects who have been
very differently organized and whose access to the instruments of governance
is invariably conditioned by the very forces they seek to deal with, creating
many spaces for complex kinds of recognition (of identities, forms of practice,
and modes of behavior), as well as confrontation and negligence. This chapter
has been especially concerned with that level of interrelation.

Second, Austin-Broos (2009) observes that indigenous people have themselves changed. The burdens and violence that Arrernte (indigenous people
of Central Australia) labor under are not just a matter of state policy in the
domineering past or more recognition-aware present but also result from
courses of change that have been set in motion in the encounter, bringing
conflict with them as people are made to revalue their world. The fact of
living with constant external pressures, reevaluation of possibilities, diversification and fragmentation of sources of value and practice, brings with it
forms of suffering that are disproportionate for people who have been recently dispossessed, devalued, and urged to remake their lives. We may also
note that this urging comes not only from outsiders and unfamiliar institutions but as well from people (for instance, indigenous politicians, community workers, family members, and so on) who assert or assume degrees of
identification with those subject to these processes and are often thought to
be more effective communicators on this basis. One implication that Austin-
Broos draws from her research is that Aboriginal adults need to recognize
schooling as essential for their children. This is by no means (yet) a universal
recognition in indigenous communities I know. Interestingly, however, in my
experience, conviction on the part of adults of the need for schooling and
capacitation of the young to take new opportunities often goes hand in hand
with a newly patent conviction that it is important for younger people to
"know" local cultural practices, even if this comes to involve explicit (rather
than implicit) teaching.

Clearly, there have been major impulses aimed at reshaping the values and
practices of indigenous people over recent decades. Some of these (discussed
in earlier chapters) have been highlighted and designated by specific policy
terms: assimilation; and then, only somewhat contradictorily, self-
determination. While the theme of self-determination places more emphasis

on continuing indigenous identity and practice, this is not to discount or be at the expense of skills and entitlements made possible by earlier programs of assimilation. Many changes that have had major effects have not been highlighted in broad policy terms (for example, the sweeping of remote-dwelling indigenous people into the expanded welfare system was not so singled out, presumably because it was not identified as a positive policy goal but an unavoidable practical measure).

Much ethnographic and critical work that has taken seriously the nature and operation of states and state bureaucracies in relation to indigenous people has shown how much of what occurs is contradictory at best. Health and other indigenously linked bureaucracies are self-perpetuating, circular, and inevitably create new opportunities for intervention (Lea 2008a). Their circularity generates aspirations even on the part of some of the bureaucratically encultured to get outside them. Versions of indigenous alterity are sometimes seen as promising ways beyond encapsulation in bureaucratic measures (as per Coulthard 2007), but difficult to achieve, and often greatly transformed in contact with a bureaucratized lifeworld (Nadasdy 2003; Lea 2008a).

Frantz Fanon (1952) and others who have seen the importance of a "psycho-affective" dimension of colonial domination have realized how, as the Amerindianist sociologist Glen Coulthard (2007:454) puts it, "the power dynamics in which identities are formed and deformed were nothing like the simplistic hegemon/subaltern binary depicted by Hegel." We have seen indigenous people become historically invisible, then visible to the state as subjects to be made to conform to recognizable ways of living, and/or to bureaucratic administration, management, and categorization. Categorization and identification, and census over time, are part of this play of (in)visibility. Such processes interact with intimate personal formation but are not reducible to the personal; they also have institutional dimensions. Recently, with the greater demand in liberal states to recognize diversity as a matter of personal freedom, we have seen the apotheosis of liberal state categorization: self-categorization, marking a break with past practice by handing over to individuals who had been closely categorized by others the capacity to elect what one is, for purposes of census, as well as self-identification. Categories are historical products, however, and so no such movement is free-form. Questions of "recognition" are made more complex in such devolution, multiplying the range of perspectives that actors may enter into with respect to specifications of identity, and evaluations of the distribution of authority and legitimacy with respect to them. On the face of it, the state devolves the role of recognition to social process conceived as taking place outside the state, but complete independence of state processes is illusory.[20]

Another complexity of recognition in historically changing situations is the fraught question of what happens when the categorized, racialized indigenous "other" is not completely distinct from oneself in a specific sense (for all its novel mutuality, one not imagined in the master-slave dialectic). This is the question of self-other in physicosocial mode, the question of "mixed race," when those deemed or self-designated indigenous and nonindigenous look at themselves and each other and recognize that they are not completely distinct, not even—or especially—on the level of physical makeup (Chapter 6). If recognition involves the formation of the self in relation to others, why is racial mixture so typically problematic and marked by many forms of denial and assertions of completeness, the refusal to see the self in the other and the other in the self? Recent Australian ethnography and reporting have documented the complexity of self-other relations in this mode, revealing both tendencies to coexistence and mutual identification, as well as strong patterns of indigenous-nonindigenous separatism (Burbidge 2014; Cowlishaw 2004). In Australia to date, recent conditions appear to have favored people with some indigenous biological background identifying themselves as indigenous without remainder. Earlier conditions favored self-identification by such people of themselves with the residual dominant category where this seemed possible. Clearly questions of power and politics of survival are involved. Australia today seems, more than before, prepared to accept as "indigenous" many people who clearly are of mixed indigenous and nonindigenous ancestry. Expectations concerning the content and meaning of being "indigenous" remain in daily negotiation in Australian life and (for many, both indigenous and not) entwined with concerns of "authenticity."

Dynamics in Review

I began by describing this book as about relationships between indigenous and nonindigenous people at different points in time and especially about "difference" as detectable and active in those relationships. I defined differences as identifiable forms of being in common, together with some sense of commonly shared values, that contrast with other forms similarly held in common by "others." The aim in each chapter has been to explore kinds of difference and the extent to which difference has served as a mode or pathway of engagement or a delimiting boundary, in the first place between indigenous and nonindigenous actors, but subsequently in more complex ways. The book's aim thus has not been to examine "culture/s" as separate but to examine what we understand as cultural by considering difference in indigenous-nonindigenous engagement and its implications.

This is a kind of field I have previously tended to call "intercultural" (Merlan 1998, 2005). I used this term mainly to go beyond what seemed to me to have been a predominant anthropological focus on continuity of indigenous "cultures" that seemed to eschew emphasis on the kinds of changes that colonization set in train. That continuity focus is less pervasive in Fourth World and Australianist anthropology than it was some time ago, but it recurs in many different forms in public, legal, and other spheres as well as in some social science styles of writing.

I take action and interaction, and the kinds of shifts that are visible through these lenses, to be central topics for anthropologists; and I take the indicators of such shifts as important indexes of what is cultural. One must take seriously the possibilities of change, often dramatic, violent, and rapid, in local cultural orders in ways that reveal aspects of what seems "cultural" as the products of encounter.

In 2016 I visited an indigenous community in northern Colombia, main elements of whose allegedly "traditional" diet, as some inquiry revealed, were apparently introduced by colonists in the nineteenth century. Similarly, I suggested in Chapter 7 that the place-based, secret-sacred ceremonial complex of Gimbat is very likely to have been, in many respects, generated in its specificity in response to the rapid changes of regional colonial incursion in the late nineteenth and early twentieth centuries (with, no doubt, commonalities and continuities with other ritual-cosmological forms of thought and action). In a broader vein, several chapters described colonial-period interrelations of a violent sort that produced differentiation within and between Aboriginal people as "insiders" (those who generally complied with colonial imposition) and "outsiders." This progressive differentiation was never absolute and always bristled with thorny issues of continuing relationship among indigenous people across the indigenous-nonindigenous divide in the light of some collaboration with outsiders (as do new events of rupture of comparable kind, such as the revolt of Larry-Boy, Chapter 6, in personal response to the introduced, racialized system of gender relations that accompanied pastoralism). On the one hand, progressive differentiation between insiders and outsiders produced a new sense for many Aboriginal survivors of their ancestors having been "wild" and unknowing, as evidence in their lack of understanding of the new order; and of themselves as different and more knowing persons, with a sense of some value in the new order, its materialities and activities. But this change was multifaceted and complicated. It involved the progress of an ever clearer indigenous realization of a divide of domination between indigenous and nonindigenous people and the racialization of blacks and whites as types (Chapters 5 and 6). In addition, it involved the collision of new categorical ways of relating to and thinking about others with particularistic, permeable indigenous ones.

For most chapters consideration of difference and its implications has involved identifying a sort of event or medium in which difference is detectable and interpretable in terms of characteristics of social action and mode of being on the parts of differing participants. Such participants interact immediately with each other, but how they do so is also shaped by prior practice, influences, and conceptualizations.

To attempt to understand what is cultural (shifting focus away from "cultures" as notionally distinct) is not, however, to dismiss questions about what persists in and through social action and how we may conceptualize this. I introduced this as the issue of "sedimentation" and return to it below.

Differences abounded and were noticed in early encounters, in ways revealing of cultural tendencies, some of which, I have argued, were and are persistent over longer spans. But difference, though observable and often attributed kinds of social value, was not necessarily boundary demarcating. Indigenous people from first encounter were keenly interested in outsiders' skin color, as compared to their own, and this was a principal ground for early designation of outsiders as ghosts. This designation now persists as a survival in many indigenous languages. For indigenous people to categorize outsiders as ancestral spirits, and even particular ancestors, did not inherently present them with an impervious boundary, but rather it presented a potential way of bridging difference. Their way of doing this was often to attribute to outsiders a particular identity and status, and thus to suggest their social incorporation in particular terms.

While indigenous people in some parts of the country continue to apply some forms of transmitted identity schemata to include outsiders (social category designations, kin identifications, and so on, that provide a social modus operandi if not more), it seems that the specific modality of identification of outsiders with ghosts is no longer current, or at least is uncommon. The conditions of its earlier general possibility included the absence of a sense of a categorical, ontological divide between living and dead, rather than produc-tive, bridgeable difference. It is not at all clear that such an ontological divide has become firmly established in many indigenous settings: I have personal experience in some of a continuing sense of ancestral presence among indig-enous people; Marie Reay (1949) long ago noted for New South Wales that ideas of spirits and ghosts were strongly persistent among indigenous people whose lives had undergone much change in other ways. But in any case, part of the establishment of a more categorical divide as one between whites and Aborigines has been the growth of other ideas about who and what whites are, much greater familiarity with their ways and the content of their lives, but not necessarily a corresponding sense of greater social involvement with them, except in specific instances and usually at small scale.

Much remarked-on tendencies toward indigenous imitation in early encounter were treated in Chapter 2 as evocations of the other in the self. The imitativeness commonly observed among indigenous people was based on their observations of difference but oriented toward possibilities of identification.

Indigenous people in early encounter were also attuned to the question of sex identity, its difference or similarity to themselves, a difference partly ob-fuscated by the unfamiliarity of clothes. The issue of sex identity was, certainly in colonial times but also thereafter, highly gendered and often led to offers of women as a bridge to identification between indigenous and nonindigenous men. This was quickly transformed in the radical development of this kind of offer toward expropriation of indigenous men, or at least sidelining of their centrality in such arrangements, sexual bombardment of indigenous women, and reorientation of sexual offers toward material exchange and rather less toward social engagement on any sort of relatively equal (male) terms, as had been practiced among indigenous men.

Chapter 3 pointed to a set of values and practices concerning materiality that historically is shown to have differed greatly between indigenous people and outsiders, was highlighted in early encounter, and has been an arena of contestation since, throughout great change in everyday materiality. Aborig-ines precolonially were hunter-gatherers with little movable property. They honed skills that allowed high performance with materials and ideological-technical assemblages they had developed. Chief among these was an orien-tation to the material world through practices of mutual identification and differentiation. The countryside was the material-ideational assemblage of highest value, involving knowing and relating to places in all the dimensions social science conventionally recognizes: economic, political, religious, and social. People and countryside were intricately linked in ways that constituted much of the emplaced and socially relational character of indigenous person-hood. This was widely and sometimes willfully misunderstood by outsiders who had little idea of the cosmological and interlinked nature of these rela-tions. On the one hand, the mobility of indigenous life was long misinter-preted as a lack of indigenous attachment to place, a nomadism (though many settlers in fact knew Aborigines to express relationships to places and regions, and said so). The network-like character of indigenous social organization, with its extension across space, was also generally classified as some sort of tribalism. But its character remained unclear to most outsiders and was usu-ally understood as determinate and bounded in a way that misrepresented indigenous sociospatial practice in which differences are sources of connection.

Outsiders came instead with their own repertoire of portable things and modalities of interpersonal engagement with which they hoped to "conciliate" the Aborigines. These were not temporally or spatially networked, as were indigenous relational modes. Early evidence shows that Aborigines did not immediately value clothes and many of the portable "things" that outsiders hoped to intrigue them with and saw as clear improvement of their condition. Aborigines are reported to have had some curiosity about many of them, but their modalities of relating to things differed then and, variably, continue to do so. Transformation of indigenous orientations to things and their uses has turned out to be a matter of long-term process, highly differentiated according to the form of colonial impact, presence, and mission (pun intended), and directly implicated in changes in the formation and character of persons.

The Tasmanians Baudin encountered immediately appreciated things that bore resemblance to those that for them embodied transcendent value, and similar patterns are reported from all over the continent. Interactions involv-ing materiality open into a vast subject matter that connects with the pro-found shift in manner of life that all indigenous social orders have undergone. Some of the kinds of changes were illustrated in Chapter 3 (on the develop-ment of indigenous livelihood as display and objectification of indigenous culture, and in commentary on transformation of livelihood and consump-tion in a market economy, and related reorientation of values). Archaeologist Denis Byrne (1996:102) argued some time ago that the tendency in his disci-pline, consistent with a nationalizing project of finding a "deep history" for Australia, had been toward valuing and retrieving distinctive and untouched indigenous material culture (the "separate cultures" approach, with its particular valuation of continuity), rather than exploring material interface. The latter would involve "that relatively horizontal (post-1788) space or terrain across which are distributed the traces of the Aboriginal contact and post-contact experience" that could yield better understanding of the course of change. In discussion of a more recent trajectory, Austin-Broos (2003) has argued that with inclusion of Aborigines in a welfare economy has come Arrernte objectification of kin relationships in terms of commodities and cash, representing a major ontological shift from a heretofore embodied, emplaced modality of relationship that emphasizes mutuality of identity. Chapter 3's coda explored the destruction of property as a way of living out conflict points to tension in the changing person-thing nexus.

Beginning with indigenous views of colonial violence as I came to know them, Chapter 5 opened out into discussion of what I called indigenous "recognition," ways of knowing others (contrasting with other acceptations of recognition, as discussed). This was identified as place- and kin-based, its genius a combination of spatial and personal extensibility and specificity. Discussion of especially the kin-based nature of indigenous organization has, in recent Australianist literature (since the influential text of Myers 1986), largely been subsumed and transformed into a discourse of "relatedness." This generalizing term may not go far enough toward suggesting the differentiated nature of practices concerning both place and kin.

Extensibility in a kinship mode and relations to places both tend to change in character in indigenous life settings that are more sedentary and reoriented toward cash and consumption. The indigenous place- and kin-based modality of recognition allowed kinds of identification even with outsiders whose relations with them were driven at personal and other levels by purposes inherently disruptive of indigenous life, as long as they could be incorporable in some ways into indigenous life at close quarters. Chapters 5 and 6 identified sexuality as a key modality of encounter and sometimes incorporation of outsiders, with the vulnerabilities as well as transformed life courses this has produced. It also produced some key kinds of difference that the Australian state (in ways partly parallel to other settler states) has taken up as matter for ordering, categorization, and management in different ways over time. Discussion of this has provided a lens through which to trace changes in state and governance. It gives a view of state powers' resetting racial terms of reference in a long-term project of national homogenization (and only much more recently, of redifferentiation and valuation of indigeneity as national cultural heritage—not at all a complete change, but one much more inflected by contemporary ideologies of personal freedom). While assimilation of people of "mixed race" to the settler category seemed at least to partly contradict earlier national emphasis on (racial) homogeneity, I have suggested that the absence of a felt structural bipolarity in the Australian context (such as existed in the United States), made racial absorption seem feasible, and stark racial difference transitory, into the postwar period with its heightened concerns of human rights and equality.

Beginning in the 1960s, "race" became unacceptable as a policy category; original issues of "assimilation" morphed into one of sociocultural assimilation, not, however, fully freed of its grounding in racial categorization. Political liberalization of the period around 1970, beyond notions of freedom and equality, also involving one of culturally specific rights, turned into a policy of "self-determination," one aspect of which was "self-definition" of people themselves as indigenous. This led to a newly fashioned bipolarity, a "postcolonial demography," of especial significance where colonization had been of longest term and most intense interaction with outsiders. People who were formerly excluded from calling themselves Aboriginal, or were reckoned in fractions and seen as on the way to assimilation, could redefine themselves. The indigenous category now is capacious, comprehending people who have highly variable ways of life, support, education, and so forth—but, I argue, has given indigenous identity, or "Aboriginality" in older terms, a certain political potency, or potential, which it did not have before.

All of the chapters have offered perspectives on distributions and exercise of power. Regarding early encounter, it was suggested that preparedness to look for and at the other rather than not look is evidence of differences in power or capacity to make arrangements in the world conform to one's intentions. Outsiders were prepared and eager to find Aborigines; the reverse was not initially the usual case. Likewise, colonial and settler modes of dealing with difference were much more boundary demarcating than permeable or relational; they placed Aborigines in a distinct and usually devalued category of persons, as compared with Aboriginal modes of recognition, which were particularistic, network-like, and of limited scale (Sansom 1982). Hence European designations for Aborigines were more thoroughly bounding, as was the later colonial generalization of indigenous people as "treacherous." Indigenous preparedness to act the other imitatively, to make bodily offers, to recognize in terms of notions of kinship and particularities of connection, all evince greater permeability.

As we might expect, permeability has the eventual consequence of considerable transformation of indigenous practice and thought, greater and more profound (I would say) than changes in settler thought and practice. There have, however, been continuing shifts in the relation to indigenous people and affairs at the level of the nation-state, in complex relation to the social bases and acceptance of change.

Chapters (especially 3–6) have pointed to many overtly violent and dramatic changes in indigenous forms of life and livelihoods, including the implications of such change for relations to country, persons, and materiality. Undoubtedly ways in which all these dimensions intersect are altered under transformed conditions of life. Although people like Phyllis Wiynjorrotj never lived a hunter-gatherer life outside colonial influence, she and others nevertheless lived a form of life in which they absorbed an embodied-emplaced sense of themselves, such as hers to Melkjarlumbu, and Peter, Sandy, and Nipper's to the initially remote, then later highly contested, region of Gimbat Station. The lengthy collision and revelation of difference of Coronation Hill occurred because (and in a period when) miners and governments had to pay attention to indigenous concerns as these were formulated in relation to resource development and a range of other contexts. The conflict brought the question of indigenous difference, entitlement, and its persistent abnegation to the surface in a space of contention occupied by a variety of powerful interests. Many of them were proponents of a political economy of development as not only in the best national interest but in the best indigenous interest in its neoliberal emphases on job readiness, assumptions of responsibility, and exit from welfare dependence. The space was occupied by many people in business, government, and the general public who were personally skeptical or derisive concerning the emerging dispensation of recognition; and others who were committed environmental and indigenist activists. The kind of difference the three male principals brought to this conflict was strangely powerful in one way and limited at the same time. The conflict exposed indigenous people involved in contentions with an intensity they had not previously experienced. It also revealed differences of experience and values going forward among those of a supposedly single indigenous socioterritorial grouping, the complex differentiating effects of change. Their descendants experience places as ones of renown, significance, and personal and family attachment, but in different terms as compared with those embodied by Peter, Sandy, and Nipper.

The kinds of profound changes this book has dealt with were prefaced in

Chapter 1 by discussion of "sedimentation." There I commented on the need for diversification of notions of habitus and sociocultural transmission in order to sharpen our capacity to distinguish among actions, processes, events in a way more consistent with emphasis on practices as cultural—learned, transmitted, in history—rather than on "cultures." This kind of move seems ever more necessary as we reflect on complexity, interconnections, and also multiple ways in which transformations occur and open up new possibilities.

To accept such complexity and interconnectedness, in other words, is not to give up on questions of what comes forward from past to present in practice, and how—that is, on the cultural—but to suggest that some aspects of this are more deeply entrenched than others and communicable in different modalities. Evidence for this kind of layering and differential sedimentation should be an important aspect of critical ethnography.

In this regard certain aspects of self-other relationship discussed in the book appeared to be deeply entrenched, transmitted, and communicated as indigenous difference in a range of otherwise rapidly changing circumstances. Observable in early historical encounters, an indigenous modality of not looking is present in many contexts: direct gaze ("lookin' at") is experienced by many indigenous people as confrontational. Aborigines were and are sometimes not prepared to look at others with whom there is no form of established being in common and not prepared to meet their looks, taking the path of refusing sensory interaction and the resulting influence that one can no longer remain outside, psychically and physically.[21] Exploring and arriving outsiders were perfectly prepared to "look at" the other and to make of the "native" an object of experience and inquiry (just as tourists at corroborees were so inclined, and many are today; in contrast, in many places Aboriginal people resist placing themselves in such a position; see Haynes 2009 on rangers in Kakadu National Park).

I observed in Chapter 1 that under many circumstances complete refusal to engage can only endure for limited periods; but a relative and more firmly institutionalized refusal can endure for long periods and through disruptions, and may be intensified in deeply unequal social interaction. Sensory circumspection—refusal of the creation of a sensory space in common—occurs often today in copresence, especially between indigenous people and outsiders, as a mode of managing lack of commonality, in an intensification of difference of a sort widely discussed in indigenous Australia as "shame" (indigenously understood as a form of respect, but also expressive of boundary demarcation, keeping the other at a distance).[22] This way of living difference is an embodied attitude that I referred to as deeply sedimented, permeating modes of bodily comportment, speech, and emotion.

At the same time, other forms of indigenous difference have some evident openness to change and may interact with sensory and affective patterns. Ways in which indigenous people and communities conceive of foreignness and nearness are undoubtedly much changed in different circumstances in various parts of the continent. Everywhere, it has shifted from the strong projection of otherness and unfamiliarity onto spatial distance (as when George Grey was told to kill everyone on his travels beyond a certain point), toward greater acceptance of possible commonalities at greater remove, including with other heretofore unknown Australian indigenous people. But sameness and difference, perhaps especially among indigenous people, continue to be significant in different ways and places—an orientation to definitions of self and other prefigured, for example, in indigenous resistance to generalization of *makarrata* (discussed above), that this might mean different things in different places; continued in forms of indigenous localisms and loyalties today, but also constantly exposed to possibilities of transformation in a whole variety of ways. Certainly in many places known and knowable people are not limited to members of a kin-based local social universe, although strong tendencies toward local Aboriginal commonalities remain significant. Undoubtedly, in many places, descendants of localized indigenous populations have a sense of (revalued) localization within wider frames, including national and international ones with the varied points of attachment these offer.

As the discussion has suggested at various points, kinds of transformation cannot be understood as simply the result of external action; nor do external influences remain purely so. Changes set in train over time have produced forms of change in habit, action, social process, vulnerability, social suffering, as well as perceptions of changing opportunity, that cannot be treated as if solely the product of colonial history or state policy (as Austin-Broos 2009:268 has observed).

First sections of this final chapter have explored the meanings and dynamics of "recognition," in relation to the current initiative Recognise. There is of course the question what *non*indigenous people expect and hope may emerge from any act of recognition of this sort. Most shared between indigenous and nonindigenous perspectives is enhancement of Australian national identity by treating the 40,000-year Aboriginal prehistory as part of the common genealogy. There is no doubt an irony here, that a long period of nonrecognition of Aborigines by the state and settler society is being followed by one in which other Australians want to treat Aborigines as "ancestors," much as some of them had earlier done to Europeans. Another product much desired by some is renewal and rededication of national identity in light of its violent and dispossessory origins. Some indigenous representatives desire recognition of indigenous autonomy—"sovereignty"—that makes anything other than recognition of indigenous political equivalence with the Australian state seem unacceptable.

Indeed, insofar as this project is understood as involving transformation of indigenous status in relation to the nation-state, changing indigenist critique and emphasis have returned to long-articulated themes of recognition with a specifically and pointedly political set of meanings: acknowledging sovereignty (or sovereignties), unceded indigenous relationship to lands (not necessarily to "Australia" as larger entity), and other forms of acknowledgment of difference. Difference between indigenous and nonindigenous people and forms of life shows some very broad, continent-wide patterning (as driven by the structures of colonization, settler political economy, state policy, and broad cultural difference). But any wider Recognise project will, I suggest, have to have the capacity to take account of the different forms of experience and the different kinds of transformation proceeding in indigenous communities and lives. Those senses of scale and recognition are partly exposed and open to change, but also deeply sedimented and constitutive of continuing difference.

Modalities of both indigenous and nonindigenous action have undergone transformations, and neither side remains unchanged, but the ways in which they change bear the imprint of the social schematizations from which they come. The quality of indigenous emphases in the matter of the Recognise initiative indicates concern with justice, enablement of freedom from domination, and distinctively political rights, alongside strong ideological insistence on cultural survival. With regard to others' dealings with indigenous people, recognition should imply more than recognizing a category or individuals as such; it implies recognizing the practices and implications of other ways of living and making relationships. One is put in mind of Hannah Arendt's (1976:479) observation that beginning is a supreme human capacity. In the series in which I have suggested Recognise be placed, above, one senses the seeking for normative authority, on both indigenous and nonindigenous parts: search for a new beginning that goes beyond what has been and does not simply respond to it. The current Recognise initiative urges interrelation but does so in ways that seem oriented (with some indigenous support and acquiescence) toward incorporation into a polity conceptualized as Australia and at large scale; in these ways, predetermined. That may be only realistic, but alternative proposals may yet seek lesser reduction of a new beginning to preceding and existing politics.

In the end, it is the process of history—former independence and way of being, invadedness and its complex, continuing aftermath—that indigenous people are asking to be recognized.

NOTES

Preface

1. The granting agency was then known as the Australian Institute of Aboriginal Studies, in Canberra, the national capital. It is now known as the Australian Institute of Aboriginal and Torres Strait Islander Studies.

2. This is related to the fact that many capital developments in the north were investment driven, restless capital in motion, and did not represent seriously assessed productive developments; see Donovan 1981.

3. Usually referring to their own condition of "wildness" as they subsequently came to see it (see Rose 1992; Trigger 1992; Merlan 1978, 1998; Lewis 2005; Cowlishaw 1999; some of these works concerning the wider region as well as the immediate Katherine area).

4. Represented in Collman's 1988 ethnography of pastoral workers in fringe camps around Alice Springs being caught in the intersection between casualized male pastoral labor and a female- and especially mother-oriented welfare system.

5. Reminiscent of White's (1991) depiction of the drastic consequences of alcohol in the Great Lakes region of North America. See Brady and Palmer 1984; Brady 2002, 2007. For Aborigines, as for Australians in general, the question of citizenship as a moment of political entitlement is elusive. Many Australians both indigenous and nonindigenous think that Aborigines became citizens as a result of a federal referendum in 1967. In fact, by altering two sections of the constitution, this referendum enabled federal censusing of them and federal legislation in relation to them and constituted a centralization of indigenous governmental management, not citizenship as a formal status. Many indigenous people equate the lifting of restrictions on access to alcohol as a moment of citizenship (as per Sansom 1980), which occurred in 1964. Until federal legislation in the post–World War II period, all Australians (Aborigines included) were British subjects. The Nationality and Citizenship Act of 1948 enabled a distinction between permanently and temporarily residing British subjects, designated Australians "citizens," and in one section confirmed the same citizen status of Aborigines. However, throughout the 1960s Australian citizens were still required to declare their nationality as British. The term "Australian nationality" had no official recognition or meaning until the act was amended in 1969 and renamed the Citizenship Act, then in 1973 renamed the Australian Citizenship Act. It was not until 1984 that Australian citizens ceased to be British subjects. With this history of blending (comparable to some other Commonwealth countries with incremental nationality and citizenship changes), it is small wonder that many, including Aborigines (whose pasts have also been characterized by continuing marginalization and discrimination), find it difficult to identify any event of

"citizenship" and in fact tend to attribute this to other events they consider signal, such as Aborigines felt legalization of access to alcohol to be.

6. In the same way white southerners in the United States felt their local knowledge of American blacks to be much more informed than that of white northerners even into the 1960s, before great black population shifts northward (M. J. Anderson 2015:212).

7. It was in the 1960s that the first former fringe-camping Aborigines were allowed to occupy houses within the town (see Chapter 5). These were slightly set off in a circuit and managed by the Department of Aboriginal Affairs (as the institution was then called), who selected tenants based on their evaluated capacity to keep a household.

8. See Thiele 1982 on the bureaucratic imperatives, which encourage wider scope.

9. By "dreaming" is meant the creative period or temporal dimension in which the landscape as indigenously understood was fashioned by creator figures, animal and human. A dreaming is an animal or human figure understood to have created particular locations in the landscape and sometimes to have traveled some distance, creating a dreaming track of linked sites. Words in some indigenous languages for this continentally ubiquitous concept may be identical or linked to words for "dream," but sometimes are not.

10. Discussed in Merlan 1998; Povinelli 2002; Austin-Broos 2011. Wolfe (1999:206–7), inspired by Herbert Marcuse's (1965) phrase "repressive tolerance," epitomizes in the adage "the more you have lost, the less you stand to gain."

11. Levitus 2009, following social scientist Charles Rowley, calls it a "carapace"; see also Rowse 2006a; Martin 2003.

Introduction

1. Illustrative of these different approaches are, first, Tonkinson 1978; H. Morphy 1991; Keen 1994; Myers 1986; and Trigger 1992; second, Cowlishaw 1988, 1999, 2004; and Wolfe 2016; third, Collman 1988; Morris 1989; Lea 2008a; and Kowal 2015. Some further commentary follows concerning these approaches.

2. And often as prolegomena to a politics.

3. I do not see this position, despite the word "ontology," as identical to the set of views advanced over the last few years in anthropology and sometimes collectively referred to as the "ontological turn" (see Carrithers et al. 2010; Viveiros de Castro 2012). That work tends to focus on standardly cultural, presumptively continuous values, practice, and materialities as ontological difference, or instantiations of irremediably "other" ways of being. The "ontological turn" thus licenses talk in terms of different "worlds" rather than of different epistemologies or representational states as per interpretive analytical positions. In my reading, Povinelli is concerned with the challenge that differences (such as queer subjectivities, indigenous forms of difference) present to global capital and liberal national forms of organization, and the question of distributions of suppressive power. Difference and undecidability, though ontological markers of different ways of being, emerge as such in the intersection with those forms of organization and not as independent "cultural" phenomena.

4. As has been reported of other colonial situations; see Chapter 1.

5. Indigenous peoples include those of the mainland, generically called "Aborigines" but who often refer to themselves in other, regional terms (Koori, Murri, and so on), and Torres Strait Islanders of the island chain between Queensland and Papua New Guinea. Possession Island, referred to in note 9 as the place from which Captain Cook designated the coast, is just off the northern tip of Cape York Peninsula.

6. Byrne (1996) argues that appropriation of this long-term indigenous presence requites Australian desire for a national past.

7. Muldoon (2008) discusses colonial (nineteenth-century) cases that potentially brought into question sovereignty as a precondition for social order and its applicability in these specific cases.

8. The present prime minister of Australia, Malcolm Turnbull, led a referendum movement for an Australian republic, against those who continue to support constitutional monarchy for over a decade and concluded that the movement had, in the idiom, "Buckley's chance of winning" because, basically, nobody was interested (in the change). The referendum did indeed fail (Turnbull 1999). William Buckley was an English convict who was transported to Australia, escaped, was given up for dead, and lived in an Aboriginal community for many years. Buckley's chance is "no chance."

9. On Possession Island, see note 5. Cook (1955–68: vol. 1, p. 387) wrote in his journal: "I now once more hoisted English Coulers and in the Name of His Majesty King George the Third took possession of the whole Eastern Coast . . . by the name New South Wales, together with all the Bays, Harbours Rivers and Islands situate upon the said coast." In 2001 the Kaurareg people successfully claimed native title rights over the island (and other nearby islands).

10. That is, land in which interests belong only to the Crown and to no other party.

11. Arendt (1976) identifies the potential in mobility to subsume by dominant power.

12. The Boyer Lectures began in 1959 as the ABC (Australian Broadcasting Commission, now the Australian Broadcasting Corporation) Lectures. They were renamed in 1961 after Richard Boyer (later Sir Richard), the ABC board chairman who had first suggested the series, broadcast every year over the period September–December on ABC Radio National. W. E. H. Stanner was the 1968 Boyer lecturer, delivering the series "After the Dreaming." The "dreaming" is the continentally known term for the creative period or temporal dimension in which the landscape as indigenously understood was fashioned by creator figures, animal and human.

13. Henry Reynolds, shortly to become involved with Eddie Mabo and the long-running *Mabo* case, began with a focus on the frontier conflict between European settlers in Australia and indigenous Australians (1972), as did Lyndall Ryan, who completed a thesis on the gruesome colonization of Tasmania in 1975 (rewritten as Ryan 1981).

14. Kelman 2013 carefully examines comparable strife over commemoration in the establishment of a battle (or massacre) site in southeastern Colorado.

Chapter 1

1. Aboriginal concepts concerning human-nonhuman and kin-stranger typifications are scattered through the literature. Hamilton (1979:44) describes a concentric arrangement of the familiar for the Desert Yankunytjatjara, from an inner circle of relatives to spheres of lesser known beings. Lesser known people could be identified as relatives under some social conditions. Nevertheless in most indigenous societies alienness, as well as a spectrum from human and possibly incorporable to unknown and nonhuman, seems to have been projected onto geographic space. See also Strehlow 1947; Musharbash 2016 for relevance of typifications to "whitefellas" (*kardiya*).

2. Sutton (2008:48) too reports this phenomenon in seventeenth-century contact of Dutch sailors with Aborigines in Cape York Peninsula, while also noting a range of other responses; he refers to it as "studious ignore."

3. As in North America, exploration and settlement occurred at very different times across the continent; cf. Nabokov 1979:22.

4. Merleau-Ponty's conceptual suggestions are useful but need to be brought to consideration of not just an immediate encounter but longer-term social contexts, their tensions and forces.

5. Anthony Pagden suggests we reinterpret this by saying that certain cultural worlds may be less adapted to resisting a colonial predator if they do not share that predator's cultural skills (Todorov 1999:xi).

6. In "Steel Axes for Stone-Age Australians," an Australianist paper of the "collapse" genre, Lauriston Sharp (1952) argued that the introduction of the steel ax changed relations among the Yir-Yoront of Cape York in manifold ways: relations of dependence of the young on the old, of women on men, in the totemic system, in religious practice, and elsewhere—such that the introduction of the steel ax could be said to presage the collapse of the entire society. Undoubtedly the introduction of foreign material items was consequential in many ways. But is this not linking too many things from the start, too deterministically, to something portrayed as "one" material introduction, just one element of change? In sum, any work of this kind needs to consider the various levels at which engagements, forms of interaction and orientation, may be understood and seek to understand the range of responses in different areas of social organization and activity.

7. Relatedly, Trouillot (2003:100) observes that in the North American context of the early twentieth century the concept of "culture/s," drawing on Enlightenment tradition and the German romantic reaction, was "launched as a shield" by such institution-building notables as Franz Boas against increasingly virulent racism and manifestations of racial power that had influenced constructions of separateness of culture/s in the first place. It was important that all peoples had cultures and also that cultures were not understood as determined and inextricably entwined with "race," a concept commonly used prejudicially. Trouillot is critical of the insistence on separateness of "race, language and culture" as a dehistoricizing and decontextualizing move that obscured power dynamics.

8. In the same way, one no longer needed to invent functional explanations for the morphological categories of language to which he also devoted much attention; rather, they were embedded in traditional language forms.

9. Many other theorists have contributed to the debate on the more or less explicitly conscious awareness, e.g., Michael Polanyi, G. H. Mead, students of emotion, social cognition, and many related topics.

10. Ramsey (1983) argues, however, that much of the prophecy so characteristic of indigenous "first contact" stories in native North America—"this was foretold"—must be seen as retroactive imaginative reworking of earlier accounts, casting events of arrival as having been predicted and prepared for in the fabulous past. In some accounts of relatively late explorer arrival, myth versions are recorded that cast explorers such as Simon Fraser (who made a canoe expedition in territory of the Lillooet, British Columbia, in 1808) as "Sun," another member of the party as "Moon." This reveals unexpected events in some of the conventional characterizations of myth (while other accounts of arrival from the region remain more "factual"). It seems strongly characteristic of the Pacific, and of Australia, that arriving explorers and whites were often understood as "ghosts" or ancestors.

11. There is debate on whether Australian languages are best classified into two large groupings: Pama-Nyungan (all historically related, even if distantly) and non-Pama-Nyungan, composed of a diverse set of subgroups. For an overview of the arguments, see Blake 1988; see also

Evans and McConvell 1997. In any case, the designation of whites as "dead" or "ghosts" occurs across this conventional division.

12. Some scholars have argued that we should therefore relativize what Westerners tend to see as world-historic colonial appearances to that understanding, rather than taking them as "firsts." This might be considered a kind of "provincializing" argument (see Schieffelin and Crittenden 1991), deflationary of colonial "first contact" rhetoric. Sahlins's argument regarding Hawaii also suggests that what might otherwise be taken to be novel occurrences can be interpreted in indigenous cultural terms as something else. The impact of that case derives in part from Cook's having been an unusually well-known historical character.

13. It is/was common in Australia for indigenous people to be envisioned as returning predecessors. Names were often recycled across alternate generations, especially between certain categories of relatives, on this assumption, e.g., from father's father to son's son. The spirits of the dead were often assumed to return to particular places in the landscape and reanimate new life. Other chapters show that race was not a solid barrier.

14. Sometimes outsiders are identified with indigenous predecessors, especially via associations with place where they are thought to have been conceived or where they have lived. My elder son, for example, was born with a particular birthmark on his chest, which led an indigenous man to identify him with himself (who had a similar mark) with a conception place and totem and his name. As this shows, there is a cluster of elements that can be involved where such forms of identifications persist and a specific set of ideas concerning recurrent elements constitutive of the person.

15. Nabokov (1979:53–55) recounts comparable stories for Jicarilla Apache; and there are many similar accounts for Australia.

16. Myers (1986), in providing accounts of movements on the part of individuals who remained longest in the desert, gives us the closest indigenous accounts of this form of life. See also Davenport, Johnson, and Yuwali 2005; Dousset and Ellis 2016.

17. For some specific descriptions, see Hiatt 1966; Haviland 1979; Merlan 1997b; Rumsey 1982; on the formal friendships and hospitality of trade partners, see Warner 1937; Elkin 1938; Kaberry 1939:1–36; Stanner 1933–34:156–75, 458–71; McCarthy 1939; Merlan 1997b.

18. In Kriol, a northern English Pidgin, "growl" means "scold," "berate."

19. See Eickelkamp 2003:319 for discussion of "lookin' at" as intrusive, but joint direction of gaze as a modality of "being with" or together, grounded in Western Desert field research.

20. Smyth (1878: 1:133) also describes for Victoria the approach taken by messengers to distant groups to whom communications were to be delivered in similar terms: "The messenger, on approaching the camp of the tribe to which he has to deliver his message, does not at once break in upon their privacy. He sits down at a considerable distance from their camp, but usually within sight of it, and makes a very small fire of bark and twigs for the purpose of indicating his presence by the smoke. After the lapse of a quarter of an hour, one of the aged blacks approaches him, carrying in his hand a fire-stick, or a piece of thick bark ignited at one end. The messenger presents his token to the old man, who scans it and orders his conduct accordingly."

21. There are category terms for these highly marked behaviors in Aboriginal languages.

22. One must be careful about what this connotes. In psychology, at least, the term "avoidance" seems strongly flavored by notions of maladaptive, coping, even illusionary, behavior that allows one to avoid dealing with stressors. In not wanting to unwarrantedly load the term with such negative connotations, the discussion resorted to a Boasian notion of the relevance of

"ordinary conditions" under which avoidance, or circumspection, became a prevalent interactional mode.

Chapter 2

1. The word apparently comes from the Dharuk language of Sydney and has become established in Australian English (now conventionally "corroboree") as the word for what Darwin called "dancing parties," both sacred and secular. See further Chapter 3.

2. Research on primate social learning typically distinguishes two forms of information that a learner can extract from a demonstrator: copying actions (defined as "imitation") or copying only the consequential results (defined as "emulation"). Questions may be roughly phrased as: how much do apes (and children) "ape" (in view of the general and approximate understanding that some of their behavior is imitative), and how may we understand what they are doing when they appear to do so? See Tennie, Call, and Tomasello (2006); Acerbi, Tennie, and Nunn (2011).

3. V. S. Naipaul evoked those formed by such mimicry, in a West Indies context, in his poignantly comic novel *The Mimic Men* (1967).

Chapter 3

1. In Yolngu dialects (northeast Arnhem Land) there is a loan word *jamah* from Malay (Macassan trepangers came from Sulawesi for over two centuries to collect sea mollusks in Arnhem waters). In Malay, Bajau, and related dialects, the main sense of *jama* is "handle, touch." *Djäma* is a Yolngu transitive verb from this source, used when people talk about work, employment, and activities related to ceremony: *buŋgul djäma* (ceremony + work.) An employed person is *djäma-mirri*, "work-having"; unemployed is *djäma-miriw*, "employment/work-lacking" (Evans 1992; Zorc 1986). Ritual as essential reproductive effort is also reflected in the main term used for "work" in Arrernte today having formerly applied to ritual preparation (Hamilton 1998; Austin-Broos 2009:118). It is also relevant that ceremony is referred to by Aborigines in English as "law" and/or "business," thus identified with what are seen as major regulatory and productive domains of European life (see Chapter 7, n. 8). Regarding "thing," in some languages there are terms meaning "bundle," "bedroll," or "stick, branch" that can be generalized to meaning something like "belongings," "stuff"; and ubiquitously, a "whatsaname" form can be used to designate an object. For example, *yuunch* = "thing" in Wik-Ngathan, a Cape York language, the primary sense of which is wood > instrument > car and sometimes "matter" or "thing with a purpose." This is different from an all-purpose word like English "thing," the primary (current) sense of which is material or immaterial object, matter. It cannot be forgotten that in the Germanic languages and into Middle English the etymon had primary senses of "creature," "assembly." I have personally worked intensively with several major (non-Pama-Nyungan) languages of the Katherine region—Wardaman, Jawoyn, Ngalakan, Dalabon, Mangarrayi, Yangman principal among them (see Merlan 1982, 1983, 1994a, 2005; Evans, Merlan, and Tukumba 2004; Wiynjorrotj et al. 2005)—of which the above generalizations are true. See J. Simpson (2016) for the diffusion of an English-derived "work" verb in Australian languages.

2. For details and images of this, see http://www.tjapukai.com.au/.

3. Cahir and Clark (2010:418) add that this adopting of commerce "operated within the cultural parameters of traditional Aboriginal commerce, reciprocity and kinship." They give no details.

4. Note the gender connotations, "slag" being originally a loose or promiscuous woman.

5. http://www.abc.net.au/news/2015-05-30/adam-goodes-indigenous-celebration-sparks-boos/6508968.

6. http://www.smh.com.au/entertainment/tv-and-radio/adam-goodes-should-admit-he-was-wrong-says-andrew-bolt-20150730-gioa1o.html.

7. Or, in some cases, had some but did not know it. Several people showed me bank books indicating they had modest cash reserves of several hundred dollars from earlier employment but were uncertain what the books represented and whether this money could be accessed.

8. The families I know who began placing photographs on graves in the 1990s had connections to Torres Strait Islanders. Since then, other families have asked me for pictures of deceased relatives, some in order to include in permanent grave markers.

9. Elsie Raymond, featured in Chapters 5 and 6, comes from this regional background.

10. E.g., Hercus and Sutton 1986; Hokari 2005.

Chapter 4

1. I set aside, for a moment, the other two: interattentionality and interaffectivity.

2. In 1919 from the brass plaque that replaced the original inscription the emotive elements—confidence, kindness, treachery—were all removed. It is worded simply: "In Memory of J. W. O. BENNETT Died May 28, 1869. Age 23."

3. It is relevant to understanding his forbearance that Goyder was a physician and Swedenborgian minister, besides being surveyor-general of South Australia.

4. Eyre was not only an explorer but also a colonial administrator, involved in varying complex colonial situations. His ideas concerning the colonized were tested, and his actions were shaped by pressures of circumstance. After his Australian explorations, from 1848 to 1853, he served as lieutenant governor of New Munster Province in New Zealand under Sir George Grey. From 1854 he was governor of several Caribbean island colonies including, controversially, Jamaica. As governor of that colony, Eyre, fearful of an island-wide uprising, brutally suppressed the Morant Bay rebellion, had many black peasants killed and hundreds flogged. He also authorized the execution of George William Gordon, a mixed-race colonial assemblyman suspected of involvement in the rebellion. This resulted in demands in England for Eyre to be arrested and tried for murder. It was John Stuart Mill who organized the Jamaica Committee that demanded his prosecution and included some well-known British liberal intellectuals (such as Charles Darwin, Frederic Harrison, Thomas Hughes, Thomas Huxley, and Herbert Spencer). A rival committee was set up by Thomas Carlyle for the defense, arguing that Eyre had acted decisively to restore order. His supporters included John Ruskin, Charles Kingsley, Charles Dickens, John Tyndall, and Alfred Lord Tennyson. Though Eyre was twice charged with murder, the cases did not proceed.

5. One cannot help thinking of a parallel: that it was not until 1967 that, by a change in a section of the Australian constitution, Aborigines came under federal census, before that having been cataloged by states only, sixty-six years after federation. See Chapter 6.

6. Drinnon (1980: chap. 9) effectively illustrates the role of writers and their literature in producing and narrativizing the difference between Indians and other Americans for reading publics. Some of the same features—including treachery—recur, as do dichotomous views of Indians as savage and noble.

7. Born in India, the son of the chairman of the directors of the British East India Company, Grant had a prominent political career as a member of Parliament, lord of the Treasury, and in

other positions. His career ended stormily over his proposals for colonial management and unrest in Cape Town and Canada. In 1835, more precisely, he became secretary of state for war and colonies, an indication of the much greater difficulties in some colonial territories than in Australia. Glenelg, like Wakefield (English politician and key figure in Australian colonization, see further) never set foot in Australia.

8. Torrens was born 1814 in Ireland, migrated to Australia at age twenty-six in 1840, pioneered and authored a simplified system of transferring land, and became third premier of South Australia in 1857.

9. At the time he received the message in 1874, Gillen was an eighteen-year-old still working for the telegraph company in Adelaide. In the 1870s he worked at various stations along the telegraph line, eventually becoming the virtual administrator of Central Australia, post and telegraph stationmaster at the present Alice Springs, stipendiary magistrate and sub-protector of Aborigines.

10. That these are widespread dynamics, readily discoverable in settler colonial contexts, is shown by the parallel dramatic account of Cayuse murder of missionaries on the Columbia Plateau in 1847, in the context of increasing streams of settlers, their abuses of Indians, a raging measles outbreak, which Indians interpreted as a settler undertaking to kill them off, and an emergent prophet cult that the Indians understood to offer them guidance under these extreme circumstances (Miller 1985:103–10). Examples could be multiplied indefinitely.

Chapter 5

1. Kriol is an Australian creole language, from pidginized English, that has developed in parts of Australia, and has spread through parts of the Roper River and Katherine region, replacing many of the indigenous languages for younger speakers. See Harris 1993.

2. The paddle steamer *Young Australian*, used to transport goods for the installation of the Overland Telegraph in the 1870s, went aground in 1874 and remained visible as a wreck.

3. A mining town about three hundred kilometers distant.

4. Probably a reference to a severe influenza epidemic of 1918.

5. The "Mrs" indexes the greater social distance of this person, an Aborigine, married to a white man. Aborigines in this area do not ordinarily refer to other Aboriginal women as "Mrs" (as they do white women), but do so in some cases like this where a principal social characteristic of the person has become her marriage to a European.

6. "Myall," used colloquially to mean an ignorant, unacculturated blackfella.

7. Barunga was first called Beswick Station, the cattle property owned first by Mick Madrill and later together with "Cowboy" Collins. It was purchased by the Department of Native Affairs and made into Beswick Aboriginal Reserve, a pastoral "training" site, in 1947. It became home base to Aboriginal people mainly originating from central and northern Arnhem Land, many of whom came into this area after the Second World War. Beswick Creek Native Settlement (established in 1951) was renamed Bamyili and from 1984 Barunga.

8. Phyllis's father worked for a storeman at Maranboy and later as a police tracker, hence his employment was one determining factor in the family's location. However, his connections to country at Beswick, his leadership role over time, and his connections by kinship and marriage were basic underpinnings of his attachment to the area.

9. An indigenous "doctor" or healer is meant.

10. Phyllis used to tell this story too. They obtained Madrill's feces, put them in a hole in a tree, covered it with wax, and "sang" (ensorcelled) the packet.

11. It may be relevant that Madrill had a wife, Connie, and apparently no reputation for having been interested in indigenous women. He died in 1942, leaving Collins and his wife as co-owners of Beswick.

12. His spelling was "Lamderod."

13. Administrators recognized Lamjorrotj's prominence but found him resistant to some of their plans—especially their effort to establish a "native camp" at Tandangal, which he regarded as a dangerous and (possibly) sacred place. They expelled him from Tandangal, but he returned to play a large role at Bamyili (Barunga) when the administrators realized they would have to shift the camp location from Tandangal for other reasons, including the lack of adequate water supply at the first two camps they had attempted to establish.

14. There were several private contractors charged with carrying the post in parts of the Top End, among them Mick Madrill and Henry Peckham, a.k.a. "The Fizzer," the postman of an Australian best seller of the early twentieth century, *We of the Never-Never* (see below).

15. This was undoubtedly not their earlier identity, but how they earlier identified themselves remains unknown to me.

16. I rely on Phyllis for these details; Laurie had died before I first visited Barunga.

17. The successful Jawoyn land claim (1982–88) included Katherine Gorge National Park.

18. These categories fascinated early ethnographers such as Spencer and Gillen as what they understood to be "marriage classes." They constitute a dimension of the complexity of Australian kin-category systems, a prevalent focus of Aboriginalist anthropology from Radcliffe-Brown (1930) for several decades thereafter.

19. Browne also had substantial properties elsewhere in the Northern Territory, e.g., at Newcastle Waters. He seems to have overextended himself speculatively.

20. The country with its hide-piercing native grasses proved unsuitable for sheep. Cotton never worked out either, with its considerable water requirements and presence of insect pests.

21. Giles had been forced to relinquish some of the vast area he had originally taken over from Browne but continued operations at Springvale, Willeroo and Delamere.

22. Nathaniel (Nat) Buchanan (1826–1901), pastoralist and explorer, was born near Dublin and came to Sydney as boy of eleven with his family. As a young man he participated in gold rushes in California, later in Victoria. He undertook pastoral exploration and operation in New South Wales and Victoria, then in Queensland, into the Northern Territory, and the Kimberley. He is sometimes said to have helped settle more country in Australia than any other man. He opened routes through Queensland to Burketown, the McArthur River, the Roper River, and Katherine, thus droving through much of the region south of and around Katherine, bringing in the herds so disruptive to indigenous life. He was part owner of Wave Hill Station on the Victoria River for a time but eventually sold his share to his much wealthier brother. He was one of the first to bring his wife to remote areas where she was often the sole white woman. He returned south as an old man and died in Tamworth, New South Wales.

23. I say this on Elsie's authority.

24. Her father, Yidorr, was known at the stations where he worked—Delamere, Willeroo, Manbulloo—as "Billycan," the names an indication of the different statuses he occupied among indigenous people and whites.

25. See "Yubulyawan Dreaming Project," http://ydproject.com/index.php/lowernav/language/, for some of Bill Harney's current activities.

26. Indigenous people at Elsey Station made a claim over the beds and banks of the Roper River in 1986 and a claim over the station in 1991. I was author of the anthropological reports

for both of these claims. The story of how Elsey became available for claim is told below. The Elsey claim took nine years to resolve and was followed by a number of land-related issues, including the Elsey residents' objections to gravel quarrying, the establishment of a national park over part of the territory Mangarrayi and Yangman people regard as theirs, questions of station management, regional water allocations, and fracking.

27. Most of Elsey was home territory of people who identified as Mangarrayi but also of some who were Yangman and had come to the station at its present location and intermarried extensively with Mangarrayi and others there. There was only a handful of Jawoyn people in the Elsey camp, but there were multiple ties of kinship to Jawoyn people whose main living areas were farther north. The three languages (Mangarrayi, Yangman, and Jawoyn) are as different from each other as, say, English and German and French, but most older people understood at least the first two, and some spoke both, while Mangarrayi was the recognized main indigenous language of the place.

28. As these indigenous placenames suggest, Elsey people's knowledge of their countryside remains rich and detailed, and they also move around it regularly to fish, forage, and hunt.

29. *The Little Black Princess*, published in 1905, was written as a children's story; see Chapter 6. Larbalestier (1990:72) calls *We of the Never-Never*, an account by Jeannie Gunn of her life at Elsey and featuring interactions with Elsey Aborigines, an expression of the "pioneer legend." As to Aeneas Gunn's premature death, indigenous people at Elsey say he ignored warnings to stay away from a "sickness dreaming" on Elsey known as Cave Creek in English (the same area in which Larry-Boy was captured; see Chapter 6). Gunn entered the limestone cavern, became sick, and died shortly thereafter. The medical diagnosis was blackwater fever, a form of malaria.

30. The report of the Gibb Committee of Review, 1971, on the condition of Aborigines on pastoral properties made recommendations sympathetic to such endeavors.

31. The change of name from Jembere to Jilkminggan (Mangarrayi: Jilgmirn.gan) had political implications to do with knowledge of the area and dreaming tracks. Retrospectively I see it as the harbinger of what was to turn into a larger dispute about entitlement and authority concerning the station when the entire property became available for claim, a situation not addressed here.

32. The situation is reminiscent of Richard Price's *First Time* (1983), which presents oral chronicles of African American maroons who escaped from slavery, in there being matter kept undercover, or at least not widely discussed publicly, but understood as foundational. But at Elsey, there was less reticence among older people in discussing the earlier situation, and a growing sense of impropriety and reserve among younger people. These stories are unlikely to remain part of the oral repertoire with the passage of the Kitty's generation and the later one of "Kayku Giles time," of whom there remain some members today.

33. Today, having won their land claim over the station, the indigenous people at Elsey are continually having to deal with a range of organizations and people concerning the management and resources of the property: livestock management, water allocations from the river, excavation of limestone by companies, which many in the indigenous community have long opposed (with little success), fracking, which is a newer development intervention, strongly opposed by some members of the community but seen by others as a source of potential income (and also contested in the wider society). In some ways this had long been the case; in other ways, many Aborigines, especially older people, continue to evaluate people, under favorable conditions, in ways that recognize difference but do not operate on some notion of "race" as unbridgeable difference. The trend, however, has been toward a more mutual racialization of difference.

34. How such nonprocreative mechanisms overlap with and differ from kin relations established in other ways and relate to genealogical relations as can be traced by the usual social scientific methodology of genealogy taking is an issue of comparative interest for different social orders of the continent. Povinelli (1993) has long argued that anthropologists have inappropriately overlaid Western (and specifically heteronormative) conceptions of kinship and family on indigenous contexts, distorting our understanding of them (see also Rifkin 2011). I am entirely sympathetic to the effort to not submerge different human experience beneath 'our' categories, and I agree this has regularly occurred. Nevertheless, we often need to use our own categories to begin to fathom kinds of difference, but need to do so with caution and awareness. There are two things that require care: one is to not ignore the nature of sexual symbolism and practice, though much of it be evidently hetero- rather than homosexual; and the second is not to subject that different human experience to yet another, different appropriation.

35. Through "classificatory" principles such equivalence of same-sex siblings, of alternate generations, and others. These are the kinds of principles that Radcliffe-Brown (1930) first began to elucidate.

36. By this I mean, a product of nearness or distance along many dimensions, including what we would see as genealogical distance but not limited to it.

Chapter 6

1. Gunn never adverts to "nigger hunts" or what she knew of them in these later comments.

2. http://john.curtin.edu.au/diary/primeminister/fulltext/fulltext%20prime%20minister_1941_6.html.

3. The government of Tasmania believed that there were no "Aborigines" left in that state, but it nonetheless legislated (in the Cape Barren Island Reserve Act 1912) in respect to "half-castes."

4. While some bureaucrats were empowered by law to approve or disallow marriages, some missionaries felt empowered to influence Aboriginal marriages by instituting dormitories where children—females in particular—could be kept out of the customary processes of bestowal. In one case, a missionary legitimized this practice by payment. From 1910 to 1938 Francis Xavier Gsell, at Bathurst Island Mission (Tiwi Islands, off the coast of Darwin) became known as the "Bishop with 150 wives" for his practice of "buying" girls betrothed to older men, thus making it possible for them to marry men of their own age and dismantling the indigenous system of long-term marriage promise.

5. Warwick Anderson (2002) provides a picture of the varieties of late nineteenth- and early twentieth-century thought and medical study concerning the character of Aboriginal Australian populations—ranging from views of them as ancient Caucasoids to racially alien peoples; and the gradual shift to preoccupation with "degrees" of black-white admixture and possibilities of absorption of the indigenous population "in order to produce a biologically consolidated nation" (p. 236).

6. The striking and widespread resort to public apology in both intra- and international contexts, particularly since the mid-1990s, has seen, e.g., apologies around this period by U.S. President Clinton to Rwandans (1998) and Guatemalans (1999) for the United States' limited action to assist; apologies by Canada to Japanese for their internment during World War II (1988); and the vexed question in Australia of apology to the Stolen Generations, among many other such issues. Characteristic is apology by powerful actors and institutions to relatively

powerless ones. The legal status of apology and its implications often remain contested issues. See Barkan 2000; Torpey 2006; Gibney et al. 2008.

7. Though this period supposedly came to an end in the 1970s, it is claimed that the Department of Community Services (DoCS) has the authority to remove children from their families if they were "at risk of significant harm" (a general principle, but one that disproportionately affects indigenous families) and that the number of indigenous children presently removed from their families equals or is greater than that of the Stolen Generations period. See Tilbury 2009, on disproportionate representation of indigenous children in the child welfare system.

8. Similar polarized and conflicting opinions have been aired around the educability, accomplishments, or definitive "otherness" of every subordinated minority population, including American blacks and Indians.

9. This doctrine was rejected by a High Court case, *Mabo v. Queensland* (no. 2) (1992), which confirmed the existence and possibility of survival of native title.

10. There never has been an Australian equivalent of the North American Indian practice of defining indigenous persons by reference to tribal enrollment. Most current U.S. tribes were organized (or reconstituted) under the Indian Reorganization Act of 1934. Although Indian nations are in a very different situation from the usual sovereign nation as understood (A. Simpson 2007), one of the features of tribal organization is "complete authority to determine all questions of its own membership" (Cohen 1942:133, cited in Simpson 2007). Tribes have adopted different criteria of membership, but a key one has involved the question of minimum "blood quantum"—how much Indian blood one must have, and its tribal attribution, in order to determine the membership of a person on a tribal roll (Snipp 1989: Appendix 4; Thornton 1997:36–37)—as well as demands for federal recognition of tribal status (Blu 1980).

11. Anthropologist Donald Thomson, known for his ethnographic research with Yolngu people in Arnhem Land and Pintupi in the Western Desert, was a notable advocate of this vision of remote reserve dwellers' future.

12. This remedialism combined with social inclusion was advocated by A. P. Elkin (1944) in his *Citizenship for the Aborigines*.

13. This is an aspect of indigenous social orders that would fall under the category of what Povinelli (2002) calls "repugnant" to modern liberal sensibilities. It confounds ideas of the individual as controller of the self, of male-female relations, of sexual propriety, and a number of other things. Nowadays many people both indigenous and nonindigenous suppress, prefer not to acknowledge, or no longer think in terms of this aspect of social practice.

14. For perspective on indigenous attraction to alcohol, see Brady 2002.

15. See Chapter 3 on the experiences of doctor, adventurer, and ethnographer Erhard Eylmann. His observations often came to rest on what seemed to him confronting and perhaps confounding—such as the fact that Aborigines newly arrived into Knuckey's Lagoon around Darwin, the "uncivilized Aborigines," manifested extreme jealously concerning their wives and women and sent them out of sight to keep them away from strangers; but rapidly took to offering them and underaged girls to anybody who had a little bit of tobacco in his possession, as well as to Chinese to obtain opium. With respect to the puzzle set up by these different behaviors, Eylmann tended to explain it simply as a difference between the "uncivilized" and more acculturated indigenes and never arrived at any deeper insight concerning gendered relations and their transformation in indigenous-nonindigenous encounter. For an account of sexual and other relations between Karajarri Aborigines and Malays on the Kimberley coast of Western Australia, see Skyring and Yu 2008.

16. One cannot, however, shy away from understanding the difference that indigenous practice and the collision of indigenous and colonial practices represent; see McGrath 1984, 1990.

17. Cameleers entered Australia from the late 1830s, and by mid-nineteenth century were seen as the solution to exploring the inland, far superior to horse and mule teams. By the late 1860s, most Australian states were importing camels and cameleers; breeding programs and trading routes were established. It is estimated that from 1870 to 1900 alone, more than two thousand cameleers and fifteen thousand camels came to Australia; and in 2007, that there remained one million feral camels that had bred and survived in Australia, most in Western Australia. The cameleers, often called "Afghans," were largely from Afghanistan, Baluchistan, and other parts of northwest India (now Pakistan) and were predominantly Muslim. See Jones and Kenny 2007.

18. Cowlishaw (1999:150) contrasts what administrators saw as the "half-caste menace" with the much greater flexibility that Aborigines, and perhaps especially Aboriginal women being sought out as partners by whites, displayed with regard to interracial sex and partnerships.

19. See extract of Northern Territory Hansard 1997, an obituary tribute to Elsie's life by the Northern Territory's chief minister.

20. As a woman, I had less occasion to hear about indigenous men's exposure to sexual curiosity on the part of white women, and it was certainly much less, given mores and the overwhelming proportions of men to women in the far north. There were men I knew well enough who recounted occasional advances to them. However, most emphasized their awareness that they would be subject to great reprisals on the part of husbands in several cases.

21. Before my time there, but the story was latent, not forgotten.

22. In this as in much else there are many parallels and interesting differences in state regulatory devices in Australia and the United States concerning indigenous people who have come to be encapsulated in successor states. As above, comments relating to North America are noted rather than treated as the major focus here, which will emerge below.

23. Len Smith (1980:68–90) estimates between a quarter and a half million; White and Mulvaney (1987), 750,000. Conservative forces in the "history wars" (see Chapter 3) have argued for a low precolonial figure in the interests of claiming lesser effects of colonization on the indigenous population. Smith clearly supports the view that the demographic effects of colonization were massive. His reconstructive demographic work is of a high standard and remains beyond any efforts to impugn it.

24. A similar principle was early applied to Indians in the United States, but arose in specific linkage with its emergent tax regime. In 1783 the U.S. Congress debated changing an article of the Articles of Confederation to create a tax assessment system based on population. This raised questions of who was to be counted. Without debate, "Indians not paying taxes" were excluded from population count (M. J. Anderson 2015:11). This exclusion began early and continued for nearly a century. A sentence in the 1870 census makes clear the reasoning. Census marshals were instructed that *Indians taxed* were "Indians out of their tribal relations and exercising the rights of citizens under State or Territorial laws" (Snipp 1989:35). More intense debate in the United States throughout the nineteenth century pivoted on whether and how slaves were to be counted, who were clearly not living under their own governments and were acknowledged to be of great value as property. Northerners wanted to lower their region's own proportional exposure to tax assessment by including slaves, who were, of course, largely in southern states, and hence favored considering each slave a complete census person. Southerners proposed various ratios of slaves to free persons to reduce their exposure to tax assessment. The controversy was eventually

resolved for a time in favor of the famous "three-fifths" ratio (M. J. Anderson 2015:13). However, closer to the time of the Civil War, when questions arose concerning possible paid emancipation of slaves, it turned out that their estimated monetary value was many times the U.S. federal budget.

25. In my experience, this was a popularly and not administratively used category, which may have arisen partly as those concerned distinguished themselves from "Aborigines." The common administrative category was "half-caste."

26. Makeshift huts or similar forms of housing.

27. The first houses in town that Aborigines could apply to live in were established in the 1960s (see Merlan 1998:8).

28. Together with myself, which may have been an important factor in their rejection and irritation.

29. CBCS (Commonwealth Bureau of Census and Statistics)/ABS (Australian Bureau of Statistics) claimed to have achieved complete enumeration by 1966. However, in my experience some people were incompletely, sometimes contradictorily, and sometimes multiply identified, without the realization that some names or forms of appellation belonged to the same person. See F. Morphy 2007.

30. The federal government was enabled to make laws specifically in relation to indigenous people for the first time under the so-called "race power" in section 51(26) of the constitution.

31. The new Commonwealth definition: "An Aboriginal or Torres Strait Islander is a person of Aboriginal or Torres Strait Islander descent, who identifies as being of Aboriginal or Torres Strait Islander origin and who is accepted as such by the community with which the person associates." This definition was developed during the period 1967 to 1978 and is now widely accepted by Commonwealth and other government agencies. As to citizenship, all Australians were "British subjects" until postwar legislation instituted Australian nationality, and a section of the Australian Citizenship Act 1948 specified that Aborigines were citizens. See also Preface, on citizenship.

32. In fact, as we have seen, "aboriginal natives" had been counted, but for the purposes of then statistically excluding them by varieties of "political arithmetic," so what the referendum really enabled was for indigenous Australians to be counted for the first time, federally, and without a need to specifically identify them as of some proportion or kind of Aborigine.

33. For the United States, too, self-definition completely altered the census concept of race, toward a constructionist interpretation of race and away from older biologized perspectives (Snipp 2003).

34. Making the extent of urbanization more comparable to that of the general Australian population, which in 2015 was 89.4 percent, with a 1.47 percent annual rate of change over the preceding five years.

35. http://www.abs.gov.au/ausstats/abs@.nsf/mf/3238.0.55.001.

36. In the United States, too, there has been substantial increase in the proportion of indigenous population in urban areas. In 1900, only 0.4 percent of Native Americans in the United States lived in urban areas (Thornton 1997:38). By 2010 that had risen to 71 percent. Amerindian material also shows that urbanized populations are proportionally much more intermarried with non-Indians than are remote and reservation-dwelling Indians (Snipp 1989:156–60).

37. "Closing the Gap" has become a key government policy rubric in the aftermath of a government intervention in the Northern Territory in 2007; see http://www.healthinfonet.ecu edu.au/closing-the-gap/key-facts/what-is-the-history-of-closing-the-gap; see also Chapter 8.

38. One gets some perspective on dimensions of indigenous people's self-representations as such from web postings, which range across ages and backgrounds. Though the evidence cannot be reviewed here, many state belonging, in terms of being a person of a particular "tribe" (e.g., Yawuru, Goenpul), a community (Oenpelli), a "nation," or a heritage (Dagoman, Torres Strait Islander). Social context or group is important, and personal identification with it, rather than a sole focus on individual identity. That people are of nonindigenous as well as indigenous family background is not apparent in most of these web presences (except through pictures). For many web entries, the "nonindigenous" side of heritage remains completely unspoken, or residual, with a few notable exceptions. And finally, since many web presences are of people of some public function and prominence, entries specify a connection between public role and indigenous identification.

39. Contrasting with the United States (Williams 2006; Snipp 2003:575–81), there has not (yet) been an equivalent census-linked movement for "multiracial" recognition in Australia. The binary Taylor identifies nevertheless may yet become more porous as more people (probably many of education and cosmopolitan orientation) begin to describe themselves, as, e.g., does medical social researcher Yin Paradies (2006:357), as "an Aboriginal-Anglo-Asian Australian."

40. Smith et al. show that the present Victorian Aboriginal population of 30,000 (as of 2001) appears to have descended from the approximately 500 individuals collected on the reserves of the Protection Board in the 1870s. The other 500 to 1,000 people recorded by the board and colonial census as living outside the reserves appear to have hardly left any discoverable descendants except for a handful of families who had some land title. Smith et al. (2008:550) explore the question of the fate of those not under board protection.

41. Sprinter Cathy Freeman, whose competitive career spanned from 1990 to 2003, won the 400 meters at the 2000 Olympics in Sydney. She took a victory lap carrying both the national Australian and the indigenous flag, the latter causing controversy (and considered unofficial). See the story of Adam Goodes in Chapter 3.

Chapter 7

1. Water buffalo were imported into the Northern Territory in the nineteenth century from Timor, Kisar, and other islands in the Indonesian archipelago to provide working animals and meat for the remote northern settlements. When the early settlements were abandoned, the buffaloes were released, where they became feral populations. The buffalo subsequently multiplied and colonized the Top End landscape, particularly the northern floodplains. Their numbers rose to the level of an infestation, as we will see in a remark concerning this part of the Top End in the chapter. A government program (the Brucellosis and Tuberculosis Eradication Campaign, or BTEC) to remove them drastically reduced their numbers in the 1980s and 1990s, but they remain a problem. See Haynes 2009, chap. 7, for discussion of a 1989 eradication program in Kakadu National Park and confrontations with indigenous park residents over the killing of animals, some of which they regarded as pets.

2. Despite claims concerning the potential goods, there is a literature on the relation of indigenous people and the mining industry that is more social analytic and more reserved. The mining industry largely embraces a governmental point of view of the "problem of indigenous dependency" as to be resolved by employment and the need for preparation of indigenous people as "job ready" (Lawrence 2005). Careful research on these relations, however, shows a considerable extent to which mining employment fails to connect with the lives of many (especially community-based, remote-dwelling) indigenous people, though does so to a greater extent with

the lives of more occupationally mobile and educated indigenous people. One of the consequences is that indigenous people employed in mining locations are typically not local to the area. O'Faircheallaigh (2006) discusses the extent to which the legal, policy, and institutional environment within which mineral development takes place has changed since the events described here. There has undoubtedly been consolidation of a stronger policy consensus that development should proceed with the agreement of Aboriginal landowners. He observes, however, that despite native title, legislative changes, and "corporate social responsibility" policies, Aboriginal landowners face formidable obstacles that, unless addressed, may mean that they continue to experience an essentially unchanged political economy of mineral development.

3. Beckett (1993) presents and analyzes a narrative from an indigenous man, Walter Newton, whom he contacted in Broken Hill, in a region of southeastern Australia that had been subject to mining and pastoralism for over a century at the time of their association (1958). Beckett shows Walter Newton's "history of the world—or Australia" to treat as commensurable and to amalgamate themes from "Dreamtime and Bible" in an expressive compound relating to a land he had learned to experience and think about in mythological and colonial terms. Newton, however, lived in "involuntary isolation" from whites and "elected isolation" from other indigenous people—he was the sole Aborigine in Broken Hill at the time. This contrasts with the relatively large number of Jawoyn and associated indigenous people of the region at the time of the Coronation Hill dispute. There are about five hundred current members of the Jawoyn Association, and most Jawoyn people tend to live in close association with Southern Arnhem Landers of other socioterritorial identities.

4. In site recording in various parts of the region I have come across dangerous sites, often ones said to be, if disturbed, the vector of disease. Cave Creek on Elsey Station (which was the cause of Aeneas Gunn's death, according to Elsey people, and where Larry-Boy hid himself; see Chapters 5 and 6) is such a place.

5. Ian Keen and I were also accused of fabricating the Bula story, on the premise (Brunton 1992) that it allegedly did not predate the Coronation Hill controversy.

6. "Footwalker" refers to a person who went everywhere on foot. It originates in the times when there were no cars or no chance of gaining access to one.

7. I adopt "double consciousness" from W. E. B. Du Bois's *The Souls of Black Folk* (1903).

8. In this, I see Peter as a rather different "personality" from Elsie Raymond (Chapter 5) and exemplary of the "assimilatory" dynamic that I have noted in this regard.

9. In Aboriginal Kriol, the English word "business" has been adopted with primary reference to sacred ceremony—not to "business" in any conventional English sense. In other words, sacred ceremony is analogized to "business" as central indigenous and nonindigenous concerns, respectively. See Chapter 3 on the indigenous connection between preparation for ceremony and postcolonial concepts of "work."

10. Section 40(a) of the Land Rights Act stated that a mining lease could not be granted unless the Land Council/s consented to it. It is also stipulated under section 23(3) of the act that Land Councils could not take any action with respect to leasing Aboriginal land unless satisfied that the traditional Aboriginal owners properly understood and consented to what was being proposed. Essentially these two sections of the legislation would presumably guarantee that the traditional landowners had the power to veto (refuse) proposals to mine in their areas. However, under section 40(b) of the act this power of veto can be overridden: if the governor-general proclaimed it to be "in the national interest" to mine, a lease could in fact be granted even if the land council and/or traditional owners had not consented.

11. Although Sandy, Peter, and Nipper were recognized by all indigenous people involved as the "right" people to speak for the area, they were sometimes impugned, especially by senior women, as irresponsible, largely because of their known abuse of alcohol.

12. John Ah Kit is an Aboriginal person born in Alice Springs, who moved with his family to Darwin in 1954 when a small child. In 1983, he was elected to the full council of the Northern Land Council (NLC) representing Aboriginal people in the Katherine region. From 1984 to 1990 he was director of the Northern Land Council. He resigned in 1990 to contest the Northern Territory seat of Goyder, encompassing large rural areas south of Darwin, for the Labor Party.

Chapter 8

1. See Rowse 2000: chap. 10; and Rowse 2006a. Herbert Cole "Nugget" Coombs, Australian economist and public servant (Rowse 2000), served as chairman of the Australian Council for Aboriginal Affairs, which was established after the referendum in 1967.

2. Several are mentioned below; many were seen by governments as extreme. In their time they constituted something of an indigenous political spokesgroup, known to urban Australia, each with a particular regional background and grounding.

3. Yolngu people had sent petitions on bark to the federal government in 1963. The bark petitions are preserved in the Australian Parliament building, regarded as the first documentary recognition of indigenous people in Australian law.

4. Six months after the conclusion of the Coronation Hill decision, his departure brought on by it (see Chapter 7).

5. For Yothu Yindi, "Treaty" video, see https://www.youtube.com/watch?v=S7cbkxn4G8U.

6. Recommendation 339 of the Royal Commission into Aboriginal Deaths in Custody.

7. As this suggests, "reconciliation" turned out to be a polysemous and contested term. For an account of its shifting meanings throughout the 1990s in parliamentary discourse, see Pratt 2005; and Short and Gunstone 2011.

8. As mentioned in the Introduction, n. 8, Australia's current prime minister, Liberal-National Malcolm Turnbull, campaigned for the republic side of this debate, without success.

9. See also Austin-Broos (2009: chap. 9), who notes the NTER's emphasis on moral renovation, attributable at least in part to the influence of Cape York indigenous leader Noel Pearson (also mentioned further below as author of an alternative proposal to "Recognise"). Pearson's views, developed over a long term, have been acceptable to some political conservatives and neoliberals because they emphasize (individual) uplift and responsibility (Austin-Broos 2009:242). Burbank (2011) treats the NTER briefly, but some of the social conditions it aimed to modify at greater length from her perspective on a remote community. In an article for which I have been extensively criticized by some (Merlan 2009), I took the view that forms of intervention are warranted, but I am well aware of the difficulties of imagining and implementing ones that might be constructive rather than destructive and of bureaucratic procedure and management that operate in ways very different from what could be constructive in indigenous settings.

10. Recognise website, http://www.recognise.org.au/. Aden Ridgeway, born in New South Wales, of indigenous (Gumbaynggirr) background, was a member of the Australian Senate for New South Wales from 1999 to 2005, of the Australian Democrats party.

11. Emphasis on inclusion in the constitution has in part been understood to recuperate a comparative neglect. American Indians are mentioned in the U.S. Constitution in three places: in Article I, section 8 (on regulating commerce); in Article VI (on the federal government's

treaties with Indian tribes as the supreme law of the United States); and in the Fourteenth Amendment to the Constitution (ratified in 1868), which refers to the exclusion of "Indians not taxed" from political representation. Indians were made citizens when subject to allotment grants in the latter nineteenth century and, later, by virtue of the Indian Citizenship Act, also known as the Snyder Act, of 1924, proposed partly in recognition of the role of Indian soldiers in World War I. These mentions are regulatory rather than explicitly recognitional, and it seems dubious that American constitutional mentions be taken as a comparator.

12. In forming his view of the constitution as a "rulebook," Pearson has relied on opinions of constitutional experts Julian Lesser and Damien Freeman. The American Constitution is also a founding, integrating document but is much more inspirational in places. However, it is certainly not so with respect to Native Americans.

13. The chair is Warren Mundine, a New South Welshman of Bandjalang background, and the former national president of the Australian Labor Party (ALP), the first indigenous person to head a major party. He quit the Labor Party in 2012 and was appointed chairman of the Australian government's Indigenous Advisory Council by (then) Prime Minister Tony Abbott.

14. Bolt has long been associated with the *Herald Sun*, a tabloid subsidiary of Rupert Murdoch's News Corp Australia. Mundine and Bolt are (otherwise) rarely in agreement.

15. See explanation of the mode of procedure adopted by the panel of experts charged with consideration of the Recognise initiative (Expert Panel 2012:4–10).

16. The High Court accepted that a modified doctrine of tenure operated in Australia, that the Crown acquired not absolute but radical title, and that this law of tenure (as a product of the common law) could coexist with the law of native title (though where there had been a valid grant of fee simple by the Crown the latter title would be extinguished). Though the comparison of native title to property law is useful in understanding the underlying movement of the *Mabo* case, it has limitations. Landholding is an entitlement within particular native title systems and hence is not capable of alienation or assignment; it does not constitute a legal or beneficial estate or interest in the land.

17. Plaintiff Paul Coe, a Wiradjuri man of New South Wales, in 1979 commenced an action in the High Court of Australia, arguing that at the time white people came to Australia, Aborigines were there and therefore the court had to recognize their rights. The case was never heard due to its being deemed inadequately prepared. Later, in 1993 after *Mabo*, Isabel Coe sued on behalf of the Wiradjuri tribe and sought declarations of various kinds and consequential relief. They include declarations to the effect that the Wiradjuri are the owners of lands constituting a very large part of southern and central New South Wales and (among other things) that they were sovereign. The justices found the claim of sovereignty adverse to the Crown, and all four justices rejected it. Justice Gibbs stated that the annexation of the east coast of Australia by Captain Cook and the subsequent acts by which the whole of the Australian continent became part of the dominions of the Crown were acts of state whose validity could not be challenged. He continued ((11) (1979) 53 ALJR, at p. 408; pp. 128–29 of ALR):

> If the amended statement of claim intends to suggest either that the legal foundation of the Commonwealth is insecure, or that the powers of the Parliament are more limited than is provided in the Constitution, or that there is an aboriginal nation which has sovereignty over Australia, it cannot be supported. . . . The aboriginal people are subject to the laws of the Commonwealth and of the States or Territories in which they respectively reside. They have no legislative, executive or judicial organs

by which sovereignty might be exercised. If such organs existed, they would have no powers, except such as the law of the Commonwealth, or of a State or Territory, might confer upon them. The contention that there is in Australia an aboriginal nation exercising sovereignty, even of a limited kind, is quite impossible in law to maintain.

18. Mabo and other Torres Strait Islanders north of the tenth latitude had made an explicit choice to remain within Australia when they had been offered the possibility of becoming part of the new sovereign nation of Papua New Guinea following its independence in 1975.

19. http://www.theaustralian.com.au/news/inquirer/uluru-statement-practical-on May 27 2017.

20. A form of this question occurs on the basis of a different (but colonial) history in countries like France, which, in keeping with liberal and Enlightenment social policy traditions and discourses of equality and common nationality, does not record ethnic or racial characteristics in its population statistics. There are nevertheless clear concentrations of populations of different origin living in differentiated social conditions, i.e., dynamics of social marginalization on racial and ethnic bases (see Jugé and Perez 2008).

21. In these respects research on dreams is informative (see, e.g., Pentony 1961) not only of this modality but also the drastic nature of colonial influence.

22. In interaction with both other indigenous as well as nonindigenous people, the latter often with particular intensity.

REFERENCES

Acerbi, Alberto, Claudio Tennie, and Charles Nunn 2011. Modeling Imitation and Emulation in Constrained Search Spaces. Learning Behaviour 39:104–14.

Akerman, K. 1979. Material Culture and Trade in the Kimberleys Today. Pp. 243–51 in Ronald M. Berndt and Catherine H. Berndt (ed.), Aborigines of the West: Their Past and Their Present. Nedlands: University of Western Australia Press.

Allam, Lorena 2010. No Ordinary Piece of Bush: The High Price of Coronation Hill. Hindsight, ABC Radio National, 4 April. http://mpegmedia.abc.net.au/rn/podcast/2010/04/hht_201 00404.mp3.

Anderson, Margo J. 2015. The American Census: A Social History. 2nd ed. New Haven, Conn.: Yale University Press.

Anderson, Warwick 2002. The Cultivation of Whiteness: Science, Health and Racial Destiny in Australia. Melbourne: Melbourne University Press.

Arendt, Hannah 1976. Origins of Totalitarianism. New York: Harcourt Brace.

Arndt, Walter 1962. The Nagorkun-Narlinji Cult. Oceania 32(4):298–320.

Attwood, Bain 2005. Telling the Truth About Aboriginal History. Crows Nest, N.S.W.: Allen and Unwin.

Attwood, Bain, and Andrew Markus 2007. The 1967 Referendum: Race, Power and the Australian Constitution. Canberra: Aboriginal Studies Press.

Austin, Tony 1990. Cecil Cook, Scientific Thought and "Half-Castes" in the Northern Territory, 1927–1938. Aboriginal History 14(1/2):104–22.

Austin-Broos, Diane 2003. Places, Practices, and Things: The Articulation of Arrernte Kinship with Welfare and Work. American Ethnologist 30(1):118–35.

Austin-Broos, Diane 2009. Arrernte Present, Arrernte Past: Invasion, Violence, and Imagination in Indigenous Central Australia. Chicago: University of Chicago.

Austin-Broos, Diane 2011. A Different Inequality: The Politics of Debate about Remote Aboriginal Australia. Sydney: Allen and Unwin.

Australia Constitutional Convention 1998. Report of the Constitutional Convention, Old Parliament House, Canberra, 2–13 February 1998. 4 vols. Barton, A.C.T.: Department of the Prime Minister and Cabinet.

Balibar, Etienne 1990. The Nation Form: History and Ideology. Review (Fernand Braudel Center) 13(3):329–61.

Banks, Joseph 1962. The Endeavour Journal of Joseph Banks, 1768–1771. 2 vols. Edited by J. C. Beaglehole. Sydney: Trustees of the Public Library of New South Wales in association with Angus and Robertson.

Barkan, Elazar 2000. The Guilt of Nations: Restitution and Negotiating Historical Injustices. New York: W. W. Norton.

Barratt, Glynn 1981. The Russians at Port Jackson, 1814–1822. AAIS, n.s., no. 21. Canberra: Australian Institute of Aboriginal Studies.

Barta, Tony 2008. "They Appear Actually to Vanish from the Face of the Earth": Aborigines and the European Project in Australia Felix. Journal of Genocide Research 10(4):519–39.

Barwick, Diana 1974. And the Lubras Are Ladies Now. Pp. 51–63 in Fay Gale (ed.), Woman's Role in Aboriginal Society. 2nd ed. Canberra: Australian Institute of Aboriginal Studies.

Batty, Phillip 2006. White Redemption Rituals: Reflections on the Repatriation of Aboriginal Secret-Sacred Objects. Pp. 55–63 in Tess Lea, Emma Kowal, and Gillian Cowlishaw (ed.), Moving Anthropology: Critical Indigenous Studies. Darwin, N.T.: Charles Darwin University Press.

Baudin, Nicolas 1974. The Journal of Post Captain Nicolas Baudin, Commander-in-Chief of the Corvettes Géographe and Naturaliste, Assigned by Order of the Government to a Voyage of Discovery. Trans. Christine Cornell. Adelaide: Libraries Board of South Australia.

Beckett, Jeremy M. 1965. Aborigines, Alcohol and Assimilation. Pp. 32–47 in Marie Reay (ed.), Aborigines Now: New Perspectives in the Study of Aboriginal Communities. Sydney: Angus and Robertson.

Beckett, Jeremy M. 1993. Walter Newton's History of the World—or Australia. American Ethnologist 20(4):675–95.

Behrendt, Larissa 2007. The Emergency We Had to Have. Pp. 15–20 in Jon Altman and Melinda Hinkson (ed.), Coercive Reconciliation: Stabilise, Normalise, Exit Aboriginal Australia. North Carlton, Vic.: Arena Publications Association.

Bellingshausen, Faddei Faddeevich 1945. The Voyage of Captain Bellingshausen to the Antarctic Seas, 1819–1821. Ed. and trans. Frank Debenham. London: Hakluyt Society.

Benjamin, Walter 1982. Konvolut N. Pp. 570–611 in Das Passagen-Werk. Frankfurt am Main: Suhrkamp Verlag.

Bennett, Mary 1928. Christison of Lammermoor. London: Alston Rivers.

Berkhofer, Robert F. 1978. The White Man's Indian: Images of the American Indian from Columbus to the Present. New York: Alfred A. Knopf.

Berndt, Ronald M. 1987. Other Creatures in Human Guise and Vice Versa: A Dilemma in Understanding. Pp. 169–91 in Margaret Clunies Ross, Tamsin Donaldson, and Stephen A. Wild (ed.), Songs of Aboriginal Australia. Oceania Monograph 32. Sydney: University of Sydney.

Berndt, Ronald M., and Catherine H. Berndt (ed.) 1979. Aborigines of the West: Their Past and Their Present. Nedlands: University of Western Australia Press for the Education Committee of the 150th Anniversary Celebrations.

Bhabha, Homi 1994. The Location of Culture. London: Routledge.

Biddle, Nick 2011. CAEPR Indigenous Population Project 2011 Census Papers. Paper 5. Population and Age Structure. Canberra: CAEPR.

Biolsi, Thomas 2005. Imagined Geographies: Sovereignty, Indigenous Space, and American Indian Struggle. American Ethnologist 32(2):239–59.

Blake, Barry J. 1988. Redefining Pama Nyungan: Towards the Prehistory of Australian Languages. Aboriginal Linguistics 1:1–90.

Blakeman, Bree 2013. An Ethnography of Emotion and Morality: Toward a Local Indigenous

Theory of Value and Social Exchange on the Yolngu Homelands in Remote North-East Arnhem Land, Australia. PhD thesis, Australian National University.

Blu, Karen 1980. The Lumbee Problem: The Making of an American Indian People. Cambridge: Cambridge University Press.

Boas, Franz 1904. Some Traits of Primitive Culture. Journal of American Folk-Lore 17:243–54.

Bourdieu, Pierre 1972. Outline of a Theory of Practice. Trans. Richard Nice. Cambridge: Cambridge University Press.

Bourdieu, Pierre 1994. Raisons pratiques: Sur la théorie de l'action. Vol. 4. Paris: Seuil.

Bowditch, Jim (1968) 2014. The Larry Boy Manhunt: Continuing Biog of Crusading Editor, "Big Jim" Bowditch. Little Darwin blog, 3 August. http://littledarwin.blogspot.com/2014/088/the-larry-boy-manhunt-continuing-biog.html.

Bradley, William 1969. A Voyage to New South Wales: The Journal of Lieutenant William Bradley RN of HMS Sirius, 1786–1792. Facsimile ed. Sydney: Trustees of the Public Library of New South Wales in association with Ure Smith.

Brady, Maggie 2002. Historical and Cultural Roots of Tobacco Use Among Aboriginal and Torres Strait Islander People. Australian and New Zealand Journal of Public Health 26(2):116–20.

Brady, Maggie 2007. Equality and Difference: Persisting Historical Themes in Health and Alcohol Policies Affecting Indigenous Australians. Journal of Epidemiology and Community Health 61(9):759–63.

Brady, Maggie, and Kingsley Palmer 1984. Alcohol in the Outback: Two Studies of Drinking. Darwin: Australian National University, North Australia Research Unit.

Brennan, Frank 1991. Sharing the Country. Ringwood, Vic.: Penguin Books.

Brunton, Ron 1992. Mining Credibility: Coronation Hill and the Anthropologists. Anthropology Today 8(2):2–5.

Bruyneel, Kevin 2007. The Third Space of Sovereignty: The Postcolonial Politics of U.S.-Indigenous Relations. Minneapolis: University of Minnesota Press.

Burbank, Victoria K. 1985. The Mirriri as Ritualized Aggression. Oceania 56(1):47–55.

Burbank, Victoria K. 1994. Fighting Women: Anger and Aggression in Aboriginal Australia. Berkeley: University of California Press.

Burbank, Victoria K. 2011. An Ethnography of Stress: The Social Determinants of Health in Aboriginal Australia. New York: Palgrave Macmillan.

Burbidge, Belinda 2014. Contemporary Wiradjuri Relatedness in Peak Hill, New South Wales. PhD thesis, Sydney University.

Bushman 1841. Corroberra. Sydney Gazette and New South Wales Advertiser, 20 February, p. 2.

Byrne, Denis 1996. Deep Nation: Australia's Acquisition of an Indigenous Past. Aboriginal History 20:82–107.

Cahir, David, and Ian Clark 2010. "An Edifying Spectacle": A History of "Tourist Corroborees" in Victoria, Australia, 1835–1870. Tourism Management 31:412–20.

Calley, Malcolm 1959. Bandjalang Social Organisation. PhD thesis, University of Sydney.

CAR (Council for Aboriginal Reconciliation) 2000. Reconciliation: Australia's Challenge; Final Report of the Council for Aboriginal Reconciliation to the Prime Minister and the Commonwealth Parliament. http://austlii.edu.au/au/orgs/car/finalreport/index.htm.

Carrithers, Michael, Matei Candea, Karen Sykes, Martin Holbraad, and Soumhya Venkatesan 2010. "Ontology Is Just Another Word for Culture." Critique of Anthropology 30 (2): 152–200.

Casey, Maryrose 2011. Cross-Cultural Encounters: Aboriginal Performers and European Audiences in the Late 1800s and Early 1900s. Double Dialogues 14 (Summer).

Cattelino, Jessica R. 2008. High Stakes: Florida Seminole Gaming and Sovereignty. Durham, N.C.: Duke University Press.

Chartrand, Tanya, and John A. Bargh 1999. The Chameleon Effect: The Perception-Behavior Link and Social Interaction. Journal of Personality and Social Psychology 76(6):893–910.

Clark, Manning 1962. A History of Australia. Vol. 1. Carlton, Vic.: Melbourne University Press.

Clarke, Philip A. 1996. Early European Interaction with Aboriginal Hunters and Gatherers on Kangaroo Island, South Australia. Aboriginal History 20:51–81.

Clendinnen, Inga 2005. Dancing with Strangers: Europeans and Australians at First Contact. New York: Cambridge University Press.

Cohn, Bernard 1987. The Census, Social Structure and Objectification in South Asia. Pp. 224–54 in An Anthropologist Among the Historians and Other Essays. Delhi: Oxford University Press.

Collier, Jane F., and Michelle Z. Rosaldo 1981. Politics and Gender in Simple Societies. Pp. 275–329 in Sherry B. Ortner and Harriet Whitehead (ed.), Sexual Meanings: The Cultural Construction of Gender and Sexuality. Cambridge: Cambridge University Press.

Collins, David 1802. An Account of the English Colony in New South Wales. Vol. 2. London: T. Cadell and W. Davies.

Collman, Jeffrey 1979a. Fringe-Camps and the Development of Aboriginal Administration in Central Australia. Social Analysis: The International Journal of Social and Cultural Practice 2:38–57.

Collman, Jeffrey 1979b. Women, Children, and the Significance of the Domestic Group to Urban Aborigines in Central Australia. Ethnology 18(4):379–97.

Collman, Jeffrey 1988. Aboriginal Fringe Dwellers and Welfare. St. Lucia: University of Queensland Press.

Commonwealth of Australia 1937. Aboriginal Welfare. Initial Conference of Commonwealth and State Authorities Held at Canberra 21st to 23rd April, 1937. Canberra: Commonwealth Government Printer.

Cook, James 1955–68. The Journals of Captain James Cook on His Voyages of Discovery. Ed. J. C. Beaglehole. 3 vols. Cambridge: Published for the Hakluyt Society at the University Press.

Coulthard, Glen S. 2007. Subjects of Empire: Indigenous Peoples and the "Politics of Recognition" in Canada. Contemporary Political Theory 6:437–60.

Council for Aboriginal Reconciliation, Strategic Plan 1998–2000, Goal 1: Documents. http://www.austlii.edu.au/au/orgs/car/finalreport/text02.htm.

Cowlishaw, Gillian 1988. Black, White or Brindle: Race in Rural Australia. Sydney: Cambridge University Press.

Cowlishaw, Gillian 1999. Rednecks, Eggheads and Blackfellas: A Study of Racial Power and Intimacy in Australia. Ann Arbor: University of Michigan Press.

Cowlishaw, Gillian 2004. Blackfellas, Whitefellas, and the Hidden Injuries of Race. Oxford: Blackwell.

Cowlishaw, Gillian 2007. No-one could Creep Up on Uncle Billy. New Critic, issue 4. http://www.ias.edu.au/new-critic/four/unclebilly.

Darwin, Charles 1896. Journal of Researches into the Natural History and Geology of the Countries Visited During the Voyage of the H.M.S. Beagle Round the World, Under the Command of Capt. Fitz Roy, R.N. New ed. New York: D. Appleton.

Darwin, Charles 1989. Voyage of the Beagle: Charles Darwin's Journal of Researches. Ed. and abr. Janet Browne and Michael Neve. London: Penguin.

Davenport, Susan, Peter Johnson, and Yuwali 2005. Cleared Out: First Contact in the Western Desert. Canberra: Australian Institute of Aboriginal and Torres Strait Islander Studies.

David, Z. R. 1986. Yolngu-Matha Dictionary. Batchelor, N.T.: School of Australian Linguistics.

Davis, Stephen L., and J. R. V. Prescott 1992. Aboriginal Frontiers and Boundaries in Australia. Carlton, Vic.: Melbourne University Press.

Dawes, William 1825. CW/0, 6, 8. Oxford: Rhodes House.

de Costa, Ravi 2002. New Relationships, Old Certainties: Australia's Reconciliation and the Treaty-Process in British Colombia. PhD diss., Swinburne University of Technology.

Dirks, Nicholas B. 1996. Is Vice Versa? Historical Anthropologies and Anthropological Histories. Pp. 17–51 in Terrence J. McDonald (ed.), The Historic Turn in the Human Sciences. Ann Arbor: University of Michigan Press.

Donald, Merlin 1991. Origins of the Modern Mind: Three Stages in the Evolution of Culture and Cognition. Cambridge, Mass.: Harvard University Press.

Donovan, Peter Francis 1981. A Land Full of Possibilities: A History of South Australia's Northern Territory. St. Lucia: University of Queensland Press.

Dousset, Laurent, and Lizzie Marrkilyi Ellis 2016. Pictures from My Memory: My Story as an Aboriginal Ngaatjatjarra Woman. Canberra: Aboriginal Studies Press.

Drinnon, Richard 1980. Facing West: The Metaphysics of Indian-Hating and Empire-Building. New York: New American Library.

Du Bois, W. E. B. 1903. The Souls of Black Folk: Essays and Sketches. Chicago: A. C. McClurg.

Eccleston, Roy 1986. Kakadu: Beauty and the Bullion. Age, 10 October, p. 11. https://news. google.com/newspapers?nid=1300&dat=19861010&id=BTspAAAAIBAJ&sjid=t5IDAA AAIBAJ&pg=1370,6013403&hl=en.

Eickelkamp, Ute 2003. Mapitjakuṇa—Shall I Go Away from Myself Towards You? Being-with and Looking-at Across Cultural Divides. Australian Journal of Anthropology 14(3):315–35.

Eickelkamp, Ute (ed.) 2011. Growing up in Central Australia: New Anthropological Studies of Aboriginal Childhood and Adolescence. New York: Berghahn.

Elkin, Adolphus P. 1938. The Australian Aborigines. Sydney: Angus and Robertson.

Elkin, Adolphus P. 1944. Citizenship for the Aborigines: A National Aboriginal Policy. Sydney: Australasian Publishing.

Elkin, Adolphus P. 1945. Aboriginal Men of High Degree. Sydney: Australasian Publishing.

Elkin, Adolphus P. 1951. Reaction and Interaction: A Food Gathering People and European Settlement in Australia. American Anthropologist 53:164–86.

Elkin, Adolphus P. 1961. Maraian at Mainoru, 1949. Oceania 31(4):259–93.

Ellis, Catherine J. 1980. Aboriginal Music and Dance in Southern Australia. Pp. 722–28 in Stanley Sadie (ed.), New Grove Dictionary of Music and Musicians. London: Macmillan.

Ellis, Catherine J. 1984. Time Consciousness of Aboriginal Performers. Pp. 149–85 in J. C. Kassler and Jill Stubington (ed.), Problems and Solutions: Occasional Essays in Musicology Presented to Alice M. Moyle. Sydney: Hale and Iremonger.

Evans, Nicholas 1992. Macassan Loanwords in Top End Languages. Australian Journal of Linguistics 12(1):45–91.

Evans, Nicholas, and Patrick McConvell 1997. The Enigma of Pama-Nyungan Expansion in Australia. Pp. 174–91 in Roger Blench and Matthew Spriggs (ed.), Archaeology and Language II: Archaeological Data and Linguistic Hypotheses. London: Routledge.

Evans, Nicholas, Francesca Merlan, and Maggie Tukumba. 2004. A First Dictionary of Dalabon (Ngalkbon). Maningrida, N.T.: Maningrida Arts and Culture.

Expert Panel on Constitutional Recognition of Indigenous Australians 2012. Recognising Aboriginal and Torres Strait Islander Peoples in the Constitution: Report of the Expert Panel. Canberra: Commonwealth of Australia.

Eylmann, Erhard 1908. Die Eingeborenen der Kolonie Südaustralien. Berlin: Reimer.

Eyre, Edward John 1964. Journals of Expeditions of Discovery into Central Australia, and Overland from Adelaide to King George's Sound, in the Years 1840–1: Sent by the Colonists of South Australia, with the Sanction and Support of the Government; Including an Account of the Manners and Customs of the Aborigines and the State of Their Relations with Europeans. 2 vols. Facsimile ed. Adelaide: Libraries Board of South Australia.

Fabian, Johannes 1983. Time and the Other: How Anthropology Makes Its Object. New York: Columbia University Press.

Fanon, Frantz 1952. Black Skin, White Masks. New York: Grove Press.

Finlayson, H. H. 1952. The Red Centre: Man and Beast in the Heart of Australia. Sydney: Angus and Robertson.

Fitzmaurice, Andrew 2007. The Genealogy of Terra Nullius. Australian Historical Studies 38(129):1–15.

Fogarty, William 2005. "You Got Any Truck?" Vehicles and Decentralised Mobile Service-Provision in Remote Indigenous Australia. Centre for Aboriginal Economic Policy Research Working Paper No. 30. Canberra: Australian National University.

Forrest, Peter 1985. An Outline of the History of Beswick Station and Related Areas. Northern Territory Library Document, mimeo.

Foster, Robert 1989. Feasts of the Full Moon: The Distribution of Rations to Aborigines in South Australia, 1836–1861. Aboriginal History 13(1):63–78.

Gerrard, Grayson 1989. Everyone Will Be Jealous for That Mutika. Mankind 19(2):95–111.

Gibney, Mark, Rhoda E. Howard-Hassmann, Jean-Marc Coicaud, and Niklaus Steiner (ed.) 2008. The Age of Apology: Facing Up to the Past. Philadelphia: University of Pennsylvania Press.

Giddens, Anthony 1979. Central Problems in Social Theory: Action, Structure, and Contradiction in Social Analysis. Berkeley: University of California Press.

Giles, Alfred 1928. The First Pastoral Settlement in the Northern Territory [compiled 1928]. Adelaide: South Australian Archives.

Glaskin, Katie 2012. Anatomies of Relatedness: Considering Personhood in Aboriginal Australia. American Anthropologist 114(2):297–308.

Goffman, Erving (1967) 2005. Interaction Ritual: Essays in Face-to-Face Behavior. With new introduction by Joel Best. New Brunswick, N.J.: AldineTransaction.

Goodall, Heather 1996. Invasion to Embassy: Land in Aboriginal Politics in New South Wales, 1770–1972. Sydney: Sydney University Press.

Goodall, Heather, and Allison Cadzow 2009. Rivers and Resilience: Aboriginal People on Sydney's Georges River. Sydney: UNSW Press.

Grant, Stan 2016. The Tears of Strangers. Sydney: HarperCollins.

Grey, George 1841. Journals of two expeditions of discovery in north-west and western Australia, during the years 1837, 38, and 39, under the authority of Her Majesty's government; describing many newly discovered, important, and fertile districts, with observations on the moral and physical condition of the aboriginal inhabitants, &c., &c. 2 vols. London: T. and W. Boone.

Grieves, Victoria, and Paulette Whitton 2013. "All My Relos": Aunty June Barker Speaks of Her Family History. Journal of the European Association for Studies of Australia 4(1):117–29.

Gunn, Jeannie 1907. We of the Never-Never. London: Hutchinson.

Gunn, Jeannie 1909. The Little Black Princess of the Never-Never. London: Hodder and Stoughton.

Haebich, Anna 1988. For Their Own Good: Aborigines and Government in the Southwest of Western Australia, 1900–1940. Nedlands: University of Western Australia Press.

Haebich, Anna, 2000. Broken Circles. Fremantle, W.A.: Fremantle Press.

Haebich, Anna 2004. Clearing the Wheat Belt: Erasing the Indigenous Presence in the Southwest of Western Australia. Pp. 267–89 in A. Dirk Moses (ed.), Genocide and Settler Society: Frontier Violence and Stolen Indigenous Children in Australian History. New York: Berghahn.

Hamilton, Annette 1979. Timeless Transformation: Women, Men and History in the Australian Western Desert. PhD thesis, University of Sydney.

Hamilton, Annette 1981. Nature and Nurture: Aboriginal Child-Rearing in North-Central Arnhem Land. Canberra: Australian Institute of Aboriginal Studies; distributed by Humanities Press.

Hamilton, Annette 1998. Descended from Father, Belonging to Country. Pp. 90–108 in William Edwards (ed.), Traditional Aboriginal Society. 2nd ed. South Yarra: Macmillan.

Hanks, William F. 2010. Converting Words: Maya in the Age of the Cross. Berkeley: University of California Press.

Harkins, Jean 1990. Shame and Shyness in the Aboriginal Classroom: A Case for "Practical Semantics." Australian Journal of Linguistics 10(2):293–306.

Harris, John 1993. Losing and Gaining a Language: The Story of Kriol in the Northern Territory. Pp. 145–54 in Michael Walsh and Colin Yallop (ed.), Language and Culture in Aboriginal Australia. Canberra: Aboriginal Studies Press.

Harvey, Roy (Bluey) 1983. Larry Boy Manhunt [from 20 September–25 October 1968]. NT Police News 6(4) and 7(1). Available at https://sites.google.com/site/ntpmhsociety/home/our-rich-history/timeline-and-events/major-crimes-and-investigations/larry-boy-manhunt.

Haviland, John B. 1979. Guugu Yimidhirr Brother-in-Law Language. Language in Society 8(2–3):365–93.

Haynes, Christopher David 2009. Defined by Contradiction: The Social Construction of Joint Management in Kakadu National Park. PhD thesis, Charles Darwin University.

Henry, Rosita 2012. Performing Place, Practising Memories: Aboriginal Australians, Hippies and the State. New York: Berghahn.

Heppell, M. (ed.) 1979. A Black Reality: Aboriginal Camps and Housing in Remote Australia. AIAS new series, no. 6. Canberra: Australian Institute of Aboriginal Studies.

Hercus, Luise Anna, and Peter Sutton (ed.) 1986. This Is What Happened: Historical Narratives by Aborigines. Canberra: Australian Institute of Aboriginal Studies Press.

Hiatt, Lester Richard 1966. A Spear in the Ear. Oceania 37(2):153–54.

Hiatt, Lester Richard 1971. Secret Pseudo-Procreation Rites Among the Australian Aborigines. Pp. 77–88 in Lester Richard Hiatt and Chandra Jayawardena (ed.), Anthropology in Oceania: Essays Presented to Ian Hogbin. Sydney: Angus and Robertson.

Hiatt, Lester Richard 1987. Treaty, Compact, Makarrata . . . ? Oceania 58(2):140–44.

Hiatt, Lester Richard 1996. Arguments About Aborigines: Australia and the Evolution of Social Anthropology. Cambridge: Cambridge University Press.

Hokari, Minoru 2005. Gurindji Mode of Historical Practice. Pp. 214–22 in Luke Taylor, Graeme K. Ward, Graham Henderson, Richard Davis, and Lynley A. Wallis (ed.), The Power of Knowledge, the Resonance of Tradition. Canberra: Aboriginal Studies Press.

Humpage, Louise 2005. Experimenting with a "Whole of Government" Approach: Indigenous Capacity Building in New Zealand and Australia. Policy Studies 26(1):47–66.

Hunter, Ernest 1993. Aboriginal Health and History: Power and Prejudice in Remote Australia. Cambridge: Cambridge University Press.

Inglis, K. S. 2012. Rowley, Charles Dunford (1906–1985). Australian Dictionary of Biography. Canberra: National Centre of Biography, Australian National University. http://adb.anu.edu.au/biography/rowley-charles-dunford-14191/text25203.

Jacobs, Patricia 1986. Science and Veiled Assumptions: Miscegenation in W.A., 1930–1937. Australian Aboriginal Studies 2:15–23.

Jones, Philip, and Anna Kenny 2007. Australia's Muslim Cameleers: Pioneers of the Inland, 1860s–1930s. Kent Town, S.A.: Wakefield Press.

Jugé, Tony S., and Michael Perez 2006. The Modern Colonial Politics of Citizenship and Whiteness in France. Social Identities 12(2):187–212.

Kaberry, Phyllis 1939. Aboriginal Woman: Sacred and Profane. London: Routledge.

Kapferer, Bruce 1988. Legends of People, Myths of State. Washington, D.C.: Smithsonian Institution.

Keen, Ian 1993. Aboriginal Beliefs vs. Mining at Coronation Hill: the Containing Force of Traditionalism. Human Organization 52(4):344–55.

Keen, Ian 1994. Knowledge and Secrecy in an Aboriginal Religion. Oxford: Clarendon Press; New York: Oxford University Press.

Keen, Ian, and Francesca Merlan 1990. The Significance of the Conservation Zone to Aboriginal People. Resource Assessment Commission, Kakadu Zone Conservation Zone Inquiry Consultancy Series. Canberra: Published for the Resource Assessment Commission by Australian Government Publishing Service.

Keller, Simon 2007. The Limits of Loyalty. Cambridge: Cambridge University Press.

Kelly, Paul 2015. The Polarising Forces Threaten to Derail Bid for Indigenous Recognition. The Australian, 2 May.

Kelman, Ari 2013. A Misplaced Massacre: Struggling over the Memory of Sand Creek. Cambridge, Mass.: Harvard University Press.

Keynes, Richard Darwin (ed.) 1979. The Beagle Record: Selections from the Original Pictorial Records and Written Accounts of the Voyage of H.M.S. Beagle. New York: Cambridge University Press.

King, Philip Gidley 1980. The Journal of Philip Gidley King, R.N., 1787–1790. Sydney: Australian Documents Library.

King, Phillip Parker 1827. Narrative of a Survey of the Intertropical and Western Coasts of Australia: Performed Between the Years 1818 and 1822. 2 vols. London: Murray.

Kockelman, Paul 2016. The Chicken and the Quetzal: Incommensurate Ontologies and Portable Values in Guatemala's Cloud Forest. Durham, N.C.: Duke University Press.

Kowal, Emma 2008. The Politics of the Gap: Indigenous Australians, Liberal Multiculturalism, and the End of the Self-Determination Era. American Anthropologist 110(3):338–48.

Kowal, Emma 2015. Trapped in the Gap: Doing Good in Indigenous Affairs. London: Berghahn.

Kupperman, Karen Ordahl 1977. English Perceptions of Treachery, 1583–1640: The Case of the American "Savages." Historical Journal 20(2):263–87.

Langton, Marcia 1981. Urbanizing Aborigines: The Social Scientists' Great Deception. Social Alternatives 2(2):16–22.

Langton, Marcia 2000–2001. A Treaty Between Our Nations. Arena Magazine 50:28–34.

Langton, Marcia 2007. Stop the Abuse of Children. The Australian, 12 December.

Laracy, Hugh 1980. Leopold Verguet and the Aborigines of Sydney, 1845. Aboriginal History 4:179.

Larbalestier, Jan 1990. Amity and Kindness in the Never-Never: Ideology and Aboriginal-European Relations in the Northern Territory. Social Analysis 27:70–82.

Lawrence, Rebecca 2005. Governing Warlpiri Subjects: Indigenous Training and Employment Programs in the Central Australian Mining Industry. Geographical Research 43(1):40–48.

Lea, Tess 2008a. Bureaucrats and Bleeding Hearts: Indigenous Health in Northern Australia. Sydney: UNSW Press.

Lea, Tess 2008b. Housing for Health in Indigenous Australia: Driving Change When Research and Policy Are Part of the Problem. Human Organization 67(1):77–85.

Lea, Tess, and Paul Pholeros 2010. This Is Not a Pipe: The Treacheries of Indigenous Housing. Public Culture 22(1):187–209.

Legislative Assembly, New South Wales 1911. Report of Board for Protection of Aborigines for Year 1910. Sydney: Government Printer.

Lemke, Jay L. 2000. Across the Scales of Time: Artifacts, Activities and Meanings in Ecosocial Systems. Mind, Culture and Activity 7(4):273–90.

Levitus, Robert 2009. Aboriginal Organizations and Development: The Structural Context. Pp. 73–97 in Jon Altman and David Martin (ed.), Indigenous Australians and Mining. Canberra: Australian National University Press.

Lewis, Darrell 2005. "Invaders of a Peaceful Country": Aborigines and Explorers on the Lower Victoria River, Northern Territory. Aboriginal History 29:23–45.

Lewis, Darrell 2012. A Wild History: Life and Death on the Victoria River Frontier. Clayton, Vic.: Monash University Publishing.

Macdonald, Gaynor 2000. Economies and Personhood: Demand Sharing Among the Wiradjuri of New South Wales. Pp. 87–111 in George Wenzel, Grete Hovelsrud-Broda, and Nobuhiro Kishigami (ed.), The Social Economy of Sharing: Resource Allocation and Modern Hunter-Gatherers. Senri Ethnological Studies 53. Osaka: National Museum of Ethnology.

Macintyre, Stuart, and Anna Clark 2004. The History Wars. Melbourne: Melbourne University Press.

Manne, Robert (ed.) 2003. Whitewash: On Keith Windschuttle's Fabrication of Aboriginal History. Melbourne: Black Inc. Agenda.

Manne, Robert. 2009. The History Wars. Monthly, November.

Marcuse, Herbert 1965. Repressive Tolerance. Pp. 81–117 in Robert Paul Wolff, Barrington Moore, and Herbert Marcuse, A Critique of Pure Tolerance. Boston: Beacon Press.

Marett, Allan 2000. Ghostly Voices: Some Observations on Song-Creations, Ceremony and Being in NW Australia. Oceania 71(1):18–29.

Markell, Patchen 2009. Bound by Recognition. Princeton, N.J.: Princeton University Press.

Markus, Andrew 1979. Fear and Hatred: Purifying Australia and California, 1850–1901. Sydney: Hale and Iremonger.

Martin, David F. 2003. Rethinking the Design of Indigenous Organisations: The Need for Strategic Engagement. Canberra: CAEPR (Centre for Aboriginal Economic Policy Research).

McBryde, Isabel 1989. ". . . To Establish a Commerce of This Sort": Cross-Cultural Exchange at the

Port Jackson Settlement. Pp. 170–82 in J. Hardy and A. Frost (ed.), Studies from Terra Australis to Australia. Occasional Paper No. 6. Canberra: Australian Academy of the Humanities.

McCarthy, Fred 1939. "Trade" in Aboriginal Australia and "Trade" Relations with Torres Strait, New Guinea and Malaya. Oceania 9(4):405–38.

McCombie Select Committee Inquiry 1859. Report of the Select Committee of the Legislative Council on the Aborigines. Melbourne: Government Printer.

McDonald, Barry 1996. Evidence of Four New England Corroboree Songs Indicating Aboriginal Responses to European Invasion. Aboriginal History 20:176–94.

McGrath, Ann 1984. Black Velvet: Aboriginal Women and Their Relations with White Men in the Northern Territory, 1910–1940. Pp. 233–97 in Kay Daniels (ed.), So Much Hard Work: Women and Prostitution in Australian History. Sydney: Fontana/Collins.

McGrath, Ann 1987. Born in the Cattle: Aborigines in Cattle Country. Sydney: Allen and Unwin.

McGrath, Ann 1990. The White Man's Looking Glass: Aboriginal-Colonial Gender Relations at Port Jackson. Australian Historical Studies 24(95):189–206.

McGregor, Russell 2011. Indifferent Inclusion: Aboriginal People and the Australian Nation. Canberra: Aboriginal Studies Press.

McKnight, David 2002. From Hunting to Drinking: The Devastating Effects of Alcohol on an Australian Aboriginal Community. London: Routledge.

Meggitt, Mervyn 1962. Desert People: A Study of the Walbiri Aborigines of Central Australia. Sydney: Angus and Robertson.

Memmott, Paul 1988. Aboriginal Housing: The State of the Art (or The Non-State of the Art). Architecture Australia, 1 June, pp. 34–45.

Memmott, Paul 2003. Customary Aboriginal Behaviour Patterns and Housing Design. Pp. 26–39 in Paul Memmott and Catherine Chambers (ed.), Take 2: Housing Design in Indigenous Australia. Canberra: Royal Australian Institute of Architects.

Memmott, Paul 2007. Gunyah, Goondie and Wurley: The Aboriginal Architecture of Australia. St. Lucia: University of Queensland Press.

Merlan, Francesca 1978. Making People Quiet in the Pastoral North: Reminiscences of Elsey Station. Journal of Aboriginal History 1(2):70–106.

Merlan, Francesca 1981. Land, Language and Social Identity in Aboriginal Australia. Australian Journal of Anthropology 13(2):133.

Merlan, Francesca 1982. Mangarayi. Amsterdam: North Holland.

Merlan, Francesca 1983. Ngalakan Grammar, Texts and Vocabulary. Canberra: Pacific Linguistics.

Merlan, Francesca 1988. A Review of Gender in Aboriginal Social Life. Pp. 15–76 in R. M. Berndt and R. Tonkinson (ed.), Social Anthropology and Australian Aboriginal Studies: A Contemporary Review. Canberra: Aboriginal Studies Press.

Merlan, Francesca 1991a. The Limits of Cultural Constructionism: The Case of Coronation Hill. Oceania 61:1–12.

Merlan, Francesca 1991b. Women, Productive Roles and Monetisation of the "Service Mode" in Aboriginal Australia: Perspectives from Katherine, Northern Territory. Australian Journal of Anthropology 2(3):259–92.

Merlan, Francesca 1992. Male-Female Separation and Forms of Society in Aboriginal Australia. Cultural Anthropology 7(2):169–92.

Merlan, Francesca 1994a. Wardaman: A Language of the Northern Territory of Australia. Berlin: Mouton.

Merlan, Francesca 1994b. Entitlement and Need: Concepts Underlying and in Land Rights and

Native Title Acts. In Claims to Knowledge, Claims to Country. Native Title Research Unit. Canberra: Australian Institute of Aboriginal and Torres Strait Islander Studies.

Merlan, Francesca 1995. The Regimentation of Customary Practice: From Northern Territory Land Claims to Mabo. Australian Journal of Anthropology 6(1–2):64–82.

Merlan, Francesca 1996. Big River Country: Stories from Elsey Station. Alice Springs: Institute of Aboriginal Development.

Merlan, Francesca 1997a. Fighting over Country: Four Commonplaces. Pp. 1–14 in D. E. Smith and J. Finlayson (ed.), Fighting over Country: Anthropological Perspectives. Research Monograph No. 12. Canberra: Centre for Aboriginal Economic Policy Research, Australian National University. http://caepr.anu.edu.au/sites/default/files/Publications/mono/CAEPR _Mono12.pdf.

Merlan, Francesca 1997b. The Mother-in-Law Taboo: Avoidance and Obligation in Australian Aboriginal Society. Pp. 95–122 in Francesca Merlan, John Morton, and Alan Rumsey (ed.), Scholar and Sceptic: Australian Aboriginal Studies in Honour of L. R. Hiatt. Canberra: Australian Institute of Aboriginal and Torres Strait Islander Studies.

Merlan, Francesca 1998. Caging the Rainbow: Places, Politics and Aborigines in a North Australian Town. Honolulu: University of Hawaiʻi Press.

Merlan, Francesca 2005. Explorations Towards Intercultural Accounts of Socio-Cultural Reproduction and Change. Oceania 75(3):167–82

Merlan, Francesca 2007. Indigeneity as Relational Identity: The Construction of Australian Land Rights. Pp. 125–50 in Marisol de la Cadena and Orin Starn (ed.), Indigenous Experience Today. New York: Berg.

Merlan, Francesca 2009. More Than Rights. Inside Story, 11 March. http://insidestory.org.au /more-than-rights.

Merlan, Francesca 2016a. Tricksters and Traditions: Story-Tellers of Southern Arnhem Land. Canberra: Asia-Pacific Linguistics.

Merlan, Francesca 2016b. Women, Warfare and the Life of Agency in Papua New Guinea and Beyond. Journal of the Royal Anthropological Institute 22:1–20.

Merlan, Francesca, and Pascale Jacq 2005. Jawoyn-English Dictionary and English Finder List. Katherine, N.T.: Diwurruwurru-jaru Aboriginal Corporation.

Merleau-Ponty, Maurice 1962. Phenomenology of Perception. Trans. Colin Smith. London: Routledge & Kegan Paul.

Merleau-Ponty, Maurice 1968. The Visible and the Invisible: Followed by Working Notes. Ed. Claude Lefort; trans. Alphonso Lingis. Evanston, Ill.: Northwestern University Press.

Michaels, Eric 1985. Constraints on Knowledge in an Economy of Oral Information. Current Anthropology 26(4):505–10.

Miller, Christopher L. 1985. Prophetic Worlds: Indians and Whites on the Columbia Plateau. New Brunswick, N.J.: Rutgers University Press.

Moore, Donald S., Anand Pandian, and Jake Kosek 2003. Introduction: The Cultural Politics of Race and Nature; Terrains of Power and Practice. Pp. 1–70 in Donald S. Moore, Jake Kosek, and Anand Pandian (ed.), Race, Nature, and the Politics of Difference. Durham, N.C.: Duke University Press.

Morphy, Frances 2007. Uncontained Subjects: Population and Household in Remote Aboriginal Australia. Journal of Population Research 24(2):163–84.

Morphy, Howard 1989. From Dull to Brilliant: The Aesthetics of Spiritual Power Among the Yolngu. Man 24(1):21–40.

Morphy, Howard 1991. Ancestral Connections: Art and an Aboriginal System of Knowledge. Chicago: University of Chicago Press.

Morphy, Howard, and Frances Morphy 1984. The "Myths" of Ngalakan History: Ideology and Images of the Past in Northern Australia. Man 19(3):459–78.

Morris, Barry 1989. Domesticating Resistance. London: Berg.

Moses, A. Dirk (ed.) 2004. Genocide and Settler Society: Frontier Violence and Stolen Indigenous Children in Australian History. New York: Berghahn.

Moses, A. Dirk 2010. Time, Indigeneity and Peoplehood: The Postcolony in Australia. Postcolonial Studies 13(1):9–32.

Muldoon, Paul 2008. The Sovereign Exceptions: Colonization and the Foundation of Society. Social and Legal Studies 17(1):59–74.

Munn, Nancy D. 1970. The Transformation of Subjects into Objects in Walbiri and Pitjantjatjara Myth. Pp. 141–73 in R. M. Berndt (ed.), Australian Aboriginal Anthropology. Nedlands: University of Western Australia Press.

Musharbash, Yasmine 2017. Predicaments of Proximity: Revising Relatedness in a Warlpiri Town. In Diane Austin-Broos and Francesca Merlan (ed.), People and Change in Indigenous Australia. Honolulu: University of Hawai'i.

Myers, Fred R. 1986. Pintupi Country, Pintupi Self: Sentiment, Place and Politics Among Western Desert Aborigines. Washington, D.C.: Smithsonian Institution Press; Canberra: Australian Institute of Aboriginal Studies.

Myers, Fred R. 1988. Burning the Truck and Holding the Country: Property, Time and the Negotiation of Identity Among Pintupi Aborigines. Pp. 52–74 in Tim Ingold, David Riches, and James Woodburn (ed.), Hunters and Gatherers 2: Property, Power and Ideology. New York: Berg.

Myers, Fred R. 2001. Introduction: The Empire of Things. Pp. 3–61 in Fred R. Myers (ed.), The Empire of Things: Regimes of Value and Material Culture. Santa Fe, N.M.: School of American Research Press; Oxford: James Currey.

Nabokov, Peter 1979. Native American Testimony: An Anthology of Indian and White Relations; First Encounter to Dispossession. With a preface by Vine Deloria Jr. New York: Harper and Row.

Nadasdy, Paul 2003. Hunters and Bureaucrats: Power, Knowledge, and Aboriginal-State Relations in the Southwest Yukon. Vancouver: University of British Columbia Press.

Naipaul, V. S. 1967. The Mimic Men. London: Deutsch.

Nash, David 1986. Motor Vehicles in Central Australian Aboriginal Society: Some Preliminary Notes. Sect. 3.17 in Barney Foran and Bruce Walker (ed.), Science and Technology for Aboriginal Development. Alice Springs, N.T.: CSIRO, Division of Wildlife and Rangelands Research.

Nettelbeck, Amanda 2008. Practices of Violence/Myths of Creation: Mounted Constable Willshire and the Cultural Logic of Settler Nationalism. Journal of Australian Studies 32(1):5–17.

NLA (National Library of Australia) MS 2. 1768. Secret Instructions for Lt. James Cook, Appointed to Command His Majesty's Bark the Endeavour. 30 July.

Northern Standard 1937. [Jeannie Gunn] first printed in Brisbane Courier Mail, 12 February.

O'Brien, Philip 2011. Gwalwa Daraniki: Land Rights Struggle on Record. National Archives of Australia, Your Memento, no. 3. http://yourmemento.naa.gov.au/2011/06/gwalwa-daraniki-land-rights-struggle-on-record/.

O'Faircheallaigh, Ciaran 2006. Aborigines, Mining Companies and the State in Contemporary Australia: A New Political Economy or "Business as Usual"? Australian Journal of Political Science 41(1):1–22.

O'Reilly, J. B. 1994. Demographic Implications of Aboriginal Out-Marriage. Journal of the Australian Population Association 11(2):149–59.

Ortner, Sherry 1995. Resistance and the Problem of Ethnographic Refusal. Comparative Studies in Society and History 37(1):173–93.

Paradies, Yin C. 2006. Beyond Black and White: Essentialism, Hybridity and Indigeneity. Journal of Sociology 42(4):355–67.

Parsons, Michael 1997. The Tourist Corroboree in South Australia to 1911. Aboriginal History 21:46–97.

Parsons, Michael 2000. Corroborees. Pp. 564–65 in Sylvia Kleinert and Margo Neale (ed.), The Oxford Companion to Aboriginal Art and Culture. Melbourne: Oxford University Press.

Parsons, Talcott 1951. The Social System. New York: Free Press; London: Collier-Macmillan.

Patton, Paul 1996. Sovereignty, Law and Difference in Australia: After the Mabo Case. Alternatives: Global, Local, Political 21(2):149–70.

Pearson, Noel 2014. A Rightful Place: Race, Recognition and a More Complete Commonwealth. Quarterly Essay, issue 55.

Pedersen, Howard, and Banjo Woorunmurra 1995. Jandamarra and the Bunuba Resistance. Broome, W.A.: Magabala Books.

Pentony, B. 1961. Dreams and Dream Beliefs in North Western Australia. Oceania 32(2):144–49.

Péron, François 2006. Voyage of Discovery to the Southern Lands. Second Edition 1824. Continued by Louis de Freycinet. Books I to III Comprising Chapters I to XXI. Trans. Christine Cornell. Adelaide: Friends of the State Library of South Australia. Orig. published as Voyage de découverte aux terres Australes. 3 vols. (Paris, 1807–16).

Petri, Helmut 1950. Kurangara: Neue magische Kulte in Nordwest-Australien. Zeitschrift für Ethnologie 75:43–51.

Petrie, Constance Campbell 1992. Tom Petrie's Reminiscences of Early Queensland. St. Lucia: University of Queensland Press. First published 1904.

Piaget, Jean, and Bärbel Inhelder 1969. The Psychology of the Child. New York: Basic Books.

Polanyi, Michael 1966. The Logic of Tacit Inference. Philosophy 41(15):1–18.

Polanyi, Michael 2015. Personal Knowledge: Towards a Post-Critical Philosophy. Enlarged ed. Chicago: University of Chicago Press. Originally published 1958.

Povinelli, Elizabeth 1993. Labor's Lot: The Power, History, and Culture of Aboriginal Action. Chicago: University of Chicago Press.

Povinelli, Elizabeth 2001. Radical Worlds: The Anthropology of Incommensurability and Inconceivability. Annual Review of Anthropology 30:319–34.

Povinelli, Elizabeth 2002. The Cunning of Recognition: Indigenous Alterities and the Making of Australian Multiculturalism. Durham, N.C.: Duke University Press.

Povinelli, Elizabeth 2005. Without Shame: Australia, the United States, and the "New" Cultural Unilateralism. Australian Feminist Law Journal 22:29–48.

Povinelli, Elizabeth 2014. Geontologies of the Otherwise. Cultural Anthropology, 13 January. http://culanth.org/fieldsights/465-geontologies-of-the-otherwise.

Pratt, Angela 2005. Practising Reconciliation? The Politics of Reconciliation in the Australian Parliament, 1991–2000. Canberra: Department of Parliamentary Services.

Price, Richard 1983. First Time: The Historical Vision of an Afro-American People. Baltimore: Johns Hopkins University Press.

Radcliffe-Brown, A. R. 1930. The Social Organisation of the Australian Tribes. Oceania 1:34–63, 322–41, 426–56.

Ramsey, Jarold 1983. Reading the Fire: Essays in the Traditional Indian Literatures of the Far West. Lincoln: University of Nebraska Press.

Read, Peter 2000. Settlement: A History of Australian Indigenous Housing. Canberra: Aboriginal Studies Press.

Reay, Marie 1949. Native Thought in Rural New South Wales. Oceania 20(2):89–118.

Reay, Marie n.d. Field notes. Butlin Library Files. Australian National University, Canberra.

Redmond, Anthony 2005. Strange Relatives: Mutualities and Dependencies Between Aborigines and Pastoralists in the Northern Kimberley. Oceania 75(3):234–46.

Reid, Gordon 1990. A Picnic with the Natives: Aboriginal-European Relations in the Northern Territory to 1910. Melbourne: Melbourne University Press.

Reynolds, Henry 1972. Aborigines and Settlers: The Australian Experience, 1788–1939. Stanmore, N.S.W. : Cassell Australia.

Reynolds, Henry 1974. Racial Thought in Early Colonial Australia. Australian Journal of Politics and History 20(1):45–53.

Reynolds, Henry 1981. The Other Side of the Frontier: Aboriginal Resistance to the European Invasion of Australia. Victoria: Penguin.

Reynolds, Henry 1996. After Mabo, What About Aboriginal Sovereignty? Australian Humanities Review, April. http://www.australianhumanitiesreview.org/archive/Issue-April-1996/Reynolds.html.

Reynolds, Henry 2001. An Indelible Stain? The Question of Genocide in Australia's History. Ringwood, Vic.: Penguin.

Reynolds, Henry 2006. The Other Side of the Frontier: Aboriginal Resistance to the European Invasion of Australia. Sydney: UNSW Press.

Rifkin, Mark 2011. When Did Indians Become Straight? Kinship, the History of Sexuality, and Native Sovereignty. New York: Oxford University Press.

Roberts, Stephen H. 1969. History of Australian Land Settlement. London: F. Cass.

Rosaldo, Renato 1989. Imperialist Nostalgia. Representations 26:107–22.

Rose, Deborah Bird 1989. Remembrance. Aboriginal History 13(1/2):135–48.

Rose, Deborah Bird 1991. Hidden Histories: Black Stories from Victoria River Downs, Humbert River, and Wave Hill Stations. Canberra: Aboriginal Studies Press.

Rose, Deborah Bird 1992. Dingo Makes Us Human: Life and Land in an Australian Aboriginal Culture. New York: Cambridge University Press.

Rose, Deborah Bird 2004. Reports from a Wild Country: Ethics for Decolonisation. Sydney: UNSW Press.

Rose, Deborah Bird 2011. Wild Dog Dreaming: Love and Extinctions. Charlottesville: University of Virginia Press.

Rose, Deborah Bird 2012. Multispecies Knots of Ethical Time. Environmental Philosophy 9(1):127–40.

Rose, Deborah Bird 2015. The Ecological Humanities. Pp. 1–5 in Katherine Gibson, Deborah Bird Rose, and Ruth Fincher (ed.), Manifesto for Living in the Anthropocene. Brooklyn, N.Y.: Punctum Books.

Rose, Deborah Bird, and Tony Swain 1988. Introduction: Christian Myth Adapted to Aboriginal

"Cosmological" Purpose. Pp. 1–8 in Tony Swain and Deborah Bird Rose (ed.), Aboriginal Australians and Christian Missions: Ethnographic and Historical Studies. Bedford Park, S.A.: Australian Association for the Study of Religions.

Roth, H. L. 1899. The Aborigines of Tasmania. Halifax: F. King and Sons.

Rowley, Charles D. 1970. The Destruction of Aboriginal Society. Canberra: Australian National University Press.

Rowley, Charles D. 1971a. Outcasts in White Australia. Canberra: Australian National University Press.

Rowley, Charles D. 1971b. The Remote Aborigines. Canberra: Australian National University Press.

Rowley, Charles D. 1986. Recovery: The Politics of Aboriginal Reform. Melbourne: Penguin.

Rowse, Tim 1998. White Flour, White Power: From Rations to Citizenship in Central Australia. Cambridge: Cambridge University Press.

Rowse, Tim 1999. A Spear in the Thigh for Senator Evans. Pp. 199–217 in Klaus Neumann, Nicholas Thomas, and H. Ericksen (ed.), Quicksands: Foundational Histories in Australia and Aotearoa New Zealand. Sydney: UNSW Press.

Rowse, Tim 2000. Obliged to Be Difficult: Nugget Coombs' Legacy in Indigenous Affairs. Cambridge: Cambridge University Press.

Rowse, Tim 2003. Historians and the Humanitarian Critique of Australia's Colonisation. Australian Journal of Anthropology 14(2):253–58.

Rowse, Tim 2006a. From Enforceability to Feel-Good: Notes on the Prehistory of the Recent Treaty Debate. Pp. 71–88 in Peter Read, Gary Meyers, and Bob Reece (ed.), What Good Condition? Reflections on an Aboriginal Treaty, 1986–2006. Aboriginal History Monograph 13. Canberra: ANU Press.

Rowse, Tim 2006b. Public Occasions, Indigenous Selves: Three Ngarrindjeri Autobiographies. Aboriginal History 30:187–207.

Rowse, Tim 2012. Rethinking Social Justice: From "Peoples" to "Populations." Canberra: Aboriginal Studies Press.

Rowse, Tim 2017. Indigenous and Other Australians Since 1901. Sydney: NewSouth Press.

Royal Commission into Aboriginal Deaths in Custody (RCIADC) 1991. Final Report.

Rumsey, Alan 1982. Gun-gunma: An Australian Aboriginal Avoidance Language and Its Social Functions. Pp. 161–82 in Jeffrey Heath, Francesca Merlan, and Alan Rumsey (ed.), The Languages of Kinship in Aboriginal Australia. Oceania Linguistic Monographs, no. 24. Sydney: University of Sydney.

Rumsey, Alan 1993. Language and Territoriality in Aboriginal Australia. Pp. 191–206 in Michael Walsh and Colin Yallop (ed.), Language and Culture in Aboriginal Australia. Canberra: Aboriginal Studies Press.

Ryan, Lyndall 1981. The Aboriginal Tasmanians. St. Lucia: University of Queensland Press.

Sahlins, Marshall 1985. Islands of History. Chicago: University of Chicago Press.

Saldanha, Arun 2006. Reontologising Race: The Machinic Geography of Phenotype. Environment and Planning D: Society and Space 24:9–24.

Sanders, Will 1990. Reconstructing Aboriginal Housing Policy for Remote Areas: How Much Room for Manoeuvre? Australian Journal of Public Administration 49(1):38–50.

Sansom, Basil 1980. The Camp at Wallaby Cross. Canberra: Australian Institute of Aboriginal Studies.

Sansom, Basil 1982. The Aboriginal Commonality. Pp. 117–38 in Ronald Berndt (ed.),

Aboriginal Sites, Rights and Resource Development. Nedlands: University of Western Australia Press.

Schieffelin, Edward L., and Robert Crittenden 1991. Like People You See in a Dream: First Contact in Six Papuan Societies. Stanford, Calif.: Stanford University Press.

Scott, James 1985. Weapons of the Weak: Everyday Forms of Peasant Resistance. New Haven, Conn.: Yale University Press.

Schutz, Alfred 1967. The Phenomenology of the Social World. Trans. George Walsh and Frederick Lehnert. Evanston, Ill.: Northwestern University Press.

Scrimgeour, Anne 2006. Notions of "Civilisation" and the Project to "Civilise" Aborigines in South Australia in the 1840s. History of Education Review 35(1):35–46.

Sharp, Lauriston 1952. Steel Axes for Stone-Age Australians. Human Organization 11(2): 17–22.

Shellam, Tiffany 2009. Shaking Hands on the Fringe: Negotiating the Aboriginal World at King George's Sound. Crawley: University of Western Australia Press.

Short, Damien, and Alex Gunstone 2011. Rejoinder to Tim Rowse,"The Reforming State, the Concerned Public and Indigenous Political Actors." Australian Journal of Politics and History 57(2):262–66.

Silverstein, Ben 2013. Native Title Within a History of Incorporation. Pp. 60–85 in Julie Evans, Ann Genovese, Alexander Reilly, and Patrick Wolfe (ed.), Sovereignty: Frontiers of Possibility. Honolulu: University of Hawai'i Press.

Simpson, Audra 2007. On the Logic of Discernment. American Quarterly 59(2): 479–91.

Simpson, Audra 2014. Mohawk Interruptus: Political Life Across the Borders of Settler States. Durham, N.C.: Duke University Press.

Simpson, Jane 2016. Working Verbs: The Spread of a Loan Word in Australian Language. Pp. 244–62 in Peter K. Austin, Harold Koch, and Jane Simpson (ed.), Language, Land and Song: Studies in Honour of Luise Hercus. London: EL Publishing.

Skyring, Fiona, and Sarah Yu 2008. "Strange Strangers": First Contact Between Europeans and Karajarri People on the Kimberley Coast of Western Australia. Pp. 60–75 in Peter Veth, Peter Sutton, and Margo Neale (ed.), Strangers on the Shore: Early Coastal Contacts in Australia. Canberra: National Museum of Australia Press.

Smith, Claire 2004. Country, Kin and Culture: Survival of an Australian Aboriginal Community. Kent Town, S.A.: Wakefield Press.

Smith, Len R. 1980. The Aboriginal Population of Australia. Canberra: Australian National University Press.

Smith, Len, Janet McCalman, Ian Anderson, Sandra Smith, Joanne Evans, Gavan McCarthy, and Jane Beer 2008. Fractional Identities: The Political Arithmetic of Aboriginal Victorians. Journal of Interdisciplinary History 38(4):533–51.

Smith, Pamela A. 2000. Station Camps: Legislation, Labour Relations and Rations on Pastoral Leases in the Kimberley Region, Western Australia. Aboriginal History 24:75–97.

Smyth, R. Brough 1878. The Aborigines of Victoria: With Notes Relating to the Habits of the Natives of Other Parts of Australia and Tasmania. 2 vols. London: Trübner; Melbourne: J. Ferres.

Snipp, C. Matthew 1989. American Indians: The First of This Land. New York: Russell Sage Foundation.

Snipp, C. Matthew 2003. Racial Measurement in the American Census: Past Practices and Implications for the Future. Annual Review of Sociology 29:563–88.

Sorensen, Roslyn, Catherine May Fowler, Chris Nash, and Wendy Bacon 2010. Addressing the

Gap in Indigenous Health: Government Intervention or Community Governance? A Qualitative Review. Health Sociology Review 19(1):20–33.

Spencer, Baldwin 1928. Wanderings in Wild Australia. Vol. 1. London: Macmillan.

Spencer, Baldwin, and Francis James Gillen 1927. The Arunta. 2 vols. London: Macmillan.

Stanner, William E. H. 1934. Ceremonial Economics of the Mulluk Mulluk and Madngella Tribes of the Daly River, North Australia: A Preliminary Paper. Oceania 4(4):458–71.

Stanner, William E. H. 1937. Aboriginal Modes of Address and Reference in the North-West of the Northern Territory. Oceania 7(3):300–315.

Stanner, William E. H. 1958. Continuity and Change Among the Aborigines. Presidential Address to Section F. Australian and New Zealand Association for the Advancement of Science, Adelaide.

Stanner, William E. H. 1966. On Aboriginal Religion. Oceania Monograph 11. Sydney: University of Sydney.

Stanner, William E. H. (1968) 1991. After the Dreaming. Boyer Lecture Series. Sydney: Australian Broadcasting Commission.

Star, Susan L., and James R. Griesemer 1989. Institutional Ecology, Translations, and Boundary Objects: Amateurs and Professionals in Berkeley's Museum of Vertebrate Zoology, 1907–39. Social Studies of Science 19(3):387–420.

Stern, Daniel N. 1985. The Interpersonal World of the Human Infant. New York: Basic Books.

Stocking, George W. 1966. Franz Boas and the Culture Concept in Historical Perspective. American Anthropologist 68(4):867–82.

Strakosch, Elizabeth 2015. Neoliberal Indigenous Policy: Settler Colonialism and the "Post-Welfare" State. London: ,Palgrave Macmillan.

Stratton, Jon, and Ien Ang 1994. Multicultural Imagined Communities: Cultural Difference and National Identity in Australia and the USA. Continuum: The Australian Journal of Media and Culture 8(2).

Strehlow, Theodore G. H. 1947. Aranda Traditions. Melbourne: Melbourne University Press.

Sturt, Charles 1849. Narrative of an Expedition into Central Australia Under the Authority of Her Majesty's Government During the Years 1844, 5, and 6. Together with a Notice of the Province of South Australia in 1847. 2 vols. London: T. and W. Boone. Reprinted as Australiana Facsimile Editions No. 5 (Adelaide: Libraries Board os South Australia, 1965).

Sturt, Charles 1984. Journal of the Central Australian Expedition, 1844–5. Vol. 2. Ed. Jill Waterhouse. London: Caliban Books.

Sturt, Charles 2002. The Central Australian Expedition, 1844–1846: The Journals of Charles Sturt. Ed. Richard C. Davis. London: Hakluyt Society.

Sutton, Peter 2001. The Politics of Suffering: Indigenous Policy in Australia Since the 1970s. Anthropological Forum 11(2):125–73.

Sutton, Peter 2008. Stories About Feeling: Dutch-Australian Contact in Cape York Peninsula, 1606-1756. Pp. 35–59 in Peter Veth, Peter Sutton, and Margo Neale (ed.), Strangers on the Shore: Early Coastal Contacts in Australia. Canberra: National Museum of Australia.

Sutton, Peter 2009. The Politics of Suffering: Indigenous Australia and the End of the Liberal Consensus. Carlton, Vic.: Melbourne University Press.

Swain, Tony 1993. A Place for Strangers: Towards a History of Australian Aboriginal Being. Cambridge: Cambridge University Press.

Taçon, Paul S. C. 1991. The Power of Stone: Symbolic Aspects of Stone Use and Tool Development in Western Arnhem Land, Australia. Antiquity 65(247):192–207.

Tasman, Abel Jansz (1642) 1964(?). The Journal of Abel Jansz Tasman 1642 with Documents Relating to his Exploration of Australia in 1644. Ed. G. H. Kenihan. Adelaide: Australian Heritage Press.

Taussig, Michael 1987. Shamanism, Colonialism, and the Wild Man: A Study in Terror and Healing. Chicago: University of Chicago Press.

Taussig, Michael 1993. Mimesis and Alterity: A Particular History of the Senses. New York: Routledge.

Taylor, Charles 1994. Multiculturalism: Examining the Politics of Recognition. Ed. Amy Gutmann. Princeton, N.J.: Princeton University Press.

Taylor, John 1996. Short-Term Indigenous Population Mobility and Service Delivery. Canberra: Australian National University, Centre for Aboriginal Economic Policy Research.

Taylor, John 2011. Postcolonial Transformation of the Australian Indigenous Population. Geographical Research 49(3):286–300.

Taylor, John, and Martin Bell 2004. Continuity and Change in Indigenous Australian Population Mobility. Pp. 13–43 in John Taylor and Martin Bell (ed.), Population Mobility and Indigenous Peoples in Australasia and North America. London: Routledge.

Tench, Watkin (1793) 1998. A Complete Account of the Settlement at Port Jackson, Including an Accurate Description of the Situation of the Colony; of the Natives; and of Its Natural Productions. Sydney: University of Sydney Library.

Tennie, Claudio, Josep Call, and Michael Tomasello 2006. Push or Pull: Imitation vs. Emulation in Great Apes and Human Children. Ethology 112(12):1159–69.

Thiele, Steven J. 1982. Yugul, an Arnhem Land Cattle Station. Darwin: Australian National University, North Australia Research Unit.

Thomson, Donald F. 1932. Ceremonial Presentation of Fire in North Queensland: A Preliminary Note on the Place of Fire in Primitive Ritual. Man 32(198):162–66.

Thonemann, Harold E. 1949. Tell the White Man: The Life Story of an Aboriginal Lubra. London: Collins.

Thornton, Russell 1997. Tribal Membership Requirements and the Demography of "Old" and "New" Native Americans. Population Research and Policy Review 16:33–42.

Tilbury, Clare, 2009. The Over-representation of Indigenous Children in the Australian Child Welfare System. International Journal of Social Welfare 18(1):57–64.

Todorov, Tzvetan 1999. The Conquest of America: The Question of the Other. Foreword by Anthony Pagden. Norman: University of Oklahoma Press.

Tonkinson, Robert 1978. Aboriginal Victors of the Desert Crusade. Menlo Park, Calif.: Cummings.

Torpey, John 2006. Making Whole What Has Been Smashed: On Reparations Politics. Cambridge, Mass.: Harvard University Press.

Trigger, David 1992. Whitefella Comin': Aboriginal Responses to Colonialism in Northern Australia. Cambridge: Cambridge University Press.

Trouillot, Michel-Rolph 1995. Silencing the Past: Power and the Production of History. Boston: Beacon Press.

Trouillot, Michel-Rolph 2003. Global Transformations: Anthropology and the Modern World. New York: Palgrave Macmillan.

Turnbull, Malcolm 1999. Fighting for the Republic. South Yarra, Vic.: Hardie Grant Books.

Veracini, Lorenzo 2007a. Historylessness: Australia as a Settler Colonial Collective. Postcolonial Studies 10:271–85.

Veracini, Lorenzo 2007b. Settler Colonialism and Decolonisation. Borderlands ejournal 6.

Veracini, Lorenzo 2010. Settler Colonialism: A Theoretical Introduction. London: Palgrave Macmillan.

Viveiros de Castro, Eduardo 2012. Cosmological Perspectivism in Amazonia and Elsewhere. HAU Masterclass Series, 1. Manchester: HAU Journal of Ethnographic Theory.

von Sturmer, John 1987. Aboriginal Singing and Notions of Power. Pp. 63–76 in Margaret Clunies Ross, Tamsin Donaldson, and Stephen A. Wild (ed.), Songs of Aboriginal Australia. Oceania Monograph 32. Sydney: University of Sydney.

Warchivker, I., T. Tjapangati, and J. Wakerman 2000. The Turmoil of Aboriginal Enumeration: Mobility and Service Population Analysis in a Central Australian Community. Australian and New Zealand Journal of Public Health 24(4):444–49.

Warner, Michael 2002. Publics and Counterpublics. Public Culture 14:49–90.

Warner, William Lloyd 1937. A Black Civilization: A Social Study of an Australian Tribe. New York: Harper and Brothers.

Watson, Virginia 2004. Liberalism and Advanced Liberalism in Australian Indigenous Affairs. Alternatives: Global, Local, Political 29:577–98.

Weatherburn, Don 2014. Arresting Incarceration: Pathways Out of Indigenous Imprisonment. Canberra: Aboriginal Studies Press.

Weber, Max 1947. The Theory of Social and Economic Organization. Trans. A. M. Henderson and Talcott Parsons. New York: Free Press; London: Collier Macmillan.

West, John (1852) 1966. The History of Tasmania. Launceston, Tas.: Henry Dowling; Adelaide: Libraries Board of South Australia.

Whimpress, Bernard 2000. Corroboree: Adelaide Oval, 1885. Kent Town, S.A.: Whimpress.

White, J. Peter, and D. J. Mulvaney 1987. How Many People? Pp. 114–19 in D. J. Mulvaney and J. Peter White (ed.), Australians to 1788. Broadway, N.S.W.: Fairfax, Syme & Weldon Associates.

White, Richard 1991. The Middle Ground: Indians, Empires, and Republics in the Great Lakes Region, 1650–1815. Cambridge: Cambridge University Press.

Wilce, James M. 2009. Language and Emotion. Studies in the Social and Cultural Foundations of Language 25. Cambridge: Cambridge University Press.

Wild, Rex, and Pat Anderson 2007. Ampe Akelyernemane Meke Mekarle "Little Children Are Sacred": Report of the Northern Territory Board of Inquiry into the Protection of Aboriginal Children from Sexual Abuse. Darwin, N.T.: Department of the Chief Minister.

Wild, Stephen A. 1977–78. Men as Women: Female Dance Symbolism in Walbiri Men's Rituals. Dance Research 10(1):14–22.

Wilk, Richard R. 1991. Household Ecology: Economic Change and Domestic Life Among the Kekchi Maya in Belize. Tucson: University of Arizona Press.

Wilkie, Meredith 1997. Bringing Them Home: Report of the National Inquiry into the Separation of Aboriginal and Torres Strait Islander Children from Their Families. Sydney: Human Rights and Equal Opportunity Commission.

Williams, Justin H. G., Andrew Whiten, Thomas Suddendorf, and David Perrett 2001. Imitation, Mirror Neurons, and Autism. Neuroscience and Biobehavioral Reviews 25(4):287–95.

Williams, Kim M. 2006. Mark One or More: Civil Rights in Multiracial America. Ann Arbor: University of Michigan Press.

Willmott, Eric 1987. Pemulwuy: The Rainbow Warrior. McMahon's Point, N.S.W.: Weldons.

Windschuttle, Keith 2002. The Fabrication of Aboriginal History. Sydney: Macleay Press.

Wolf, Eric R. 1982. Europe and the People Without History. Berkeley: University of California Press.

Wolfe, Patrick 1994. Nation and MiscegeNation: Discursive Continuity in the Post-Mabo Era. Social Analysis 34:93–152.

Wolfe, Patrick 1999. Settler Colonialism and the Transformation of Anthropology: The Politics and Poetics of an Ethnographic Event. London: Cassell.

Wolfe, Patrick 2016. Traces of History: Elementary Structures of Race. London: Verso.

Woodward, Robert 1990. Coronation Hill—Wealth vs. the Environment: Wilderness; The Mineral-Rich Area in Australia, Where Crocodile Dundee Roamed, Has Become a Classic Ecological Battleground. Los Angeles Times, 19 August.

Wortham, Stanton 2006. Learning Identity: The Joint Emergence of Social Identification and Academic Learning. Cambridge: Cambridge University Press.

Wright, Judith, and Jean Conochie 1985. We Call for a Treaty. Sydney: Collins/Fontana.

Wiynjorrotj, Phyllis, Sarah Flora, Nipper Daybilama Brown, Peter Jatbula, Judy Galmur, Margaret Katherine, Francesca Merlan, and Glenn Wightman 2005. Jawoyn Plants and Animals: Aboriginal Flora and Fauna Knowledge from Nitmiluk National Park and the Katherine Area, Northern Australia. Northern Territory Botanical Bulletin No. 29. Ethnobiology Project, in collaboration with Department of Natural Resources, Environment and the Arts, Palmerston, N.T., and the Jawoyn Association, Darwin, N.T.

Young, Diana 2001. The Life and Death of Cars: Private Vehicles on the Pitjantjara Lands, South Australia. Pp. 35–59 in Daniel Miller (ed.), Car Cultures. Oxford: Berg.

Zhao, Yuejen, and Karen Dempsey 2006. Causes of Inequality in Life Expectancy Between Indigenous and Non-Indigenous People in the Northern Territory, 1981–2000: A Decomposition Analysis. Medical Journal of Australia 184(10):490–94.

Zlatev, Jordan 2005. What's in a Schema? Bodily Mimesis and the Grounding of Language. Pp. 313–33 in Beate Hampe (ed.), From Perception to Meaning: Image Schemas in Cognitive Linguistics. Berlin: Mouton de Gruyter.

Zorc, R. David Paul 1986. Yolngu-Matha Dictionary. Batchelor, N.T.: School of Australian Linguistics, Darwin Institute of Technology.

INDEX

Aboriginal and Torres Strait Islander
Commission (ATSIC), 179, 221, 223
Aboriginal Land Rights (Northern Territory)
Act (1976), ix, xv, 162, 184
Aboriginal Sacred Sites (NT) Act (1978), 184
Aboriginal Treaty Committee (ATC), 214,
216, 218, 230
Aborigine, Commonwealth definitions of, 3,
158, 172–79, 181, 236, 242, 262 n.31. *See
also* natives, categorization of
Aborigines Protection Act (Victoria) (1869),
158, 172
acculturation, 9, 260 n.15; lack of, 136, 159,
160, 163, 164, 172, 256 n.6
adaptation, 9, 139, 253 n.22; to Australian
environment, 8, 160, 200; cultural, 91, 208,
252 n.5; to European contact, 41
Ah Kit, John, 208, 265 n.12
alcohol, 69–70, 119, 198, 208, 249 n.5;
addiction, xii, xxi, 87, 169; availability, 143,
145, 147, 187, 198; drunken behavior, 40,
146; exchange of women for, 165, 167;
restriction of access to, xxi, xii, 168, 173,
223, 249 n.5; as social burden, xii–xii, 87,
220; and vehicles, 97, 143, 169; and
violence, xiii, 146, 147
Alligator Hole (Nimarranyin), 128, 152
alterity, 49, 91, 233, 235
ancestors, 132, 237–38, 246; Aboriginal terms
for, 31; Europeans seen as, 29, 32, 34, 56,
238, 246, 252 n.10. *See also* ghosts
apocalypse, 191, 197
apocalyptic: figures, 188, 195; sites, 188, 191,
192, 193, 200; tradition, 189, 191, 193, 194,
198
apology, as reparation, 160, 212, 221–22, 259
n.6

Arendt, Hannah, 246, 251 n.11
army camps, internment in, xi, 169, 185,
195
Arndt, Walter, 193
Arnhem Land, 75, 131, 132, 134, 185, 186;
impact of colonization on, 126, 166;
indigenous reserves, 90, 160, 194–95;
kinship systems, 37, 150; and land rights,
162, 216, 221; music, 130. *See also*
Murngin; Yolngu
Arrernte, 11, 228, 234, 241, 254 n.1
Asians, 157, 160
assimilation: concepts of, 9, 159, 162, 242;
dynamic, 264 n.8; expectation of, 158–59;
forced, 158; inability to assimilate, 160;
lack of, 4, 148; of mixed races, 158–59, 160,
163–64, 242; phase, 161, 162; policy, 160,
163–64, 168, 182, 234; practices, 179;
programs, 161, 235; sociocultural, 161,
242; successful, 130; and survival, 12;
theory, 181, 214
assimilationism, 179, 181
Austin-Broos, Diane, 11, 96, 101, 233, 234,
241
Australia Day, 94
Australian Constitutional Convention, 222
authenticity, xvi, 198, 208, 236. *See also*
inauthentic
autonomy, 9, 10, 12, 16, 21, 165, 195, 246
avoidance, 20, 21, 38, 253 n.22; of kin, 36, 42,
131, 154; practices, 37, 124. *See also*
circumspection; refusal; refusal to engage

Bamyili, 95, 131, 161, 186, 188, 256 n.7, 257
n.13. *See also* Barunga; Beswick
Banks, Joseph, 19
Barraway, Sandy, 188, 189, 190, 195, 196, 198

ACKNOWLEDGMENTS

The ideas for this book had two sources. First, in reading the Australian and global literature on colonial contact, power, inequality, and culture over years I became convinced that much of the diversity of indigenous people's behavior in their interaction with outsiders that is evident in the historical sources remained insufficiently examined and slanted toward what have subsequently become consensual commonplaces. Further, these commonplaces needed unsettling. Second, as a result of my own field research experience, I sought clarification of the cultural character of social process and action over time. This book represents the marriage of these concerns, with its examination and analysis of indigenous-nonindigenous interaction at different points in time and over long spans. Early parts of the book are mostly grounded in historical sources, and later parts in my own field research experience and in analysis of policy, action, and interaction at a range of levels, including that of the changing nation-state of Australia.

With a project resulting from long incubation it becomes difficult to fully recognize contributors to it. My first and greatest debt is to the indigenous people and communities in the region of the Northern Territory of Australia to which I have returned over decades since 1976, and where I retain lively contacts, but in many cases two and three generations on from my original ones. Those relationships and people have been unforgettable, life-changing ones. Special debt to particular people, families, and communities in and around Katherine and other Northern Territory towns, at Jilkminggan within Elsey Station, and Barunga and Beswick communities on the Central Arnhem Highway is evident especially in latter chapters of this book. I also want to express thanks to those associated with particular institutions in my fieldwork region with which I have had long-standing working and research relationships: the Northern Land Council, the Commonwealth Scientific and Industrial Research Organization (CSIRO) in its Katherine branch, the Aboriginal

Areas Protection Authority in Darwin, the Northern Territory Archives, Transport and Works in Katherine, the Katherine Language Centre, the Jawoyn Association, and the Katherine Historical Society.

I thank the institutions that have supported research contributing to this project. The Australian Institute of Aboriginal and Torres Strait Islander Studies (originally Australian Institute of Aboriginal Studies) was the source of my first research funding from 1976 to 1979 and at other times throughout the next two decades. The impetus to write up this project in a systematic way came in the form of an invitation to me to deliver the Jensen lecture series at the Frobenius Institut, Goethe-Universität, Frankfurt am Main. I did so under the title "Anthropologies of Encounter: From 'First Contact' to the Everyday" and delivered the lectures during May–June 2010, several of which became draft chapters for this book. I am grateful for support I have received subsequently for preparation and publication of this book from the Frobenius Institut. Australian Research Council Discovery Grant (DP 120100960), for a project entitled "Inside Alice Springs: Diversity in a Central Australian Town," 2012–16, also provided forms of support for this project. Small grants from Sydney University and the Australian National University enabled me to carry out aspects of relevant research and documentation. I was elected to membership of the Princeton Institute of Advanced Study, Social Sciences, for the academic year 2015–16, which enabled me to complete the manuscript.

I am grateful to colleagues at the Australian National University, at Sydney University, at Frankfurt, Hawaii, University of Virginia, and at Princeton IAS who listened to, read, and/or commented on chapters of this book. At Frankfurt I was cordially received and assisted by Professor Karl-Heinz Kohl; at Princeton by the School of Social Science, led by Professor Didier Fassin, and most exceptionally assisted administratively and in readying material for publication by Donne Petito, Nancy Cotterman, and Linda Garat. Among colleagues who have been of great support in correspondence and conversation at various stages of this project I must single out Diane Austin-Broos, David Dinwoodie, Tim Rowse, Alan Rumsey, and Rupert Stasch. In my view, Diane's work on the Hermannsburg mission in Central Australia has been a particularly successful integration of history and culture. David's comments have always been considered and helpful. In latter stages of writing Tim helped me edit and cut the manuscript down to size and provided critical and substantive comments and suggestions. Rupert's work on otherness and tourism among Korowai people in West Papua, and conference participation to which he invited me, have been stimulating. Alan is not only an acute commentator but also my husband and most tried veteran of chapter drafts.

Only one chapter of the book (Chapter 2) is related to another publication on imitation. Some of the ideas are to appear in a somewhat different form in a volume entitled *Mimesis in the Pacific*, edited by Jeanette Mageo and Elfriede Hermann (Berghahn), deriving from a presentation of the material at the Association for Social Anthropology of Oceania conference at Kona, Hawaii, in 2014.

My love and thanks for long-term staying power and encouragement go, as always, to Alan, to my sons James and Jesse, and to all the new people, big and now also little, they have brought into my life.

CPSIA information can be obtained
at www.ICGtesting.com
Printed in the USA
BVOW09*0851130418
512930BV00001B/1/P